PEOPLES OF THE WORLD

The Middle East and North Africa

PEOPLES OF THE WORLD

The Middle East and North Africa

Joyce Moss • George Wilson

The Culture, Geographical Setting, and Historical Background of 30 Peoples of the Middle East and North Africa

FIRST EDITION

Gale Research Inc. • *DETROIT* • *LONDON*

Joyce Moss
George Wilson

Gale Research Inc. staff

Coordinating Editor: Linda Metzger
Associate Editor: Victoria A. Coughlin

Production Manager: Mary Beth Trimper
Production Associate: Mary Winterhalter

Art Director: Arthur Chartow
Keyliner: C.J. Jonik

The paper used in this publication meets the minimum requirements of American National Standard for Information Sciences—Permanence Paper for Printed Library Materials, ANSI Z39.48-1984.   ∞™

Printed in the United States of America
Published in the United States by Gale Research Inc.
Published simultaneously in the United Kingdom
by Gale Research International Limited
(An affiliated company of Gale Research Inc.)

10 9 8 7 6 5 4

Contents

Countries Today

Preface

Attempting to draw a picture of the modern Middle East by describing cultural differences that distinguish the various groups living there brings one face to face with ambiguity. On the one hand, qualities such as Arabism and Islam cross societal and national boundaries. Yet coexisting with these qualities is a strong inclination toward nationalism—begun under the rule of the Ottoman Empire, fostered by European colonialism, and accentuated in the latter part of the twentieth century by the presence of oil in the region.

In the 700s-1000s, warriors in the name of Islam carried the message of the new religion throughout the region and across Northern Africa into Spain. They were girded with powerful religious concepts, aided by religious rules that allowed Muslim men to wed non-Muslim women—more than one at a time provided only that the man be able to support them—and to adopt the children into Islam. Using a language that was superior in its poetical sound to most it encountered, the warriors for Islam quickly populated the region and transformed its politics, religion, and language.

Those who came under the rule of the Arab invaders soon adopted Arabic as their language and with it the customs of those rulers—including a fondness for poetry, to which the Arabic language is so well adapted. But "Arabism" held other attractions. The Arab world had a centuries-old literature and records of achievements in science and medicine. Arabic allows for descriptions of the achievements of other regions such as the invention of the wheel, potter's wheel, and windmill in the region of the Fertile Crescent. The people who adopted Arabic as a language became "Arabized"—accepting Arabic cultural mores and governing styles described by the new language.

In some areas this "Arabization" was tempered by relations with other countries. Tunisians, for example, while long Arabized, were deeply influenced by the French, Greeks, and Italians, as the Egyptians have been influenced by their long association with the British. The result is an Arab world with differences accentuated by exposure to other societies.

Islam itself was such a powerful force that it extended sometimes beyond the Arabized region. Those people west of the Zagros Mountains became Arabized and for the most part adopted Islam. Those east of the mountains adopted Islam but remained Persian in their cultural influence. Islam, therefore, extends throughout the region and beyond, isolating other long-standing religions into small separate societies, some of which have been Arabized, and almost all of which are tolerated by the teachings of Islam. Of the 200,000,000 people of the Middle East, including Arabized North Africa, more than ninety percent are Muslims. Fewer than five percent represent the religion that is next in size in the Middle East—Christianity. Perhaps 4,500,000 (slightly more than two percent) are Jewish—living in very small pockets in almost every Middle East country, forming a majority only in Israel.

Over this unity of religion and language was superimposed nationalizing boundaries—first as provinces of the Ottoman Empire, then as "protectorates" of British and French forces after World War I. The nationalization has been accentuated by the discovery of oil in the Middle East, a discovery that made some nations immensely wealthy while their neighbors remained poor.

The Middle East today represents four forces: Arabism, Islam, nationalism, and oil. The contradictions among these forces are seen in religious differences in Lebanon, the territorial conflicts among Iraq, Iran, and Kuwait, and the attempted unity of the Organization of Oil Producing and Exporting Countries (OPEC) and the Arab League.

This volume attempts to explore the differences and similarities among Middle Eastern peoples as a result of these forces.

Acknowledgements

The authors are particularly indebted to Dr. Afaf Lutfi al-Sayyid-Marsot, Professor of Middle Eastern History, University of California at Los Angeles, who read and added valuable information and significant accuracy to the entire manuscript. Thanks also to Rabbi Stanley F. Chyet, who reviewed the sections on Israeli Jews, Judaism, and the ancient Hebrews.

We are also grateful to the following people who contributed to the research and writing of various sections of the book:

Shiva Rea Bailey	Paulett Shapiro
Monica Gyulai	Suzanne Smith
Marjorie Kelly	Lisa Velarde
Harvey Shapiro	Colin Wells

A special acknowledgement is extended to Dr. Nikki Keddie, University of California at Los Angeles, Dr. W. Paul Fischer, Redlands University, and David Tuch for allowing us to select photographs from their private collections. Other illustrations came from the Smithsonian Institution and the University Museum of the University of Pennsylvania.

Introduction

Civilization as represented by the development of towns and cities arose first in the fertile river valleys of India, China, and the Middle East. It was in these valleys that people discovered the benefits of labor specialization. Here it was not always necessary for every person in a community to farm in order for all to survive. The fertile lands made it possible for some to farm, while others sewed, painted, formed tools, traded, and so on. In these river valleys, people developed ways to live together under law and to communicate in writing as well as voice. The Middle Eastern cities became model trade centers. Middle Eastern merchants carried their goods first east and later west to the societies bordering the Mediterranean Sea, where another great civilization had been established centuries earlier along the Nile River in Africa.

Two great rivers followed parallel courses from north and east of the Mediterranean Sea southeasterly to the Persian Gulf. A delta region near the Persian Gulf provided especially attractive soil to early farmers—as soon as the skills had been developed to separate the farmland from the waterways. In the delta, the early kingdoms of Sumeria and Babylonia arose in the land between the waters, "Mesopotamia."

Self-Rule in the Middle East

A sweeping arc on a map describes the path of the Tigris and Euphrates rivers and curves toward the south and west along the coast of the Mediterranean Sea to end near modern-day Israel. Along this "Fertile Crescent," city-states rose and fell, and kingdoms expanded, aged, and were replaced by new kingdoms. Trade routes to the east and west made this an attractive land for many foreigners.

New Asian groups (the first known inhabitants had probably come from Asia) were almost constant threats to the native peoples. As a result, the peoples of the crescent frequently found themselves without self-rule. The ancient kingdom of Sumeria fell to the rule of Babylonia. From the east, Assyrians attacked and destroyed the city of Babylon in 689 B.C. Restored a few years later, Babylonia joined its neighbor, the Medes, to regain control and capture the Assyrian stronghold at Nineveh. Along the coast, a group of city-states formed the loose association referred to as Greater Syria. A king of Persia overran Babylonia in 539 B.C. and made that people of the crescent subject to the coastal rulers for more than 200 years. Alexander the Great defeated the Persian armies and ruled the region from Greece.

After another disintegration of Babylon, the governments of the region fell into disarray, but were finally organized into a single unit as part of the Ottoman Empire, which had Constantinople as its base. Ruling a large expanse of land from Greece and the north coast of the Middle East to what is now Iraq and Iran, the Ottomans replaced many of the old rulers with their own administrators. Resentment throughout the empire eventually eroded Ottoman power, at first in the Mediterranean region, then by a growing nationalism in Iraq and Iran. By the end of the nineteenth century, the Ottoman Empire had begun to crumble.

The end finally came with World War I, when the Ottomans allied with the Germans and lost the war. The allies, particularly France and Great Britain, with a promise of self-determination, had encouraged a rebellion in the Arab regions of the Ottoman Empire that aided in defeating the Ottomans. Still, self-government was slow to arrive in the Fertile Crescent region. France and Great Britain had agreed to separate spheres of influence—Britain expanding its base from Egypt through Iraq, and France attempting to control Syria. However, the nationalism that had begun to take form under the Ottomans made life difficult for the new "rulers."

By the 1920s, the region of the Fertile Crescent could be described as a series of mixed Arabic, Christian, and Jewish societies beginning in the southwest with Palestine, sweeping north through Syria, and arcing along the rivers of Iraq. These societies were more often than not tribal in nature. Iran, a non-Arab, society formed a limit to Arabism east of the rivers, as did Turkey to the north.

The Middle East in the Twentieth Century

A time line of events from World War I to the 1960s is useful in understanding the state of this section of the world today:

Early 1900s   The Ottoman Empire is declining, with growing nationalism in the regions of Syrian, Palestine, Iraq, and Egypt.

1916	France and Britain sign the Sykes-Picot agreement dividing much of the Middle East between the two of them and Russia. Sharif Hussain, without knowledge of the British-French agreement, is persuaded by Sir Henry McMahon to join the allies against the Ottomans. Later Hussain will lose control of Arabia to King Ibn Saud of the Nejd, but his sons will become British-appointed rulers in Iraq and Transjordan.
1917	The Balfour Declaration. Britain recognizes the Jewish demand for a homeland by declaring its intent to create a Jewish state in Palestine so long as it does not prejudice the rights of other inhabitants in the area.
1922	Britain begins to withdraw from the area by canceling its protectorate status for Egypt and Sudan, but British military influence remains.
1930	Iraq becomes an independent nation, but again the British military influence remains.
1937–1938	Arabs demand an Arab Palestine.
1939	A "white paper" declares British intent to limit Jewish migration to Palestine and to create an Arab state in part of Palestine. Two-thirds of the population is Arab.
1945	An Arab League is formed to counteract the Jewish plan for an independent state, which the Arab groups vow never to recognize.
1947	The Palestine problem is addressed by the United Nations, which proposes that Palestine either be a mixed Arab/Jewish state, or that the land be divided fifty-six percent to a Jewish state, forty-four percent to the Arabs. Having already begun to develop an independent nation, the Jews rebel along with the Arabs at this solution.
1948	The United States and Russia recognize Israel as a member of the international community of nations. As many as 800,000 Palestinian Arabs leave the country.

1956 President Nasser of Egypt moves to unify the Arab world by a show of force against the British and Americans as he nationalizes the Suez Canal. For a short time, Egypt and Syria join to form the United Arab Republic. Until Syria withdraws, Nasser guides the new republic.

1967 In an early skirmish, one of many that have occurred through three decades, Israelis capture the Gaza Strip, a Palestinian "finger" of land pointing northeast from the Sinai Peninsula, and the Golan Heights on the Syrian border, as well as the West Bank of the Jordan River, which has been under Jordanian occupation.

The people of the region were long sorted into Arab and Jewish groups by religion. Most of the Arabs were, over the centuries, loosely united by their common faith and language, and shaped into national identities by outside forces. These national societies, bound by "Arabism" and Islam, are new and have rapidly replaced older, smaller societies.

The Middle East today is composed of these new national societies sprinkled with small, most often religiously determined, subsocieties, and a few societies, such as the Kurds and Armenians, that cross national boundary lines.

Format and Arrangement of Entries

Reflecting the influences on today's configuration of the Middle East (including Arabized North Africa), this book is divided into four sections—Ancient Cultures, Middle Eastern Religions, Cultures Today, and Countries Today. **The Ancient Cultures** entries provide a brief overview of the Middle East before the Common Era and the contributions of the Middle Eastern societies to the birth of civilization. The short sections about the three great **Middle Eastern Religions** attempt to position these influences in that region today.

Organized alphabetically by people names, **Cultures Today** includes a sampling of the hundreds of societies giving color and variety to Middle East. Because of their importance in the area with a population spanning most of the nations of the Middle East, the entry on the Arabs precedes that of the other cultural groups. Each culture entry is arranged as follows:

A dictionary-style definition introduces the entry, pronouncing the people's name, describing the group in brief, and furnishing the key facts of population, location, and language.

Following this introduction are detailed descriptions under three main headings: Geographical Setting, Historical Background, and Culture (for the old societies) or Culture Today.

For quick access to information, subheadings appear under main headings. The Culture Today section, for example, may include the following categories—Food, clothing, and shelter; Religion; Education; Business; Family life; and The arts. (Due to the unique experience of each group, the subheadings vary somewhat across the entries.) The entries conclude with a section headed For More Information, which is a selective guide for readers wanting to conduct further research on the featured group.

Each culture entry also includes a map showing the location of the society within the array of political states in the Middle East. Photographs illustrate the entries and assist the reader in understanding cultural differences.

The country briefs in The New Middle East section include two maps, one to locate the country in the region known as the Middle East and another to show some geographical features and to indicate the country's relationship to some of the societies living there. The briefs contain information about population, languages, and cities as well as a description of the topography of the nation and current events and issues within each country.

Other Helpful Features

A Bibliography of sources used to compile this work is included in the back matter. Although every effort is made to explain foreign

xviii

or difficult terms within the text, a Glossary has been compiled to further aid the reader. A comprehensive Subject Index provides another point of access to the information contained in the entries.

Comments and Suggestions

Your comments on this work, as well as your suggestions for future *Peoples of the World* volumes, are welcome. Please write: Editors, *Peoples of the World*, Gale Research Inc., 835 Penobscot Bldg., Detroit, Michigan 48226-4904.

Table of Middle Eastern Countries and Societies

The table below illustrates the relationship of Middle Eastern countries to the societies described in this book.

Country	Societies Within the Country
Afghanistan	Baluch, Hazara, Pushtun, Qashqa'i
Algeria	Algerians, Arabs*, Bedouin, Berbers
Bahrain	Arabs
Egypt	Arabs, Bedouin, Copts, Egyptians, Nubians, Palestinians
Iran	Armenians, Azerbaijani, Baluch, Iranians, Kurds, Pushtun, Qashqa'i
Iraq	Arabs, Armenians, Iraqi, Kurds, Palestinians, Yazidis
Israel	Arabs, Druze, Israeli Jews, Palestinians
Jordan	Arabs, Bedouin, Jordanians, Palestinians
Kuwait	Arabs, Palestinians
Lebanon	Arabs, Druze, Lebanese, Maronites, Palestinians
Libya	Arabs, Bedouin, Berbers, Libyans, Palestinians
Morocco	Arabs, Bedouin, Berbers
Oman	Arabs, Bedouin
Qatar	Arabs, Bedouin
Saudi Arabia	Arabs, Bedouin, Palestinians, Saudis
Syria	Arabs, Bedouin, Druze, Kurds, Palestinians, Syrians, Yazidis
Tunisia	Arabs, Tunisians
Turkey	Armenians, Kurds, Turks, Yazidis
United Arab Emirates	Arabs, Baluch, Bedouin, Iranians
Yemen	Arabs, Bedouin, Yemenis

* This list is a mixture of titles that reflects the influences on the Middle East today. "Arabs" is a language-based segmentation of the society. It represents not only all the people who originated in the Arabian desert region of Saudi Arabia, Iraq, Kuwait, Yemen, and Oman, but also those peoples who have become "Arabized"—using Arabic as their language and having by virtue of the language adopted many cultural traits that are Arabic. In this sense, the term "Arabs" includes all the country-based societies except for Iranians, Turks, and Israelis. There are a number of smaller societies in the region. These may or may not be "Arab." Bedouins are "Arab" but are identified as a separate society by their lifestyle. However, most of the cultures described in this volume are nationally inspired.

THE ANCIENT CULTURES

SUMERIANS
(sue mehr' ee uhns)

Early inhabitants of the delta region of the Tigris and Euphrates rivers.

Population: Unknown.
Location: Present-day Iraq; the delta area of the Tigris and Euphrates rivers.
Language: Sumerian.

Geographical Setting

Thousands of years ago, the land that is now Iraq began as much as 100 miles north of the present-day coast where the Tigris and Euphrates Rivers flow into the Persian Gulf. Here the two rivers flowed near each other and built up a delta area of silt from the distant mountains. The land here was broken by the many streams of the two rivers as they found their way to the gulf. Between the streams lay rich soil, but soil that was subject to frequent flooding as the rivers swelled seasonally. Fish were abundant in the streams, and if the floods could be controlled, the land was capable of producing crops in quantities unknown in many other areas. The land could be expanded if the floodwaters were redirected. The delta area between the two rivers came to be known as Sumer.

Historical Background

Origin. Perhaps as early as 5000 B.C., farmers moved into the delta area and established villages of mud-plastered reed houses. The discoveries of their villages were made in excavations begun in 1932 that gave the ancient society its name—the Ubiad society. About 3500

B.C., these early settlers were joined by settlers from the west and northwest, and a new city-state, Uruk, was formed near the present-day town of Warka. A thousand years later, a great ruler of a state upriver from Warka, Sargon, led Akkadians to victory over the people of Uruk. Sargon reformed the society, establishing the idea of private ownership of the land, to be recognized by deeds issued by the government. The area was further unified and the earlier Sumerians regained control between 2050 and 1950 B.C., during which time another city-state, Ur, came to power. But in 1950 B.C., the city of Ur was destroyed and the land divided into independent, warring villages. Merchants took advantage of no governmental controls to become very wealthy in this period. They became, in effect, the heads of state (their word for "head" became the present-day word for wealth, "capital"). Local leaders arose, who freed slaves and created social rules. About 1700 B.C., people of the west, Amorites, took control and built a great city upriver, Babylon. The people of the delta area are known from the language they developed, Sumerian.

Culture

Food, clothing, and shelter. The early Sumerians were planters. They cleared the land, draining it of swamps with elaborate systems of ditches, and building canals for irrigation. On the land thus separated from the water, they planted grains, vegetables, and fruit trees. These farmers lived in houses built from available materials—reed and mud—but erected towering holy places such as the ziggurat uncovered at Erech (Warka). These holy places often included storage facilities for grain. For it was in these holy places that priests allotted the land to be farmed and supplied seed and tools for the planting and harvesting. Dressed in skirts, farmers worked the land using metal sickles and plows, eventually hitching oxen to the plows to till the land and to pull wheeled carts for transporting the harvest. Others tended goats and sheep. All the farm products were recorded and counted in the temples. Along the rivers, fishermen and merchants built boats with high prows and sterns for carrying goods from city to city along the two rivers.

The soil provided the people with enough food that some could turn from farming to establishing villages throughout the delta area and to becoming merchants, toolmakers, and craftspeople. Sumerian people also became adept as potters and basketmakers. Potters of ancient Sumer had learned to use the potter's wheel.

Language and mathematics. Early in their history, the people of Sumer began to keep records in writing and to use a system of mathematics based on sixty, the same base as our time-keeping today. At first, the writing was a system of pictures of important activities. These gradually changed to a pictograph representation of words and sounds, including as many as 2,000 different symbols. The writing was done on clay tablets that were then baked to preserve the records. The pictographs were drawn into the tablets using reeds as markers. The reeds left a wedge-shaped mark in the clay. A system of such wedge-shaped symbols, called cuneiform, finally formed the Sumer written language. Patterns carved in small cylinder-shaped stones

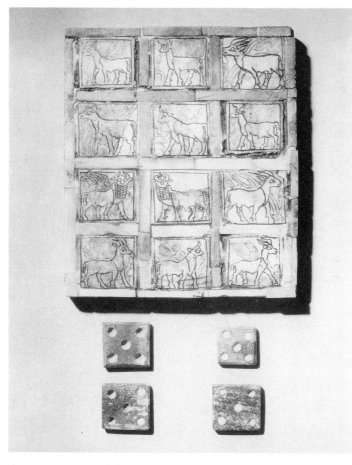

A game board and pieces from a royal tomb at Ur.
Courtesy of the University Museum, University of Pennsylvania.

were pressed into the clay to identify the writers. The language was used by future societies, including the Hittites, Babylonians, and Persians.

Religion. The people of Sumer revered a number of local gods. For these gods, they built pyramidlike towers of worship. Since the ruler of the city often claimed kinship with the favored god, many of a ruler's activities took place in the temple. Scribes of the temple counted sheep and goats to determine the proper sacrifices. Grains were also stored there and allocated to the citizens. Wage lists were kept there and wages paid at the temple. The holy place was both a

A bullhead in gold and lapiz lazuli created about 2600 b.c. *Courtesy of the University Museum, University of Pennsylvania.*

place of worship of the gods and the seat of government of the kingdom.

For More Information

Braidwood, R. *The Near East and the Foundations of Civilization.* Portland, Oregon: University of Oregon Press, 1952.

Scarmuzza, V. M. and P. MacKendrick. *The Ancient World.* New York: Holt, 1958.

ANCIENT EGYPTIANS
(ee jip' shuns)

Early inhabitants of the Nile River Valley.

Population: 7,000,000 (estimate at the time of Roman dominance).
Location: Egypt.
Language: Egyptian.

Geographical Setting

Ancient Egypt began with the settlement of farms and farm villages
along the Nile River. A long narrow band of fertile land is bordered
on both sides by desert, and spreads into a wider delta area as the
river flows toward the Mediterranean Sea. Flood waters annually
widened the river, covering much of the fertile soil and adding new
soil to it. As a result, the early Nile River Valley was one of the most
fertile areas of the world. The first kingdoms in the region avoided
the delta area, where much labor was required to separate livable
land from the many streams that made up the mouth of the Nile.

Historical Background

Origins. By 5000 B.C., farmers were settled along the Nile River,
cultivating the land using stone and wooden tools and harvesting
wheat and barley. As harvests increased, not all the people needed
to farm to sustain the population. Village people began to create
copper tools, silverworks, and lapis lazuli jewelry for trade, and to
move up and down the river by boats, selling these products as well
as excess farm products. Gradually the populations in the trade centers grew into city-states and the Nile River Valley became the location of many small kingdoms.

By 3100 B.C., some of these small city-states had been consolidated under a single governing unit with its capital at Memphis just south of the delta area and not far south of present-day Cairo. Ruled by men who claimed membership in the family of gods, the empire was marked by remarkable constructions of burial sites for the rulers. The construction of these pyramids continued through most of the reigns of the pharaohs from Memphis. Much of the work force for these monuments to the god-kings was provided by workers from the southern river. The kingdom at Memphis lasted until about 2270 B.C. After its collapse, there followed 200 years of civil war as the various city-states competed for power and space.

By 2060 B.C., a new empire had come into being farther south along the river. This new empire, with its capital at Thebes, once more united the valley under a single ruler. This time, however, emphasis turned from monument-building to public works. For 200 years, the Egyptians were employed in great public-works projects, reclaiming more farmland from the flood plain, and increasing the arable land through irrigation projects. However, this empire, too, was to decay and become prey to Hyksos invaders from the northeast. The Hyksos may have been related to the Hebrews, and it may have been their promise of friendly welcome that inspired Joseph to travel to Egypt in search of aid for the famine-stricken Hebrew region in what is now Israel and Lebanon.

The Hyksos loosely ruled the far southern Nile region, making it possible for the old princes of the region to unify and defeat the Hyksos, thus restoring the empire. The new empire ruled intermittently until 1085 B.C. During this time it was periodically being invaded by people from Syria, Phoenicia, Palestine, Nubia (part of what is now far southern Egypt and adjacent Sudan), and Northern Sudan. All of these claimed at some time to be rulers of the Egyptian Empire. Eventually, Egyptians took control and began to expand their trade routes around the Mediterranean Sea, trading bronze, woven goods, leather, glass, and embroidery for such items as cedar lumber from Lebanon and copper from the Sinai area. So skilled were these early traders at shipbuilding and navigating, that before 600 B.C. Egyptian sailors had survived a three-year journey in which they circumnavigated the whole of Africa.

Culture

Tools. Each of their invaders and trade partners brought new ideas to the Egyptians, so the origin of early Egyptian tools is not well known. What is known is that by 3500 B.C., sailboats traveled the Nile River. Plows were used to till the soil as early as 1300 B.C., the potter's wheel had come into use in Egypt by 2750 B.C., bronze replaced copper for tools and weapons by 2000 B.C., and the wheel was in common use by 1600 B.C.—too late to be of help in building the pyramids.

Village life. While great monuments were erected by the god-kings, perhaps to reinforce the idea of their divine right to rule, most of the early Egyptians worked in the fields. But most of these fields were owned by the empire, and allotted to farmers in exchange for substantial taxes. Families in the early empires passed their rights to farm the land from generation to generation through either the mother's or father's lineage.

The majority of the Egyptian villagers lived in small houses made of mud and straw bricks, the houses clustered tightly together to save the fertile farmland. One- or two-stories tall, the houses were squarish with small, high, slit-like windows. The poorest of the workers lived in small mud-brick houses with palm-leaf and straw roofs held in place by palm trunks. Often, several houses were built around a square courtyard. Inside, only the wealthy people furnished their home with beds and tables. But the most prosperous citizens decorated their homes with rugs, chests, and bowls of copper, bronze, or gold. The average home, however, might be furnished with a stool, earthen pots for cooking and for carrying water, and mats for sitting and sleeping. Cooking was done outside on open fires or in a brick oven. Many homes were surrounded by gardens or orchards.

Food and clothing. Men of the village wore linen skirts in the fields— skirts that evolved from the loincloth worn by the very early Egyptians, and that, in later periods, became nearly ankle-length pleated skirts. Women also dressed in linen, a draped and pleated dress falling below the knees and held at the shoulders with straps or sleeves. Egyptians used eye makeup and red makeup to enhance their appearance, and if they could afford them, necklaces, bracelets, and rings. Men shaved their faces using bronze razors, cut their hair short, manicured their nails, and frequently wore wigs of sheep hair.

The farmers grew wheat, barley, vegetables, and fruits for food, and supplemented this diet with fish from the river. Women ground the grain into a coarse meal and then formed the meal into loaves of bread to be baked on the outdoor oven. An Egyptian meal included this bread along with fish, vegetables, fruit, or meat.

Economy. As agriculture developed, allowing some of the people to devote time to other activities, villages grew and some of their inhabitants spent their time making tools and weapons of bronze, crafting leather products, creating glassworks, or embroidering and weaving. Some built high-ended boats of reeds bound together, and used the boats to carry on a brisk shipping trade with other villages along the river and between the major cities of Thebes and Memphis. This river travel was important in uniting a kingdom whose capital was frequently located near the delta area, and whose religious center was far upriver at Thebes.

Religion. Early Egyptians held many gods in high esteem. One of these, the sun god Ra, was particularly venerated. Another important god was the Thebes' god of wind, Amon. At one time the Egyptian Empire worshiped a dual sun-wind god, Amon-Ra. Included among the gods was the ruler of the empire. This ruler made periodic visits to villages and towns along the river to perform special ceremonies in which he or she interceded with the other gods on the village's behalf. At one time a trinity of gods was worshipped—the goddess Isis, and the gods Osiris and Horus.

The Egyptian legacy. Most of the Egyptian peasants could not read or write, but one of the major contributions of ancient Egypt to world society was a system of pictures called hieroglyphs, which was eventually refined so that the later Egyptians were able to write much more easily with symbols stylized from the old picture writing. Historical records of the early people have been found in three forms of writing, recorded at first on clay tablets, and later on a paper made from the common Nile reed, papyrus.

Egyptian sailors greatly expanded the known world, circumnavigating Africa, and traveling to Greece, Persia, and Phoenicia. Much of this travel was done by sail, a device that came into Egyptian use early in the development of Nile civilization.

Egyptians were not as innovative as their eastern trading partners in basic arithmetic. However, one branch of mathematics was important to the management of the land. Egyptians, early in their history, began to contribute to our knowledge of geometry and its use in plotting farming areas and constructing such monuments as the pyramids.

Egyptian art was preserved in the artifacts buried with the dead rulers. Gold, silver, and bronze works of exquisite designs have been found in such explorations as that of the tomb of King Tutankhamen (1362-1352 B.C.). Besides fine jewelry, early Egypt contributed to the cosmetic industry. Cosmetics were in common use among wealthy Egyptians at least by the time of the establishment of the first rule from Thebes. The artistic ability of Egyptians was also illustrated in their houses. The walls of most homes were painted with bright colors or with murals, while some of the finest household articles might have been made of glass. Egyptians were able to make and form glass early in their history, and some believe that glassmaking was invented in Egypt.

The ancient Egyptian language began to disappear 1,000 years ago. It was a language that was written without vowels and with twenty-four symbols for consonants and other sounds. Today that language is known only as it evolved over several millennia into a form that is used in the liturgy of Coptic churches in Egypt.

The pharaohs of ancient Egypt built monuments to themselves along the Nile River. *Courtesy of Dr. Paul Fischer.*

For More Information

King, Joan Wucher. *Historical Dictionary of Egypt.* Metuchen, New Jersey: Scarecrow, 1984.

Wallbank, T. Walter, Alastair M. Taylor, and Nels M. Bailkey. *Civilization.* Chicago: Scott, Foresman and Company, 1965.

HITTITES
(hit' eyets)

Rulers of the northern Middle East in the second millennium B.C.

Population: Unknown.
Location: Northern Middle East: present-day Turkey, Syria, and Iraq.
Language: Hittite.

Geographical Setting

The land of northern Syria and Iraq is mountainous, with the mountains giving way in Turkey to the Anatolian plateau and in southern Syria and Iraq to desert and the valleys of the Tigris and Euphrates rivers. These rivers originate in the mountains of northern Turkey. It is a region of harsher winters and milder summers than the deserts to the south.

Historical Background

Origin. Some time before 2000 B.C., invaders from the north descended upon the inhabitants of the mountain valleys of the northern Middle East, probably entering the area first in present-day Syria. Having already developed the ability to fashion weapons, particularly short daggers, from bronze, these invaders easily defeated the native population of the region. From this beginning, the newcomers roamed over present-day Syria, Turkey, and Iraq. So widespread was their travel that a Babylonian king in 1932 B.C. noted that the Hittites had come to the land of Akkad.

A warlike people who were scattered by the mountains they invaded, the Hittites were at first separated into many small tribal units, then grew to be city-states as the people settled and became skilled farmers. However, by the middle of the second millennium B.C., most of the Hittites had united under one leader, Labarna, and the Hittite Empire had begun an expansion that was to include the people of Akkad and Babylon in the Fertile Crescent, to unite most of present-day Syria, and to see Hittites enter Palestine and invade Turkey as far as Aleppo.

About 1225 B.C., Egypt controlled the region of the Mediterranean coast as far as Syria and had ambitions to rule over that land. At the end of the century, the Egyptian ruler Ramses II (1310-1244 B.C.) sent his army to conquer the Hittites in Syria. After many years of bitter fighting, Ramses was driven back to Palestine by the forces of King Khattushilish III of the Hittites. So bitter was this defeat that Ramses elected to establish peaceful relations with the Hittites by marrying one of Khattushilish's daughters.

The Hittite Empire was to be short-lived, however. Greek armies moved along the Mediterranean coast and forced the people of the coastal nations of the Middle East inland. These people eventually defeated the Hittites and the Hittite kingdom fell in 1190 B.C.

The Hittites survived in a number of city-states for nearly 500 years before being finally defeated in 717 B.C. Even then their influence was felt in other societies. For example, one of King David of Palestine's military leaders was a Hittite. By the time of their disintegration, the Indo-European Hittite peoples had helped to form a bridge between the older cultures of the east and the emerging cultures of the west.

Culture

Overview. For many years, knowledge of the peoples known as Hittites was limited to brief references in biblical writings. For example, two of Solomon's wives were from the Hittites. However, in 1906 a great library was discovered in the ruins of the ancient Hittite capital of Khattushash. Located ninety miles east of present-day Ankara in central Turkey, this royal library contained 10,000 clay tablets on which the literature and daily records of the Hittites were recorded in a cuneiform manuscript. These clay records and other discoveries, particularly discoveries made after World War II, have provided us with the knowledge now available of an ancient empire that stretched from the coast of the Mediterranean Sea in a sweeping arc down the Tigris and Euphrates valleys.

Pictures show a people in appearance not unlike today's Armenian people but dressed in high peaked caps, knee-length tunics, and pointed shoes designed for easier movement in the heavy mountain snows. These adventurers had begun to use chariots before they came to present-day Syria and to manufacture weapons and tools from bronze. Their language quickly became merged with that of the Babylonians and Armenians, so that Hittite writing adopted the script of the Babylonians. Some of the Hittites chose to speak in the Babylonian tongue, while others adopted the Aramaic language that was used in Syria and in Palestine in biblical times. Hittite writing followed other languages in alternating direction. A line reading from left to right was followed by one reading from right to left, and so on.

Government and economy. The records tell of a military government that dictated almost every aspect of daily life. Farmlands were allocated by the government. Wages were set by the government, and trade was carefully regulated. Even the price of cattle hides was set by the government

The Hittites were feared warriors of the ancient Middle East because of their organization and because they were the first to use iron weapons and tools. Some of the writings tell of manufacturing iron tools for nearby rulers and of gifts of iron knives or daggers.

Most of the Hittites, however, were farmers, raising barley and wheat, and harvesting fruits that grew in the area. They also herded sheep, goats, and cattle, which they used for food and for making cloth. The Hittites were proficient manufacturers of fine cloth, which they used both for their own needs and for trade.

Religion. Aside from the military, another major force in Hittite life was religion. The Hittite religion included many gods, some venerated universally and some locally. Pictures of the gods show human figures with bird heads and wings. Sometimes called the people of a thousand gods, the Hittites gods included both males and females. There was a male storm god, for example, and a goddess of the sun. There was also a god who oversaw male virtues, and other gods and goddesses responsible for nearly every natural event. The Hittites paid respects to their gods through sacrifices, prayer, oath, ceremonies of purification, and exorcism.

Arts. As in other societies, religion inspired much of Hittite art. Many artistic monuments are recognitions of the gods; others tell of Hittite war might. The Hittites had developed great skill in architecture, devising stone foundations for great wooden columns to support their palaces and temples. Hittites were skilled potters, making clay products in intricate forms and designs. One excavated pottery example of this skill revealed a teapot-shaped vessel with a lid that slid along an extension of the handle for easy carrying and to keep the lid from getting lost. Cups, jars, and other vessels showed a variety of forms and original designs. Clay and stone figures used as decorations for buildings included exquisite sculptures of lions, which were common in the Syrian area of Hittite times. But perhaps the greatest artistic and industrial contribution of the Hittites was the use of iron. These people appear to have been among the first to learn to use this metal to fashion tools, jewelry, and weapons.

The Hittites were great borrowers of culture. Many aspects of their literature and their business practices were adopted from the Babylonians, and many of their words show a relationship to early European languages. Hittite mythology borrowed from the Babylonians. The Hittites also used a system of trade exchange similar to that of the Assyrians and Babylonians, which included weighted silver pieces as a sort of money.

Law. In law, however, the Hittites differed from the "eye-for-an-eye" stance of their neighbors. Hittite laws, rather, were based on a system of fines. While certain matters, particularly matters of a sexual nature, were tolerated in Hittite law and not in other societies, punishment of Hittite crimes most often involved paying of fines rather than execution, imprisonment, or other physical retributions that were common in Babylon, Assyria, and other dynasties. For example, Hittite law required that a person breaking a free man's arm or leg should pay him twenty shekels of silver and then be allowed to go home. The crime of murder thus became very expensive. Hittite law was very explicit about crime and the compensation for it. The law as it is understood today exists in a 200-paragraph Hittite record.

For More Information

Gurney, O. R. *The Hittites.* New York: Penguin, 1954.

Wallbank, T. Walter, Alastair M. Taylor, and Nels M. Bailkey. *Civilization: Past and Present.* Chicago: Scott, Foresman, 1965.

HEBREWS
(he′ brews)

Ancestors of the Israeli Jews, who occupied the area first called
Canaan from around 2000 B.C.E. (before the common era of
Christians and Jews) to 70 C.E. (the common era).

Population: Variable (about 800,000 around 950 B.C.E.).
Location: Southern and northern areas of present-day Israel.
Language: Hebrew.

Geographical Setting

Central Arabian deserts sit in southwest Asia on a peninsula between
the Red Sea and the Persian Gulf. A comparatively well-watered
region rims these deserts on the north. Called the Fertile Crescent,
this region includes one-time Canaan (today's Israel) in its southernmost corner.

Water lies to the west, great deserts extend to the east, mountainous areas spread to the north, and wilderness and water cover
the south. Also in the south is an expanse of desert known as the
Negev, reaching all the way to the Red Sea's Gulf of Eilat (also called
Gulf of Aqaba). Flowing north to south through the land is the Jordan
River. In the east lies the Dead Sea, a salt lake that is the lowest
point on Earth. Much of the land is dry.

Its soil made ancient Israel mainly an agricultural land. The valleys, coastal plains, hill country, and even the Negev when irrigated
could be successfully farmed. Positioned between Asia and Africa,
the land also served as a throughway for trade caravans and for
invasions from expanding empires.

Historical Background

Abraham of Ur. The history of the Hebrews begins with Abraham of the city of Ur located in what is now the southern part of Iraq. Abraham is recognized as a patriarch by today's Muslims and Christians, as well as Jews, so the early history of the Hebrews is a history of all three of the major religions of the area.

Hebrew origins—the patriarchs. A number of semi-nomadic, or partly settled, groups called Habiru appeared in the region once known as Canaan from about the year 1900 B.C.E. They roamed the land with livestock—goats, sheep, and cattle—settling in one area for a time, then moving onward. Among these semi-nomads lived Abraham and the early leaders who descended from him. They came to be called the patriarchs.

Born in the city of Ur in Mesopotamia, Abraham first lived in a community of well-built, two-story houses, and was a wealthy herdsman of cattle and sheep. Moving into Canaan, however, he began quite a different existence. The tent became his home, and family was his society. The family's structure was simple. At the helm was the father, the patriarch, with sons, daughters, and wives all subject to his authority. The tribe (family) lived off their herds and the labor of family craftsmen such as musicians or smiths. When Abraham died, his son Isaac succeeded him as patriarch, or leader of the family and its religion. (In this era, a family had its own religious traditions and burial grounds.) Isaac, in turn, was succeeded by his son Jacob, and Jacob by the twelve tribes of Israel. It is said that Jacob once wrestled all night with a stranger in the desert until the stranger blessed him and gave him the name *Isra-el*, meaning "wrestler with the Lord." From this incident comes the name Israel.

Two tenets of a new faith emerged from the period of the patriarchs. The first concerned the covenant. Applied to the whole family, the covenant was an agreement with one God. The family would worship only this deity, who in exchange would be devoted to the family's welfare. Abraham initiated the covenant, which was renewed by Isaac and then by Jacob. The second tenet concerned the nature of this deity. Abraham's God was no distant, impersonal force but rather a deity with whom he could reckon and reason, one who could be questioned by any individual member of the covenant. Thus, the

Bible relates incidents such as Abraham's convincing God to spare the evil town Sodom if at least ten righteous men lived there.

Slavery and exodus. When drought descended on Canaan, it was common for herders to wander into Egypt, where the Nile River nourished the land. Biblical lore holds that first Jacob's son Joseph and later the rest of the family (seventy members) moved to Egypt. The Hyksos were the rulers in power at the time and Jacob's family was on friendly terms with these rulers. They therefore lived securely until the Hyksos rulers fell. Into power came new Egyptian rulers, who enslaved foreign settlers, including Jacob's descendants.

One estimate places the total Hebrew sojourn in Egypt under 150 years, sometime between 1720 and 1220 B.C.E. (Klein 1986, p. 32). Jacob had ten sons who joined Joseph in Egypt: Reuben, Simeon, Levi, Judah, Dan, Naphtali, Gad, Asher, Issachar, and Zebulun. Over time they multiplied into ten tribes of *Israel* plus two more tribes named not after Joseph but after his sons, Manasseh and Ephraim.

Belonging to the tribe of Levi, the leader Moses organized Hebrew and non-Hebrew slaves to escape to freedom. For years he led them through the wilderness of the Sinai Desert, losing the weak and aged to death and fending off challenges to his authority. Moses himself perished before reentering the land of the patriarchs, but not before spearheading a pivotal change in their covenant with God. During the desert trek, the covenant between the issue of Abraham and the Lord was expanded. Now it included not only his family but the entire nation of refugees who embraced it.

Period of the Judges. The retaking of Canaan by the Hebrews was a long-term conquest that spanned at least a century. It entailed the Hebrews' destruction of places sometimes retaken by the Canaanites, then reconquered again. Although the Hebrews themselves did not at first fight as a united group, they finally succeeded in the conquest, defeating the Canaanites, an accomplished society whose alphabets and dialects the Hebrews adopted. One of these dialects they shaped into biblical Hebrew.

The Israelites, as they were now called, settled in tribes. The large tribe of Judah positioned itself west of the Dead Sea, while the tribespeople of Ephraim moved north of the sea. Occupying the coastal area were two outside groups—the Philistines and to north of them the Phoenicians. The Israelites formed rural communities, each of them governing themselves through a Council of Elders (made up of notable individuals) and a "Judge." The term Judge was used loosely for the local military leader who distinguished himself in battle. Among the Judges of the time were Deborah, Gideon, and Samson, a Judge who came to lead the tribe of Dan.

Bordered by the Phoenicians, the Israelites were influenced by their customs. Foremost among the Phoenician gods was Baal, god of rain and agriculture. Some Israelites borrowed rituals from the worship of Baal and incorporated them in the worship of their own Lord. When camel raiders overran Israelite communities, prophets explained the defeat as punishment for the Israelites' desertion of their own customs. Time and again, straying from the faith would be linked to military defeats.

Kingship—Saul, David, and Solomon. The Philistines seemed to be constantly on the warpath, and the separate Israelite tribes needed a champion to marshal a unified force against these foes. A simple farmer named Saul rose to the position. One day, while he was plowing behind a yoke of oxen, a crisis arose. Ammonites had surrounded an Israelite city, and, according to folklore, Saul cut a pair of oxen into pieces, then sent the pieces through the land with messengers to recruit soldiers, threatening that anyone who failed to come would have the same done to his oxen. Saul defeated the enemy and remained in power for nineteen years, without a palace or royal court, but as a type of supreme Judge. He was heroic but jealous of his power. One of his aides, a boy named David, defeated the great Philistine Goliath in man-to-man combat about 1010 B.C.E., then married Saul's daughter. The two men feuded and David escaped to the desert, where he organized outlaws into a small army of professional fighters. Shortly thereafter, David rose to leadership after Saul killed himself while losing in battle, preferring suicide to death at the hands of the Philistines. His eldest son, Esh-baal, claimed the throne, but David returned home and won some support. The two leaders battled, with David's experienced fighters winning. David became king by about age thirty-three.

In the tenth century B.C.E., the Israelites entered a golden era. David and then Solomon ruled, developing the land into the major force in western Asia. Though young, King David of Israel was multitalented: a military leader, poet, musician, family man, and builder. He made a brilliant political move, capturing Jebus, a city that belonged to none of the twelve Israelite tribes, and making it a physical symbol of the united people—Jerusalem, the City of David. David planned the building of a royal chapel there, and also established the priesthood and musical guilds. A bureaucracy was formed, which included scribes, ministers, a standing army, and royal officials to collect taxes. Despite this glory, David had public and personal troubles. His rule embittered many of the people and they rebelled at hardships such as unbearable taxes. All but the tribe of Judah grew disenchanted. Even David's own son Absalom perished in a revolt against his father in 978 B.C.E.

After David died, his oldest son, Adonijah, and Solomon, the son of his favorite wife Bathsheba, competed for kingship. Solomon won, killing or banishing Adonijah's supporters. He then reigned for some forty years (968–928 B.C.E.), concentrating not on war but on business and material splendor. Solomon built the temple his father had originally planned, intending it to be the sole worship center for Israelites. His reign brought prosperity to the wealthy but not the commoners. The worship of Phoenician gods spread, intermarriage increased, and Solomon built pagan shrines for his foreign wives. Taxes continued, and forced labor began for the common folk as well as the slaves. When Solomon died in 928 B.C.E., only the tribe of Judah accepted his son Rehoboam as successor. The other tribes demanded that he lessen their burdens, and when Rehoboam refused, the northern tribes revolted, beginning a period of the Divided Kingdom.

Divided Kingdom. The nation split into the northern Kingdom of Israel and southern Kingdom of Judah. The separation would last from 928 to 600 B.C.E., during which time the records of the Hebrews were written in the Jewish Bible, or Old Testament.

Sometimes Judah and Israel fought together against outside enemies; they also battled each other. Murders were rampant as brother killed brother and there was perpetual plotting for succession to the thrones. Phoenician idols found their way into both kingdoms, and prophets of the time, Amos and Hosea, protested the desertion of the Lord and warned that the Israelites would suffer dire consequences. Such warnings were confirmed around 722 B.C.E., when Israel fell to the Assyrians. The conquerors emptied the land, forced the northern Israelites into exile, and repopulated it with foreign peoples.

The Israelites of Judah to the south held on until 587–586 B.C.E. Here Jeremiah the prophet warned the people to rely on the Lord, not military might, but they refused to listen. Falling under Babylonian rule, Judah revolted and Babylonia retaliated, crushing the Judeans and leveling their temple. Nebuchadnezzar, the ruler of Babylon, deported 10,000 to 12,000 of the leading scholars, priestly families, and craftspeople in order to prevent future rebellions, ushering in the period of Babylonian exile.

Exile and return. The Babylonian exile was the first major scattering, or diaspora, of Jews, and it lasted from around 589 B.C.E. to 539 B.C.E. Not all the Judeans cooperated. Some fled to Egypt, where they served pharaohs as fighters. Meanwhile, the fortunes of those in Babylon depended on their social status. Commoners were enslaved, while scholars, priests, and landowners had limited freedom. About 545 B.C.E., Persia under Cyrus II conquered Babylon and freedom increased. Subjects could worship their gods, own property, and so on. The Judeans could even return to Israel.

Not all Judeans returned, but enough came to dedicate a small second temple in Jerusalem about 515 B.C.E. Some sixty-five years later the Jewish governor Nehemiah arrived and was shocked by the sorry state of the holy city. Jerusalem's people were poor, unhappy, and sacrilegious—they did not even abstain from business activity on the Sabbath. Aided by a priest named Ezra, Nehemiah wrought major changes. He brought with him the Five Books of Moses, the Jewish Bible, which in 444 B.C.E. Ezra read to an assembly of the adult population and established as the basis of Judaism. Ezra ordered every Judean to divorce his gentile (non-Jewish) wife, and Nehemiah arrested those who broke the Sabbath laws.

Roman rule. In 332 B.C.E. Alexander the Great conquered the Judeans, bringing Western ways to the holy land. Called "hellenism," the new lifestyle was Greek in essence. About 200 B.C.E., Syrians known as the Seleucids gained control and promoted these same ways. Life became much harsher than it had been under the Persians. The new government appointed corrupt Judean priests, who worked in league with the outside rulers, and passed decrees banning Jewish worship, diet, circumcision, and other religious traditions. In the temple the outsiders set up a shrine to Zeus and ordered the Judeans to make sacrifices to the Greek gods. Not everyone cooperated. A local priest, Mattathiias Hasmonean, fled to the hills with his five sons, then mounted three years of guerrilla resistance against the Seleucids. One of his sons, Judas Maccabeus, staged one surprise attack after another in the years 165–164 B.C.E. until he reached the sanctuary in Jerusalem itself. There he dismantled the shrine to Zeus and lit the Judean menorah, or seven-branched candleholder. Over the next

100 years several other Hasmoneans (Maccabeans) came to power as the High Priest of Judea. In the end, though, these Hasmonean rulers cooperated with Rome.

From 37 to 4 B.C.E. not a Hasmonean, but a converted Jew named Herod, reigned as king. He had crowned himself with Rome's approval. Herod, in quest of favor from those subjects who hated and mistrusted him, built a new, majestic house of worship in Jerusalem, traditionally called the "Second Temple." Of white marble and gold, Herod's temple rested on a platform whose western supporting wall still stands in Jerusalem. Herod's rule gave way to rule by corrupt Roman governors and a General Council of "acceptable" Judeans, the Sanhedrin. The seventy-one-member council of priests and notables governed under the watchful gaze of the despised Roman governors. Many Judeans looked for a Messiah, or deliverer, to relieve them. Some believed Jesus was this savior.

Nero rose to power in Rome in 66 C.E., and conditions worsened until, finally, the Israelites rebelled. Zealots (a Judean sect that resisted Roman rule) under the leader Menahem overcame a Roman garrison at Masada on a mountain that loomed above the Dead Sea. He then captured Jerusalem, but was assassinated by another sect of Jews, the Sadduccees. Opposition weakened and the Romans rallied. They retook all but Jerusalem and Masada by the middle of A.D. 60. The Zealots held Jerusalem until 70, when Romans broke through and amidst heavy bloodshed destroyed the "Second Temple." Thousands of Jews were marched out of the land, many to become slaves or victims in Roman gladiator games. But Menahem's nephew, Eleazar ben Yair, escaped to Masada where he held the fort until 73 C.E. In the same year the Romans built a ramp to the summit. Mounting it, they found only a few children and two women alive. The other 960 defenders preferred suicide at Masada to being taken captive by the Romans.

Culture

Food, clothing, and shelter. Religion became part of everyday life for the Israelites. A portable tent first housed the Ark, or cabinet that held the Ten Commandments. These ten rules were reported to have been given Moses during the Hebrew wandering after escaping from Egypt. In similar fashion, the early patriarchs dwelt in tents. Made of dark-brown or black goat hair, these portable homes apparently stood higher in the center (about seven feet) than at either end. A straw mat served as a bed, some leather as a table, and a few stones just outside the tent as a stove. Utensils included earthen bowls, water jars, goatskin bags, a copper pot, and rough-hewn knives, forks, and spoons.

More permanent housing was later adopted from the Canaanites. In the low-lying plains were small, boxlike homes of mud-brick walls sealed by mortar and whitewash. More popular in the central highlands were stone houses made of ill-fitting, uncut stones pasted together with mortar. One room inside, about ten feet square, served for sleeping, eating, entertaining, and fulfilling religious obligations, such as circumcision (removal of the foreskin of a son on the eighth day after his birth). Religious symbols decorated the home, and by the era of Roman rule some houses already affixed to their doorposts *mezuzot*, narrow containers with a scroll declaring dedication to the one God.

Diet, too, was intimately connected with religion. The everyday fare included barley bread, milk, dates, figs, pomegranates, melons, grapes, and wine. Probably the most common meal was stew prepared from beans, lentils, and peas. Vegetables (lettuce, beets, cucumbers, and onions) added flavor and variety. Only rarely did the people eat animals, and biblical laws specified which ones were permitted (animals with hooves cleft in two and that bring up their cud). Pigs were unacceptable (did not bring up their cud), as were camels (did not have split hooves). Biblical law also prohibited cooking a kid goat in its mother's milk, probably to prevent creating pagan charms of the time. In post-biblical times, religious leaders expanded this law to prohibit eating milk with meat.

Clothing first consisted of a loincloth, then the tunic. Close-fitting shirtlike garments, tunics were made either of wool or linen as biblical law prohibited mixing both materials in the same garment. Often white, the tunic came in various styles; one type draped over one shoulder and reached slightly below the knees. A belt, or folded length of cloth, encircled the waist. Usually a loose cloak covered the tunic, and sandals were standard footwear. Probably by 538 B.C.E., such outfits had given way to Persian styles such as coats, trousers, and boots.

Religious clothing differed from everyday wear. The high priest wore eight garments—tunic, sash, breeches, and turban, covered by a gown, breastplate, robe, and crown all woven from gold, blue, and purple wool. Lesser priests wore ceremonial caps while common men went bareheaded. Covering the head was not required by the Bible. Tearing one's clothes to mourn the death of a family member was.

Family life. Families were father-centered, but mothers occupied a place of honor, respected as the ones who through child bearing insured the continuity of the family. Regarded as a father's property, children under thirteen (twelve and one-half for a girl) could be sold by him. Marriages, arranged by parents, occurred around the age of eighteen, and marriage to more than one wife was permissible. Though rare, divorce was possible, for example, if a wife proved unable to bear her husband children. Adult children honored their parents by caring for a mother's and father's worldly needs. Respect meant children followed certain behavior patterns; they did not sit in their parents' seats or interrupt them in conversation. Parents, in turn, had obligations to the child. Besides circumcising a son, a father, for instance, had to teach him the Torah (the five books of Moses), find him a wife, and train him in a trade that made him self-sufficient.

Religion. The Israelite religion developed over the ages. It proceeded from sacrifices at high places to worship in a central temple to local synagogues. At first, it was a sacrificial cult that used a portable tent and ark to house the stone tablets on which the commandments were inscribed. On an alter outside the tent, the worshippers offered animal sacrifices. *Kohanim* (priests) conducted the ceremony to the musical accompaniment provided by their assistants, the *Levites*. The belief was that all things belonged to God, so that a man should sacrifice, or surrender the first produce, livestock, even human life in his family. An animal could substitute for a first-born child.

The permanent temple in Jerusalem was a house of worship whose inner precincts only the priests could enter. These priests carried out rituals on the people's behalf. Though the people themselves could not enter the sanctuary, they gathered outside and made pilgrimages to the grand house of worship. At the same time, the people were expected to contribute to the temple upkeep with money or farm products.

After 70 c.e., the synagogue and *Bet Midrash* (study hall) grew popular, having arisen out of the ongoing conflict between the prophets and priests. In temple times and after, priests were the official leaders, while prophets were individuals who warned against hypocritical worship and idolatry. The prophets held that the holy covenant bound Jews to ethical relationships with one another and that the formalities of the religion were valueless unless people lived ethical daily lives. Some prophets offered their homes as synagogue-type meeting houses, providing an an alternative type of spiritual experience. Ezra, the prophet who read the Torah to the public in 444 B.C.E. and made it the Jewish constitution, began certain enduring customs, including the practice of holy leaders standing on a dais at meetings, the raising of the scroll to full view of congregants as they rise, and the reading of the Torah on Monday and Thursday mornings, when people came to local markets.

Already celebrated in ancient times were sacred days—the Sabbath, Feast of Weeks (Shavuot), New Year (Rosh Hashanah), Day of Atonement (Yom Kippur), and the Festival of Booths (Sukkot). As time passed, some of these took on an added dimension, commemorating and keeping alive historical events. The Festival of the Booths is a celebration of thanksgiving for the harvest. In ancient times, it is believed people actually dwelt in booths by their homes for seven days in commemoration of how the Israelites dwelt in the desert when they left Egypt.

Education. The great scholar Hillel lived at the time of King Herod (37–34 B.C.E.). The Romans were in power, and Herod supported them, building gymnasiums and adopting elements of the Greek and Roman language, literature, and philosophy. In response, Jewish sects arose, among them the Sadducees—an upper class of landowners, merchants, and official priests—and the Pharisees. The Pharisees were a group dedicated to the Torah and common folk. Its members held that the Torah, set down during the time of the Divided Kingdom, provided guidance for every situation in life. Developing this line of reasoning, a poor but esteemed teacher named Hillel rose to fame. He became regarded as a prince of the community, a counter king, a more legitimate ruler, in fact, than Herod himself. His impact was summarized in the following (Glatzer 1966, p. 31).

In ancient days when the Torah was forgotten from Israel,
Ezra came up from Babylon and reestablished it.
Then it was again forgotten
until Hillel the Babylonian came up and reestablished it.

Hillel spread universal precepts, such as not judging your fellow man before you have been in his situation; knowledge will shrink unless it grows; and one who studies Torah has life in the world to come. (The Pharisees believed in an afterlife.) A champion of the common man, Hillel advocated education for everyone. Although he had opponents within the Jewish community, his teachings and causes prevailed. In the first century C.E., Joshua ben Gamla arranged for teachers to be appointed in every town at the town's expense. Subsequently, Jewish law would pay special heed to schooling, even limiting permissible class size (one teacher per twenty-five students).

Law and art. Beyond influencing education, Hillel formed seven rules that helped make the Jewish Bible a timeless guide. One was his "generalization of a special law." The Torah, or Five Books of Moses, set down specific laws. When harvesting a crop, for example, a corner of the field was to be left unharvested for the poor. Also, in loaning money one should not take a mill as security from the borrower because doing so would jeopardize the borrower's life. This last rule was generalized into "do not take anything used to prepare food." Hillei seized on the general intention of the law and applied it to the society of the time.

Aside from relating the law, the Jewish Bible told an awesome story that constituted the major artistic achievement of the time. There were other achievements, such as the melodies and poetry of King David's and Solomon's time. The Bible was the monumental work, though. It is divided into three parts, the first being the Torah (Five Books of Moses), which formed a complete narrative from creation to the time of the patriarchs to Moses's death before entering Canaan. The second part, the prophets, continues the story from the conquest of Canaan to the early Second Temple. In the third part are a great mix of literary genres from poetry to proverbs to historical books.

For More Information

Frankel, Ellen. *The Classic Tales: 4,000 Years of Jewish Lore.* Northvale, New Jersey: Jason Aronson Inc., 1989.

Glatzer, Nahum N. *Hillel the Elder: The Emergence of Classical Judaism.* New York: Schocken, 1966.

Klein, Herbert. *The Peoples of Israel: Fifty-Seven Centuries of Presence.* Malibu, California: Pangloss Press, 1986.

Orlinsky, Harry M. *Ancient Israel.* Ithaca, New York: Cornell University Press, 1954.

BABYLONIANS

(bab ih lone' euns)

Early inhabitants of the Kingdom of Babylon in the Tigris-Euphrates River Valley whose civilization paralleled and was similar to that of the Assyrians to the north.

Population: Unknown.
Location: Present-day Iraq, principally the region north and south of Baghdad along the Tigris and Euphrates rivers.
Languages: Sumerian, Akkadian.

Geographical Setting

Before the time of Babylon, there were many small city-states along the Tigris and Euphrates rivers. One of these was in the delta area of the two rivers, with its capital at the city of Ur. Another was Kish, located to the north of Babylon. These city-states carried on an active trade, using the rivers to travel north and south. At that time, before 2000 B.C., the great rivers flooded annually beginning about April and city-states were largely determined by the locations of canals for drainage of the land. As these canals filled with silt, cities were relocated from place to place along the rivers. At that same time, the distance between the two rivers narrowed below where present-day Baghdad stands. Here, in a place where elaborate drainage canals were constructed and where irrigation systems were extensive, the city of Babylon was constructed. It was a city that could control river traffic along both rivers, lying on a branch of the Euphrates River near the present-day city of Hilla. In this city, near the end of the third millennium B.C., a ruler by the name of Sunu-abu established a kingdom.

Historical Background

Beginning. About 2400 B.C., the ancient empire of Sumer was conquered by the ruler of a state upriver, which had been inhabited by Semitic people perhaps coming from the north. The ruler of this kingdom of Akkad—Sargon, of the Arabian desert—and his sons and grandson held the land of the southern river valleys until 2230 B.C., when a new group from the north, the Guti, overran Akkad and controlled the land until 2130 B.C. The area then broke again into several city-states before coming together to form two kingdoms. North of Babylon was the kingdom of Insin, and south lay the kingdom of Larsa. About the end of the third millennium B.C., these two kingdoms were united under one ruler, Sunu-abu. Thus the Tigris and Euphrates river valleys were the sites of many civilizations before the rise to power of one of the most famous kings of Babylon, Hammurabi, about 1770 B.C. This powerful ruler gathered the laws that governed the earlier states and added his own to form one of the earliest codes of law in the world. About this same time, another kingdom was rising far to the north in present-day Iraq—the Assyrian Kingdom, with its capital at Ninevah.

Hittites. About 1600 B.C., Hittites, a warring band from Asia Minor, invaded the declining Babylon, and the old kingdom was disbanded. Centuries later, the city of Babylon arose again, this time as a vassal state of Assyria, and in the 600s B.C., a leader of the city attempted a revolt against Assyrian domination. Besieged by the army of the Assyrian leader, Assur-bani-pal, the city fell again. However, Assyria itself soon weakened and disintegrated, because the Assyrians, according to the Babylonians, refused to worship the Babylonian city-god Marduk. Again the region fell into disunion, with various local rulers taking turns at attempts to dominate.

Nebuchadnezzar. Not until the end of the sixth century B.C. was Babylon again a power under its ruler Nebopolassar. Under his rule, and that of his son Nebuchadnezzar, Babylonian (now Chaldean) influence grew and spread so that by 586 B.C. it held power as far distant as Judah, from where the Jewish people were relocated to Babylon to become prisoners and slaves. Later in that same century, Persians captured Babylonia and the Jews were permitted to leave. Still later, armies from Greece attacked the land under Alexander the Great, who died while in possession of much of the Middle East in

323 B.C. Then in 275 B.C., Babylon fell to a band known as Seleucids, descendants of Alexandrian forces governed by Seleucus. The inhabitants of the city were moved to Selucia, and the influence of Babylon vanished.

Culture

The city of Babylon. A visitor to old Babylon would find a walled city ten miles or more square, with canals coursing toward the river. Small mud-brick or mud and reed houses sheltered most of the in-

Found at Nippur, this tablet is one of the world's oldest medical journals, written about 2100 B.C. *Courtesy of the University Museum, University of Pennsylvania.*

habitants of the city and the fields surrounding it. Stone towers—the sites dedicated to the gods and also used as centers of commerce, employment agencies, and governmental agencies—arose in several places in the city. The government controlled much of the life of a city that was held together partly by religion, with priests among the city officials. Streets within the city were lined with more substantial structures of mud-brick or stone that were used for commerce and for the homes of wealthier merchants. Certain streets were dedicated to the growing diversification of artisans, some of whom were becoming well-known along the river for their ability to weave products from imported flax. For Babylon was a trading city, in its peak times controlling trade along the rivers. Here also, from early times, were palaces of the rulers, and works of beauty commissioned by them. Babylon was the site of a great tiered garden that became known as one of the "seven wonders of the world"—the Hanging Gardens of Babylon.

Farming. From early times, the land around the city was privately owned. Workers dressed in skirts tilled small plots of land owned either by them or by a wealthier landlord. Chief agricultural products were barley, dates, sesame, and wheat. The farmers of the valley learned very early how to climb the date trees and assist in fertilizing the female flowers to produce more fruits. The more affluent farmers used metal sickles to clear the land and metal plows to work it like their predecessors, the Sumerians, whose language they had borrowed.

Language and literature. Using this language and later the newer Akkadian vocabulary, Babylonians kept records of history, wrote pieces of literature, and tallied hours of labor and products by writing on soft clay tablets and then leaving them in the sun to bake dry and harden. Among the writings left behind are stories of the city-god Marduk, the special god who looked after the city. The "Epic of Creation" tells of Marduk's encounter with a monster Tiamat. Marduk killed the monster and, out of her body, created the world. Other stories tell of an ancient king Gilgamesh and his many exploits. And, of course, there were the records of business and the written laws that evolved into the more than 300 laws that formed the Code of Hammurabi.

Religion. Marduk was the central god of Babylon and the ruler was one of his court—holding power by reason of godliness just as the rulers on the other great river, the Nile. But other gods through the ages included Anu, the god of heaven; Innini, goddess of heaven; Enlit, the earth god and his mate the goddess Nintel; Eu, god of water; Babbar, god of the sun; and Sin, the moon god. Agents of the gods were the priests of the temples. These priests also kept the government records and performed some of the municipal duties.

Business. Life in Babylon was controlled by the religious sector. The god-king controlled traffic on the river, eventually devising a system of licensing shippers and merchants. Lands were held independently except that the Babylonian rulers early learned to tax property owners and to charge for transfers of lands and buildings. Although property was privately owned, priests assigned workers for the fields, counted the harvests, and provided seeds and tools as they had in the older land of Sumer. At a site ideally situated to control river traffic, Babylonian merchants grew wealthy, and acquired larger and larger portions of the land.

Arts. Some of the people of Babylon became skilled artisans and were employed in the preparation of religious sculpture. Other craftspeople used the potter's wheel to make a variety of pots and dishes, on which they painted designs and illustrations in black, white, and red. Other artisans were employed in decorating public places with wall paintings of the royalty and of scenes important to the time and the city.

Law. By the end of the Babylonian era, a substantial set of laws governed almost all aspects of daily life. The Code of Hammurabi, created "to establish justice in Sumer and Akkad," began: "Let any oppressed man, who has a cause, come before my image as king of righteousness!" It went on to define laws about trade, property ownership, repayment of debts, marriage, divorce, and the care of children. This code suggests the pattern of life in Babylon and also reveals the long history of some of the mores of the Middle East today.

Under the law, claims to private property were to be justified by ownership of a deed. This deed could be transferred by sale, gift, or partitioning, or used as collateral on a loan or pledge. It was the buyer's responsibility to be sure that the seller had legal right to the property.

On the vast amount of land owned by the government, workers were allowed to lease houses for a period of a year, and were required to pay rent twice yearly. Some land was leased to farmers for a period of up to ten years. Each time land was transferred a tax was to be paid, often to help pay for the support of soldiers in the army of the ruler.

In any transaction, should a party default on payment, that person could assign his wife or children to work to pay off the debt for a period of up to three years. The man controlled the family and had ownership of the children in Babylonia.

Marriages were arranged by purchase of the bride. The groom's family paid a bride-price, while the bride's family helped the new-lyweds by supplying a dowry of money or household goods. Under

This ivory plaque came from Assyria, Babylon's neighbor and rival about the eighth century B.C.
Courtesy of the University Museum, University of Pennsylvania.

the law, men could divorce their wives by repaying the price of the dowry. In a divorce, the children became custody of the father. A woman could also sue for divorce on the basis of cruelty or neglect. But in this event, should the woman prove to be at fault in the marriage, she was penalized by drowning. If she was proven correct, suitable alimony was arranged. A man and wife could adopt a child, but then were obligated to treat that child as their own.

Grievances were penalized by exact repayment. Stolen articles required repayment of the value of the article. A person whose actions resulted in the death of another's son or daughter, was punished by the death of his own son or daughter.

The Code of Hammurabi, reveals a male dominated society, but one in which women had rights under the law and in which the rights of children were protected.

For More Information

Swain, J. W. *The Ancient World.* New York: Harper and Row, 1950.

Wallbank, T. Walter, Alastair M. Taylor, and Nels M. Bailkey. *Civilization: Past and Present.* New York: Scott, Foresman and Company, 1965.

PHOENICIANS
(feh neesh' uns)

Early inhabitants of city-states around the Mediterranean Sea.

Population: Unknown.
Location: The Mediterranian coast of what is now Syria and Lebanon.
Language: Phoenician, one of the Semitic languages.

Geographical Setting

The land that is now Syria and Lebanon borders the Mediterranean Sea. It rises rapidly in the east to mountains, leaving a rugged coastal area twenty miles wide and two hundred miles long. In this narrow area, there are not many natural resources. Cedar trees once covered the mountains, and a few mineral deposits are found in the foothills. One of the few favorable seaports today is Beirut, Lebanon, but 3,000 years ago there were several small ports with names such as Simyra, Sidon, and Tyre that could accommodate the sailing boats of the time.

Historical Background

Origin. For thousands of years, the land around the eastern arch of the Mediterranean Sea has been contested by rival peoples. Before 1500 B.C., groups of migrants from the east followed the mountains that border the Persian Gulf and settled in small kingdoms along the sea. To the north people known as Hittites settled what is now southeastern Turkey. Hebrews followed the coast south into the region that is now Israel, where Philistines and Canaanites had settled. Between the peoples north and south of them and intermixed with them, along the coast of present-day Syria and Lebanon, a group known as the Phoenicians settled in a number of city-states bound together by their main industries: sea trade and fishing.

Egyptians. About 1500 B.C., the pharaohs of Egypt began to expand their realm. The Egyptians moved northeastward along the coast, and the Egyptian ruler Ahmosi took possession of the city-states of the Phoenicians, leaving the princes of the cities in charge, but exacting tribute that had to be paid to an Egyptian governor.

For a time, Egypt held the region firmly. However, eventually the area reverted to its previous owners. Still later, Ramses II conquered the land and claimed it for Egypt once again. Again, in the tenth century B.C., the Egyptians withdrew from present-day Syria.

Independence. For two hundred years, the Phoenicians were governors of their own destiny. From their central city, Tyre, they scattered around the Mediterranean, building ships and trading with people as far away as England. The rulers of Tyre, Sidon, and other city-ports sent settlers to Cyprus and to the northern coast of Africa beyond Egypt. Across the sea from the toe of Italy, Phoenicians built Carthage, a great shipping center in north Africa. By 1100 B.C., Phoenicians had settled near the Strait of Gibralter, and other stopping places for their ships were built as far away as present-day Spain.

In the period from 970 to 930 B.C., the city of Tyre was governed by Hiram I, who unified the Phoenicians by making alliances with leaders of other cities. This was the time of the great Hebrew leader Solomon. Hiram I and Solomon became allies and friends. When Solomon began to build a large palace in the city that is now Jerusalem, Hiram sent materials and workers to help with the building. In exchange, Solomon granted Hiram rights to land in Galilee. The Phoenicians were now extended into Palestine (present-day Israel and Jordan).

Assyrians. In the next century, Assyrians from the north had begun to raid Phoenician ports and threaten the Phoenician union. By 725 B.C., the bases of the Phoenicians had been overrun by the Assyrians. That was not the end of land disputes, however. By the sixth century B.C., the Egyptians had captured the land from the Assyrians, only to lose it to people from the east known as the Chaldeans, who under Nebuchadnezzar marched onto Phoenician land.

In the fourth century B.C., Alexander the Great claimed this region for Macedonia. Still later, Egypt and Syria took turns at ruling over the Phoenicians. Between 264 and 146 B.C., Phoenicians based at Carthage engaged in three long wars with the Romans for control of Carthage and part of Italy. Known as the Punic Wars, these wars ended in defeat for the Phoenicians and the complete destruction of Carthage. The Phoenician city-states finally disappeared when Pompey of Rome claimed the land in 64 B.C.

Culture

Industry. The Phoenicians lived in a land where the major resources were the sea and the trees of the nearby mountains. Once described as providing more fish than there was sand, the area was uninviting for agriculture but the sea encouraged its people to become shipbuilders and traders. Phoenician ships were the fastest on the sea, and their navigators the best. Some claim that the Phoenicians sailed around Africa into the area of the Red Sea.

Phoenician sailors traveled along the coast of Africa in search of trade. Certainly their ships traded along the Atlantic coast of Africa and north into the British Islands. They traded fish to Palestine in exchange for cloth. From a small shelled sea animal, the Phoenicians made a rich purple dye, which they used to color silk and other cloth to trade around the Mediterranean Sea.

Government. Each Phoenician city was ruled by a prince or king who often paid allegiance to the king of Tyre. The people of Tyre were ruled by a king who was to follow agreed-upon guidelines, a sort of constitution. So, Phoenicians were among the early practitioners of some sort of constitutional government.

Arts. Because of their primary industry, trading, the Phoenicians were in a position to borrow ideas from other people and to improve upon them. They became highly skilled glassworkers and metalsmiths. Early users of iron, they manufactured knives, swords and daggers. Other Phoenician arts were borrowed from the Egyptians.

Food, clothing, and shelter. The name Phoenician may have originally come either from their words for "red skin," from a Greek name for palm trees, or from the word for a scarlet dye that the people made and sold. Phoenicians were known throughout the Mediterranean area as "red skins" for their perpetually sunburned skin—an outcome of their occupations: fishing, sailing, and trading. Phoenician diets consisted of the fish they caught and the cereal obtained from trading with nearby peoples.

These seafaring people lived in communities established around the port facilities and temples. There they constructed homes of stone and mud with thatched roofs. While in the cities, people wore long robes and pointed hats for protection against the sun. On ship, the crews wore a single piece of cloth wound around the waist and between the legs to form a sort of short pants. Their clothes were patterned after the clothes of their Egyptian conquerors.

Language. Hebrews, Philistines, and Phoenicians may have all come to this area from farther east, perhaps from the region of Babylon near the Persian Gulf. They brought with them a Semitic language that was modified and developed into different versions as the different groups became isolated and formed their own communities. The Phoenicians probably borrowed the idea of a written alphabet from other peoples, then shaped it into an alphabet with twenty-two consonants. Later the Greeks added vowels, which led to our present alphabet. The practical nature of the Phoenicians is illustrated by this alphabet, which took the names of common items as the names of the letters. For example, the first two letters in the Phoenician alphabet were *aleph* and *beth.* In their language, *aleph* meant ox, and *beth* meant house.

Religion. Phoenicians worshipped many gods. The city-states worshiped different gods of the land. Each state took gods they thought would protect them from immediate dangers and look after those items of nature that were important to them. One city-state might worship gods of the forest; another, gods of the wind. The choice of gods to worship depended on local conditions. Finally, one name, *Ba'al,* came to identify the chief god, whether it was the god of war, forests, sea, wind, or whatever was of dominant importance to the local community. To the gods, Phoenicians built temples consisting of an enclosed court and a roofed shrine. There were altars of stone and bronze on which sacrifices were made to the important gods. The sacrifices allegedly included humans.

Conclusion. Contributions to a constitutional form of government, systems of navigation, and our present European written languages are legacies from the Phoenicians who lived more than 2,500 years ago.

For More Information

Harder, Donald Benjamin. *The Phoenicians.* New York: Prager, 1962.

Herm, Gerhard. *The Phoenicians; The Purple Empire of the Ancient World.* New York: William Morrow, 1975.

Wallbank, T. Walter, Alastair M. Taylor, and Nels M. Bailkey. *Civilization Past and Present.* Chicago: Scott Foresman and Company, 1965.

MIDDLE EAST RELIGIONS

ISLAM IN THE MIDDLE EAST

The number of Muslims—followers of Islam, or "submission to god"—in the world today is approximately 900,000,000. It is a growing worldwide religion that arose in the Arabian Peninsula and has spread to the extent today that the largest populations of Muslims are in Indonesia and Pakistan.

In A.D. 610, according to Muslim belief, the angel Gabriel ordered Muhammad to recite the Word of God as it was delivered to him. This was the same basic message that had earlier been revealed to the Jews and later to the Christians, but the Word had been misinterpreted over the years and had to be restated. Over a period of twenty-two years, Muhammad received revelations from the angel, revelations incorporated in the Muslim holy book, the Quran. This is a detailed guide to behavior toward God, fellow humans, and the self.

As with Christ before him, Muhammad—the last prophet—was not accepted in his own state of Mecca, which was at that time a center for worship of pagan gods and therefore enjoyed a large income from visitors. The most powerful people of this city-state were active traders and were exposed and dedicated to many different gods. Muhammad's revelation that there "is no god but God" was threatening to them. In 622, Muhammad was forced to flee Mecca and establish home in Yathrib (now Medina). This departure from Mecca marks the establishment of the Muslim community and the beginning of the Muslim calendar. From then on, Islam—not the family or the tribe—was to be the basis of personal identity and social life.

Muhammad became both the religious and political leader of Yathrib. In a series of military victories and negotiations he established Islam and by 630 had such a large following that he was able to reenter Mecca with little opposition. There the prophet performed the first pilgrimage, entering the ancient shrine founded by Abraham, the Ka'ba, and destroying idols that had been placed there. The Ka'ba was thus established as the major religious site in the Muslim religion. Thousands of followers visit the sacred center each year on a pilgrimage, or *Hadj*, that fulfills one of the basic requirements of the faith, one of five Pillars of Islam:

1. Confession that there is "no god but God" and that Muhammad is the messenger of God.
2. Daily prayer (five times).
3. Giving of alms.
4. Fasting in daylight hours for the Muhammadan month of Ramadan.
5. Pilgrimage to Mecca at least once in a lifetime.

Prayers are said five times daily wherever one finds oneself, but on Friday the community gathers at the mosque for noon prayer. But prayer is not the only Muslim practice. The religion bans eating pork, drinking alcohol, gambling, and usury (loaning money with excessive interest). There are also specific laws concerning marriage, divorce, and inheritance. In some interpretations, art representing human figures is discouraged. The prophet Muhammad is never portrayed unless veiled, even in motion pictures.

Following Muhammad's death in 632, Islam was governed until 661 by a series of caliphs, or successors, accepted by the majority of the followers. The coming to leadership of the fourth caliph, Ali, cousin and son-in-law of Muhammad was challenged by the governor of Syria. The movement split those who felt that leadership should fall to Muhammad's blood relatives and those who believed that leadership should be decided by consensus of the followers. Despite this difference, Muslims were united in spreading the message revealed to Muhammad. Within a hundred years, Islam had swept across North Africa to Spain and southern France, and as far as the Indus River in the East. Most of these areas remain Islamic, and in addition have become Arabized by adopting the Arabic language.

Sunni. One governor established a Sunni dynasty with its capital at Damascus and his followers formed the division of Islam known as Sunnis, or orthodox Muslims. The majority among Muslims are of this Sunni sect, who believe that the community as the whole is the guardian and guarantor of Islamic law. This law, shari'a, is based on four sources, which in descending order of importance are: the Quran, the examples and teachings of the prophet, communal consensus on Islamic principles and practices, and reasoning by analogy. In later years the consensus was reduced to a consensus of religious scholars. This four-pronged determinant of the law provides great unity, but also provides for a variety of interpretations. Perhaps the most graphic example of this is the treatment of the law relating to modesty among women. In some places this law is accommodated by the wearing of a veil in public; in others, simply by avoiding male company when possible; and in others, is left to the discretion of local leaders.

Shi'ites. The followers of Muhammad's cousin, Ali, who believe that Muslim religious leadership descends through blood lines, are called Shi'ites. This group became more concentrated in Iraq and Iran. About 15 percent of today's Muslims are Shi'ites. Except for this difference in belief about the right to religious government, Muslims are united in their adherence to the basic tenets of the religion. However, lesser differences in worship procedures has divided both Shi'ites and Sunnis into subsects. One of these is Sufism.

Sufism. Many Muslims were influenced by a movement that started in Arabia and extended in the eighth and ninth centuries to Iraq and Persia. Called Sufism, this movement sought to temper the legalistic Islamic religion with mysticism. Sufism sought to appeal to the emotions to escape from one's self and unite with God. Ritual music and dance and constant awareness of God through prayer and the use of His name were the vehicles for unity with God. Sufism stressed the immanence of God but allowed for sainthood, elevating local heroes—both men and women—to higher religious status. Sufis believed in the unity of all parts of the world, as illustrated in this translation of a thirteenth century poem by Mawlana Jalal ad-Din Rumi (Nicholson 1975, p. 168):

I died as mineral and became a plant,
I died as plant and rose to animal,
I died as animal and I was man.
Why should I fear? When was I less by dying?
Yet once more I shall die as man, to soar
With angels blest; but even from angelhood
I must pass on: all except God doth perish.

While Muslims ruled in Spain (750-1492), the region functioned as a cultural transfer point between Europe and the Muslim world. A listing of objects that came to Europe via the Islamic world in-

An ink, gold, and pigment cover of a Quran prepared by Mahmud ibn al-Husayn al-Kitab al Kirmani about 1164 A.D. *Courtesy of the University Museum, University of Pennsylvania.*

dicates the latter's wide trade network. Even though not all items originated in the Middle East, Europeans came to know them by their Arabic names. Among the agricultural and food products were rice, sugar cane, eggplant, oranges, lemons, dates, and coffee; in cloth, the trade brought taffeta, muslin, damask, and satin. The divan, sofa, ottoman, lute, and guitar were also Islamic introductions. During this period, Islamic medicine and science were more advanced than those of Europe, as seen by a list of Arabic mathematical and chemical terms: cipher, zenith, nadir, algebra, algorithm, alchemy, alkali, talc, alcohol, arsenic, soda, and syrup. The equivalent of "the" in Arabic is *al*, suggesting that many English words have an Arabic origin and were delivered to the West in the great Islamic expansion. This movement also left its mark on the architecture of east and west. The Alhambra in Spain and the Taj Mahal in India are famous examples.

The best-known Muslim shrine outside of Mecca and Medina is the gold, marble, and mosaic Dome of the Rock in Jerusalem. Here Muhammad is believed to have met and prayed with the ancient prophets Abraham, Moses, and Jesus, and to have climbed a ladder of light through the seven stages of heaven. This episode has given Jerusalem its status as the third holy city of Islam.

Reform and renewal. Islam has a long tradition of renewal and reform. Its purpose is not to reinvent or recreate the already perfected

The Mosque of Omar in Jerusalem. *Courtesy of the University Museum, University of Pennsylvania.*

message, but to implement an already existing ideal. Periods of openness and experimentation are often followed by calls to return to the strict interpretation of the Quran and strict enforcement of the shari'a. In the eighteenth and nineteenth centuries, calls for religious and social reform often acquired political overtones as they challenged Western interests. Western power was military, political, economic, and social, and these elements along with a cultural dimension were communicated through a new educational system. This was a civilization that refused to be absorbed into the Islamic belief system. The Islamic opposition was total.

However, reaction to the West was varied; it came to be either ignored, escaped, integrated, accepted, or fought. Islamic revivalists completely rejected Westernization and sought to circumvent it by returning to past glory. Modernists among the Muslims wanted to reform society by applying the essence of Islam to contemporary issues. For them, there was not inherent conflict between Islam and modern science. There was, however, endless debate about how best to integrate Islam and Western thought. Amid this arose a movement toward nationalism, supported frequently by pointing to religion as the element most threatened by foreign rule. Islam was uniquely theirs, and had a great history of military and political success.

In the end, this difference resulted in some states, such as Iran and Libya, becoming disillusioned with Westernization and its various ideologies. They looked unfavorably on such Western societal issues as crime, divorce, and drugs. The result has been a recent and widespread movement toward more conservative forms of Islam. An example of this is the veil, which many women today wear more as a symbol of their unity with Islam than for its traditional implications of modesty. However, Islamic women today enjoy varying degrees of freedom and independence. In Egypt, for example, women are members of parliament; there are more women in the Egyptian parliament than in the United States Congress.

Islam today. In the Middle East today, orthodox Islam is enjoying a strong resurgence. However, in other regions thrives a popular form of Islam that is adapted to the traditions of the people. While orthodox Islam is mostly practiced by the wealthy, educated, and urbanized population, popular Islam is the choice of the lower classes.

One concept of popular Islam is *baraka,* or "divine grace," which is a sign of God's blessing manifest in a material form. Baraka is particularly sought by the poor, and attempts to gain it usually involve visits to the tomb of a holy man or woman who may have been a saint.

In Morocco, the Marabout, or "one tied to God," is a popular tradition. The Marabout is believed to have a special relationship with God, and thus able to intercede for others. Those who qualify for the position are popular patrons of the poor. Tombs of these "patron saints" are found throughout Morocco.

Popular practices are particularly associated with women since they are removed from the religious establishment and less exposed to Quranic readings or prayer at the mosque. Women use this exclusion by holding religious meetings in their homes, using the occasion as a social event. While women never preside over a mixed audience, they can pray at the mosque, fast during Ramadan, and make the pilgrimage to Mecca.

Over its 1,400-year history, Islam has spread across continents, unified millions of people, and supported a rich and diverse civilization. While Muslims regard the message of Islam as eternal and universal, their individual lives have demonstrated a variety of orientations towards traditional and popular patterns.

The Dome of the Rock, built as a mosque in the 600s, is a disputed area. It may have been built on the site of the altar of Solomon's temple. *Courtesy of the University Museum, University of Pennsylvania.*

For More Information

Cambridge Encyclopedia of Islam. Cambridge, University of Cambridge Press, 1970.

Mostyn, Trevor, editor. *Cambridge Encyclopedia of the Middle East and North* Africa. Cambridge: Cambridge University Press, 1985.

Nicholson, Reynold A. *The Mystics of Islam.* New York: Schocken, 1975.

CHRISTIANITY IN THE MIDDLE EAST

About two thousand years ago, Christianity arose from dissident Jews who felt that Judaism had wandered from the instructions of God. Their leader was Jesus, a Jewish man born of working parents in the Palestinian town of Bethlehem, who Christians came to believe was the Christ, the Son of God. The small group taught a religion based on love, helping others, forgiveness, and a version of the much earlier Eastern concept known as the golden rule (which encouraged people to treat others in the same way they would like to be treated). For a period after the death of its founder, Jesus Christ, the new religion was treated as a sect of Judaism. But with its acceptance by Roman leaders, the sect became separated from its Jewish heritage and went on to become the largest of today's religions.

The Christian church was born in the Middle East and had its earliest growth there. For roughly six centuries, from the death of Christ to the death of Muhammad, Egyptian, Syrian, and Greek church leaders in great cities such as Antioch and Alexandria shaped the beliefs that Christians hold today. These beliefs center upon a trilogy of God the father of all, his son in the person of Jesus Christ, and a Holy Spirit. Also central to the Christian faith is the belief in a life after that on earth and the intercession of Christ, whose death is believed to make ascension into heaven possible for all.

The faith was predominant in the region by the 600s. However, after the death of Muhammad, the Muslim religion swept through the Middle East, North Africa, and into Spain and France. In the 1000s, Christians rebelled against Muslim threats to Europe and occupation of areas held sacred to the Christians. A series of crusades temporarily restored Christian rule to Palestine. However, since then, the Muslim religion has spread widely. Today Christians in the Middle East are estimated to number about 10,000,000, or five percent of the area's population, and are a minority in a region dominated by Islam.

The early church. In the first few centuries of the Christian era, the Roman Empire encompassed the entire Mediterranean coast, including much of the Middle East. Most of Arabia was independent; Mesopotamia (modern Iraq) and Persia (modern Iran) were ruled by the Parthians, a people of what is now northern Iran, and later by the Persian Empire. These empires were in almost constant warfare with Rome. During a 300-year period, Christianity grew in popularity within the area which Rome controlled. The two most important Christian centers were Antioch, then a Syrian city but now part of Turkey, and Alexandria, the great Egyptian city which was also the major center of Greek learning. In these and other cities, Christian leaders such as Clement and Origen founded the new religion's theology (religious code).

As Christianity grew, it encountered increasing opposition from the Roman state. Roman religion was closely connected to the state, so that what threatened one was seen as threatening the other as well. Roman governors executed many Christians for refusing to recognize the emperor's divinity. Christians were attacked throughout the empire, but especially in the more heavily populated east. Many renounced their faith. Those who did not, however, saw their fallen comrades as glorious martyrs and were strengthened in their resolve. The worst persecutions occurred in Egypt, particularly under the emperor Diocletian in the late 200s and early 300s A.D.

Byzantium and Orthodoxy. The situation changed dramatically when Diocletian's successor, Constantine, himself converted to Christianity. During Constantine's rule (A.D. 312-337), Christians were accorded equality before the law, confiscated church property was returned, and old state religious cults were abolished. In 330, Constantine refounded the ancient Greek city of Byzantium as the new, and Christian, imperial capital. Called both Byzantium and Constantinople, the "second Rome" occupied a strategic site on the Bosporus, a narrow strait that divides the Mediterranean and Black seas and separates Europe and Asia. Soon its church became a new focus of Christianity, equal in seniority to that of Rome and surpassing in power those of Antioch and Alexandria. Eventually the Roman Empire split into eastern and western halves. Religious life reflected this division, with the Latin West coming under the Catholic Pope in Rome and the Greek East under the Orthodox Patriarch of Constantinople.

Politics and religious dissent. As the church's following and power expanded, its unity became more difficult to maintain. Different factions arose to challenge and help define what would become the Orthodox position. These breaks with Orthodoxy (which means "right believing") tended to center around the interpretation of Christ's nature. The Nestorians, followers of Nestorius, emphasized Christ's human nature and refused to recognize Mary as the Mother of God. In contrast, the Monophysites stressed Christ's divine aspect ("monophysite" comes from the Greek term for "one nature"). These controversies gave rise to great arguments within the church, which were decided by the Ecumenical Councils of the 400s.

The councils decreed the Orthodox position: that Christ combined two natures, human and divine, in one person. Attempting to enforce this creed, the church moved from the religious realm into the political. Nestorious came from Antioch, and it was in that city that Nestorians were most numerous (though later gaining a wide following among Mesopotamian Christians). Similarly, it was the Patriarch of Alexandria, Cyril, who led the Monophysite reaction to Nestorianism. The Monophysites nearly succeeded in making their view the Orthodox one, and for several hundred years remained widespread in the empire. However, they were predominant only in Egypt and parts of Syria, as local populations, resenting imperial rule, embraced beliefs that differed from those of the Orthodox church.

The Orthodox Byzantines energetically persecuted the Syrians, Egyptians, and smaller groups of Christian Arabs who held to their non-Orthodox beliefs. In Mesopotamia, the Persian Empire encouraged its large Nestorian population in their resistance to Orthodoxy, but also persecuted them as Christians. In both empires, the persecutions inspired strong resentment among the people. Meanwhile, continual warfare between the two states weakened both of them.

Christians under Islam. Consequently, when Muslim Arabs began their conquest of the Middle East in 633, they encountered weak imperial defenses and populations that often welcomed the invaders. By 641, all of Egypt, Mesopotamia, and Syria were in Muslim hands. At first, the Christians were a majority in the newly conquered lands. The Muslims allowed them to keep their churches but levied a head tax (*jizya*) on non-Muslims. Muslim law recognized both Jews and Christians as *Ahl al-Kitab*, or "People of the Book," meaning that, like Islam, the older religions were based on sacred scriptures. Therefore, Jews and Christians enjoyed *dhimmi* or "protected status" in

Muslim society, in exchange for which they were prohibited from bearing arms. The Ottomans, who ruled the region from 1516 to 1917, employed a similar system, in which separate religious groups (*millets* or "sects") maintained separate civil administrations. Most Christians in the early years of Muslim rule fared better than they had under the Byzantines.

Beginning in the 700s, however, large numbers of Muslim Arab immigrants settled in Christian areas. Many Christians, seeking political or social advancement, or simply wishing to avoid the *jizya*, converted to Islam. Other factors contributed to declining numbers of Christians: the men were not allowed to marry Muslim women without converting to Islam, and the children of a Muslim man and a Christian woman were considered Muslim. While permitted to maintain religious institutions and to live under their own legal systems, Christians could not build new churches or seek converts. By the 1200s Christians in Syria and Egypt made up less than half the total population.

By then, the religious divisions of Byzantine times had crystallized into isolated groups. In Egypt, descendants of the Monophysites, the Copts, comprised the majority of Christians (see COPTS). Smaller Orthodox communities in Egypt and Syria endured in coastal cities, where during the Byzantine era they had been protected by the emperor's troops. (Their members were called Melkites, after *melk*, the Syrian word for "king.") In rural inland areas of Palestine and Syria, Arab Monophysites called Jacobites herded and tended small farms. The Maronites occupied parts of Lebanon, vying for dominance with other Christian and Muslim groups there (see MARONITES). In both rural and urban Mesopotamia, large numbers of Nestorians survived until modern times.

The fortunes of these Christians have varied with the times. Often, they have coexisted peacefully with their Muslim neighbors. At one time Christians were ruthless toward Muslims as they joined "crusades" to recapture what the believed to be their holy land. Yet they have also suffered persecutions and even mass slaughter, particularly in wartime. Large population shifts have resulted at such times, as when Armenians fled from Turkey in World War I (see ARMENIANS). Substantial numbers have emigrated to Europe or America, further depleting Christianity's shrinking numbers in the Middle East. Most recently, the Islamic fundamentalist movement of the 1980s has heightened tensions between the two communities. Christians in some countries play down their faith in public. Religion aside, however, many Christian groups share cultural affinities with Muslims, and both Christians and Jews have become Arabized over the centuries.

Ancient rites in the Middle East. The religious isolation of Christian sects in the Middle East has meant that the churches preserve practices that date from the earliest days of Christianity. Liturgies are conducted in Greek, Syrian, Armenian, and Coptic as well as Arabic. The congregation prays standing up in orderly rows, sometimes with arms half-extended and hands palm upward. Often during worship the group is divided by sex. Priests are permitted to marry, celibacy being required only of monks, bishops, and patriarchs. The people continue to put faith in miracles and divine apparitions as do some Christians everywhere. In 1970, for example, thousands of Lebanese witnessed what appeared to be the Virgin Mary hovering over a Jacobite church in Beirut.

Western connections. Since the time of the Crusades, in the eleventh and twelfth centuries, Christian communities have acted as intermediaries between Middle Eastern and Western cultures. Many of the churches have also established formal ties with Roman Catholicism. Breakaway groups from some churches have reunited with Rome, adopting Latin rituals in their services. In most cases, these "Uniate" Catholic churches are smaller than the parent church. The Nestorian Catholics, however, have surpassed their non-Catholic counterparts in Iraq since the nineteenth century. Among the more prosperous Uniate communities are the Maronites, who in 1180 became the first to embrace Catholicism and did so as a whole, and the Greek Catholics of Lebanon, Syria, Jordan, and Israel. Maronites, who live in Lebanon, have had traditional ties to Europe, particularly to France, since the sixteenth century.

Social standing. The standing of Christians in Middle Eastern societies can often seem paradoxical to Westerners. Fiercely loyal to their own exclusive and ancient communities, they also feel a need to take part in the larger, mostly Islamic, Arab world. The older groups point to heritage that predates Arab arrival: Copts to the Egypt of the pharaohs; Nestorians and Chaldeans to ancient Assyria; Melkites and Orthodox to imperial Constantinople; and Maronites to ancient Phoenicia. Yet most of these groups also take pride in Arab heritage and culture. Except for the Copts, they have intermarried over the centuries with Christian Arabs, descendants of settled Bedouin tribes who became Christian in the centuries before Muhammad.

If their self-perception is complex, so is the way that the Muslim world views them. Muslims have often scorned the Christians as unbelievers, looking down on them for being outside the faith that occupies such an important place in their lives. Increasingly, however, they are looking to Christians as models for educational and economic achievement. In part because of the social barriers they have faced, Christians have relied more on education than their Muslim neighbors, for whom lessons often consisted simply of memorizing passages from the Quran. Since the seventeenth century, mission schools from the West have provided education for Christians. In most countries, Christians have had significantly higher literacy rates than Muslims. Similarly, Quranic injunctions against usury have meant that in some societies Christians have become wealthy bankers and merchants.

Keeping the faith. In almost every aspect of their daily life, Christians are reminded of their status as a religious minority in a culture dominated by religion. They hear and see radio and television broadcasts that are almost always Muslim; they wake to the call, issued five times daily, for Muslims to pray; all around they see evidence of Muslims practicing their faith, kneeling on prayer rugs in the street or entering the grand mosques with their needlelike minarets. Churches in some areas cannot be built within a certain distance from mosques, are often small and inconspicuous, and must not have steeples higher than the minarets (such restrictions vary from place to place). Especially since the revival of Islamic fundamentalism in the 1980s, Christians have felt increasingly uncomfortable in Muslim societies. Tens of thousands emigrate and some convert to Islam each year. Their steadily shrinking numbers cause some to fear for Christianity's survival in the land of its birth.

For More Information

Betts, Robert Brenton. *Christians in the Arab East.* Atlanta: John Knox Press, 1978.

British Library. *The Christian Orient.* London: British Museum Publications, 1978.

Hoffmeier, Jakes K., et al. "The Church in Egypt," *Christianity Today*, June 17, 1988, pp. 25-39.

Ostling, Richard N. "Fear in the First Churches," *Time Magazine*, April 23, 1990, pp. 66-68.

JUDAISM IN THE MIDDLE EAST

Of the close to thirteen million followers declaring Judaism as their faith, nearly four million reside in the Middle East and North Africa. They have maintained a continuing presence in this region since the first diaspora (scattering) in 587 B.C.E. (before the common era of Christians and Jews) At times many Jews lived outside the Holy Land, but today the majority live in Israel. Elsewhere the Jewish population has decreased in recent decades. Some 88,000 Jews lived in Iran around 1950, for example. Now, from available figures for 1988, a drastic drop in the country's Jewish population is evident.

Estimated Jewish Population in Parts of the Middle East and North Africa, 1988

Egypt	200	Morocco	10,000
Iran	20,000	Syria	4,000
Iraq	200	Yemen	1,000
Israel	3,659,000		

*Abstracted from *American Jewish Year Book 1990*, p. 528.

Rabbinic Judaism. At first, Judaism was a highly centralized religion. Its growth before 70 C.E. (the common era after the birth of Jesus)(see HEBREWS) resulted in hereditary priests, a central temple at Jerusalem, and sacrifices of animals and crops. This whole ensemble would change with the advent of rabbis.

Already the religion had stirred differences of opinion on practices, which gave rise to various sects. One sect, the Pharisees, consisted of religious leaders concerned for the welfare of common folk. These Pharisees developed *halakhah*, Jewish law, in organized academies. One such academy operated at Yavneh (near present-day Tel Aviv) before 70 C.E. and grew into a center of Jewish authority. A scholar of the time, Yohanan *ben* ("son of") Zakkai (73–132), helped establish the tradition of ordaining *rabbis*, that is, officially recognizing individuals as religious leaders. This challenged the hereditary priesthood; leadership fell to those who earned it through study and ability instead of priests who inherited it. As consolation, Yohanan gave the priestly families ceremonial honors during worship, which continue to this day.

The manner of worship changed too, with animal and vegetable sacrifices giving way to prayer. By 132, the Yavneh scholars had arranged a fixed worship service. At its core was a prayer called the *Amidah*, which proclaimed monotheism, or dedication to only one all-powerful god. Other parts of the prayer covered the major tenets of the religion: its concepts of creation, revelation (of the law to Moses at Mount Sinai), and redemption (afterlife in a world to come). The rabbis favored public over private worship, regarding the community as more likely to prompt compassion from God. They set a minimum, a quorum of ten adult males, for joint prayer.

Talmud. Scripture, that is, the Five Books of Moses recording events from creation to the Second Temple era, formed the basis of Judaism. The rabbis, however, maintained that Moses had received not only written text but also oral law. The written law commanded no work on the Sabbath, for example; the oral law defined what was meant by "work." Between 200 B.C.E. and 200 C.E., individuals were charged with passing down the oral law by word of mouth. Judaism credits Rabbi Judah the Nasi (135–200 C.E.) with finally recording oral law in the *Mishnah*. Like the Jewish Bible, the Mishnah soon became a subject in religious schools. Sages would study a law, then ask, "From where do we know this?" and trace it back to some verse of the Bible. They ultimately recorded their opinions in a work called the *Gemara*. Together the Mishnah and the Gemara that explained it became known as the *Talmud*.

About this time the religious center shifted from Palestine (now Israel) to Babylonia (now Iraq). Jews had occupied Babylonia ever since the first diaspora (see HEBREWS) and enjoyed a limited type of freedom there. More Jews joined them after the second diaspora in 70 C.E., and academies of learning grew. From these academies came a flurry of Jewish scholarship. Two Talmuds appeared. The Palestinian Talmud (completed in the 300s) preceded the Babylonian Talmud (completed in the 500s), the latter becoming the more popular version. From about 600 to 1000, Babylonia became the spiritual center of Judaism. The religious leaders who rose to position of *gaon* (head of an academy) received credit for spreading a unified way of life.

Karaites. Not all Jews accepted the rulings of Babylonia's rabbis. By 1300, some seventy-one Jewish sects had appeared; most notable is *Karaism*, which has survived, albeit in small numbers, to the present day. The term Karaism means "belief in the scriptures." In keeping with this definition, Karaites rejected the oral law and abided only by scripture. Moses, they insisted, had received the Five Books at Sinai and nothing more. Karaites rejected rabbinic practices of the day—for example, the prohibition against mixing meat and dairy foods. They celebrated neither Hanukkah nor Purim, since these holidays were not designated as such in the Bible. Finally, while the rabbis promoted a lenient approach to the law (allowing various viewpoints), the Karaites steadfastly opposed such a liberal attitude.

Rabbinic Judaism simplified. Meeting the challenge posed by the Karaites, the rabbis made their form of Judaism more accessible to

The Torah, the five biblical books recording the history of the Hebrews, is written on scrolls. *Courtesy of David Tuch.*

the average Jew. Saadia ben Joseph (882—942), a *gaon* in Babylonia, first translated the Bible into Arabic. After him came the Spanish-born philosopher Moses ben Maimon (1135-1204), or Maimonides. The oral law as documented in the Talmud was a complicated mix of law and literature. A few sentences of Mishnah would lay down the law, followed by maybe a page of legal interpretation in Hebrew and Aramaic, which sometimes veered off into tales, poems, and so forth. While the Talmud held rules for all aspects of human life from religion to marriage to property, only the most studious scholars could trudge through it. Maimonides aimed to remedy this problem (Wouk 1986, p. 177).

> . . .I have undertaken to write a book making plain what is forbidden and allowed, impure and pure . . . all in clear language and a brief style. So that the oral law can be on everybody's lips . . .

Later a court physician to the sultan in Egypt, Maimonides met his goal. His book, the *Mishneh Torah* ("Second" Torah), has since been hailed for its success, but scholars of his time objected to its making decisions without crediting them to respected sources. The Mishneh Torah nevertheless became the basis of another work, the *Shulkhan Aruch*, a digest which, with later decisions and commentaries, is used today. Written by Joseph Caro (1488-1575), it presents the laws in categories, and credits the sources on which they are based. Both Maimonides and Caro were *Sephardim*, and their works reflect this.

Sephardim. Muslim control extended across the Middle East into Spain from the early eighth century until about 1212. During the first few centuries of Muslim rule, immigrants flocked there from the Middle East and North Africa, and Spain became the most populous Jewish settlement after Babylonia.

Sepharad means "Spain." Known as *Sephardim*, the Spanish Jews promoted their own style of Hebrew pronunciation and prayer. Jews of northern and eastern Europe pronounced Hebrew differently. Called *Ashkenazim*, this group also followed its own set of religious customs. Ashkenazim and Sephardim became two main divisions in Judaism. *Oriental Jews* (those native to the Middle East) have been regarded as Sephardim, since they worshipped in much the same style.

Already in the 1200s some Jews focused on the mysteries rather than on the study of the religion. These mystics strove for an immediate connection with God. Called *kabalah*, their movement rested on ideas recorded in a guidebook, the *Zohar*, written in Castile, Spain. Kabalah ultimately faded, perhaps due to its disdain for anything non-Jewish, but it did not go out of existence. Some of its followers migrated to the Holy Land during the 1400s, infusing the religion with added spirituality.

All Jews were expelled from Spain by the Christians in 1492. Along with the mystics, many of them fled eastward. Resettling in Palestine, Morocco, Turkey, and Egypt, they joined (but remained separate from) the native Oriental Jews. Slight differences in religious customs existed between the Sephardim and Oriental Jews, and the ways of the Sephardim became more popular as the years passed. Still, some of the native ways persisted and even influenced the Sephardim. Moroccan Jews, for example, displayed great reverence for individual holy men. After death, they elevated these *saddiquim* (holy men) to a type of sainthood, then would invoke the name of a particular saint in times of hardship. They made pilgrimages to saints' tombs, sometimes passing the night in the sacred spots. (In Israel today, Moroccans have substituted places of pilgrimage for Moroccan Jewish saints.) On holidays other customs surfaced, some shared by Jews elsewhere. Jews in Morocco as elsewhere prepare for spring's Passover with a feverish cleaning (Stillman 1988, p. 119).

> When we got to Passover, there would not be a table or any of the walls (not cleaned). The mattresses of wool or straw and the pillows would be opened, washed and plucked and afterwards restuffed.

On Shavuot, which celebrates receiving the Torah, Moroccan Jews once observed a more unique custom, playfully spraying each other with a water pistol, the *bu titu*. Later in the day they would attend synagogue to hear King David's psalms. The Jews of Morocco were themselves highly reputed religious poets, who adapted verse to popular Arabic and Turkish songs.

Haskala—enlightenment. The 1500s and 1600s saw a fervent outpouring of new secular ideas that upset old notions about the shape of the earth and so on. Meanwhile, Jews studied only the Bible and Talmud, concentrating almost wholly on the Talmud. Reaction to such intense study gave rise to an East European movement, *Hasidism*, under Rabbi Israel Baal Shem Tov (1700–1760). Like Kabalah, Hasidism stressed the spiritual side of the religion. Its followers aimed to reach emotional heights through singing, dancing, and losing oneself in prayer.

Outside in the larger world, Europe was experiencing an upheaval in basic notions about human rights. From about 1770 to 1880, new ideas about an individual's rights resulted in a movement that brought about more civil liberties for Jews. Called emancipation, this movement affected the Ashkenazim who would, in the next century, establish the State of Israel. There was, at the same time another movement called enlightenment, which involved the toppling of old ways in favor of new ones. In Judaism this meant changes in religious ideas and practices. Those Jews who entered the *Haskala* (enlightenment) movement advocated more interaction with the everyday world. Judaism and Jewish history should be studied, they said, but so should secular subjects, and religious habits should change to keep pace with a changing world. From this last notion came the growth of different types of Judaism.

Divisions in rabbinic Judaism. From about the 1780s, a reform movement in Western and Central Europe introduced novelties such as the organ and mixed male-female choirs to worship services. Its leaders held that Judaism should discard "obsolete" rituals. They abandoned strict observance of rabbinic law and reworded certain prayers to include all humanity, not only Jews. Then came the less radical Positive Historical (Conservative) School. Its members valued old rituals as symbols. Favoring a judicious number of changes in the religion, they insisted on retaining old prayers that roused the emotions. In contrast to both approaches was the neo-Orthodox movement, which continued most of the old practices. Orthodox Jews observed rabbinic rituals with little change. Among the new concessions they adopted were prayer in languages other than Hebrew and secular as well as religious education.

The Holocaust and Israel. Two pivotal events affected all Judaism in the twentieth century: the Holocaust of World War II and the 1948 founding of Israel. The Holocaust came crashing down on the European Jews, murdering six million of them. Many of the survivors moved to the Holy Land. Mostly Orthodox Jews before the war, some lost their faith during the Holocaust. Where was God, they asked, during the horrific suffering of millions of innocents? Others fiercely held onto Judaism as the faith that had sustained them through the nightmare. They accepted mystery in the religion, believing there were limits to their human understanding of events.

Joining survivors in Israel around 1948 were Jews from other areas of the Middle East and North Africa, who experienced new hardships after the founding of the state. Synagogues were bombed, stores looted, and Jewish lives lost. Now that Israel existed, Arabic- and Persian-speaking Jews could take refuge in the homeland. Many have proceeded to settle in Israel.

Today's Israeli population is about eighty-two percent Jewish. Most are not religious, but the minority of observant Jews wield great power. Survival of the state appears tied to the religion and vice versa. In fact, some believe the time of the Messiah (described below) has begun with nationhood and Israel's military successes. Others disagree, arguing that Israel has strayed from its holy goal, succumbing to worldly tactics and concerns.

Judaism today—beliefs. Judaism was the first religion to believe in only one all-powerful God. Unlike a sun deity, for example, this force was not tied to a single natural object or phenomenon. The religion holds that God the creator made a covenant with Abraham, led the Jews out of slavery in Egypt, and broadened the covenant to include them at Sinai. There they were "chosen" to uphold Jewish law. The main concern of this law is ethics, or right conduct to others in this world. In the Talmud is a story about the sage Hillel and a man who asked to learn all Judaism while standing on one foot. Hillel replied: "Do not do to your neighbor what is hateful to you. The rest is all commentary. Now go and study it." Right conduct, the religion teaches, hastens the coming of the Messiah, a figure who will usher in an age of peace and plenty as life was before human beings erred in paradise. After the Messiah arrives, righteous souls will enter Paradise while wicked ones are sentenced to the netherworld. Always a practice-oriented faith, Judaism focuses mainly on life in this world. Humans, it holds, have free will to choose good over evil. God punishes sins but is also forgiving, and compassionate. Banning idol worship, perjury, murder, theft, and so on, the Ten Commandments cover the basic precepts. There are more commandments. Rabbinic tradition, in fact, speaks of 613 negative and positive commandments, many of them obsolete (for example, a sacrifice without salt should be punished with a whipping). Only about 100 apply to observant Jews today (for instance, a divorce requires a religious bill of divorcement, or *get*). While outdated laws are no longer observed, their intent is retained. Judaism prescribes charity, for example. Once it required leaving a corner of a field unharvested for the poor; this changed to reserving a portion of one's earnings.

Worship service. Jewish prayer rests on the belief that individuals can communicate directly with God, who is able to hear and respond. The observant Jew prays three times daily, chanting morning, afternoon, and evening services. On holy days, observers chant an additional (*musaph*) service. The quorum of ten, established in early rabbinic times, is still required for collective worship, and *kohanim*, Jews whose ancestors were priests, still receive ceremonial honors.

The heart of the services is Torah reading. One of 52 portions is read each week; an entire cycle of Torah reading is completed each year and then begins anew. In the Five Books (Genesis, Exodus, Leviticus, Numbers, and Deuteronomy) is the story of ancient Israel (see HEBREWS). Mideast and North African Jews have long displayed a close familiarity with the text, quoting passages from memory. In Israel today, Bible study is part of a Jew's basic education.

Prayer leaders. Central to the service is the cantor, whose fine voice qualifies him as lead singer of the *nigun*, or melody. The cantor, not a typical figure in synagogues until the 12th century, became essential by the 18th century. If a community could not afford both a rabbi and cantor, it was obliged to engage the cantor to serve as the mes-

All that remains of the early Jewish temple in Jerusalem is the Western Wall. *Courtesy of David Tuch.*

senger of the community before God. The rabbi, in contrast, taught and made decisions for the community concerning Jewish law.

In the Mideast and North Africa, the rabbi's role changed little over the years. The Muslim rulers who governed habitually gave the religious leaders authority over a group's personal affairs. This system has persisted to present-day Israel, which has an official body of rabbis (rabbinate) that controls marriage and dietary laws. Of course, new rabbis appear in each generation. Rabbinical students attend *yeshivot*—schools that teach Jewish law. To qualify for ordination, they take a bar exam in religious law, the *semikha* test, covering Talmud, codes, and decisions.

Factions. While the only offical form of Judaism in Israel is Orthodoxy, other forms have taken root here. Reform (Progressive) and Conservative (Modernist Traditional) Judaism both have organizations in the country (the Reform group moved its world headquarters there in 1970). Most observant Jews are Orthodox, though. They follow a mix of traditions. There are Hasidim who observe eighteenth-century customs and train students at their own yeshivot. Other divisions exist. Orthodox Ashkenazim and Sephardim have different synagogues (the Sephardim are in the majority in Israel though they are a minority in world Jewry). Some of the Sephardi synagogues are Syro-Lebanese. Frequented by Jews from Syria and Lebanon, these synagogues practice a distinct custom: midnight and early morning singing of sacred Hebrew songs that are called *Bakashot.* The songs, set to Arab musical arrangements, are sung on Sabbaths between the fall holiday Sukkot and spring holiday Passover.

Holy days. A historical dimension appears in most Jewish holy days. Shavuot is a summer agricultural festival that celebrates also the Day of Lawgiving to Moses. During Sukot, the fall agricultural festival, Jews decorate huts with the harvest, the huts symbolizing the years of wandering in the desert after escaping slavery in Egypt. The shofar (ram's horn) ushers in the Jewish New Year (Rosh Hashanah) and is sounded on the Day of Atonement (Yom Kippur); Middle East legend says Moses used such a horn to signal the Egyptian slaves of the time for return to Israel. In Israel, the above holidays are annual events on which work ceases. The weekly work stoppage occurs on the Jewish Sabbath, Saturday.

The Sabbath also celebrates history—the creation of the universe and of the people of Israel from ex-slaves who could finally chose their own day of rest. A minority of Israelis attend synagogue on Sabbath, to the surprise of some Arabic-speaking immigrants. Jews from Sefrou, Morocco, recall Sabbath there. In 1972, most everyone filled the synagogue Friday night and Saturday. When the Torah was removed from the ark, men rushed up to kiss it. Saturday afternoon they studied *Gemara* (see above) in the synagogue library, then joined their families to eat and drink *mahya* (a fermented beverage once prepared in rooftop stills). Still later they ate some *sxina* stew, rested, and finally returned to synagogue for the late afternoon and evening services.

Life rites. Most Jews continue to undergo life cycle rituals even if they do not regularly attend synagogue. This is no small matter, for the life rites signify entrance into and dedication to the Jewish faith. Just as the patriarch Abraham circumcised his son Isaac on the eighth day after birth, so do most Jews today. The circumcision, which sealed the pledge between Abraham and God, is a sacrifice of flesh and blood that harks back to ancient times. Another almost universally observed rite is bar mitzvah, a boy's religious entrance into manhood at the age of thirteen. Its most outstanding feature is a public reading of the Torah by the adolescent, acknowledging his attainment of adult privileges and obligations. In relation to marriage, weddings and divorces are strictly religious affairs in Israel. The traditional wedding ceremony is performed under a *huppah*, or canopy, which symbolizes the home of the married couple. The bride receives a *ketubah*, religious marriage certificate, and the union is blessed. In the ceremony, bride and groom drink from a cup of wine that recalls the altar offering of ages past. The groom afterward breaks the glass, showing that even at the height of happiness the newlyweds recall world suffering. Among death rites for immediate kin are rending a garment, mourning at home for a week (sitting *shiba*), and reciting memorial prayers every anniversary of the death. There is widespread observance in reciting these prayers.

Symbols. Like holidays, Jewish symbols are tied to history. The six-pointed star is said to have been the form of the shield carried by the biblical King David. Early rabbis taught followers to begin Sabbath with a hearty meal even if this meant doing without on weekdays. So that the people would not concentrate on their appetites, the rabbis added rituals (the lighting of Sabbath candles, the prayer over wine) to mark the sacredness of the meal. Not ordained by

Jewish law, the wearing of a head covering during worship arose in controversy during the Middle Ages. In time it came to suggest piousness and certain headgear grew common: turbans and skullcaps in the Middle East and North Africa. The tallit, another worship garment, is a prayer shawl with *zizit*, fringed corners to remind wearers of the commandments. At one time such fringes were supposed to appear on everyday garments, then were limited to prayer shawls. A final "garment" is *tefillin*, two boxes with Torah verses, including both the *Shma*, a basic verse that declares God's oneness, and the command to fasten such boxes to the hand and forehead.

Arabic-speaking Jews. Religious rights vary in Arabic lands today. In Syria, where emigration is forbidden to Jews, 1980s' reports say secret police watch synagogue services. Egypt's Jews have been relatively free to worship as they please since 1970, but few Jews remain in the country. Once Egypt even had a large Karaite community, but it has mostly moved to Israel. The Karaites opened their own synagogues in Israel, yet their children were exposed to mainstream Judaism in the army and school, and some left the Karaite community. Overall, Arabic-speaking families tend to experience less religious observance across the generations after moving to Israel. At first the parent-immigrants appear to be more traditionally observant than most parents from Europe and America. The difference, however, seems to dimish as generations pass. Perhaps living in Israel makes the children feel as religious as their parents. In fact, the idea that living in Israel confers holiness on a person is supported by the Talmud, which declares Israel more holy than any other country.

For More Information

Gross, David C. *1,001 Questions and Answers about Judaism.* Garden City, New York: Doubleday, 1978.

Maimonides. *The Commandments.* 2 vols. London: Soncino Press, 1967.

Seltzer, Robert M. *Jewish People, Jewish Thought: The Jewish Experience in History.* New York: Macmillan, 1980.

Singer, David. *American Jewish Year Book 1990.* New York: The American Jewish Committee, 1990.

Wigoder, Geoffrey, editor. *The Encyclopedia of Judaism.* New York: Macmillan, 1989.

Wouk, Herman. *This Is My God: The Jewish Way of Life.* New York: Touchstone, 1986.

THE ARABS

ARABS
(air′ abs)

Inhabitants of countries throughout North Africa and the Middle
East whose native tongue is Arabic.

Population: 200,000,000 (1988 estimate).
Location: The Middle East; Northern Africa.
Language: Arabic.

Geographical Setting

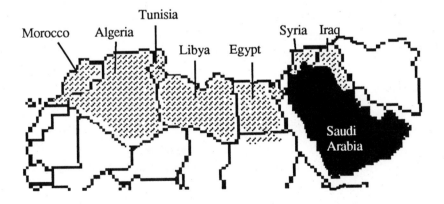

In contrast to other groupings in this book, which are based on geography or on religion, the division Arabs is based on language.

Originally from the Arabian Peninsula, Arabs in the name of Islam marched more than 1,300 years ago across North Africa and north and east toward present-day Iraq and Iran. Aided by religious tenets that allowed the soldiers, and indeed all men, to claim more than one wife, and that held that the father's children were Islamic, Arab traditions spread from Mauritania, Morocco, and Spain, to Pakistan. Today, therefore, many people have adopted the language and customs of the once nomadic Arabs—they have become "Arabized." Language binds the Arabs, and national identities and local customs separate them. Today the Arabized peoples, most of whom call themselves Arabs, populate a variety of geographical settings from the Mediterranean coast, to the mountains of Iraq, to the deserts of the Arabian Peninsula. In this sense, since they speak Arabic and have adopted some Arab mores, more than ninety percent of the people of the Middle East who are described in this book are Arabs.

Historical Background

Origin. Although ancient kingdoms existed in Arabia, Arabs can be thought of as beginning to unite as a people with the revelation of the Quran in Arabic—the message from God via the prophet Muhammad to the Arabs of Mecca, Medina, and, later, far beyond. After the death of the prophet Muhammad in A.D. 632, Muslim armies set about restoring order. As their expeditions went ever farther afield, they discovered how ripe Syria, Iraq, and Egypt were for conquest. Alienated from their Byzantine and Persian rulers, the inhabitants of the region welcomed the Muslim forces and regarded them as liberators.

Umayyad dynasty (661-750). Centered in Damascus, the Umayyad dynasty consisted of an aristocracy of Arab warriors based in garrison towns throughout the empire. While theoretically all converts to Islam enjoyed equal status, in fact all non-Arab Muslims (*Mawali*) became politically integrated by functioning as clients of Arabs and were, therefore, their social and economic inferiors. Eventually the *Mawali* greatly outnumbered the Arabs. Faced with the growing discontent and increasing unrest of the *Malawi*, the Umayyad fell to the Abbasids of Baghdad. The Muslim Empire was at a point when it no longer needed a caste of warriors at the top, but instead it did require administrators, merchants, bankers, and religious officials.

Abbasids. Along with a full-fledged bureaucracy came a less accessible ruler or caliph. No longer was his title Deputy to the Prophet of God. Now he was known as Deputy of God and the Shadow of God on Earth. This was the period of the caliph Haroun ar-Rashid (786-809).

The empire's incredible wealth was reflected in trade routes that ranged from China to northern Russia. Arab coins from the era were found as far away from Baghdad as Scandinavia. In return, Abbasid merchants imported silks, spices, tin, paper, felt, brocades, silver and gold, slaves, tigers and panthers, elephants, rubies, ebony and sandalwood, coconuts, furs, and amber. So sophisticated was the supporting financial system that a check drawn in Baghdad could be cashed in Morocco. In fact, the Arabs invented the bank check.

Eventually the size of the empire made it too unwieldy. Corruption and inefficiency drained the economy as well. With its political disintegration, the region became more vulnerable to incursions from the outside. First various Turkic peoples entered Baghdad as the military force that would become the power behind the throne. Then—in contrast to the Muslim Turks from the East—Christian Crusaders arrived from the West. After nearly a century of sporadic fighting, the religious impetus collapsed under defeat by Saladin in the twelfth century, and the Crusaders either returned to Europe or stayed and became assimilated within Islamic civilization. By far, the most disruptive force was that of the Mongols from Central Asia. In 1258 these fierce warriors put an end to the Abbasid caliphate. The Mongols cared little for settling the land. Their plunder and move tactics were so devastating that some areas have never recovered. The Mongol push westward was stopped in Palestine by the Mameluk dynasty based in Cairo.

War and redevelopment. With the region exhausted, the power center of the Muslim world moved both east and west in the hands of the Moguls of India, the Safavids of Persia, and the Ottoman Turks. By 1517, much of the Arab world was incorporated into the Ottoman empire, where it remained for centuries. In addition, a new and crippling blow was delivered: rich trade routes were weakened with the European discovery of sea routes around Africa. The Middle East's role as commercial middleman began to wane. Even worse, the discovery of the New World and its gold disrupted the economy of the Old World. Muslim empires had access to none of this new wealth.

Engaged elsewhere, even Europeans believed that the Ottomans were stronger than they actually were. The empire continued to disdain things European or even knowledge of them. The Renaissance, the Reformation, and the Enlightenment came and went. Then, in 1798, an event occurred that demanded attention: Napoleon Bonaparte invaded Egypt. The Ottoman Empire found itself confronted by an opponent whose strength it had not imagined.

The Colonial Age. Napoleon had been sent by France to capture Egypt, Syria, and Iraq in response to the British conquest of India thirty years before. Although Napoleon did not get much farther east than Gaza, and the French occupation of Egypt lasted only three years, the episode had a profound impact. Accompanying the French forces were scientists, scholars, and artists who investigated and recorded ever aspect of Egyptian life and filled volumes with their findings. A mania for Egyptian antiquities had begun. For their part, the Egyptians resented the French for their harsh taxation policies and were offended by such uncivilized behavior as drinking in public. Unable to protest the occupation effectively, the Egyptians were nonetheless rid of the French when the British and Ottomans forced them out. Indeed, over the next 150 years, the colonial rivalry between Britain and France was a greater factor in determining the geopolitical fate of the Middle East than was anything the local residents did.

Muhammad Ali (ruled 1805-1849). During the nineteenth century, Egypt experienced the fastest and most thorough change of any country in the Middle East. Reform efforts began under Muhammad Ali, who arrived in Egypt as the second-in-command of an Albanian regiment sent by the Ottoman government to face the French. Within a few short years he was recognized as leader by the religious establishment in Egypt, had replaced the Ottoman governor with the approval of the government in Istanbul, and had massacred rivals for power who were members of the Mameluk dynasty.

Having achieved a monopoly on political power, Muhammad Ali next turned to establishing an economic monopoly. In claiming most of Egypt's land for the state, he was able to shift agriculture from subsistence level to a cash-crop economy. Peasants were instructed which crops to plant and forced to sell their harvests to the government—which resold them at a profit. This meant that Egypt was now subject to the fluctuations of the world market. A boom or bust abroad heavily impacted the peasant, the state, and the latter's development plans. Every bit of income was needed for the roads, canals, irrigation works, schools, factories, and railroads that were being built by the government.

Muhammad Ali also expanded his military expeditions. Egyptian troops occupied parts of Greece, Syria, and Arabia, supposedly to restore order on the Ottoman sultan's behalf but actually because the countries lay along the major Egyptian trade routes. In reality, their presence threatened the sultan until the European powers once more stepped in. Individual Europeans, mostly French, were brought to Egypt to instruct Egyptians in all manner of military and economic reform. Conversely, large numbers of Egyptians went abroad to study.

Political awakening. Egyptians abroad learned more than Muhammad Ali and his dynastic heirs bargained for. Along with the ability to read training manuals in French, they were also able to read newspapers and books. Consequently, this educated vanguard became exposed to concepts such as democracy, political parties, and constitutional government. They believed political reform was in order as much as military and economic. When political parties were eventually formed in the twentieth century, they were granted only limited responsibility. Neither the British (who occupied Egypt in 1882 and remained until the 1950s) nor Egypt's ruler, the *khedive,* would allow parties to function freely.

In addition to the political awakening, another long-term effect of establishing a Western-educated class was that growing numbers of what became society's elite were neither completely Western nor were they any longer completely Arab. Thus, along with the imported economic and military reforms, there arose imported cultural institutions to service this new social group: museums, a national library, a geographic society, an opera house, schools run by missionaries, civil law courts, newspapers. The yawning chasm that divided the Western-educated elite and the illiterate peasant was more than a matter of relative wealth; it was also a cultural outlook.

The Arab world reemerges. The Ottoman Turks entered World War I on the side of the Germans, thereby raising the stakes for Britain and France in the Arab world. Seeking to undermine Turkish control of the region, Britain encouraged the Arabs to declare their independence and stage a revolt. In the exchange of correspondence between

Sharif Hussein of Mecca and the British High Commissioner in Egypt, Sir Henry McMahon, Britain pledged military and financial assistance if Hussein would proclaim a revolt. The outcome of the revolt was to be the creation of an independent Arab state, minus some vaguely defined territory. The debate continues as to whether the territory in question included a Jewish homeland as well as a Christian Lebanon.

On June 5, 1916, Sharif Hussein declared Arab independence. By September of 1918, the British and the Arabs had pushed the Turks out of Arabia and Syria, and an Arab government was headquartered in Damascus. It was only in 1917 that the Arabs learned of the secret Sykes-Picot Treaty, signed by Russia, Britain, and France in 1915. The Communist revolution in Russia forced that country to drop out, but Britain and France maintained their agreement to divide up the Arab Middle East between them. Although the takeover was camouflaged as mandates awarded by the League of Nations, the results were the same: France got Lebanon and Syria, Britain got an arc of land from the Persian Gulf to the Egyptian border (now known as Iraq, Jordan, and Israel). Britain had long since occupied Egypt, and France retained control of the rest of North Africa. Only the supposedly useless wastes of Arabia were left for the Arabs to use for their independent state.

But that was not all. On November 2, 1917, Britain issued the Balfour Declaration in support of establishing a Jewish homeland in Palestine. It also recognized the civil and religious rights of the non-Jewish inhabitants, who comprised ninety percent of the population. Nothing was said, however, about their political rights. The American King-Crane Commission went to Palestine to verify local support for the declaration and found that the overwhelming majority rejected it. Instead, they wanted complete independence under Faisal, the son of Sharif Hussein who had been driven from his throne in Damascus by the French.

The Arab revolt that began with such high hopes and great expectations ended with betrayal, political subjugation, and bitterness. Sharif Hussein lost his own throne in Mecca to the Sa'ud family, who incorporated the holy cities of Mecca and Medina into Saudi Arabia. The British decreed that Faisal be king of Iraq, and Abdullah (another son of Sharif Hussein) became king of Transjordan. Lastly, Palestine became Israel in 1948, thereby giving rise to hostility that still plagues the region. Ironically, only Saudi Arabia—as the least advanced politically and the least promising economically—was left alone to enjoy independence.

Between world wars. The years between the world wars were characterized by demands and sometimes violent demonstrations for independence. France followed a "divide and conquer" policy of rule, fragmenting Syria into several districts. The British style was more that of the "power behind the throne." With Europe exhausted after World War II, political control was loosened. The expectation among Arabs was that, since European might alone had separated the Arabs, independence would automatically bring reunification as a single Arab state. However, each Arab country expected to have the lead role for different reasons. Iraq had been independent longest, Egypt was the most developed, King Abdullah harbored hopes of leading a Greater Syria, and Syria saw itself as the Arab heartland and natural center of any future state. Surely, they thought, the overwhelming force of their combined efforts would result in the removal of what was regarded as the only remaining European colony, Israel.

But the Arabs had not been politically united since the caliphate of roughly 1000 years before. Neither had they been politically independent and experienced in self-government, nor even experienced in cooperative efforts. Above all, they did not trust each other and eyed one another as potential rivals in the rescue of Palestine. They were also concerned about maneuverings of Britain and the United States that appeared to be efforts to control the region from outside once more. The lack of planning, coordination, and resolve doomed their efforts to failure. Israel was born under difficult conditions.

Domestic difficulties. What proved to be impossible was explaining the failure to Arab citizens back home, after raising their expectations so high. Within a few years, one Arab regime after another fell. Syria experienced three coups in one year. King Abdullah was assassinated in Jerusalem in 1951. Egypt's King Faruq was overthrown in 1952 and put out to sea in his yacht, where he died. Lebanon experienced civil unrest in 1956, and Iraq underwent a bloody revolution in 1958.

Arab unity. It was thought that a government that was truly representative of the Arab people would be able to harness the strength of the nation and channel it toward success. If Arab countries were not the equal of Europe, it had to be because someone was sabotaging the effort. The key, therefore, lay in identifying the traitor, and rival political factions were only too willing to point the finger. Finally, in Egypt's Gamal Abdal Nasser, the Arab world had found a hero who was so popular that no one dared point a finger to challenge him.

Arab political unity was a relatively new phenomenon—perhaps about 100 years old—when Nasser came to power in the 1950s. Nasser's great success was in extending the concept of Arab nationalism beyond the intellectual elite, where the idea was born, and making it real for the masses. At least temporarily, he managed to bridge the gap between the Western-educated elite and illiterate peasants. "Arabism" originated in many minds, among them students at the Syrian Protestant College (now the American University of Beirut) in the nineteenth century. Unlike other missionary schools, this college was open to students of all religions. In raising the standard of literacy, the school unwittingly created a literary revival in Arabic in Lebanon. By aiming at religious conversion, it made students cherish their heritage all the more and unite on the one factor they had in common: their language.

When the Ottoman government in Istanbul pursued a more pronounced policy, "Arabness" became even more distinctive and a badge of pride that set the Arabs apart. Prior to the revolt, some Arabs wanted to be free of the Turks, while others recognized the value in having the Ottoman government as a shield to fend off the more dangerous threat from Europe. Buoyed at the end of World War I by their expectations of statehood, Arab nationalists became disillusioned and embittered at the Versailles Peace Conference. United States President Woodrow Wilson's call for self-determination was clearly not going to be applied to them.

Gamal Abdal Nasser. The Arabs believed they had found in Nasser the means of redressing the balance. The son of a postal clerk and grandson of a peasant, Nasser was the first Egyptian to rule Egypt in many centuries. He came to power as one of the revolutionary officers who overthrew King Faruq in 1952. By 1954, his dominant rule became public. It was not until 1956, however, that he became widely popular as the hero of Suez who had successfully defied the West and expressed the anger and resentment that had been smoldering for decades.

Nasser's purchase of 200 million dollars in weapons from communist sources vividly demonstrated that a new age had dawned. Pursuing a course of "positive neutrality" between the Communists and the West, Nasser had also accepted an offer of financial aid from the United States to build the High Dam at Aswan. However, the offer was withdrawn as punishment for Nasser's Communist arms purchase, and he decided to get the funding elsewhere and to nationalize the Suez Canal. The Canal, which lay completely within Egyptian territory, had been built and paid for by Egyptians but never run by them, although the concession to run it was due to end within a decade and revert to Egypt.

Unable to accept the fact of Egyptian control of the Canal, Britain joined with France and Israel in attacking Egypt, then claimed it was just protecting the Canal by intervening to separate the combatants (i.e., Israel and Egypt). When both the United States and Soviet Union condemned the invasion, a pull-back by all three parties was inevitable. A United Nations Emergency Force was sent to Sinai to serve as a buffer between Egypt and Israel, and played that role until Nasser ordered it off Egyptian soil to touch off the 1967 war. The immediate result of the 1956 war, however, was the adulation of Nasser. Not only was he a hero to Egyptians but to other Arabs as well. He had withstood the combined military forces of the West and they had been forced to withdraw.

The next two years were the high point of Arab nationalism as well as a period of great unrest. Any Arab government allied with the West came under tremendous pressure to prove its nationalist credentials. This generally meant falling into line with Nasser's chosen policy. After Syria merged politically with Egypt to form the new entity of the United Arab Republic, the pressure became even more intense. In 1958, King Faisal II lost his throne and his life in a military coup in Iraq. King Hussein of Jordan held on to his throne with the help of British troops. American Marines helped quell unrest in Lebanon. The tide had turned. Yemen was the only other state to merge with the United Arab Republic and, in fact, in 1961 Syria pulled out of the union. It had found that what worked in Egypt did not necessarily work in the very different social and political environment of Syria.

Nasser's biggest failure was, of course, Egypt's crushing defeat at the hands of the Israelis in the 1967 war. Believing his own rhetoric and pushed along by the expectations of others, events overtook Nasser, and the result was that Egypt lost a war for which it was utterly unprepared. Israel's devastating strike against three Arab states in six days left no doubt about the Arabs' military preparedness. Aside from the physical loss of territory to Israel, the war's outcome was twofold: a sharp restructuring of reality on the part of the Arabs and the realization on the part of Palestinians that there was no one left on whom to call for help. If they were ever to achieve their dream of statehood, they now had only themselves to depend on. That meant that the Palestine Liberation Organization assumed a much more militant, activist stance.

Culture Today

Overview. Arabs are the inhabitants of those countries stretching across North Africa and the Middle East as far as the Turkish and Iranian borders whose native tongue is Arabic. The Arab language is of two varieties: a written form of Arabic used in books, magazines, and newspapers, as well as in formal situations like public speeches, and a colloquial or spoken form that functions like a regional dialect. While written communication across the Arab world is readily intelligible, Arabs from opposite sides of the region sometimes have difficulty understanding each other when speaking. There are more or less five colloquial dialects spoken in Arabic: that of North Africa, Egypt, the Fertile Crescent, Iraq, and the Arabian Peninsula—the last often referred to as Gulf Arabic.

Originally the term "Arab" was used among Arabic-speakers to mean the nomadic Bedouin of the Arabian desert. Today, however, the word has long since been used to describe all Arabic-speakers, no matter what their mode of living. It is not unusual for the term to imply more than language, however. "Arab" frequently includes a cultural component and may refer to a religious identity as well. Certainly most Arabs are Muslims (that is, followers of Islam), but there exist Christian and Jewish Arabic-speakers as well. While the number of Jews living in Arab countries has greatly decreased since 1948 due to mass emigration to Israel, some Arabic-speaking Jewish communities still remain.

Arabs after Nasser. The post-Nasser era (beginning in 1970) has been characterized more by bilateral activity than by international movements. Nasser's successor, Anwar Sadat, felt that the success of his 1973 invasion of Israeli-occupied Sinai provided him with enough political influence to negotiate peace terms with Israel from a position of strength. His people's halfhearted acceptance of the Camp David Accords and Sadat's own assassination proved that others assessed the situation differently. Egypt's resulting political isolation from the rest of the Arab world left it leaderless and attention was turned inward. The more conservative Arab monarchies experienced economic growth on one hand and political uneasiness on the other. One resulted from the oil boom; the other from the Islamic revolution in Iran. Iraq was busy fighting a war with Iran. Lebanon was in chaos with its never-ending civil war, in which Syria was bogged down as well, attempting to influence events in Lebanon.

When national borders are arbitrary, populations diverse, political procedures weak, if existing at all, and arms plentiful, fighting is often the outcome. Violence is also probable when parties refuse to speak to each other for fear of losing support at home. This was the condition in the Arab world. However, this is not the whole story of the Arab world. Enormous strides have been made in the fields of health, education, and social services.

What Arabs have in common beside their Arabic language is a sense that their culture's potential has yet to be tapped. They point to Western imperialism, regional hostility, government corruption, political divisiveness, and economic wastefulness as reasons for delayed development. But they can also point with pride to dams, factories, transportation networks, television stations, hospitals, universities, and refineries.

Values. Many of the traditional values of Arab society are well worth preserving. Arab streets are crime-free compared to the West. Family life is much stronger. Manners and courtesy are taught early and held in high esteem. The pace of life is slower and decision-making deliberate. The key question is, can one enjoy the benefits of technology and modern life and still preserve aspects of traditional life? The resolution to this dilemma will vary according to the perception and experience of each person, but all seek to live in a society characterized by political security, social justice, and human dignity. Beyond that, different aspects of Arab life are described in some of the following sections that reflect both the interest in Arab unity and the national differences of the Arab and Arabized people.

POPULATION OF MEMBER STATES OF ARAB LEAGUE

Algeria	24,194,777	Oman	1,265,382
Bahrain	480,383	Qatar	328,044
Egypt	53,347,579	Saudi Arabia	15,472,123
Iraq	17,583,467	Somalia	7,990,085
Jordan	2,850,482	Sudan	24,014,495
Kuwait	1,938,075	Syria	11,569,659
Lebanon	2,674,385	Tunisia	7,738,026
Libya	3,956,211	United Arab Emirates	1,980,354
Mauritania	1,919,106	Yemen	9,158,020
Morocco	24,976,168		

For More Information

Egan, E. W., editor, *The Middle East: The Arab States in Pictures.* New York: Sterling Publishing, 1978.

Mansfield, Peter. *The New Arabia*ns. Chicago: J. G. Ferguson Publishing Company, 1981.

The Middle East and North Africa, 37th edition. London: Europa, 1991.

CULTURES TODAY

ALGERIANS
(al jeer' ee uns)

People of Algeria, mostly Muslim and Arab or Berber.

Population: 24,000,000 (1989 estimate).
Location: North Africa, bounded by Niger, Mali, Mauritania, Western Sahara, Morocco, the Mediterranean Sea, Tunisia, and Libya.
Languages: Arabic; Berber; French.

Geographical Setting

Two broad mountain ranges and an intervening plateau roughly parallel the Mediterranean Coast and separate a narrow coastal plain from the great expanse of the Sahara Desert. The Tell Atlas Mountains run southwest to northeast, ending near the coast in a series of mountains (the Kabyle and the Aries mountains) and valleys. The Kabyle Mountains lie near the border with Tunisia. Historically, these coastal mountains have been havens of safety in which Berber villages allow for a distinctive Berber lifestyle.

Southward the Tell Atlas Mountains are cut by a plain that is fertile soil in the north and occasionally spotted with shallow lakes in the south, a region known as the High Plateau of Shotts. Farther inland, the plateau is separated from the Sahara Desert by another range, the Saharan Atlas.

Northern Algeria has warm wet winters and hot dry summers. In the mountains, winters are colder and dry spells last for five or six months each year. Much of the north is fertile land on which grapes and grains are grown. South of the mountains, Algeria is an expanse of rock and sand, part of the Sahara Desert.

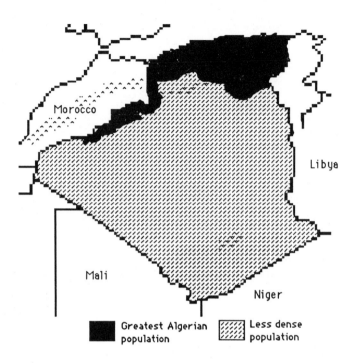

Greatest Algerian population   Less dense population

Historical Background

In the last days of the famous port city of Carthage (in Tunisia), most of current coastal Algeria was included with present-day Tunisia in the country of Numidia. As Carthage declined so did Numidia, finally breaking into several tribal organizations after 146 B.C. Many of these tribal groups were Berbers who, in various times, came under the rule of Rome, the Vandals, then Rome once more. During these reigns, the Berbers in the Auries and Kabyle mountains remained stubbornly independent until the area was invaded by Arabs bringing the new Muslim religion to the area in the A.D. 700s. At first resistant to these invaders, the Berbers were gradually converted to Islam.

Taken into the Arab Ummayad Empire and then placed under the rule of the Abbasid Caliphate, the Berbers rebelled in 756 and there followed hundreds of years of dispute between Berber and Arab ruling factions. Finally brought together in the 1100s, the country had become politically unstable again by 1250. Reaction to European inroads of the Arabs brought an invasion from Spain and then, by request of the native population, military intervention by the Turks.

A series of rulers, called beys, then governed the area at the will of the Turkish sultan.

Disturbing political issues at home caused France to take advantage of a reported insult cast by the ruling bey at a French council in 1827. France invaded Algeria, but withdrew because of unrest at home only to continue to attempt to dominate its African neighbor. For the next twenty-five years, France struggled with the Algerian people. By 1957, however, the Berber groups in the mountain outposts had capitulated to the French, who had made peace with the desert tribes. France ruled Algeria until 1962.

In the first seventy years of its rule, France encouraged immigration to Algeria with large grants of land to the European settlers. Algerian farms supplied grain for the French armies, and the Algerians were reduced to poverty.

After World War I, the sentiment for independence grew steadily, and by the end of World War II, most of the people of North Africa were demanding self-rule. Still, France continued its control even though a full-fledged war for independence began in Algeria in 1954. Five years later, French president Charles DeGaulle declared France's intention to allow an election in the country. Three years later, after more war, Algeria became an independent nation—part of the Arab Maghreb.

In its last days in power, France had begun to develop the oil reserves in the country while retaining control over Algerian exports. Eighty-two percent of the farm, mineral, and oil production of Algeria was purchased by France. When France finally quit Algeria, most of the European settlers abandoned the country as well. This left an Algerian population that had been deprived of its land, moved to the cities, and become a citizenry of factory workers in French-owned industries.

The new president, Houari Boumedienne, initiated land reforms and, to help his struggling government, declared Algerian ownership of fifty-one percent of the two French oil companies. This was one of many actions taken by the Boumedienne government to socialize the foreign dominated industries of Algeria. Over the years of his rule, Boumedienne attempted to make Algeria an important, independent part of North Africa. He became a staunch supporter of Arab causes, such as the demand for a Palestinian homeland. Algeria also became a factor in North African politics—supporting Western Sahara in its struggles with Morocco.

In 1978, Houari Boumedienne died and Colonel Ben Djidid Chaldi was chosen to replace him. Chaldi rapidly abandoned the totalitarian policies of Boumedienne and established a broader-based authority. This government has lowered taxes and lessened restrictions on land ownership in an attempt to make Algeria a self-supporting nation. From 1978 to 1991 the Algerian government has been working to improve relations with other countries. Foreign manufacturers have been encouraged to invest in plants to manufacture goods in partnership with the government-controlled businesses. A plant for assembling Fiat automobiles, providing jobs for thousands of Algerians, is planned for 1992.

Culture Today

The more than one hundred years of oppressive French government left Algeria with confusing land ownership, mostly controlled by French settlers. Except for the Berber villages in the mountains, and the nomadic Berbers of the Sahara, Algerians mostly formed a lower class in their own country, living in squalid housing on the outskirts of the big cities and earning their living by factory work.

People. The people of Algeria are Berbers and Arabs. However, through the years, the Berbers have become Arabized so that today distinctions between the two groups are dim. In some places language separates the two groups, which are otherwise bound by religion and occupation. In other places, Berbers and Arabs are distinguishable only by their own declaration of heritage. The major distinguishable Berber groups are the Kabyles of the coastal mountains, the M'zabites of the northern Sahara (who do not claim relationships with either Berbers or Arabs), and the Tuareg of the southern desert.

Family life. Until French domination of land rights, the basic unit of Algerian life was the extended family—a father and mother, their unmarried children, and the families of married sons. The senior male member of this family was the ruler of the group. These extended families lived together with fifty or sixty members sharing land and income, and living in a single compound. Extended families joined others in a small kin group, the *ayla*, for additional economic support. In Arab areas, these groups were ranked, with the highest class of Arabs being the *shurfa*, who claimed descent from Muhammad. Women married young (in their teens), most often by arrangement between families.

As these Algerians were disenfranchised by the immigrating French, they flocked to the cities in search of work. There the extended family tended to become a smaller unit as fathers and sons found separate occupations and chose to be independent. Since land reform later restored some of the old farmland to the native owners, recent years have seen some return to the previous lifestyles.

Early Algerian farmers raised wheat and barley for food, while herders kept goats and sheep. These farm products formed the base of the Algerian diet. Meat would be eaten on festive occasions, often with bits of sheep combined with semolina to form the North African dish called couscous. Among the desert dellers, where grains have not been readily available, dates serve as a staple food. French intervention introduced French cuisine into the diet and converted coastal farmlands to raising grapes for the French wine market. The Algerians were then forced to import a large portion of the food they eat.

Algerian men wore loose-fitting shirts that hung to the knees and covered these with cotton or woolen outer garments. Women were heavily clothed, especially when outside their own homes. In clothing, too, French intervention brought European styles. Most city-dwelling Algerians changed to this dress. But with the demand and eventual achievement of independence, the older costumes came to be accepted or, in some places, even preferred.

Algerians once lived in small villages or clusters of family compounds near their farmlands. As they lost these lands to the French, the farmers moved to cities that were ill-prepared to house them. There they built homes of whatever material was available. Since tin cans were often in supply, this became a major housing material. Some city slums became known as *Bidonvilles*, tin can cities.

Women. Women in Algeria have not been secluded as in the most fervent Arab-Muslim areas. Still, the women have not been encouraged to join men in social affairs. Over the ages, Algerian women have virtually established their own society, visiting with other women and avoiding encounters with unfamiliar men. In one group, the Chaouia, this separation has even resulted in a distinctly female language. The separation of sexes was interrupted by the French-inspired need to find factory and office work for support.

Some women today wear European-style clothing at home and work. Still, modern women follow the older traditions. Many wear face veils and cover their European dress with wraparound robes when outside the house.

Arts and literature. Algerians have a long history of accomplishments in architecture. Pyramids date from the third century B.C. and mosques of the exceptional Moorish design are represented by the famous Grand Almoravid Mosque at Tlemcen, which was built in the thirteenth century. Rural Algerians, especially the Kabyles, are

Many musicians entertain in the streets of major Algerian cities. *Courtesy of the Smithsonian Institution.*

well known for their tapestries and rug weavings that feature geometrical designs.

Algerian interest in literature is equally long-standing. However, one of the most well-known Algerian writers was an immigrant from Haiti. Frantz Fanon moved to Algeria in 1952, became immediately involved with the movement toward independence, and wrote a world-acclaimed book about the state into which the Algerians had been forced. His book *Les Damnés de la Terre* has been translated into English as *Wretched of the Earth.*

Religion. Almost all Algerians are Muslims and most of these followers of Muhammad are of the Sunni sect. However, the Muslim tenets are not as closely followed as in some other regions. Algerian men sometimes omit the mandatory prayers, or the practice of kneeling and bowing in submission as they pray. However, these omissions, too, are changing as the dependence on and influence of France diminishes. Many Algerians, as with Muslims throughout the Maghreb, are returning to more strict submission to the teachings of Islam.

For More Information

Abercrombie, Thomas J. "Algeria: Learning to Live with Independence." *National Geographic*, August 1973, pp. 200-233.

Nelson, Harold D., editor. *Algeria: A Country Study.* Washington, D.C.: American University Press, 1979.

The Middle East and North Africa, 37th edition. London: Europa, 1991.

ARMENIANS

(ar mee' nee uns)

Ancestors of people who settled the plateau region south and west
of the Caucasus Range in the Soviet Union, Turkey, and Iraq by
600 B.C.

Population: 6,000,000 (worldwide; 1989 estimate).
Location: The Soviet Union; Iran; Turkey; Iraq.
Language: Armenian, an Indo-European language.

Geographical Setting

Greatest Armenian
population

The Caucasus Mountains form a barrier, stretching between the Black Sea and the Caspian Sea, that separates the Soviet state of Georgia from the states of Armenia and Azarbaijan. South of these mountains, the land drops into a wooded grassland, the *steppe*, which rises to a plateau 2,000 feet above sea level and then to 16,000-foot Mt. Ararat. This plateau extends into northern Iran and northeastern Turkey at an average altitude of 6,000 feet. The high plateau is cut by deep gorges and fertile valleys. In the south, the plateau drops to juniper-covered foothills and mountain slopes where olive and fig groves thrive along with grape orchards. The overall climate is dry, with short hot summers and long cold winters.

Historical Background

Origin. Four thousand years ago, the plateau south of the Caucasus Mountains was an important trade route from the Mediterranean Sea to Central Asia and the Middle East. By the end of the second millennium B.C. bands of people had begun to migrate to this region from locations between the Danube River and the Black Sea. These migrants came to a land inhabited by tribal groups organized into small kingdoms, who throughout their history were subject to invasion from Trojans, Hittites, Assyrians, Persians, and Arabs and were also accustomed to Greek refugees fleeing from strife in their country. The early Armenians, people who called themselves the Hayk, settled the land near Lake Van on the upper Euphrates River as skilled farmers and pastoralists by 800 B.C. on the fringes of the Urartu Empire, one of the largest states in western Asia. When Urartu (Ararat is a distortion of this name) collapsed under attack of the Medes about 600 B.C., the Hayk spread over the old kingdom, assimilated the people into their own culture, and began the Armenian tradition. Armenian oral tradition traces their origin to Hayk, great-grandson of Noah, who lived in the land near Mt. Ararat. He named the area around the lake the Valley of the Armenians, and the neighbors began to refer to the area as the land of the Armens.

Persians. At first under the rule of Cyrus II of Persia, the Armenian region was divided into tribute-paying units led by Persian governors, or satraps. These units were fortified towns known throughout their history for their abundance of farm products. When Persia fell to Alexander the Great in 331 B.C., the Armenian state became a part of Greece, but by now a satrap had become king of the loosely united satrapies. King Orontes IV adopted Greek ways and spread Greek culture through Armenia, eventually proclaiming himself King of Armenia. However, Greek rule gave way to Roman domination in 190 B.C. and Armenia was again divided, with part of it claimed by the Roman conquerors. Nearly 100 years later, the land was reunited under the ruler Tigranes. When Persians again invaded the land, the Armenian kingdom was divided into two vassal states and a feudal noble/peasant society developed. The land was redivided after 301 A.D., when the western part of the kingdom adopted Christianity.

By about 400, an alphabet had been devised for the oral language, and a written language developed for the translation of holy books. Other literature in the Armenian language began to form an Armenian tradition opposed to that of their eastern Persian neighbors.

Turks, Mongols, and Egyptians. Domination by other peoples continued through the ages. Arabs invaded and divided the land, and a new Armenia appeared in 884. From the eleventh through thirteenth centuries, Turks, Mongols, Christian Crusaders, and Egyptians encroached on Armenian land and the Armenians finally moved northwestward to form a new state of Lesser Armenia that was supported by European nations. Again Egyptian forces overran the kingdom and many Armenians were forced to abandon their land. Those who remained in the west fell under the rule of the Ottomans and now are governed by Turkey. Those in the east were ruled by Persia (now Iran) and Russia (now part of the Soviet Union).

Armenians after World War I. In the late nineteenth century, political unrest in the Ottoman Empire resulted in the deaths of 300,000 Armenians. Difficulties between Armenians and Turks arose again during World War I when the Turks feared that the Armenians would side with their enemies in Russia. Most of the Armenians living in Turkey were deported to the Syrian desert. Resistance by the Armenians resulted in an estimated one million deaths. Others fled behind Russian lines, and in 1936 part of historic Armenia became a Soviet Republic. Armenian troubles have not always been entirely with other people. In 1988 a massive earthquake struck two major Armenian cities, leaving 25,000 dead.

Today, their land limited to the border of Soviet Armenia, Turkey, and Iran, Armenians have spread throughout the world while maintaining a strong affiliation as a people and with their homeland. Two-thirds of these people live in the Soviet Union.

Culture Today

Economy. One-third of the population of Soviet Armenia is engaged in agriculture. The people live in small isolated villages and are employed in several hundred state collective farms that produce a large portion of the food of the Soviet Union. Armenian farmers grow grapes, fruit, cereals, tobacco, and cotton. Often these villagers live in homes without electricity or running water, as do peasant farmers in many other countries throughout the world.

As in other areas around the world, Armenians are moving to the cities, where production of chemicals, precision instruments, metals, and machinery provide jobs, and where universities, libraries, performing arts, and modern restaurants are available.

As in other parts of the housing-scarce Soviet Union, many urban Armenians live in block-long apartment buildings of pink stone or concrete. Still, these people are more prosperous than many other Soviets, owning television sets, modern appliances, and some private cars.

Houses. Because natural stone is abundant, it is the major construction material in the rural areas of Armenia. Huge stone slabs are used for housing, monasteries, monuments and domed churches. The typical village house is a square of stone blocks with a corrugated metal roof pierced by a stone chimney. The rough-hewn stone homes provide shelter for extended families who work in the fields. In more remote mountain villages, these homes often have very small windows in order to conserve heat, and areas within the home are reserved for farm animals.

Family life. The Armenians have a deep sense of ethnic and cultural identity, preserved by their language, religion, and strong family attachments. Set apart by their beliefs and language, families live near each other throughout the world. Large extended families, encompassing several generations, live in the same community.

It is important for Armenians to marry and to have children. Children are taught strict manners, in addition to respect for and submission to the authority of elders. They learn to speak the Armenian language at home and in parochial schools and are expected to follow cultural and religious traditions.

Preparation of food and dining are symbols of family togetherness, especially during the Christian holidays of Easter and Christmas.

Young girls are taught to prepare Armenian dishes by their mothers and grandmothers, and meals are family social events. Family reunions are festive celebrations of food and conversation, as are the popular and enthusiastically attended Sunday family picnics.

Food and clothing. Armenian food is complex and diverse—featuring many combinations of available fresh produce with meat, olive oil, fowl, and fish. These are served with pilaf (rice), yogurt, and bread. Marinated eggplant salad, grape leaves stuffed with rice, pine nuts, or currants, homemade yogurt (*mazdoon*), finger-shaped raw bits of lamb (*chee keufteh*), and bulgar wheat patties are typical Armenian foods. Lamb is frequently used to make a stew or shish kebab, and is stuffed with wheat and baked to form the dish *sini keufteh. Kinaafa*, a shredded dough pastry with cheese filling, *baklava*, layers of wafer-thin dough and butter filled with chopped walnuts and honey, and *kurabai*, butter-almond cookies, are typical Armenian desserts. Many of these foods are prepared and eaten by other people throughout the Middle East and are not exclusively Armenian.

Today, most Armenians wear Western-style clothing, the older generation tending to dress conservatively in suits and ties, and plain dresses. Occasionally, a widowed grandmother wears a black dress and shawl.

Arts and literature. Historically, Armenians are known for the architecture of their churches, early mosaic work, illuminated manuscripts, and religious paintings, poetry, and music. Much Armenian music resembles the music of Asia or Turkey and is played on such instruments as the *oud*, which resembles a lute, and the clarinet. Frequently, this music accompanies popular Armenian folk dances, which resemble Greek dances.

A long and distinguished literary tradition includes the contemporary works of the Pulitzer Prize-winning author and dramatist William Saroyan, best remembered for his *The Daring Young Man on the Flying Trapeze* and *The Time of Your Life.* Novelist Michael Arlen wrote *Passage to Ararat*, Richard Hagopian wrote *Faraway the Spring*, and Marjorie Housepian wrote *A Houseful of Love.* Distinguished historians are Sirarpie Der Nersessian and Richard G. Hovannisian.

Armenian performers have gained international reknown in many fields. They include opera singers Lucine Amarda and Lili Chookasian, film director Rouben Maloulian, pop singer Cher, actors Mike

Connors and Arlene Francis, and musician Cathy Berberian. Aram Ilich Khachataurian is an internationally known composer who creates symphonies that include Armenian folk tunes. Other composers include Alan Hovhaness and Richard Yardumian. Yusuf Karsh is an award-winning photographer.

Religion. Under Persian rule, Armenians lived among people who followed the religion known as Zoroastrianism, and old Armenian beliefs incorporated this and other religions of the area as the different peoples were assimilated into the society. When Christianity was accepted by most Armenians, they patterned religious literature after the Greek and Roman churches and after the writings of Cyril of Jerusalem. To this they wed their own interpretations to form a Christian faith based at the church of Gregory at Ashishat. Armenians add religious celebrations of John the Baptist and of Mary, the mother of Christ, to traditional celebrations. An ancient feast of Anahite, the chief female god of ancient Armenians, became a celebration dedicated to Mary, and the celebration of the New Year—once dedicated to Vanatur, one of many gods of the ancient world—was rededicated to John the Baptist.

For More Information

Arlen, Michael J. *Passage to Ararat*, New York: Farrar, Straus and Giroux, 1975.

Maclean, Fitzroy. *To the Caucasus; The End of All the Earth.* Boston: Little, Brown and Company, 1976.

Mirak, Robert. *Torn between Two Lands; Armenians in America 1890 to World War I.* Boston: Harvard University Press, 1983.

AZERBAIJANI

(a zur by john' ee)

People of mixed descent who inhabit the neck of land known as
Azerbaijan, lying between the Caspian Sea and the Black Sea in
the Soviet Union and extending south into Iran.

Population: 12,000,000 (1988 estimate).
Location: Iran; the Azerbaijan Republic of the Soviet Union, ex-
tending into the Soviet Republics of Georgia and Armenia.
Language: Azerbaijani, a Turkic language.

Greatest Azerbaijani
population

Geographical Setting

The rolling countryside of Azerbaijan is divided between the Soviet Union and Iran by the Araks River Valley. The two northwestern provinces of Iran lie between Turkey in the west and the Caspian Sea to the east, while Soviet Azerbaijan lies between the Black Sea on the west and the Caspian Sea. Rolling hills are broken by barren mountain peaks rising more than 10,000 feet and by fertile plains. Two principle waterways, the Kura and Araks rivers, flow south-easterly through the region to empty into the Caspian Sea where fields of lush pasture and cultivated orchards form a coastal lowland. The mountainous areas are rich in petroleum and mineral resources, but agriculture remains the major economic factor. Winters are short and cold while summers are long, hot, and dry throughout most of the country. However, average annual rainfall ranges from eight inches in the drier zones to forty inches in the coastal lowlands near the Caspian Sea.

Historical Background

Early history. Written records of the ancient Assyrians refer to the land of present-day Azerbaijan as an extensively green and fertile region, which they called Georgia. In this region about 600 B.C., Zoroaster, the founder of the religion that once (before Islam) was the state religion of Iran, was born in the town of Reza'iyeh.

This was an ancient land bridge through which trade flowed between the Black and Caspian seas. Inhabited early on by small tribes of people, the land was the subject of frequent disputes by Medes and Persians, both of whom sought to control the profitable trade. In 1226 A.D., a group from Iran, the Sassanians, became rulers of Persia. These rulers spread the Persian culture among the various feudal tribes. These tribes became Persian-speaking followers of the Persian state religion. When the Arabs conquered Persia in the seventh century, the inhabitants of Azerbaijan became subjects of the government in Baghdad, and Islam replaced Zoroastrianism as the preferred religion. Ancestors of today's Azerbaijanis were not a distinct group until the eleventh century, when the groups were assimilated by Seljuk Turkic warriors who invaded and colonized land from present-day Iran to Soviet Georgia. These invaders populated the region in such numbers that a new Turkic-speaking Azerbaijani culture emerged. The Azerbaijani, converted to the Sunni Islamic religion and speaking a Turkic language, varied considerably from other Persians. Their Turkish customs and social order bound them in a new identity.

Mongols and Persians. In the fourteenth century, Mongol followers of Ghengis Khan rampaged through Persian land and invaded Azerbaijan and Iraq. They established a new dynasty, the Ilkhans, with its capital in Azerbaijan. Fighting among the Mongols soon led to the collapse of this government and the land was claimed by the Ottoman Empire. Persians from the Azerbaijan town of Ardabil, however, pushed back the Ottomans and reinstated a Persian dynasty.

The Persian rulers made their capital at Tabriz, expelled foreign influences from the lands, and unified their people under the mantle of the Shia form of Islam. Although the Azerbaijani continued to speak their own language, Turkish tribes among them supported the Persians who controlled Azerbaijan for 200 years.

Iran. In the sixteenth century, Shah Abbas opened Iran to the West by inviting diplomatic relations with the British and establishing peace with the Ottomans. Shah Abbas brought ethnic and religious minorities together with a new sense of national identity. He used Armenian architects to restore and beautify the cities, and built holy shrines at Tabriz, Ardabil, and Meshed.

Russia. In the eighteenth century, neighboring Russia began to expand its empire and temporarily occupied Azerbaijan. Despite Azerbaijani resistance, the Russians increased their efforts so that by 1828 the Persians had lost control of all Azerbaijani territory north of the Araks River. Undertaking a land-reform program initiated by the Russians, this portion of Azerbaijan had begun to develop a modern agricultural economy by the end of the nineteenth century. After some attempts to gain independence, the Azerbaijani outside of Iran came under communist control and were formed into a Soviet Socialist Republic in 1920, with its capital at Baku.

Azerbaijani under the Shah. In Iran, Reza Shah Pahlavi, the country's leader from the 1950s to the 1970s, worked to erase regional and tribal customs. Religious leaders lost much of their authority, as the Shah sought to Westernize the country. Western clothes, education, and civil law were introduced and many of the customs of the Azerbaijani and other societies were outlawed. The Iranian Azerbaijani joined with their Soviet counterparts to gain independence. In 1945, with Soviet support, the Iran group declared an independent state, but this state lasted only one year before again becoming part of Iran. Then, when the Shah was overthrown with the help of the Azerbaijani, this group found itself in greater conflict with the regulations of the religious fundamentalists who took charge of the country, and many moved to Turkey. Since that time, the Azerbaijani majority in the Soviet state of Azerbaijan has been agitating for independence.

Culture Today

Overview. Almost as many Azerbaijani live in the Soviet Republic as in the two northwestern provinces of Iran. In both countries they are mainly rural people engaged in agriculture. With the exception of the few who still lead nomadic lives and those who are educated and employed in large industrial centers, most Azerbaijani are settled farmers and herders. Modern Azerbaijani have given up many of their old clan traditions.

Economy. Soviet Azerbaijan is a modern agricultural state, even though only a small portion of the land is fertile. Using modern technology and systems for irrigation, the farmers produce wheat, barley, sesame, vegetables, cotton, tobacco, and grapes. In the lowlands they produce citrus fruits and raise tea and rice. Fruit orchards cover the cooler southeastern slopes and valleys. Here mulberry trees provide homes for silkworms. Livestock provides meat and dairy products for both local use and for the state-owned economy. The livestock also provides wool, which is made into textiles for clothing and woven into hand-loomed carpets for which Azerbaijani craftsmen are famous.

The Azerbaijan Republic is a major petroleum center. Because of this, the Azerbaijani enjoy private housing, roads, transportation systems, and health and recreational facilities more abundantly than many other people in the Soviet Union. An increasing number live in cities and work in industrial plants or as teachers, policemen, taxi drivers, university professors, government officials, and other urban occupations.

Iran's Azerbaijani are mostly farmers who live in villages in densely populated valleys. Tabriz and Reza'iyeh, the capitals of the two Azerbaijan provinces, are ancient market towns famed for their oriental bazaars held in domed marketplaces. These two cities are also known for their Islamic mosques, the Blue Mosque in Tabriz and the Friday Mosque of Reza'iyeh. The markets and mosques of Iranian Azerbaijan are popular tourist stops, as are the medieval houses, mineral-spring spas, and beaches of Soviet Azerbaijan.

Food, clothing, and shelter. The majority of Iran's modern-day Azerbaijani remain rural people who live in their ancestral villages in the densely populated valleys. Farm villages of fifty or so houses and scattered towns of more than a thousand residents are surrounded by fields and orchards. In Iran, the availability of well water is the single most important factor determining a village location.

Rural homes in Iran are single-story, mud-brick and stucco structures of square or rectangular construction. These homes generally have flat roofs and front porches supported by wooden pillars. Soviet farmers, too, live in small homes constructed of available material—sandstone, fired bricks, and stucco. These homes have flat roofs, wooden window frames and doorways, and plastered interior walls. Floors in Azerbaijani farmhouses are often covered with layers of Persian carpets. Most Soviet farm homes have electricity and electrical appliances. Furniture in Azerbaijani homes is simple. People traditionally sit on mats and cushions laid on the carpets. In some

These Azerbaijani men are building a tent frame.
Courtesy of Dr. Nikki Keddie, U.C.L.A.

homes cooking is done on the traditional stone oven in the center of an open kitchen area.

The Azerbaijani diet has been influenced by Persians, Turks, Armenians, and Georgians. It is varied and highly spiced. Soviet Azerbaijani boast of unusual longevity, which some attribute to diets of fresh vegetables, sour milk, and spring water. Azerbaijani are famous for their rice dishes called *pilaf*, which are prepared in many different ways, using bits of chicken, dried fruits and nuts, prunes, apricots, almonds, pistachios, and sesame seed. Pilaf is usually sauteed with onion in butter and cooked in a chicken or meat broth to provide a base for a variety of meat and poultry dishes, vegetable stews, and salads.

Sour milk products are staples of the Azerbaijani diet. From sour milk, they make a yogurtlike food called *kefir* and a drink much like buttermilk. The curds are used to make a tangy, white cream cheese that is spread on flat unleavened bread. Milk is churned into sweet butter and boiled to a golden liquid for cooking.

Meat dishes are also varied. *Yariakh dalmassy* is a combination of minced lamb and rice wrapped in grape leaves. *Nur kurma* is lamb marinated in pomegranate syrup, onions, oregano, and olive oil; *kababe morgh* is chicken marinated in citrus juices; and *chelau kebab* consists of lamb strips, beaten thin and served with rice to which beaten egg has been added.

Most modern-day Azerbaijani wear European-style clothing. Rural women keep their heads covered with scarves and shawls and tend to wear layers of sweaters and jackets over loose-fitting peasant dresses. Men wear woolen caps and coarse woolen trousers and jackets. This dress varies in Soviet Azerbaijan where trendy European styles are available, and in the religious regime of Iran. In Iran, women wear more completely covering dresses, and veils or shawls covering the face. In public, these women often wear a *chadoor*, a long black garment, over their usual dress.

Only among the few nomadic Azerbaijani is the older style worn—for men, baggy pants held up by a sash, boots and a furry hat called the *karakul*, and for women, a long habit called an *atlas* with a loose blouse over baggy pantaloons and with a shawl.

Family life. Iran's Azerbaijani are Muslims of the Shi'ite sect. In addition to the usual lifetime marriage, the more traditional followers practice a temporary form of marriage called *mutah*. This union is made for a specific period of time and its dissolution is built into the time arrangement. As is common in Islamic tradition, men hold leadership roles in the family. They are expected to support the family and to help in the instruction of the children, particularly of the older boys. Women care for the homes and tend to the needs of the young children. Both women and men have the right to inheritance, to own property, and sometimes to vote.

Language. Language is the main binding force among the Azerbaijani. The Soviet Azerbaijani have purged Russian words from their language and favor an old Slavic alphabet, the Cyrillic alphabet. The Iran Azerbaijani, too, use the Azerbaijani language, but write using Persian and Arabic script.

Religion. Iranian Azerbaijanis are Muslims of the Shi'ite sect. In Iran they follow the guidance of the learned holy men, the *mujtahids*, who are identified by long brown robes (*aba*) and turbans. Religion is discouraged in the Soviet Union, so the Soviet Azerbaijani practice their religion in semisecrecy, a pattern known as parallel Islam. In Iran religious celebrations are important events, including *Nauruz*, the Iranian New Year, *Ashura*, which commemorates the martyrdom of Imam Husayn, and *Ramadan*, the month of fasting, among others.

Arts and literature. Azerbaijani literature dates to the tenth century, at which time writers began to write in Turkish as well as continuing to write in Persian. Modern writers include novelists Sultan Medjit Ganizade and M. S. Ordubardy, playwright D. Dzhabarly, and poets Hussein Djavit and S. Vergung.

The first Azerbaijani opera was written by U. Gadzhibekov in 1908 and began a tradition that continues in Soviet Azerbaijan. The Soviet people enjoy symphony, musical comedy, and drama as well as opera.

Azerbaijani are well-known for their stone carving, ceramics, carpet weaving, metalware, and architecture. Throughout their history, artists have created miniature paintings that are common throughout Islamic societies.

For More Information

Abrahamian, Edward. *Iran: Between Two Revolutions.* Princeton, New Jersey: Princeton University Press, 1982.

Bennigsen, Alexander, and S. Enders Wimbush. *Muslims of the Soviet Empire: A Guide.* Indianapolis: Indiana University Press, 1986.

Shaw, Stanford. *History of the Ottoman Empire and Modern Turkey.* London: Cambridge University Press, 1977.

108

BALUCH
(bal ooch')

Herders and farmers of the Iranian-Afghan desert.

Population: 5,000,000 (1983 estimate).
Location: Pakistan (the two Baluchistan provinces), Iran, Afghanistan.
Language: Baluch, an Indo-European language.

Geographical Setting

Located west of the Indus Plains and bordered by the rugged mountain ranges of Iran in the west and Afghanistan in the northwest, the land of the Baluch—Baluchistan—is an arid plateau of sand and stone bordered on the south by a subtropical coastal strip on the Arabian Sea, and a fertile but harsh winter region in the north. Water in most of this area is scarce, less than eight inches of rain falls per year, and temperatures are extreme—hot in the summer and cold in winter—sometimes rising to 125 degrees Fahrenheit or falling below zero degrees.

Historical Background

Origin. In a traditional ballad, Baluch claim to be followers of the Imam Ali who once lived in the low hills around Allepo in present-day Syria. According to this story, when their leader was killed by the caliph of the region, the Baluch were forced to migrate to the southern shores of the Caspian Sea. This claim is supported by the writings of the Persian King Naushirwa. So great were their numbers, the king wrote in his *Shah Namah*, that "the ground has become black with Biloches."

The Baluch language has been traced to the early Median and Parthian cultures of ancient Iran. Because of the language and because the Baluch use the image of a tiger as their national emblem, it is believed that they originated on the southern shores of the Caspian Sea, where the tiger is known to have lived. They moved to their present lands between the sixth and fourteenth centuries. The region was a historical crossroads and subject to centuries of conflict and conquest.

Baluch and outsiders. Meeting Arab invaders in the seventh century, Baluch groups accepted the Muslim faith and associated with the Sunni sect. Joining the Arabs, they spread the religion as the armies marched on Persia and Afghanistan. This movement added to the Baluch culture from such people as the Paktuns of Afghanistan. At first, organized in a collection of small independent societies, the Baluch were first united in the tenth century under Ilmash Rumi. They settled in Kirman as a nation of loosely allied societies. They had been pushed back and forth across the desert by battles with the Kirman and were later invaded by the Mongol armies of Ghengis Khan. Through centuries of struggle, the Baluch remained fiercely independent, even when the area became part of the empire of the Moguls of India. In the sixteenth century, the Moguls were driven out by the Baluch under Ibrahim Mirwari. Organized by one of his successors under an Ahmadzai dynasty, the Baluch fell under the control of India, and then, in 1839, to British influence. In 1893, an international border area known as the Durand Line was negotiated with Afghanistan as a buffer zone and British-ruled Baluchistan as part of the British Indian Empire.

Baluch in Pakistan. When India was partitioned in 1947, the Baluch chose to join Pakistan. Still, isolated Baluch tribes refused to give up their autonomy and pushed for an independent Muslim state. The Khan of Kalat, ruler of Baluchistan, revolted against the merger with Pakistan and was deposed in 1958, but regained his throne in 1962.

A bitter civil war among Baluch societies erupted in the 1970s, slowing the struggle for independence. The immigration of people from Punjab in India to work in mines in the area caused the Baluch to be concerned for their nomadic lifestyle. The result was another rebellion by the Baluch living in Pakistan. In 1975, Pakistan's Prime Minister Zulfikar Bhutto suspended the Baluch local government and dismantled their chief and subchief system of government. Since then, continuous friction between Baluch societies and between these societies and the governments of the various countries has resulted in the movement of many Baluch to Pakistani cities to seek protection and employment.

Change. The nomadic life of the Baluch has been altered by politics and poverty. Many Baluch have migrated to the large cities of Pakistan in search of work, while others labor in the oil fields of the Persian Gulf. Typically, the migrants are the young unmarried men who send a portion of their incomes to support the families left behind. These migrant workers generally live in squatter settlements near their work, often in concrete-block houses.

Culture Today

Nomadic life. Those Baluch who remain in Baluchistan, an area that spreads across three nations, cling to their herding and planting way of life. Nomadic Baluch travel with their herds as the seasons change. In summer they move sheep, goats, cattle, horses, and camels to the hills where they set up tents (*khizdis*) or build huts (*jhuggis*) of branches and straw. In winter they return to the plains where they live in earthen homes. These Baluch depend on a combination of herding camels, sheep, and goats, and on farming They plant seeds along embankments where water from the slight rainfall has collected, wherever they stop to pasture their sheep and goats. However, most of their farming is concentrated near oases. Using underground channels called *karez*, they bring water from spring and river sources many miles to irrigate their plants. Water is a most precious commodity in Baluchistan, where it is considered community property to be shared between camps and even with rival societies. Still, the Baluch depend mostly on the products of their sheep and goats for their own food needs and for meat and wool to market.

City life. Quetta, the capital of old Baluchistan, was begun in the tenth century. Since then, other towns in Baluch territory have been established by the British. In these towns and cities, the Baluch lifestyle shifts toward European influences.

Quetta, on the eastern limit of Baluchistan in Pakistan, is a crossroads of transportation routes to Iran and Afghanistan. It is a modern city of more than 100,000 people, which was almost completely rebuilt after a disastrous earthquake in 1935. Tourism is a major industry for the Baluch in Quetta. In the smaller cities, landless poor work in light industry and craft-oriented jobs. Some work in mines exploiting the rich mineral deposits of the area, in oil production, or in the natural gas fields discovered near Quetta. However, more than seventy percent of the Baluch live in rural villages. Most are tenant farmers or sharecroppers. Electricity is available to only one-fifth of the population.

Social organization. Baluch society is divided into *hakim,* who are ruling landowners or prosperous farmers, *baluch,* who are businessmen and professional people, and *hizmatker,* the landless tenants and former slaves. The right to tax and therefore the right to govern is controlled by the *hakim,* who compete with each other under a system labeled feudal militarism. Leaders buy support with property rights. Losers of the power struggle then must share their wealth with the winners or with other Baluch societies.

Purda, the practice of seclusion of women, is a mark of wealth among the Baluch. In the poorer nomadic societies, such strict Islamic practices cannot be observed. Only the wealthy can afford to hire male servants for such chores as going to market, thus ensuring that women will not encounter outsiders or other men.

A chief, or *sardar*, makes decisions regarding the larger society with smaller units governed by *malik* or *takkari* subchiefs who are members of the council of elders, *shahi jirga*.

Family life. Although the Baluch would rather marry their cousins, they tend to consider land and water rights when choosing partners. The marriage between cousins, an arrangement that tends to keep landholdings within the family, is fading. Today seventy percent of the Baluch landowners are married to non-kin. However, marriage between cousins is still preferred among the Zikris, a religious sect of Baluch who are coastal fishers. The Zikris, whose beliefs differ from the majority Sunni Islamic Baluch, view others as less devout Muslims and hold to cousin-marriage as a means of self-unification rather than as a landholding method. They refuse to marry non-Baluch, and prefer to marry within the Zikris society when cousin-marriage is not available. Throughout the villages of Baluchistan, marriages are often arranged by the families of the bride and groom, and a bride-price (*lab*) is paid to the bride's family. In Muslim tradition, divorce is a choice of the husband and is accomplished by repeating "I divorce you" three times before a chieftain, the *Sardari*. Also, polygyny is allowed wherever the husband can afford to care for more than one wife.

Among the nomadic Baluch, women have more freedom. They take part in politics and warfare alongside their menfolk, and in some groups segregation of sexes is not at all practiced. Nomads view this practice as an imposition on Baluch life by foreign groups who have visited or controlled the area.

Women in Baluch farming society tend the animals, help with the farm work, care for the children, and prepare meals. They also weave on handlooms and embroider clothing. Nomadic women once preferred to marry a man who had committed a robbery and escaped, murdered at least one man, and who possessed a swift and sturdy mare. The qualities of bravery, strength, and wealth represented by the old symbols are still criteria for families offering their daughters in marriage.

Among the nomadic Baluch, wedding celebrations take place in an encampment (the *mena*) at night. The women sing the *Halo*, a wedding song of the camp, and a series of questions are posed to the man throughout the night. The mullah recites passages from the

Quran while the men touch their foreheads to the ground in prayer. The bridegroom is asked if he will marry the woman and, after he has answered affirmatively, a messenger is sent to ask the bride if she consents. Traditionally, the woman shows reluctance by refusing this request twice before accepting it. The bride and groom then see each other for the first time at the ceremony.

Food, clothing, and shelter. At a typical meal, milk and cheeses are supplemented with meat, rice, and flat breads called *nan, kak,* or *chapati.* In camp, the food is cooked in an open-sided hut called a *cherri* where pottery jars filled with hot ashes are sunk into the sands and used as ovens. Saffron rice is cooked in large iron pots hung over the ovens. Goat meat and mutton is roasted on spits over wood fires. The bread dough is shaped into round, flat cakes and placed on the side of the heated pots to cook. Goat milk is used to make *mast,* a food similar to yogurt, and is also the base of a popular drink, *lassi,* a mixture of curds, herbs, and spices.

Baluch summer camps consist of tents called *kirris.* These are constructed by standing fork-shaped tree branches and placing a ridgepole between them. Woven reed mats are suspended over the poles to form the tent and are used inside for ground covering. Winter dwellings are more permanent open-sided houses constructed of tree trunks, with roof and walls made of mud-reinforced reeds. Sometimes the floors of these homes are concrete covered with Persian rugs. The home is furnished with cushions and reed mats, woven saddlebags for storage, ceramic and brass pottery for water, string beds, and goatskins for milk storage.

Clusters of kirris house extended families within compounds. The head-wife and her children live with the husband, and the lesser wives and their children with the husband's mother. Brothers and their wives, as well as other close relatives and friends, are housed in nearby separate houses.

Baluch men wear a loose, knee-length tunic called a *chola* over billowing white trousers with narrow cuffs, or over a cloth wrapped around their middle, the *languatta.* Over this, they wear a sleeveless vest or a long white cotton overcoat, the *kirta.* A *pushti,* a long shawl, is draped over the shoulder or wrapped around the face to keep out heat and dust. Under large, white turbans, a small, red, embroidered and decorated cap covers long hair arranged in ringlets. The men go barefoot or wear curled, pointed-toe leather shoes called *jittees* or sandals woven from palm fiber.

Women part their long, dark hair in the middle and style it into braids using fat from sheep. Women's clothes are colorful, usually bright red or made of red-patterned fabrics. The common dress, the *pushk*, is loose and calf-length with elaborate embroidery around the shoulders. Under this dress, women wear *shalvar*, baggy pants caught at the ankle. A long shawl, the *siree*, is draped over the hair and shoulders. Women wear a great deal of jewelry, including silver ankle bracelets, gold bangles, rings studded with precious and semiprecious stones, and silver ringlets used as earrings. Married women often wear a gold ring inserted in one side of the nose. Baluch women use black *kohl* to make their eyes appear larger, and red henna to dye the soles of their feet, palms of hands, and their fingernails. Men also use the red henna to dye their beards as an indication that they have made the holy pilgrimage to Mecca.

Arts. Nomadic Baluch are fond of displaying their horses and the weapons used in battle. Men wear curved *talwar,* swords with silver hilts that have been handed down from father to son. They carry muzzle-loading *tupaks*, homemade guns with brass decorations that show the number of men killed by the owner. They also carry hatchets called *tawa* and rhinoceros-hide shields studded with brass and gems.

Women take pride in weaving and embroidery. They use wool to weave textiles and beautifully patterned carpets of geometric design. They also produce mats, baskets, sandals, and eating utensils from the dwarf palm.

The Baluch enjoy music and poetry. Their oral history is delivered in song and rhyme. They employ professional storytellers, *davtars*, and minstrels, *doms* and *loris*. Baluch songs and poems describe genealogy, epic battles, and love songs. The singers and professional dancers are accompanied by a wooden fiddle, the *sarinda*, a three-stringed lute, the *dhambiro*, a drum, the *dohl*, and a flutelike pipe, the *nal.*

Religion. The Baluch are Muslims of the Sunni sect. However, traveling Baluch have much faith in superstitions, trial by ordeal such as walking on fire, and miracles, and place their faith in the power of their chieftains. These Baluch dispense with the Muslim prayers and fasting. Some prefer pilgrimages to their own shrines than to Mecca. Two important shrines are the Pir Suhri and Pir Durbar on the crests of the mountains in Baluchistan.

Recreation. The Baluch enjoy riddles and games. A favorite game is *chonk*, which is played with dice made from cowry shells. Children play a hide-and-seek game using a bone. They throw the bone as far as possible and rush to find it; the finder is rewarded by being roughed up. A most popular form of entertainment for everyone is posing and solving riddles.

Many sports events take place at a ten-day fair held once a year in February. The fair is called *mela* and is attended by thousands of Baluch from throughout the area. These visitors watch and participate in such sports as spear-throwing, sword-fighting, wrestling, and camel and horse racing.

Conclusions. These traditional lifestyles of the Baluch are rapidly changing as the people move to the towns and villages, adopt European-style clothing, and are exposed to opportunities in business, labor, and education.

For More Information

Dodwell, Christina. *Travelers on Horseback.* New York: Walker and Company, 1989.

Matheson, Sylvia. *The Tigers of Baluchistan.* London: Arthur Barker, Ltd., 1967.

New Faces of Baluchistan. Islamad, Pakistan: Pakistan Publications, 1979.

Pakistan: A Country Study. Washington, D.C.: American University Press, 1983.

BEDOUIN
(bed' oo in)

Desert dwelling nomads who speak Arabic.

Population: 4,000,000-6,000,000 (1980 estimate).
Location: North Africa; the Middle East.
Languages: Arabic; Berber.

Geographical Setting

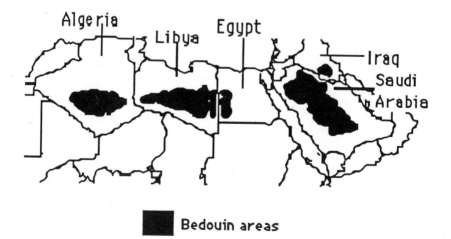

Bedouin areas

The Bedouin are scattered across the deserts of a huge area from Syria, Jordan and the Arabian Peninsula in the east to Egypt and Saharan North Africa (including much of Libya, Algeria, and Morocco) in the west. Though uniformly barren and dry, the landscape varies considerably in other respects. In the Empty Quarter of Saudi Arabia and the Ergs of the Sahara, great sand dunes roll and shift with the wind; in certain areas, such as the Hijaz of western Saudi Arabia, formidable mountains rise from the desert. While some Bedouin live in such environments, most occupy the less-fierce plains. In addition to the constant problem of water, the Bedouin have also learned to cope with violent, sand-bearing winds and temperature extremes. Nights are often chilly, even in summer, while winters in northern Arabia can bring frost and even snow. Summer days, by contrast, can exceed 120 degrees Fahrenheit in the scant shade.

Historical Background

Rise of camel nomadism. Wild dromedaries (camels with one hump) seem to have lived in both North Africa and the Middle East in prehistoric times. It is thought, however, that the animals were first domesticated in southern Arabia, perhaps as early as 2500 B.C. In taming the dromedary, which is calmer and more suitable for riding than its two-humped Bactrian cousin from Asia, the Arabs made possible a way of life that has existed until modern times. While goat- and sheepherding nomads might subsist on the desert's edge, only with the camel could men survive in the inner desert. Quicker over long distances than the horse, and able to carry greater loads, the camel can travel for days without water on a diet of shrubs and bushes that even sheep and goats will not touch. At such times, the animal subsists mostly on fat it has stored in its hump.

The camel's importance extended far beyond its basic function of transporting the people and their goods from one grazing ground to the next. The Bedouin relied on the camel in almost every aspect of desert life. The animal's milk and flesh supplied nourishment, and in emergencies it might be killed for the liquid it collects in its paunch. Its hair has been woven for saddlebags, blankets, sacks, and clothing, and its skin used for various leather goods, including weatherproof tents. The size and quality of a man's herd was a measure of his wealth and an indication of his status. Thoroughbred camels were raised for riding or carrying baggage. Each time an animal was sold, the new owner marked the camel with his brand, or *wasm.* Camels were used for payment of taxes, awarded to enemies to settle feuds, and sold for money to buy food or manufactured goods.

Caravans. By Biblical times, great trade routes had arisen across the deserts of the Middle East. Long camel caravans negotiated these routes, at the ends of which their goods were traded to settled farming communities. From southern Arabia the caravans transported frankincense and myrrh to the wealthy Mediterranean of the Holy Land. Other cargoes included gold, silver, lead, iron, elephant skins, ivory, precious stones, spices, and cloth. The Bible story of the Queen of Sheba (c. 1000 B.C.) depicts such a caravan. Similar caravans traveled north to Mesopotamia. The Bedouin guarded the routes and supplied water, in exchange for a toll of perhaps twenty-five percent of a caravan's worth. They sold camels to the traders, acted as guides, and raided those caravans that refused to pay the toll. For centuries the nomadic Arabs' prosperity relied on the state of the caravan trade. A slow decline accelerated during Roman times (c. 100 B.C. to A.D. 600), when the Romans opened sea routes to the east that circumvented those across the Arabian peninsula.

Raiding. Warfare between the Roman and Persian empires added to the disruption in Arab lands, and it is during this period that the earliest true Bedouin raids—using camels for long-distance travel and horses for the final attack—were recorded. Bedouin society was organized by tribes, and trading for camels usually took place inside a single tribe. Raiding thus became the way in which camels, the basis of the Bedouin economy, were exchanged between tribes. The raid (*ghazu*) became a source of excitement as well as of revenue. A system of rules guided the behavior of the raiding parties: women and children were not to be touched, and booty was the aim rather than the deaths of defending tribesmen. The raiders must not leave their victims completely destitute. Upon returning safely, the party divided the spoils, each man receiving a portion according to his performance on the raid.

Warriors of Islam. After emigrating from Mecca to Medina (a settled oasis) in A.D. 622, the prophet Muhammad set about converting Bedouin tribes to his new religion. Eight years later, an army of 10,000 Bedouin warriors helped him capture Mecca. Within a hundred years of Muhammad's death in 632, Arab armies under Islamic banners had conquered territory from India through Egypt and North Africa to Spain and France. The Bedouin warriors contributed to this advance, and in the process integrated some of the teachings of Islam into their own desert code of ethics; for example, the Islamic mandate for alms-giving and aid to the needy. In centuries to come, the Bedouin would continue to supply power bases for Arab movements. In the eighteenth century, for example, tribes in Arabia fought behind the puritanical Wahhabi religious revival. This dynamic movement, allied to the powerful ibn Saud family, still influences social and religious life in Saudi Arabia.

Bedouin in North Africa. In their conquest of North Africa, the Arabs at first occupied coastal areas, where the Bedouin soldiers intermarried with the original inhabitants (see BERBERS and MOROCCANS) to form a small urban elite. In the centuries that followed, however, larger numbers of Bedouin migrated westward. They found that their lifestyle could easily be transplanted from the deserts of the Middle East to those of North Africa. In the Sahara, the Bedouin vied with the Taureg (see BERBERS) for control of the rich Arab caravans that brought slaves and gold from sub-Saharan Africa to the Middle East.

Pressures for change. The Bedouin survived as masters of the desert until the modern age. In World War I, led by urbanized Arabs such as the Hashemites, Bedouin tribes allied themselves with the British and French against the Turks (whose Ottoman Empire at that time ruled most of the Middle East) and the Germans. After the defeat and expulsion of the Turks, however, victory turned to frustration as the European powers either ruled directly (as did the French in Syria) or supported weak central governments whom they controlled and manipulated. In both cases, Bedouin autonomy, which had begun to give way to a settled lifestyle in the century before, was severely curtailed. The European forces patrolled with aircraft and automobiles, gradually penetrating farther and farther into the deserts. In the newly created states of Iraq and Transjordan, central governments used cars, planes, and machine guns to end raids and tribal warfare. Camel caravans had declined in the nineteenth century. The disruption of raiding and this decline in trade—the old sources of income—created widespread poverty among the people. In Arabia, King Abd al Aziz ibn Saud (who gave his name to Saudi Arabia, his new state) likewise employed modern weapons to consolidate his leadership of the Bedouin there. Abd al Aziz, who called himself "King of the

Bedouin," also used older methods of gaining allegiance, such as marrying the daughters of powerful sheikhs. The newer ways, however, allowed him to exercise power on a scale previously unknown. In Saudi Arabia as elsewhere, the technology and political realities of the twentieth century diminished the nomads' exclusive command of the great deserts.

Culture Today

While the modern governments often used military force to bring the Bedouin under control, they have since relied on more peaceful means. They cannot allow autonomous nomads to cross international boundaries at will with their animals, following traditional routes, or avoid taxes. Nor can these governments let tribes threaten travelers or permit tribal justice to supersede municipal courts. Consequently, they have discouraged such practices by providing the Bedouin with schools, health care, and jobs, in exchange for establishing settled communities. Such measures may represent a genuine attempt to improve the Bedouin's lot, but are generally incompatible with nomadic life.

Adding to the pull toward settled communities is the harshness of nomadic life. Old sources of income have largely disappeared. In addition, herds have declined in value with the advent of industrial society. Similarly, the expansion of cultivated lands has reduced available pasturage near the desert oases. On the edges of the desert especially, pick-up trucks supplement or replace camels for transporting goods. Yet the Bedouin remain central to Arabic culture. Both they and other Arabs see desert life as a model of purity impossible in the towns or cities. On a smaller scale, the nomadic life persists in the deserts. In fact, one national leader, Muammar Qadaffi of Libya, was born and raised among tent-dwellers.

Tribes and territories. The flexibility of tribal organization enabled the tribe to meet a wide range of challenges. The Bedouin could unite when numbers counted, as in a war, or they could disperse when resources were limited. Such dispersals have meant that many tribes have sections in different regions. In Arabia and its nearby deserts there are about 100 large tribes (those numbering 1,000 members or more) and many smaller ones. Other tribes live in Egypt or North Africa. The camel nomads of the inner desert have been considered the most noble of the Bedouin (perhaps because untainted by the crassness of city-life, they are healthier and tougher). The sheep and goat herders of the desert fringe, closer to settled communities, are lower on the social scale.

Tribal territories were well-defined and their boundaries known to all. Within them, tribesmen knew every well and grazing spot, rotating among them at intervals that best ensured the welfare of the herd. These resources were jealously guarded, and to enter another tribe's territory without permission—even if only to cross it—was to risk attack. Territories constantly changed as new tribes became stronger and formerly strong ones declined. Today, a number of factors has weakened these territorial distinctions. Most important, the suppression of raids and attacks prevented the enforcement of tribal rights. National borders were drawn without regard for tribal territories, and the Bedouin were discouraged from crossing from one nation to another. Governments dug wells in the desert, which helped supply water, but since the wells were open to all, they further cut across old rights. The Saudi government abolished tribal grazing rights in 1953, opening the land for all to pasture herds. Such measures led to severe overgrazing in some areas, as there was no longer a strong incentive to preserve the quality of the pasturage.

Food, clothing, and shelter. Food is scarce in the desert, and most Bedouin have suffered undernourishment at some time in their lives. Dairy products have been the traditional staple: the milk of camels and goats is drunk fresh or made into yogurt and clarified butter called *ghee*. Many meals consist of a bowl of milk or yogurt, or rice flavored with ghee. This simple main meal is eaten in the evening, and may be followed by a handful of dates, which commonly grow in the desert oases. Women make round loaves of unleavened bread from coarse, stone-ground wheat. Regardless of their poverty, however, even the poorest Bedouin will struggle to present a guest with the finest fare obtainable. They admire generosity perhaps more than any other trait, and the desert code dictates that a guest—whether friend, stranger, or enemy—be protected and well fed (for a maximum of three days). Meat is usually eaten only on such occasions, whereupon a lamb, goat, or young camel is slaughtered and roasted.

On the guest's arrival, the host will spread a rug for him before the fire and serve coffee. Preparing coffee is the important way of showing hospitality. In the guest's presence, the beans are roasted over the fire in a long-handled skillet, then pounded with a mortar and pestle. These utensils are decorative, as are the ornate brass or copper pots in which the coffee is boiled.

The Bedouin wear light, loose-fitting clothing that covers them almost completely, allowing air circulation and free movement yet affording protection from the sun and wind-blown sand. The main garment for men is the cotton *thawb*, a long straight-cut gown of white, brown, or gray. Over the thawb, men wear a silk or cotton *kibr*, a long jacket open in the front and secured with a leather belt. For warmth, a one-piece coat which falls to the fingertips called the *aba* is woven from wool or camel's hair. Men also wear the traditional Arab headgear, the *keffiyah*, a square cloth folded into a triangle and kept in place with a double loop of woven cord. The keffiyah is helpful in keeping blowing sand from blowing into the nose and mouth. Women and girls wear one or two long-sleeved, ankle length dresses, whose color depends on the tribe. Some women also wear different types of black veil-like face masks with eye-slits, for modesty and protection against the elements. They cover their heads with a piece of cloth to keep sand away and for protection from the sun, and most adorn themselves with jewelry and black eye makeup called *kohl* (again protection from the sun as well as for decoration).

Most Bedouin live in long, low tents woven from camel or goat hair. A line of poles supports the center of the tent. A wealthy sheikh

Coffee-making is an important social event among the Bedouins. *Courtesy of the University Museum, University of Pennsylvania.*

will have a longer tent with more poles. The tent's sides and end panels may be rolled up to let in breezes, or closed up tightly in rain or sandstorms. The hairs from which the tent is made expand when wet, making the tent waterproof. Inside, ornate, woven partitions called *gata* divide the tent into sections. The men's part includes a fireplace, scooped out of the sand, and an area for entertaining; the woman's part is used for storage and sleeping, and has a second fire for cooking. The tent and belongings inside may be dismantled and packed up several times a year.

Family life. Until they are seven years old, Bedouin children remain with their mothers, living in the women's compartment of the tent. Older boys may help with the herds and wait upon guests. Girls learn their duties at an early age by watching their mothers cook, weave, and care for the tent. Marriage ideally occurs within the extended family; custom dictates that the prospective bride's cousin (her father's brother's son) have first claim. Should this cousin desire the marriage, the father and brothers of the bride then must consent to the union. The cousin must give consent to a woman who aims to marry someone else. Few Bedouin men have more than one wife, since Islamic law requires that he be able to support the wives equally. A married woman can own and control her own possessions, which may have been inherited, given to her by her family or husband, or be the result of her own efforts. She is free to do with them as she pleases, but she must have her husband's approval to buy or sell any family property. Women are responsible for child-rearing, meal preparation, sewing, collecting and weaving animal hair, pitching, striking and loading the tents, gathering fuel, nurturing the young and elderly, and drawing water for the household. The senior woman in the family owns the tents. Men's duties include hauling water from distant sources, tending the flocks and herds, raiding, defense, and entertaining guests.

Economy. In the past, the Bedouin considered it shameful to accept a wage-paying job. Today, however, many rely on part- or full-time employment for their incomes. The men have supplied a labor pool for the development of oil in the Arabian Peninsula since the 1950s and 1960s. Income from oil has brought immense wealth to some Arab states, and the Bedouin have benefited somewhat from it, though education and health care remain poorer than in towns and cities. Bedouin men also serve in the armies and police forces of states such as Saudi Arabia and Jordan. Former Bedouin, now settled, raise crops for sale in local markets.

Arts and literature. Most Bedouin arts and crafts involve the ornamentation of various tools, weapons, utensils, clothing, and jewelry. Weaving is highly developed, and decorative patterns adorn tents, rugs, storage bags, saddlebags, and outer garments. The patterns are often geometric, with bright colors produced from natural dyes. Women also exercise their talents in leather work, constructing and decorating cradles, storage bags for coffee, food, and water, and various other items for household use. Jewelry and weapons (usually daggers and sheaths) are often ornamented with highly wrought designs of silver.

Poetry has been transmitted orally for centuries, and is often regarded as the height of the Arab literature. Today, this art has largely moved to the cities where former Bedouin write about urban themes. The Arabic language is rich and pure, evoking the atmosphere of desert life. Themes of poetry include love and war, great journeys, and legendary acts of honor. Many of the poetic forms were developed before the advent of Islam in the seventh century. Poetic conventions glorify the nomadic life, and include descriptions of great battles, noble acts of generosity, the quality of a camel or a horse, or memories of an abandoned campsite. The poems are imbued with the sense of honor that governs Bedouin life.

For More Information

Abbu-Lughod, Lila. *Veiled Sentiments: Honor and Poetry in a Bedouin Society.* Berkeley: University of California Press, 1986.

Alotaibi, Muhammed. *Bedouin: The Nomads of the Desert.* Vero Beach, Florida: Rourke Publications, Inc., 1989.

Kay, Shirley. *The Bedouin.* New York: Crane, Russak and Company, 1978.

BERBERS

(burr' burrs)

Members of a Muslim Caucasian group in North and West Africa.

Population: 14,000,000 (1984 estimate).
Location: North Africa; the Sahara Desert; Sahelian West Africa.
Languages: Berber; Arabic.

Geographical Setting

Most Berbers live in the two North African countries of Morocco (about eight million) and Algeria (about four and one-half million), where they form isolated pockets, mostly in mountainous areas, among the majority Arabic-speaking population (many of whom are partly or wholly descended from Berber stock). Smaller numbers are

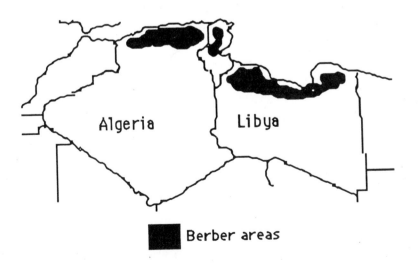

Berber areas

scattered in nomadic groups or oasis settlements in the Libyan and Sahara deserts, from Libya in the west to Niger, southern Algeria, Mali, Senegal, Mauritania, and Western Sahara (claimed by Morocco) in the south and east. Only in the last two areas—both sparsely populated—do Berbers predominate numerically.

The rugged mountain ranges of Morocco and Algeria have provided refuge for Berber tribes since the Arab conquest of the early 700s. In both countries, the mountains are mostly arid and rocky, inhospitable even when only of moderate height. Those of the Rif Range in northern Morocco, for example, have few peaks above 6,000 feet, yet deep gullies and ravines make movement difficult. In the equally convoluted terrain of Morocco's High Atlas range, some peaks are nearly twice that height. South of these northern ranges in Morocco and Algeria, arid tablelands and valleys give way to the vast Sahara Desert, which extends in a broad belt across North Africa. The more heavily populated area to the north—between the Sahara and the Mediterranean—is called the *Maghreb*, an Arabic word meaning "the sunset."

Historical Background

Origin. Berbers are the earliest identifiable inhabitants of the Maghreb, having arrived sometime around 2000 B.C., perhaps in a series of migrations from southwest Asia. These immigrants mixed with other peoples during and after their movement to the Maghreb, so that today the Berbers are a mixed people. By 1200 B.C., Phoenician traders had made contact with them, establishing trading outposts along the Mediterranean coast. The greatest of these colonies, Carthage (established about 750 B.C. near the site of modern Tunis), founded a commercial empire that came to control much of North Africa. The Greek historian Herodotus, writing around 450 B.C., describes good relations between the indigenous Berber tribes (whom he calls "Libyans") and the Carthaginian traders. "Libyans" on the Atlantic coast of present-day Morocco, Herodotus relates, would barter gold for goods brought by the Carthaginians.

Client kingdoms of the Roman Empire. In the 200s B.C., Carthage fought a series of wars (called the Punic Wars, after the Roman word for Phoenician) with the increasingly powerful Romans, finally resulting in the defeat of Carthage and its complete destruction in 146 B.C. Berbers served in the Carthaginian army, and Berber king Masinissa (c. 240-148 B.C.), threw his support to Rome in 204 B.C. and was able to extend his own territory at the expense of the declining Carthaginians. A skilled soldier and statesman, Masinissa encouraged the continuance of Carthaginian culture among the Berbers of Numidia, as his kingdom was known. (From "Numidia" comes the word "nomad.") Masinissa's descendants continued to rule in North Africa as Roman clients until A.D. 40, when the client kingdom of Mauretania (in present-day Morocco, and not to be confused with modern Mauritania) became—as had Numidia—a Roman province under direct Roman control. For the next 350 years, however, Rome continued the practice of using client kings on the frontiers, enlisting them to protect the coastal areas from the fierce, independent inland tribes—the "barbarians," or (in Latin) *barbari*, from which the word "Berber" probably derives.

Arab conquest and the spread of Islam. Roman control weakened in the 400s, and for the next 300 years, Berber tribes contended for their independence with the Romans and the Vandals, a Germanic tribe that crossed from Spain and established a kingdom centered in Carthage in 429. The turbulence of these centuries culminated in the Arab invasion of the late 600s and early 700s (see ISLAM), when Roman power was overthrown forever in North Africa. At first, the Berbers resisted the Arabs as intensely as they had the Romans, but by 710 Arab armies had penetrated as far as Morocco. In towns and farming areas, Berbers began to rely on Arabs (as they had on Romans earlier) to protect them from the wilder inland tribes. The Arabs established garrisons rather than colonies, and marriages between Arab soldiers and Berber women led to a ruling Arabic elite that was actually a mix of the two races. Islam also spread slowly in the towns. The nomadic desert tribes and isolated mountain villages, by contrast, more quickly accepted Islam, but at the same time resisted Arab political and cultural domination. An important exception was a Berber tribal chief of the Rif who converted to Islam, took the Arab name Tariq ibn Ziyad, and with his warriors was sent by the Arab governor of North Africa, Musa ibn Nusayr, to lead the Muslim invasion of Spain in 711.

Islam and the tribes. Some Berbers accepted a Muslim movement begun in Mecca, the Kharidjite movement, that believed in both the right to depose an unjust ruler and in non-Arabs becoming caliphs. In this belief, they were often in opposition to other Berber tribes or to the Arabs of the Maghreb. The Kharidjite movement appeared in Morocco in 739 and attempted to open Islamic religious leadership to Berbers and other non-Arab Muslims. Kharidjite Berbers rose against Arab taxation policies across the Maghreb, establishing a number of theocratic kingdoms. However, their power was shattered in the early 900s by the Fatimids, militant Shi'ite Arabs (see ISLAM) who gained support first among the Kitama Berbers of the Kabyli mountains in Algeria, and later conquered much of the rest of North Africa and Egypt. Eventually, however, Berbers returned to Sunni Islam, rebelling against the Fatimids, who as punishment encouraged the emigration to the Maghreb of Arab tribesmen known as the Banu Hilal and Banu Sulaim. A mass migration of 50,000 of these tribesmen followed. For two hundred years, beginning in the mid-1000s, the Hilalians, as the newcomers were known, ravaged the Maghreb lowlands, Arabizing the Berber population more radically than the previous, comparatively small garrisons had done. In particular, the Arabic language became widespread for the first time.

As the coastal lowlands became Arabized, the entire Maghreb fell under the influence of two successive Berber dynasties, the Almoravids (c. 1000-1150) and the Almohads, who unified the Maghreb under a single rule for 100 years (1150-1250). These were competing tribal confederations that cohered around strict, austere interpretations of Islam, and each in turn controlled the distinctive Moorish society that arose in the Maghreb and Islamic Spain. In the mid-1200s these confederations broke up into a series of smaller Berber dynasties not so concerned with religious interpretation: the Merinids in Morocco, the Zayanids in Algeria, and the Hafsids in Tunisia. Such kingdoms endured until 1500, even though for the next 200 years instability remained the rule, as Christian armies won back control of Spain (1300s–1400s) and then launched repeated incursions into the coastal Maghreb (1400s–1500s).

Ottomans, Arabs, and Marabout states. From the early 1500s to the early 1800s, the political forces that would define the borders of modern Algeria and Morocco began to emerge more clearly. In Algeria, the Ottoman Turks (see TURKS) extended their empire to the eastern Maghreb, centering their authority in the port city of Algiers. In Morocco, Arabic dynasties retained power, most notably the Alawis, who contested Ottoman control of Algiers. In the hinterlands of both areas, however, a Berber and Arab religious movement known as Maraboutism weakened the authority of these centralized regimes.

The marabouts were holy men, Berber mystics whose localized and originally spiritual influence became more political during the instability that followed the Almohads. The Alawis of Morocco were able to temporarily repress the Marabouts, but the Ottomans recognized a number of small, independent Marabout states in the eastern Maghreb. In the 1700s the Alawis were forced to enlist the Marabouts' support by conceding authority to them.

European influence. The weakness of these central governments allowed European powers—especially France and Spain—to become powerful in the Maghreb during the 1700s and 1800s. Spanish fortresses, established during the Christian offensive of the 1400s to 1600s, continued to dot the Moroccan coast, while exploitative French companies and speculators virtually controlled the Moroccan economy by the end of the 1700s. During the 1800s, British, German, and Spanish interests competed with the French for influence in Morocco, with its strategic location at the entrance of the Mediterranean. In Algeria, a dispute set in motion by France between that country and the weakened Ottoman ruler ended in the French invasion and conquest of Algiers in 1830. The subsequent French occupation of Algeria provoked unrest among Berber tribes there, who had attained virtual autonomy under the Ottomans. In the mid-1800s some Algerian Berbers, led by Abd al Qadir, conducted raids into Algerian territory from the Moroccan hinterland. The French used the opportunity to attack Morocco, forcing the Alawi king to cooperate in France's campaign against Abd al Qadir. French influence steadily increased in Morocco during the 1800s and early 1900s, although the Berbers, along with others, kept up their fierce and traditional resistance to central authority.

Emergence of nationalism. Throughout the 1900s, the Arabic majorities in Morocco and Algeria became more and more dissatisfied with French rule. Nationalist movements emerged, dedicated to the struggle for independence, but with a strongly Arabic, urban constituency. A short-lived exception was the Islamic republic founded by a Berber leader, Abdel Krim, in the Moroccan Rif in the 1920s. Created to oppose European colonialism, this briefly successful political experiment ended after invasion by the combined forces of the French and Spanish. Moroccan independence came only in 1955, under an Alawi monarchy. In Algeria, a long and bitter war ended with French withdrawal in 1962. Berber uprisings against the French contributed to both processes, but the Berbers also protested what they perceived as the Arabic domination of the nationalist forces and of the national governments that followed.

Culture Today

The Berbers remain an essentially rural and tribal society, although less so than in the past. The growth of North African cities since World War II has attracted many Berbers to urban life. In the cities, most take jobs as unskilled laborers; job shortages have forced some to seek such employment in Europe. Also, increasingly stronger central governments have limited tribal autonomy. In the past, when greater isolation allowed a larger measure of self-government, tribes separated into flexible and roughly equal political divisions called *leffs*, based on affiliations between extended families and clans. The leffs' most important governing function was to oversee defense of the tribe against other tribes. As central authorities increasingly inhibited warfare between tribes, the leffs' role became social rather than political. Although some institutions have weakened, tribal membership remains the most important way in which Berbers identify themselves. They tend to discount any notion of "Berberism," despite religious and racial background. When they do refer to themselves in this larger context they use not the word Berber but *Imazighen*, meaning "Free Men."

Tribal groups. In Morocco, where Berbers make up about thirty-four percent of the population, Berber tribes fall into three main groups. About thirty tribes live in the Rif, traditionally the most isolated part of Morocco. Of these settled farmers the most powerful are the Ait Uriaghil, the tribe around whose leadership Abdel Krim formed the Rif Republic. In the Middle Atlas, where harsher winters discourage agriculture, live the Berrabers, a seminomadic group that practices transhumance, or the shifting of livestock between summer and winter pastures. Farther south, in the western High Atlas and Anti-Atlas ranges, the Shluh, like the tribes of the Rif, are mostly agriculturalists.

The largest tribal group in Algeria, the Kabyles—also sedentary farmers—traditionally inhabit the rugged mountains east of Algiers. The Chaouias, though less numerous than the Kabyles, occupy a larger area to the south, the Aures Mountains of eastern Algeria. In the northern Aures the Chaouias are settled farmers, but where the southern mountains give way to low plains they live a seminomadic life, farming small plots but also driving flocks to the high plains in summer. In central Algeria, on the northern edge of the Sahara, stand the seven walled cities of the M'zab, descendants of a Kharijite band that fled to the desert in the 1000s. The M'zab strongly distinguish themselves from both Arabs and other Berbers. They are an urban society, whose cities preserve a long tradition of rule by the Islamic clergy. Farther south, across the Sahara from Libya to Mali, live the Tuareg, a group of nomadic tribes that for centuries controlled the profitable trade routes across the Sahara. More recently, governmental restrictions on movement and (in the early 1970s) severe drought have forced many Tuareg to give up their nomadic life.

Food, clothing, and shelter. The sedentary mountain tribes rely primarily on grains in their diet: millet, barley and corn especially, but also wheat and rye. Seminomadic groups like the Berraber build massive stone granaries in their main villages, leaving guards behind while the rest are away at the seasonal pasture. Where water permits, Berbers grow vegetables such as potatoes, tomatoes, onions, garlic, squash, and peppers. Most families also keep livestock consisting of small herds of goats or sheep, and perhaps some chickens. This secondary food supply provides eggs, milk, butter and meat, as well as a prestigious way to accumulate wealth. Nomads like the Tuareg have relied more on livestock, both as a primary food source and to trade for other foods. However, many now tend gardens around the oases of the Sahara, where (like sedentary Berbers in lowland valleys) they grow dates, citrus fruits, and figs as well as grain and vegetables.

Most Berbers have adopted as their ordinary dress the Arabic *djellaba*, a long-sleeved tunic usually of cotton, often worn with a cotton turban or cap. In the high mountains, villagers wear heavy woolen capes and robes. Most distinctive in their dress are the Tuareg, often called the People of the Veil, because the adult men cover their faces with an indigo-dyed cotton veil, which is tucked into the turban. Tuareg aristocrats—unlike most Berber tribes, the Tuareg have several different social classes—wear cotton robes of rich blue to show their noble status. Unlike Arab women, Berber women do not wear veils.

Berber houses in the mountain villages are of stone reinforced with dried mud, are flat-roofed and, when built on slopes, often interconnected so that the roof of one forms the courtyard of another behind it. Seminomadic groups like the Berraber, when away from their main villages, live in circular tents of woven grey or black-striped goat hair.

Family life. Though practices vary from group to group, most Berber families are both patriarchal and patrilineal, with authority and inheritance centered on the men. In the traditional extended family, authority resides in the father, whose household will include his wife, his children, the wives of his sons, and his son's children. By the 1980s, however, even in remote mountain villages such families had become rare, as smaller nuclear families increasingly came to predominate. Yet even if the extended family no longer lives together, in most Berber communities the father's authority remains paramount, even over a married son. Many tribes have a series of social ranks, through which a man ascends as he gets older; usually he cannot reach the higher ranks, no matter what his age, until his father has died. Male children are more desirable than female. The birth of a son is celebrated, and conversely, when a woman cannot produce a son, her husband may seek divorce or seek a second wife. Seven days after a child's birth, the extended family—especially both parents' siblings—offer gifts at an elaborate naming ceremony, which represents the child's initiation into society. For an uncle not to attend this important family gathering is considered particularly disgraceful, a repudiation of the entire family.

Berber marriages, known for their spectacle and complexity, traditionally represent an alliance between different families. Before the wedding both sets of parents engage in delicate negotiations, some-

Berber Women of Tunisia. *Courtesy of Dr. Nikki Keddie, U.C.L.A.*

times without the knowledge of the children concerned. These negotiations are almost always begun by the prospective groom's father, and during them the man's family gives presents to the woman's family. The negotiations concern the amount of the dowry, or *sdaq*, that the girl's father will receive, and how much the boy's father will spend on the celebration. The celebration itself takes place over several days, during which the bride and groom, in separate parties with friends of the same sex, go singing from house to house in the evening. Both groups collect gifts, called *grama*, from the households they visit. Then the couple are married at the bride's house, where her girlhood friends sing and dance, and the bride is brought to the groom's house, where more singing, dancing, feasting and gift-giving follow her arrival.

Religion. Although Berbers trace their history only from the arrival of Islam (knowledge from earlier times comes from other sources), many Berber religious practices apparently reflect pre-Islamic beliefs. As in Muslim popular beliefs, the hereditary saints (Marabouts, or in Berber, *igurramen*) continue to play an influential role in local affairs. Believed to possess the power to heal (*baraka*) as well as to intercede on behalf of a suppliant, the igurramen also supervise local elections, arbitrate disputes at the market (*souk*), settle feuds between rival clans, and impose fines or other punishments. Animal sacrifice also features in daily religious life, occurring at virtually all public occasions in the village, such as a naming day or wedding celebration. Some old practices have been absorbed by Islam. Magic, for example, can be practiced by a *fgih*, a learned Muslim who derives his powers from his knowledge of the Quran, or by a female witch, whose knowledge passes from mother to daughter.

Language. Since many Berber dialects are mutually unintelligible though related, many Berbers use Arabic to communicate with members of tribes other than their own. Each of the major tribal groups has a separate dialect: the Rifians, Berraber, and Shluh of Morocco, and Kabyles and Chaouias of Algeria. These dialects are all unwritten as well as complex; only the Tuareg have both a spoken (Tamarshak) and a written (Tifinagh) language. Tifinagh uses pictographs composed of lines, circles, and dots rather than letters. In addition to its attraction as a universal language, Arabic also displaces Berber by virtue of being writeable, and by its prestige as the language of the Quran (see ISLAM).

Although individual Berbers have played important political roles (Morocco's first prime minister was a Berber), nowhere have Berbers cohered as a distinct political force. To different degrees, the traditional disjunction between central authority and tribal autonomy continues. National governments allow the villages to administer customary law, rather than holding them to national codes, as long as there is no threat to state security. In the same way, earlier Arabic and Ottoman rulers allowed customary practice to supplement *shariah*, the Islamic law code. Traditional ways are more difficult for nomadic tribes like the Tuareg, whose way of life included crossing what are now national borders.

For More Information

Gellner, Ernest. *Saints of the Atlas.* Chicago: University of Chicago Press, 1969.

Nelson, Harold D., editor. *Algeria: A Country Study.* Washington, D.C.: American University Press, 1985.

Nelson, Harold D., editor. *Morocco: A Country Study.* Washington, D.C.: American University Press, 1985.

COPTS
(kahpts)

Members of the Coptic Orthodox Church of Egypt.

Population: 4,000,000 (1988 estimate).
Location: Throughout settled areas of Egypt, with concentrations in Cairo and the South.
Language: Egyptian Arabic.

Geographical Setting

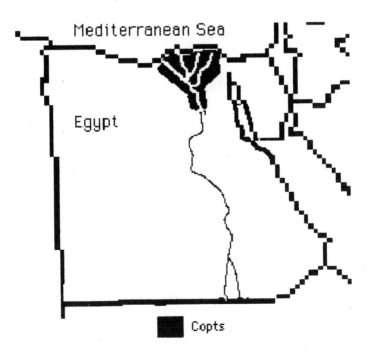

Copts

Like the rest of the Egyptian population, the Coptic minority (estimated at six to ten percent) resides almost entirely in the fertile Nile valley and delta. Protected by vast deserts to both east and west, their soil enriched by the river's yearly flood, the valley and delta have supported Egypt's primarily agricultural population for over 5,000 years. The Western Desert, covering two-thirds of Egypt's area, stretches from the Nile west to Libya and from the Mediterranean Sea south to Sudan. Immense, inhospitable and flat, the Western Desert is permanently inhabited only at its six freshwater oases. The Eastern Desert rises quickly from the Nile to a sandy plateau, which stretches 80 to 130 kilometers and is broken by a chain of rocky, arid hills running from the delta to the Gulf of Suez and the Red Sea, where a string of coastal villages constitute the desert's only permanent communities. East of the delta the desert runs into the Sinai Peninsula, whose southern reddish hills meet the Red Sea and give it its name.

Egypt's climate is dry and sunny, hot in summer and slightly cooler in winter, with these temperature changes offering the only seasonal variations. The lack of a rainy season has heightened the importance of the Nile, which in ancient Egypt was worshiped as divine. Its dependable annual flood, which deposited a new layer of rich silt each year until the High Dam was built in the south and controlled the Nile flow, has long been the central feature of life in this agricultural land.

Historical Background

Origin. The Copts, Christians in a Muslim society, are not ethnically distinct from other Egyptians. They embody instead the small part of Egypt's once Christian population that clung to Christianity following the Arab conquest of Egypt in the mid-600s (see ISLAM). The word "copt" may have come from the Arabic *qubt*, which derives in turn from the Greek *Aigyptios*—meaning "Egyptian," or from *kift* meaning "black soil." The Copts thus represent Egypt's pre-Islamic past, during the last stage of which Egypt was a province of the Christian, Greek-speaking Byzantine Empire.

Early Christians. The Coptic Orthodox Church claims an unbroken line of bishops reaching back in time to the see (the domain of a bishop) of Alexandria founded by St. Mark. Christianity had probably come to Egypt by about A.D. 150; within forty years a bishop had been installed in Alexandria, Egypt's great port city. As subjects of the Roman Empire, Egyptian Christians were persecuted like Christians in other Roman provinces until the early 300s, when the Emperor Constantine became a Christian and made Christianity the official religion of the state. In 451 the Egyptian church broke away from the main body of eastern Christians over a doctrinal question. The Egyptians, like the Ethiopians and Armenians, held that Christ was of one nature (divine) while the rest of the church decided that he was of two natures (divine and human).

Conquest and conversion. For the next two hundred years, the Orthodox Church in Constantinople pressured the Copts, trying to make them renounce their Monophysite (from the Greek for "one nature") doctrine. In the early 600s, Byzantine persecution was particularly fierce. Hence, the Copts did not resist the Arab invasion of the 640s, and even assisted the Arabs against the Byzantines. At first, Arab rule was indeed easier for the Copts, who were allowed to worship as they wished, and were taxed more lightly than under the Byzantines. By the 700s, however, the taxes had increased, and the delta Copts' armed resistance to them was met by increasingly severe punishment. Some Copts began to convert to Islam to escape the taxes since Muslims were exempt from a poll tax. This conversion was accelerated in Lower Egypt by heavy Arab immigration. Under Islamic law, children of mixed marriages were raised as Muslims. Also, Muslim men were permitted to marry Christian women, but Muslim women were not permitted Christian husbands. By the 800s, Copts were a minority in the delta. Islam penetrated the relatively isolated south (Upper Egypt) more gradually over four centuries. Here Coptic monasteries and the powerful Nubian kingdoms, who also believed in one nature of Christ, afforded protection from persecution by the invaders. Violence reached a peak in the early 1300s under the Mameluks (ruled 1250-1517), and mass conversions in Upper Egypt occurred. Despite the incentive of tax exemption, Copts had remained the majority in Upper Egypt until the 1300s.

Ottoman rule and the *millet* system. Under Arab rule, the Coptic Church was allowed a measure of independence. This policy was formalized under the Ottomans, who ruled in Egypt from 1517 to 1798. The Ottomans allowed Jewish and Christian religious leaders to retain authority, even strengthening the leaders' power by giving them civil jurisdiction as well. Each religious administrative unit, called a *millet*, registered its own births, deaths, wills and marriages; maintained its own law courts; and collected taxes among its people. The millet system still influences Egyptian law; for example, some Copts convert to Islam to obtain divorces, which are easy under Islamic rules but are forbidden, with a few exceptions, by the Coptic Church.

1801-1922. Napoleon's brief occupation of Egypt (1798-1801) shattered Ottoman power there, and began a slow acceptance of the Copts into positions in government. A former Ottoman officer named Muhammad Ali was chosen by the tribal sheikhs to take the rule of Egypt when they were no longer willing to follow Ahmed Pasha Khorshid, the ruler supported by Albania. Ruthless but highly efficient, Ali encouraged loyalty to his rule (rather than religious rule) massacred some of the tribal rulers (beys), repealed repressive laws against Christians, and allowed them to serve in high government positions but then replaced Coptic members of an advisory council while suppressing violent Muslim outbreaks against his government. His successors, Said and Ismail, continued his secularizing policies, opening military service to Copts and improving their schools.

Coptic participation in civil service continued to increase under British occupation (1882-1922). At first, Copts welcomed the British, who defeated the anti-British militant leader Arabi Pasha. Soon, however, they felt that British concessions were coming too slowly. They began to support Egyptian nationalism, which grew in the early 1900s. Mustafa Kamel and later Saad Zaghlul led the Muslim-Coptic coalition that eventually succeeded in achieving independence from the British in 1922. Several Copts helped draft the 1923 constitution, which guaranteed religious and legal equality. Installing two Copts in senior cabinet positions, Zaghlul declared, "Egypt belongs to Copts as well as Muslims." (Wakin 1963, p. 17). Coptic leaders continued to play an important role in the coalition, known as the *Wafd*, until the 1940s, when the alliance fell apart and most Copts left the party. Nevertheless, it was customary procedure to have a Copt as a cabinet member in the Egyptian government until 1952.

Tensions and conflict under Nasser and Sadat. After the 1952 Revolution, Egypt's new leader Gamal Abdul Nasser continued the suppression of religious involvement in politics that had come to be associated with one section of the nationalist movement. In particular, he outlawed the powerful and militant Muslim Brotherhood, a move which to some degree counterbalanced the effective exclusion of Copts from positions in the government. Anwar Sadat, who succeeded Nasser in 1970, under mounting pressure from fundamentalists, abandoned Nasser's policy of reestablishing Islam as the state religion and lifted the ban on the Muslim Brotherhood. Copts protested, demanding protection from discrimination in universities and government posts and an end to restriction on the building of Christian churches. Sadat refused. Sectarian violence between Muslims and Copts flared in 1972 and renewed between 1978 and 1980, when Sadat was assassinated by Muslim fundamentalists enraged by his peace accord with Israel. Sadat's successor, Hosni Mubarak, has managed to clamp down on extremism once more, reestablishing an atmosphere of religious moderation and national unity.

Culture Today

Their common ethnic background with the dominant community distinguishes the Copts' situation from that of most other minorities. They are as "Egyptian" as the Muslims—more so, they often claim, in their connections to the ancient past. Like other Egyptians, they speak Arabic, while the Coptic language (ancient Egyptian written in Greek letters) survives only in church liturgy. Some wear the same clothes as Muslims and eat the same food, yet in subtle ways Copts remain isolated, a seemingly ever-dwindling minority. Many Copts have emigrated from Egypt to other areas such as the United States. Among those remaining, incentives to convert to Islam remain numerous and strong: easier divorce and remarriage, a better position under the law, and social acceptance by the dominant Muslim majority.

Urban life. Although substantial numbers of Copts live as peasants, especially in Upper Egypt, Copts have, more than Muslims, historically tended to concentrate in cities and larger towns. In a 1986 study, roughly sixty percent of Copts lived in urban areas, as compared with forty-three percent of Muslims. This tendency stems from the Copts' earliest times as a minority, when security from an angry mob could be found in numbers, a strong, nearby central authority, and the professions they chose to follow. The nature of Islam encouraged the Copts to specialize in occupations associated with cities. The Quran discourages Muslims from usury, for example, so Copts became the money-lenders of Egypt (as did the Jews in medieval Christendom for the same reason). The Arab conquerors' general lack of understanding of Egyptian administrative affairs traditionally gave the Copts opportunities as accountants, tax-collectors, and other low-level administrators. In the Middle Ages, Copts who came from the country brought traditional trades, such as building, weaving, and making jewelry, which they plied in the cities. Today, Copts continue to stand out in urban occupations, especially the professions: law, medicine, engineering, accounting, pharmacy, and architecture.

Education. For related reasons, Copts have maintained an educational advantage for nearly two centuries. As a minority engaged in accounting and later in commercial activity, they have had both the incentive and the resources to educate their children. As young children, Muslims were taught the Quran while Copts educated children for the guild of accountants. In 1976, the proportion of Copts completing university degrees was twice as great as that of Muslims. Copts tend to study practical subjects, and not concern themselves with academic or literary pursuits. Unlike the Muslims, they have no strong literary tradition outside of religious writings or political argument.

Family Life. With their religious injunction against divorce standing in sharp contrast to the easy divorce available to Muslim men, Copts emphasize family solidarity and affection. Coptic men spend much time at home, less frequently gathering in exclusively male settings (such as coffeehouses). Like Muslims, Coptic parents instill in their children a deep sense of family unity that extends to distant relatives, who share in religious occasions such as Confirmation and First Communion. Until recently, Copts often married within the extended family, even with first cousins. As in the rest of Egyptian society, marriages must usually have the parents' approval, and courtship is often conducted with other family members present. Many Coptic children are sent to study abroad, however, and bring back Western ways, which are replacing older traditions. In general, upper-class Copts are among the most Westernized of Egyptians.

Religion. The Copts' religion has not only provided the context for their tenacious survival, but has also contributed much to the development of Christianity as a whole. For example, Copts played a central role in the emerging importance of martyrdom for early Christians. Under the persecutions of the Roman Emperor Diocletian between A.D. 303 and 311, nearly 150,000 Egyptian Christians perished. These early martyrs have inspired Copts through Byzantine and Arab occupation to the present, and remain a crucial element of Coptic faith. In commemoration of their suffering, the Coptic calendar begins in A.D. 284, the year of Diocletian's accession to power. The second pillar of the Coptic Church, monasticism, had an even greater impact on future Christianity. Egyptian Christians were the first to seek solitude in order to reflect on Christ and his teaching. Groups of these religious hermits began pooling their spiritual and worldly resources, and thus, the first monasteries arose in the harsh Egyptian desert. In Upper Egypt Coptic monasteries became fortresses that temporarily stopped the Arab attack. Today, tradition demands that the Coptic Patriarch (the head of the church) be chosen from among the monks, who remain unmarried, although priests of lower ranks are permitted to wed.

Copts employ religious symbols more than both their Muslim compatriots or fellow Christians in the West. They hang crosses around their necks, or tattoo them inside the right wrists of their children. Such tattoos served the purpose, in the days of persecutions, of preventing Copts from denying their faith. Today they are believed by rural peasants and the poorer urban Copts to ward off the evil eye. Crosses also decorate the walls of houses and other buildings, and, above all, figure in the colorful, geometric patterns of the well-known and traditional Coptic textiles. Other favored symbols, such as the Virgin Mary, Jesus, and St. George, adorn posters and automobiles.

In other ways, also, Copts celebrate their religion differently from Western Christians. They celebrate four annual periods of fasting. One of these, Lent, lasts nine days longer than in the West. And Copts do not agree with the Roman Catholic Church on the two natures of Christ, believing only in his godliness.

A tradition of the Copts, now fading as European-style clothing gains in popularity, was to wear clothing similar to those of their Arabic Muslim neighbors, but to distinguish themselves by wearing black turbans. In compliance with Muslim traditions, Coptic women once were veiled when appearing in public.

Coptic names reflect their religious affiliation. Copts and Muslims both use Old Testament names, e.g., Da'ud (David) and Ibrahim (Abraham). Muslims alone use names from the Quran, e.g., Mustafa and Muhammad. Meanwhile, Copts alone use New Testament names, e.g., Butrus (Peter) and Hanna (John), or names associated with Christianity, such as Ghattas ("baptized one"). Egyptians can often tell whether someone is Christian or Muslim just from hearing a name, though less so in recent years as names without obvious religious significance have become more popular. Copts can almost always identify a Coptic last name, however, and can often recount a distant, or not so distant, family relationship.

For More Information

Chitham, E. J. *The Coptic Community in Egypt: Spatial and Social Change.* Durham, England: Centre for Middle Eastern and Islamic Studies, University of Durham, 1986.

Wakin, Edward. *A Lonely Minority: The Modern Story of Egypt's Copts.* New York: William Morrow & Co., 1963.

Worrell, William H. *A Short Account of the Copts.* Ann Arbor: University of Michigan Press, 1945.

DRUZE

(drewz)

People of Lebanon and Syria who follow the Muslim faith along with some elements of Christianity.

Population: 350,000 (1988 est.).
Location: Syria; Lebanon; and Israel.
Language: Arabic.

Geographical Setting

Three Druze settlements

Syria is a border country between the tectonic plates, segments of the earth's crust, that include the continents of Europe and Africa. The collision of the two plates has resulted in a rugged northern region of folded mountains. South and east of it is a plateau that extends into Jordan. The Druze live in the mountains bordering this southern plateau. Many are farmers and sheep and goat herders, but in the Druze-majority region, they are occupied in nearly all vocations.

The Druze, a people bound together by a common and semisecret religion, occupy an area in each of three countries: Syria, Lebanon, and Israel. Originating in Lebanon, the Druze moved to Syria where they lived for many years isolated from other Syrians in their own district on the border of Jordan and Syria. They have now spread into Lebanon and other parts of Syria. A few Druze live in the mountains of Israel. Among these groups, the Druze in the mountains of southern Lebanon have frequently migrated to their stronghold in the extreme south of Syria, prompted by the unfriendliness of their majority neighbors, the Maronite Christians. In Syria, outside of their southern base, the Druze are a minority among Syrian Muslims and Orthodox Christians. Most of them farmers, many Druze live in the mountain valleys of Lebanon. About six percent of the population of Lebanon is Druze.

Historical Background

Origin. In the A.D. 1000s, there arose a caliph of Egypt, the son of a Russian mother, whose minister, al-Darazi, governed Cairo erratically. Believing himself to be the voice of God, the caliph spread a reign of terror throughout Egypt. About 1016, this caliph, El-Hakim-Biamr-Allah, came to believe he was a reincarnation of God, and attempted to convince the people of Cairo of this idea through a missionary named Ismael Ad-darazi. The idea was so unpopular with the people of Cairo that Ad-darazi was forced to flee the country. But in Lebanon, he found a more receptive audience, and his followers established communities in what is now western Lebanon near Mt. Hermon. As the number of people accepting this new religion grew, their communities spread throughout Lebanon and Syria, encompassing Arabs, Turks, Kurds, and Syrians. The name of the new group (Druze) bound together by religion was taken from that of the missionary, Ad-darazi, who spread a gospel of absolute allegiance to El Hakim, who the Druze believe to be the final reincarnation of God. Soon the religion spread to Arabs who had migrated from Yemen and to migrants from such places as Turkey and Saudi Arabia. Having settled along the coast of Lebanon before the tenth century A.D., the Druze came to control much of the coast, particularly the area around Beirut. Here they were subject to frequent attacks from Egypt and Turkey. In the eleventh century, the door of the Druze religion was closed. No outsiders were let in, and no Druze were allowed to leave the religious community.

As a unified group with a religion that dictated every aspect of their lives, the Druze prospered as farmers in the mountains of Lebanon and on the plateau of southern Syria. But other people were interested in this land. Turkey, had control of Lebanon in the sixteenth and seventeenth centuries, but left the people in the cities of Lebanon to fend for themselves. The result was that small groups quarreled with one another, leaving the Druze to deal with invaders alone. Syrian cities had long been trading partners with the Arabian Peninsula. Since the Druze lived in the path of the trade routes, they became acquainted with and were subject to raids by Arab marauders.

Conflict with Maronites. Then in the 1800s, the Druze became alarmed at the rapid growth of another religious group in the mountains of Lebanon, the Maronite Christians. War over economic differences between the two groups erupted in 1860. Thousands of Maronites suffered death at the hands of the Druze and were caught in disputes between Sunni Muslims of Damascus and Greek Orthodoxy. Eventually, the Maronites were forced to flee inland. The fighting finally ended when the Ottomans took command of the area and established a separate governmental system for the Christians. In 1921, the French, who had been granted rule over Syria by the League of Nations, reached an agreement with the Druze that provided for Druze independence. A condition of this semi-independence was that the French could monitor Druze behavior and require changes in any policies that were not in conformity with "modern" civilization. Eventually, the Druze objected to this requirement and, in 1925, rebelled against French control. Although the rebellion was suppressed after two years, the French adopted a more accepting attitude toward the Druze. When the French abandoned Syria and Lebanon in 1945, the Druze began a struggle, along with other factions, to gain participation in the local government. Factional disputes grew, erupting into civil war in Lebanon by 1970. In 1977 the leader of the Druze, Kamal Jumblatt, was assassinated. His murder aggravated the civil war, which has continued into the 1990s.

Meanwhile, the Druze in Syria saw that nation become an independent socialist republic. In the process they became citizens of the country in which they had long been a small minority in the midst of a Muslim majority.

Culture Today

Religion. The Druze are bound as a people by their religion. Before Ismail Ad-darazi, they were part of a Muslim community, so their roots are partly in that religion. Earlier, they seem to have held to a nature-based faith and to some degree this early religion has been incorporated into present beliefs. In 1021, Al Hakim, the caliph of Egypt, disappeared mysteriously. His followers today believe that he did not die, but disappeared to reappear at another time. The faith that binds the Druze holds that God reappears on earth from time to time and has done so as many as seventy times in the past. Al Hakim was the final reincarnation. There are to be no other incarnations of God until Al Hakim, himself, reappears. In the form of Al Hakim, God gave his final conditions for salvation to mankind. Outside this secret religion, the other incarnations have not been made known. It is believed that Jesus is recognized by Druze as an incarnate God while Muhammad is not. At some time, Al Hakim, the last reincarnation of God, will reappear. At that time, the Druze will gain the power to overcome Muslims and Christians, capturing Jerusalem and Mecca. Members of the Druze believed to be in Asia will return to the homeland, and the whole world will be unified. Since the Druze see themselves as the force to unite all peoples of the world, they call themselves by a name that means "unitarians."

The Druze religion is based on seven principles. Five of these are Druze interpretations of the basic conditions of Islam: belief in one God and Muhammad as his messenger, prayer five times a day, giving of alms, fasting during the month of Ramadan, and making a pilgrimage to Mecca. To these the Druze added the necessity of allegiance to the leading religious leader (the *imam*) and strife in God's way (variously interpreted to mean commitment to military action for the sake of Islam, or commitment to pursue greater knowledge of the will of God). These seven tenets dictate Druze life. One outcome of the Druze religion is that the Druze believe they must be honest in their words, but only with other Druzes.

The religion has built a class structure. A group of elders amounting to two percent of the population, the *Ajawid,* are supposed to be fully aware of the many facets of the religion. Another group, those over forty years old, who make up fifteen percent of the people, know many of the religious secrets and meet frequently to study their own scriptures from the *Kitab al-Hikma*. Druze scripture is not the Koran, the Bible, or the Torah. They believe these works to be good guides but not divinely set.

The majority of the Druze are *Juhha*, the class of followers ignorant of the religious secrets but aware of and bound by seven basic tenets: recognition that Al Hakim is a reincarnation of God, rejection of all other religions, avoidance of unbelievers, truthfulness to other Druzes, submission to Al Hakim, charity, and protection to other Druzes. The policy of secrecy has helped to isolate the Druze people from the rest of the world.

Food, clothing, and shelter. Many Druze are farmers. They successfully raise wheat, fruits, vegetables, sheep and goats, which they trade with others. Today, Druze have become traders, businesspeo-

A Druze man. *Courtesy of the University Museum, University of Pennsylvania.*

ple, managers, and laborers in many industries of the countries in which they live.

Modesty is a key to Druze dress. The women uniformly wear long black dresses. Their only display of color are standard red slippers. Men traditionally wear black robes over which they have a white girdle. Members of the upper classes top their dress with a white fez, or cap. The lower-class Druze wear a white cloth formed into a roll around the fez.

Women. Women are treated with great respect in the Druze community. They share in all religious functions. In marriage the husband

Druze women once wore distinctive hats. *Courtesy of the University Museum, University of Pennsylvania.*

must treat his wife as an equal. Husbands can take only one wife, and the wife is the family member who can initiate divorce. Druze cannot remarry after a divorce. On the other hand, Druze women must practice extreme modesty. They wear a veil to cover their faces, sometimes even while sleeping, and certainly whenever they may encounter someone who is not a Druze.

Today. Every aspect of life is governed by the Druze religion. They believe that God appeared through Al Hakim and that "Universal Intelligence" is reflected through one of his officers, Hamzah ibn Ali. The beliefs that bind the Druze are found in their religious text, the *Kitab al-Hikma* ("book of wisdom"). This book contains letters written by Al Hakim and Hamzah. The beliefs describe a God who is unknowable, unfathomable, and passionless.

In 1983 the Druze of Lebanon allied with the Shi'ite Muslims of that country and forced the predominately Maronite Christian government to change. Thereafter the Christian-dominated Lebanese government has struggled over admitting more input from the other Lebanese groups. The Christians have not relinquished their hold on the government easily, and fighting between the two factions has continued into the 1990s.

For More Information

Abu, Izzeddin and M. Nejla. *The Druzes: A New Study of Their History, Faith and Society.* Leiden: E. J. Brill, 1984.

Berger, Morro. *The Arab World Today.* Garden City, N.Y.: Caravan Books, 1974.

Fisher, W. B. *The Middle East: A Physical, Social and Regional Geography*, 7th edition. London: Methune and Co., 1978.

Mukarem, Sami Naseb. *The Druze Faith.* Delmar, N.Y.: Caravan Books, 1974.

EGYPTIANS

(ee gyp′ shuns)

People of Egypt who are largely peasant farmers along the Nile
River.

Population: 51,900,000 (1988 estimate).
Location: Egypt.
Languages: Arabic; also English and French.

Geographical Setting

Egyptians

Located in the northeast corner of the African continent, Egypt consists almost entirely of desert except for a narrow strip of fertile land located along the banks of the Nile River. This river stretches the length of Egypt, 550 miles from Aswan in the south to Cairo at its mouth on the Mediterranean Sea. Until the High Dam was built in the 1950s and 1960s, the river valley was flooded annually, bringing new soil from the highlands and making the valley one of the most fertile in the world. This dam eliminated the flooding and replenishing of the soil, but promised to give Egyptian farmers a more consistent water supply for their crops. Most Egyptians live on the four percent of the land near the river that can be cultivated, making this a very densely populated region.

Rainfall in most of Egypt is low, averaging five to ten inches a year. Temperatures are hot in summer and moderate in winter, with above ninety-degree Fahrenheit temperatures normal for the summer months, and in the sixty-degree range in winter.

Historical Background

Ancient Egyptians. With the Indus River in Asia, and the Tigris and Euphrates rivers of the Middle East, the land of Egypt was the site of the earliest development of towns and cities that mark the beginning of civilization. Today's people of the Nile Valley consider the ancient Egyptians to be their ancestors. Here, as early as 4,000 years before the Christian era, people had come together and formed societies—towns, cities, and small kingdoms. By 3100 B.C., the ruler Menes had united the peoples of the Nile delta with those living southward along the river into a single empire. Empire after empire grew and thrived in the valley. These developed trade with the Middle Eastern and Asian powers and other peoples who visited and stayed in Egypt. The land became a center for learning and art. But by 1085 B.C., the empire of Egypt had begun to decay and again divided into Upper and Lower—the kingdom of the delta and that of the river. Many sought to conquer the valley and claim its riches: Greeks, Romans, Arabians, North Africans, Turks, French, and, most recently, the British. All these people contributed to the rich culture of Egypt.

The Nile traditions. Throughout the centuries, the way of life along the river remained relatively constant. Land was possessed by wealthy landowners and worked by a peasant class, the fellahin, yielding two or three crops a season. Before the 1850s, when irrigation projects began to provide more stability, the fellahin lived in easily rebuilt mud houses and then moved to higher land as the river overflowed its banks. Many of these peasants worked as sharecroppers, farming the landowner's soil and keeping only one-fourth to one-half of a crop for themselves. But in the second half of the nineteenth century this lifestyle began to change. Egypt's ruler, Muhammad Ali, began agricultural reforms to bring the farmers from subsistence farming to a market economy. The major crop changed from food products to cotton, which had been introduced a century earlier. However, when other world suppliers reduced the market for cotton, the plan failed and many peasants suffered.

In 1882, the British occupied Egypt to assume economic control and settle the country's debts for roads, railways, telegraph systems, and canals built by the British. The royal family and the large landholders benefited from the increased activity. The lives of the vast majority of Egyptians, the fellahin, changed also, as peasants had to work more of the year to pay the heavy taxes, and as some prospered and formed a new class of rich peasants.

Land reform. It was only after a revolution in 1952 that the majority of Egyptians, through the armed forces, gained power and their living conditions became a matter of concern. It was not until 1962, under the leadership of Gamal Abdal Nasser, that the National Charter

An old fort at Alexandria. *Courtesy of Dr. Paul Fischer.*

officially limited the amount of land held by farm owners to 100 *feddans* (acres), a decrease in the earlier allotment of 200 acres decreed in 1959. Beyond 100 feddans, the land was claimed by the government. Some of this was divided into plots and awarded to the fellahin peasantry. Water-pumping stations were built. Land ownership was limited so that small farmers could own the land they worked. Government cooperatives were organized to provide seed, insecticides, animal feed, and fertilizer. Although this development did not produce all the results hoped for, it did bring the average Egyptian farmer some benefits. Radios and television sets became available and brought the farmer into closer touch with the outside world. Transportation improved, as did health care. However, as health care improved, the population grew—doubling in fifteen years—and added to the problem of providing enough farmland for everyone. Despite strong efforts from leaders such as Nasser (who tried to industrialize the country) and Anwar Sadat (who created an open economy) to modernize the Egyptians, inflation, overpopulation, and the general unrest in the Middle East have slowed progress for the Egyptian peasant. With a shortage of land to cultivate, many have migrated to the crowded urban centers. In 1991, Cairo (in Egyptian, El-Qahira) has a population of nearly 10,000,000 people, Alexandria (El-Iskandariyah) nearly 3,000,000, Giza (El-Jizah) nearly 2,000,000, and fifteen other cities have populations greater than 100,000. More than

Cairo, Egypt, is a modern city of twelve million people. *Courtesy of Dr. Paul Fischer.*

one-third of Egypt's population lives in these cities, which are located mostly in the delta area of the Nile River or near the Suez Canal. In these cities, the peasant farmers have exchange their old lifestyles for life in suburban, low-cost housing.

Culture Today

Economy. Although agriculture today is the occupation of slightly less than half the Egyptian population, the economy for most Egyptians remains dependent upon agriculture. On their small plots of land, farmers use hand tools, such as the hoe and a palm trunk for leveling ground in the manner they have practiced for centuries, but now supplement these practices with a growing use of mechanization. The primary grain crops are wheat and barley, and in the summer millet is grown. The grains are made into round bun-shaped loaves of bread that constitute the staple of the fellahin diet, which also includes vegetables, dates, and melons. Some chicken, goats, and sheep are raised for food along with cattle, which yield foodstuffs such as eggs, butter, and cheese. Egyptians have run artificial hatcheries for breeding chickens since the 1700s. Wherever the land is sufficient, cotton is raised to sell or trade for other necessities. As a cash-crop, cotton first became important in the 1860s when shipments of raw cotton from the American South to Europe were dis-

Highway vendors are a common site in Egypt.
Courtesy of Dr. Paul Fischer.

rupted by the Civil War in the United States. Other cash crops include rice and sugar cane.

Traditional peasant industry includes pottery-, brick-, and basket-making. The pottery may be formed by hand or turned on a wheel. Bricks are sun- or fire-baked. Baskets are made from the leaves and branches of date palms.

Social structure. Villages were once generally organized along family lines. Extended families formed lineages, lineages formed clans, clans formed villages. The village head, or *omda*, was the respected leader of a clan, and generations of omdas were drawn from the same family. The position required only that the omda be male, an elder, literate, and a landowner. His responsibility was to settle feuds and disputes among villagers, supervise the village guards, and interface with outsiders. He was the contact of the village with outside government, was obligated to provide hospitality for guests, and acted as a buffer in local disputes. Therefore, the omda needed to be one of the more affluent members of the village. The close family ties and some aspects of leadership remain. However, in the 1970s, when the central Egyptian government began extending services to the villages, it also assumed greater control. Villagers were threatened by this loss of identity and resented being forced to participate in a political system that they felt put them at a disadvantage. Judges who implemented legal codes were regarded as less understanding than the omdas whose authority they had usurped. Frequently, villagers undergo two settlement procedures: a legal one administered by the government and a "fair" one administered by the omda.

This dualism applies to areas other than legal ones, such as education and medicine. Villagers seek folk remedies in addition to the medicine of the government clinics. This action is particularly the case if the government-supplied care is too expensive or too slow to act.

In the past, villagers sent their children to the *kuttab*, the local school. There they learned to read, write, and recite the Quran. This Muslim holy book also contains all the rules of Arabic grammar. The instructor was a strict disciplinarian who did not hesitate to apply corporal punishment. Learning was by memorization. Attendance was spotty, even for the three or four years that children generally bothered to go to school. Helping in the fields or at home was considered more important than education, and educating girls was considered a waste of time. Today children have access to government-run schools.

Houses. Along the Nile, mud is plentiful and rainfall is limited. Using available materials, the Egyptians build their customary dwellings—low structures with two- to three-foot-thick mud walls made of unbaked adobelike bricks. For more affluent citizens a home's entrance opens onto a roofless, dirt-floored courtyard, part of which serves as a kitchen. A large door gives access to a wide courtyard, around which there are one or two rooms for the family, reception rooms for guests and possibly the family's animals. Roofs are rough wooden beams covered with sticks, bamboo, or straw overlaid with mud. Most peasant homes are single-story units, with flat roofs made of beams covered with straw and mud. Better homes have an upper story that may include a sitting room with rug-covered, cushioned benches, while the best homes are furnished structures made of brick. Today, unbaked mud brick has been replaced, particularly in the towns, with oven-baked bricks and reinforced concrete walls. Windows may contain glass panes, and floors may be tiled. A growing number of homes have running water and electricity. The homes shelter an extended family that is the basic social and economic unit: parents, married or unmarried sons, and unmarried daughters. Residences are built with the anticipation of a second story being added to house sons and their spouses and children. In rural areas, mud-brick houses have been replaced by houses of stone or concrete, even though concrete walls are not as good as the old adobe for controlling temperature.

Family life. The family consists of a father, mother, married sons and their wives and children, unmarried sons or daughters, or divorced daughters. The father's unmarried sisters and widowed mother may also reside with the household.

Children are married young, particularly the girls, who are often married before they are sixteen years old. Marriages are usually arranged between parents, although this practice is less frequently the case if the children have attended elementary school. The bride and whatever children she may have are considered to be part of the groom's family. Consequently, daughters are less regarded than are sons. A wife's primary function is to bear children, particularly sons. If she does not fulfill this duty, she may be divorced and returned to her father's house, or remain in her husband's house while he takes a second wife who will bear him children. In Egyptian society inheritance of property rights is decreed by the writings of the Quran. Under this system women inherit one-half the amount that males do. To keep property within the family, the ideal marriages are regarded as those between children of brothers. An additional factor in this decision is bridewealth, which is lower in the case of cousin-marriage.

Bridewealth is used to buy all the necessities that the bride needs to set up the household. It may also include personal items of adornment for the bride herself. Although the families agree on an amount, only a portion of the bridewealth is actually paid. The unpaid portion becomes due only in the case of divorce. Women seeking divorce forfeit the bridewealth, so divorce is limited and is more often the action of the husband. In divorce, the husband takes custody of the children as soon as they are considered separable from their mother; for girls this custody lasts until marriage. Egyptian city women have been fighting this tradition of divorce and child custody for many years. Divorcing couples also quarrel about ownership of the house in a country with a great housing shortage. However, the only issue on which legislators have agreed is a minimum age for marriage.

Under Islamic law, each child inherits a portion of the father's estate, with the daughters receiving lesser portions than their brothers. This would divide the landholdings into small, insufficient parcels, so in practice the land is divided among the children. These small plots are sometimes made more effective by growing crops such as jasmine for a profitable perfume trade.

Food and clothing. The word used for bread in Egypt is *aish,* or "life"—an indication of the importance of bread in the Egyptian diet. Bread, in fact, is often the only item consumed at a meal. From their fertile land, Egyptians derive cereals, tomatoes, cucumbers, eggplants, squash, cabbage, and beans, all of which add to the Egyptian diet. Tea—thick, sweet, and syrupy—is drunk with meals of vegetables, stews, and some meat. In the cities, these ingredients are frequently bought at market by the men, and the meals.are prepared by the women. Today's markets also provide cigarettes, beer, soft drinks, and other European innovations.

Traditional clothing is often worn in the farm villages, while European-style clothing dominates in the cities. The traditional male dress consists of the *galabiya,* a full, ankle-length gown, worn over a cotton undershirt and knee-length shorts. The galabiya is well suited to the climate in that it covers the entire body as protection from the sun while allowing air to circulate freely beneath it. Galabiyas usually have pockets at the hips and an opening at the neck and down the chest similar to a shirt front.

A woman's clothing is similar to the male galabiya but fuller. The dress is usually made of black cotton or, in rare cases, silk, and is long-sleeved, high-necked, and ankle-length. Women cover their hair with a shawl or a veil, and sometimes wear European-style dress under the galabiya, removing it when inside the home.

Leisure activities. Visiting with relatives and neighbors is a major relaxation for Egyptians. In villages, even with running water in the homes, women still gather at the local well to visit. In cities as well as villages, men gather at the barbershop or the coffeehouse to talk, play cards, or listen to the radio. Egyptian city workers have movies, restaurants, sporting events, and bars available. However, with a swelling number of migrants from farm areas, the cities are often referred to as ruralized, with the newcomers, unfamiliar with city amenities, opting for the ways of the village.

Pigeons are encouraged to nest in coves built for them, and then are used as food. *Courtesy of Dr. Paul Fischer.*

Religion. While most Egyptians are Muslims, a small percentage belong to the Coptic Church and practice the Christian faith. Religious leaders, either Muslim Sheikhs or Coptic priests, are generally the leading men in a village. Muslim mosques are part of all communities. Friday communal prayers are observed, as is the month of fasting during daylight hours known as Ramadan. Individuals who have made a pilgrimage to Mecca return to paint the story of their trip on the whitewashed outer walls of their homes, celebrating their status as pilgrims.

Other traditions. Alongside these orthodox practices of Islam are the local customs brought from other places in Africa to the villages. Medicine men and women are highly regarded in the more remote villages. The more downtrodden women tend to practice *zar* ceremonies—ceremonies aimed at releasing the woman from the spirit or demon that possesses her. The center of a public ceremony, the woman in question may be subject to verbal outbursts or to almost uncontrollable dancing to the beat of the drums. Eventually, it is believed that the spirit will make known what is required to release the woman from her demons: a new dress of a certain color, specially prepared food, or a particular activity. Once the prescribed item has been achieved, the woman resumes her previous role peacefully.

Egyptian camel drivers now cater mostly to tourists.
Courtesy of Dr. Paul Fischer.

Related to the medicine practitioners are the celebrated magicians who reportedly go beyond curing illness to performing such mystical deeds as discovering hidden treasure or prescribing effective love charms.

Arts and literature. Among the earliest written languages, Egyptian first was written as a series of pictures, or hieroglyphics, then evolved to symbolic writing, or demotics. Much later, after the acceptance of Islam, the Egyptians adopted the Arabic language. In all these forms, the Egyptians have a legacy of literature. One of the earliest literary works, *The Book of the Dead*, was written on papyrus perhaps 3,000 years before the Christian era. Inscriptions in the stonework of tombs hint at a wide range of subjects written about mostly by court scribes. This rich heritage is reflected in recent times in the writings of such authors as Muhammad Mandur, whose writings as a spokesman for socialism have been translated into many languages. Salamah Musa (1887-1958), born of Coptic parents, was an advocate of Western-style governments and customs, and Ahmad Amin gained an international reputation as a historian.

Egyptian music has an equally long history. Egyptians were early users, if not inventors, of such musical instruments as the flute, guitar, harp, lyre, and trumpet.

Egyptian interest in sculpture and architecture is well-known because of the great pyramids and the ancient royal throne, the Sphinx. Murals decorated tomb and temple walls from early days. Made of bronze and gold, jewelry and housewares of great beauty and excellent design appeared early in Egyptian history. The interest in art and beauty is reflected today in such finely tiled buildings as the mosque and university El Azhar, whose use by the French during their short rule offended the Egyptians to rebellion, and in the exquisitely designed metal and clay pots found in every marketplace.

Conclusion. Many of the mores of the Egyptian peasants are based on the value of social harmony over consumption and materialism. Smooth relations with neighbors are far more important than a competition for possessions, which instills rivalry and bitterness. This value system has sustained Egyptians and given them a reputation for gentleness and humor.

For More Information

Brugman J. *An Introduction to the History of Modern Arabic Literature in Egypt.* Leiden: E. J. Brill, 1984.

Old and new merge as automobiles and goats share Egyptian streets. *Courtesy of Dr. Paul Fischer.*

Marsot, Afaf Lutfi Al-Sayyid. *A Short History of Modern* Egypt. London: Cambridge University Press, 1985.

The Middle East and North Africa, 37th edition. London: Europa, 1991.

HAZARA
(huh zar′ uh)

People of Afghanistan who are of mixed Iranian and Mongol descent.

Population: 1,500,000 (1985 estimate).
Location: Central Afghanistan.
Languages: Hazaragi, a Persian dialect; Dari.

Geographical Setting

Hazara area

Most Hazaras live in the Hazarajat, a mountainous, roughly circular area in central Afghanistan. The Hazarajat comprises the western part of the Hindu Kush mountain range, which stretches west from Pakistan deep into landlocked Afghanistan. Though not clearly defined, the Hazara homeland extends from the northern Koh-i-Baba ridge, a high offshoot of the Hindu Kush, south to the Helmand River, and from the Paropomisus Mountains eastward nearly to the national capital of Kabul. Most of the terrain is rugged and supports only sparse plant life. The Hazaras farm the lower valleys, up to about 10,000 feet; in the summers some herd sheep and goats to the higher valleys for pasturage. Farmers use all the land possible for growing crops, often plowing steep hillsides above the valley floors.

Rainfall is scarce; agriculture relies on the rivers fed by melted snow from the high mountains, and on simple irrigation techniques. In years with little mountain snowfall, such as those of 1969 through 1971, the rivers can run dry, causing widespread hunger and hardship. When snowfall is heavy, the small mountain villages are isolated for months at a time. While winters are severe, summers are temperate, though short in the higher altitudes. The Hazarajat is densely populated considering its harsh terrain, and despite the migration of many Hazaras to cities such as Kabul in the twentieth century.

Historical Background

Persians, Greeks, and central Asians. Throughout historical times, the land today called Afghanistan has been a melting pot of influences and peoples from east, west, north, and south. By 550 B.C., Achaemenid Persian rulers had conquered the local inhabitants, about whom little is known. Then in the 330s B.C., the Greek armies of Alexander the Great shattered the formerly mighty Persian Empire. Alexander advanced through Afghanistan and into India, bringing a Greek cultural influence that lasted for several centuries after his death in 323 B.C. Persian influence, however, proved longer lasting. Nomads from central Asia established control of the region in about A.D. 150. Their empire, surrounded by the powerful Indians, Chinese, and (in Mesopotamia) Parthian states, lasted 400 years. The gradual expansion of another Persian empire, the Sassanids, was slowed in the 300s and 400s by the continuing immigration of more central Asian peoples.

Islam. Arab Muslim armies (see ISLAM) swept into the region about 700. The Arabs conquered the Persians, then slowly incorporated modern Afghanistan, Pakistan, and parts of northern India into the Islamic domain that stretched west to North Africa. Over the next 200 years, most of the region's inhabitants became Sunni Muslim. Eventually, the Ghaznavid Empire arose from southern Afghanistan. The Sunni Ghaznavids assured the continuation of Sunni Islam to the east of Shi'ite Iran. By the 900s, a new central Asian people, the Turks (see TURKS), had settled the area of the Hindu Kush. As elsewhere in the eastern Islamic world, Turkish leaders slowly eroded Ghaznavid power with various Muslim Turkish dynasties controlling Afghanistan by 1200.

Mongols. Beginning in 1220, several waves of Asiatic conquerors overran central Asia and much of the Middle East. Mongol leaders such as Genghis Khan (1155-1227) and Tamerlane (1336-1405) commanded huge armies and subdued lands from China to Turkey. They destroyed many civilizations, ravaging the land and ruining the cities. It was out of this turbulent era that the Hazaras emerged as a distinct people. They are believed to be the descendants of Mongol soldiers and the area's previous Persianized inhabitants—who themselves probably included the blood not only of Persians, but also of Greeks, Arabs, Indians, and Turks, as well as other central Asians. The group adopted Farsi, the Persian language, but also preserved Mongol social ways.

Withdrawal to the mountains. The empire controlled by Tamerlane's successors began breaking up in the late 1400s and early 1500s. In the 1500s and 1600s, empires in India (Moguls) and Iran (Safavids) struggled for dominance over strategic Afghanistan, which could serve as an invasion route for either side. As these empires waned, tribal groups in Afghanistan competed for power. Other groups slowly pushed the Hazaras from the fertile lowlands around the Hindu Kush into the higher, narrow valleys they occupy today. In the north, Uzbek tribes raided the Hazara villages for slaves. In the south and west, the land was claimed by the strong Pushtun tribes, whose leaders created the first centralized Afghan state in the mid-1700s. In the late 1800s, the Pushtun leader Abdur Rahman waged a concerted effort to dissolve tribal loyalties and consolidate his own power. He forced whole communities to move to new areas, weakening both those who were uprooted and those whom they replaced on the land. Further Hazara land was lost in this way.

War and defeat. Within the Hazarajat, the Hazaras remained stubbornly independent. Their enmity with the Afghan Pushtuns and with other groups in the culturally diverse land was increased by religious tension: nearly all Hazaras are Shi'ites like the Persians whose language they used, while other Afghan groups are mostly Sunni. While the Hazaras constantly warred among themselves, they also waylaid unwary travelers to the Hazarajat. Nomads from other regions and even caravans avoided the Hazara land, or were attacked. By the 1880s, the dominant Afghan confederation (led by Abdur Rahman) demanded taxes from all the Hazara groups, even as it continued to whittle away at the fringes of Hazara territory. In the winter of 1891, the Hazaras rebelled against outside control. Each side declared jihad, or holy war, against the other. After initial victories, the Hazaras were defeated and ultimately crushed by the Afghan forces in 1893. Some Hazaras fled to Iran; others were sold into slavery.

Defiance and disunity. War impoverished the people and ruined their homes and crops. In the following years, as throughout the twentieth century, many migrated to cities such as Kabul, Ghazni, and Mazar-i-Sharif to work at casual day labor. Yet the spirit of resistance persisted. The Hazaras were among the first to declare independence following the advent to power of the Russian-backed Communist government in 1978. The Hazaras were unable to unify, however, and their disunity prevented them from mounting effective opposition during the 1980s Soviet-Afghan War. On the other hand, it also kept the Russians from attacking the Hazarajat as they did much of the rest of Afghanistan. Following Soviet withdrawal in the late 1980s, the government of Afghanistan was slow to reestablish firm control over this Hazara homeland. Still, the Hazaras remain poor and downtrodden in Afghan society, barely able to survive in the Hazarajat, and comprising an ethnic underclass when they move to the cities.

Culture Today

Overview. Afghanistan's past has made the country a patchwork of separate yet often composite ethnic groups. No such thing as "a typical Afghan" exists. Aside from the dominant Pushtuns and the Hazaras, Iranian-related groups include the Farsiwan (Persians), the Qizilbash, the Nuristanis, and the numerous but ethnically diverse Tadjiks. All of these speak dialects of Dari, the Afghan version of

Persian, and some, like the Hazaras, have substantial Shi'ite populations. (The Pushtun, however, are nearly all Sunni.) Turkic speakers include the Uzbeks and Khirgis (both mostly Sunni). Substantial numbers of Mongols and seminomadic Arabs also live in Afghanistan, though both have mostly abandoned their original languages in favor of Dari. Finally, two groups often associated with Hazaras are the Taimanis and Aimaq, who like the Hazaras may be of mixed origin. The Hazaras' Mongol background can be seen in their appearance—often light-bearded, with characteristic high cheekbones. The Persian dialect of Hazaragi contains many Mongol words.

Family life. Mongol elements also appear in the Hazara family structure. Some Hazaras follow the Mongol practice of using different words for older and younger siblings, for example. The family unit is headed by the father, and usually includes his wife, their unmarried children, and married sons with their wives and children. Hazara women are reported to be more independent than is common in some Muslim societies. Though she will conform to most Muslim ideas of modesty, for example, a wife controls her household and often plays a role in village affairs commensurate with her family's prestige. The father's authority is limited by the tendency of the family to act as a unit. If a member's behavior requires correction or punishment, the family usually meets to decide on appropriate action, which the father might then carry out. Family lineage is often traced by a village or group of villages back to a common ancestor.

While the Hazaras were once nomadic, herding sheep and goats and raising horses for fighting, most now are settled farmers. The men tend the fields; in some groups, women and children continue to herd flocks to higher summer pastures while the men remain to look after the crops. Women are also responsible for domestic tasks such as weaving.

Food, clothing, and shelter. Grains such as wheat or barley are staple foods, along with dairy products such as milk, buttermilk, curds, and butter. Meat is eaten only sparingly, as the flocks of goats and sheep represent the people's wealth. However, during the ten days of Muharram, the holy period commemorating the death of the Shia leader Husain, many animals are slaughtered and eaten in celebratory feasts. The meals take place at the village mosque, and the whole village takes part. Where possible, the Hazaras also grow a few vegetables and fruits—peas, carrots, beans, lentils, potatoes, onions, melons, apples, mulberries, grapes, and apricots.

Hazara clothing is similar to that of other Afghans. Men and women both wear knee-length cotton shirts with loose pants (*perane-tambon*). Women often incorporate large pleats in their pants, considered a sign of wealth. The Hazara women knit wool gloves and thick, knee-length wool stockings, which are worn in winter inside boots. Both are decorated with traditional designs. In the summer, boots are often discarded in favor of cheap, colorful plastic shoes or sandals that are made in Kabul or imported from Pakistan, India, and Japan. While the women rarely cut their hair, the men shave each other's heads frequently.

Settled Hazaras live in solid houses of dried mud or baked mud bricks, with a central courtyard surrounded by a high mud wall. The enclosure often holds some or all of the family's livestock, and is guarded by the vicious watchdog that is a common feature of Afghan villages. The dogs have their tails and ears clipped off, to avoid their being shredded in fights. Often, a felt and reed *yurt* (nomad tent) stands in the courtyard, both a useful summer hut and a reminder of the Hazaras' nomadic past. The groups who continue to seek summer pastures for their flocks live in *yurts* from May to September. Either women and children go to tend the flocks, or selected village families amounting to about one-third of the village population tend them.

Religion. The Sayyids, a group of religious figures claiming descent from the prophet Muhammad (see ISLAM), play an important role in Afghan daily religious life. Most Sayyids are Sunni, but the Shi'ite Hazaras have their own group of Shi'ite Sayyids. These religious leaders live among the Hazara laypeople and are highly respected for their learning and piety. While Sayyid daughters rarely marry non-Sayyids, the Sayyid men take Hazara wives, with the result that over the years they have become indistinguishable from the Hazaras.

After the 1979 Islamic revolution in Iran, which brought the Shi'ite Ayatollah Khomeini to power, young Hazara militants attempted to mobilize a similar movement. They wished to oppose not only the Russian-backed Communist government, but also the seizure of Hazara lands by Sunni Pushtuns and the generally poor condition of their people. However, the movement quickly splintered into groups that warred among themselves.

Urban life. The Hazaras who have migrated to cities like Kabul are known for keeping their religious and cultural ways. Almost always, these easily identifiable differences mark them for low-paying, menial jobs that others will not take. Some are seasonal workers in construction or unskilled labor, returning to their villages in the slack winter months. Others pull carts (*karachis*) for hire, or rent themselves as water or grain carriers. They live in mud huts on the slopes above the cities, and often subsist on restaurant scraps. Western clothing is common in the cities and, like others in the urban centers, Hazaras buy secondhand clothing from such countries as the United States. Such clothing is widely available in cheap, open-air markets. In the mornings, men in Kabul trade vegetables to the restaurants in exchange for bread left over from the previous evening meal of meat and rice. Juice from the rice is soaked into the bread, adding flavor and substance to the meal.

For More Information

Bonner, Arthur. *Among the Afghans.* Durham, North Carolina: Duke University Press, 1987.

Canfield, Robert. *Hazara Integration into the Afghan Nation.* New York: Afghanistan Council of the Asia Society, 1972.

Dupree, Louis. *Afghanistan.* Princeton, New Jersey: Princeton University Press, 1978.

IRANIANS
(ihr ay′ nee uns)

Native speakers of various Persian dialects.

Population: 23,500,000 (1988 estimate).
Location: Iran; Western Afghanistan.
Language: Persian.

Geographical Setting

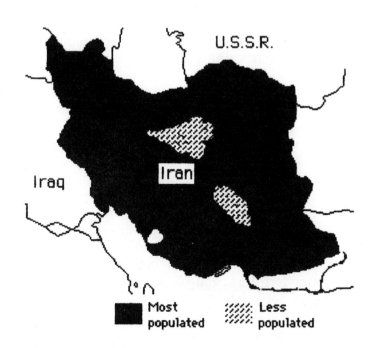

The Iranian plateau, heartland of the Persian language and culture, includes mountains, deserts, and irrigated farmland. Occupying central Iran, the plateau is divided from the coastal lowlands of the Caspian Sea in the north and the Persian Gulf in the south by the Elburz and Zagros mountain ranges, respectively. The Zagros range also forms a natural border with Iraq to the west, while in the east the plateau gradually blends with the highlands of Afghanistan and the deserts of the southeastern Iranian province of Baluchestan. Water from the surrounding mountains drains into the interior basin, which contains two great deserts, the Dasht-e-lut in the north and the Dasht-e-Kavir in the south.

Iranians have traditionally settled the arable lands between mountain and desert. The most prosperous urban centers—Tehran, Mashhad, Kerman, Shiraz, and Ishfahan—lie in this roughly circular strip, in the *mo'tadel*, or "temperate" zone, between 3,000 and 6,000 feet above sea level. Above and below the mo'tadel region, in the *sardsir* ("cold lands") and the *garmsir* ("warm lands"), extremes of climate have prohibited regular cultivation. These areas are generally inhabited by nomadic societies. Some of these societies, which include Kurds, Gilakis, Mazanderanis, Lors, Baluch, Azarbaijani, Qashqa'i and Turkomans, are represented elsewhere in this book. Settled Iranians described in this chapter constitute fifty percent of Iran's population, with the nomadic descendants of the ancient Persian peoples adding a further twenty percent. Those not descended from ancient Persians make up the remaining thirty percent.

Historical Background

Ancient empires. The position of the Iranian plateau, with the Caspian Sea to the north and the Persian Gulf to the south, has made it a land bridge between Europe and Asia, an intersection of many different cultures and civilizations. Despite repeated invasions from both east and west, however, Persian culture has persisted for nearly 3,000 years. The Persians arrived on the plateau around 1000 B.C., coming with other Iranian (Aryan) groups from the plains of central Asia. One of these groups, the Medes, developed a powerful empire in the 600s B.C., defeating the once-mighty Assyrians and occupying Mesopotamia (modern Iraq) and much of Asia Minor (modern Turkey). The Persians were subjects of the Medes, but in 553 B.C. their leader, Cyrus, overthrew the Median king and established the first Persian empire. Cyrus and his descendants (called Achaemenids, after an ancestor) expanded Persian power by conquering Egypt and Greek city-states on the western coast of Asia Minor. Persian attempts to conquer Greece itself were turned back by the Greeks beginning in 490 B.C., and in the late 300s B.C., the Greeks, under Alexander the Great, conquered the Achaemenids, ending their dynasty.

Although Alexander's successors were unable to retain power, Greek cultural influence persisted under the Parthians, an Iranian group that replaced them in the 200s B.C. Like the Greeks, the Parthians had a weak centralized state, relying instead on local lords and independent governors. Inscriptions on stone recording the acts of Parthian kings are in Greek. The Parthians held sway from India in the east to the borders of the Roman empire in the west, often coming into conflict with the Romans.

Eventually, the Persians, led by the Sassanid family, rose against the Parthians and overthrew them in the A.D. 200s, creating a new empire that ruled until the 600s. The Sassanids attempted to recreate the glory of the Achaemenid Empire, reestablishing a strong central government and reconquering much of the territory that the Achae-

Ancient rock carvings found near Routan, Iran. *Courtesy of the University Museum, University of Pennsylvania.*

menids had controlled. Still, the disruption brought by Alexander's conquest and the years of Greek influence meant that the Sassanids lacked a clear picture of the past. It is from Greek literature and archeology that we know of these early Persian empire builders.

The coming of Islam. The Sassanids continued the Parthians' warfare against the eastern half of the Roman Empire, whose capital became the Greek city of Byzantium. Constant warfare had weakened both empires by the mid-600s, when a strong new power emerged. Persians had come into contact with Arabs for centuries, but the Arabs had always been disunited nomadic tribes whom the Persians kept in check and from whom they occasionally exacted tribute. In the early 600s, however, the Arabs united under the prophet Muhammad, and with Muhammad's death in 632 began a campaign of conquest in the name of the new religion of Islam (see ISLAM). By 641 the power of the Sassanids had been shattered, and the Persians were absorbed into the new Islamic empire. Yet Persian elements survived. The Arabs had no ready institutional structure that could cope with such a large and varied empire, for example, so they adopted most of the Sassanids' administrative and taxation systems. The Persian language also persisted, and would lend itself to a distinctive and important branch of Islamic literature. As Arab conquerors mingled with their new subjects, the differences between them became fewer and less significant. Most Persians converted to Islam, and Persian dynasties such as the Samanids came to power in the 800s. Persia became part of a new Islamic world that stretched from Spain to the China Sea.

Invasions from the east. Soon this new world was itself disrupted by external threats. As early as the 800s, Turkish soldiers began entering Iran from central Asia, setting up small local dynasties in isolated areas. In addition, Persian rulers such as the Samanids began using Turkish troops. By the late 900s, many of these soldiers had overthrown their Iranian rulers to take power for themselves. Still, large numbers of Turks did not begin migrating westward until the 1000s, when the Seljuq Turks conquered territory extending from northeastern Iran to Asia Minor. Three factors combined to minimize the disruption caused by this influx. First, the Turks who had already converted to Islam when they arrived in Iran shared a common religion with the Persians. Second, the Seljuq rulers encouraged many Turks to continue west, where they could be used against the Byzantine armies, rather than to settle in Iran. Finally, like the Arabs, the Turks in Iran adopted Persian cultural and administrative institutions rather than imposing their own.

In the 1200s, however, came new invaders from the east whose conquest and rule were not so tempered. Mongol armies under Genghis Khan swept into Iran, killing millions of Iranians and displacing the ruling Turks. The warlike Mongols looked down on Islamic culture, and their leaders were interested only in squeezing the highest taxes possible out of their new subjects. Destroying agriculture and trade, the Mongols inflicted damage so great that many parts of Iran have never recovered. The Turks gradually regained control of Iran as the Mongol Empire broke up in the 1300s, and they would continue to rule Iran until 1925.

Safavids and Iranian Shi'ism. In the 1400s a Turkish-speaking dynasty called the Safavids became powerful in Azarbaijan, from where they expanded, conquering all of Iran by 1510. The Safavids brought Shi'ism to Iran, which henceforth would be closely identified with Shi'ite beliefs (see ISLAM).

Persian feelings of national identity resurfaced under the Safavids, and these feelings became and have remained closely intertwined with Shi'ism. It was in this period that the borders of modern Iran were defined.

Qajars. After the downfall of the Safavids in 1722, a long period of invasion and civil war, culminating in the victory of the Qajar dynasty in 1797, brought social and cultural stagnation to Iran. The Qajars, a Turkish tribe whose rulers gained power by allying themselves with the northern Iranian aristocracy, ruled until 1925. Under their rule, Iran suffered economic exploitation, as Europeans grew more powerful in Asia, and military defeats mounted as Russia carved away much of her territory to the north. During the 1800s, when newspapers and a university were founded, Western democratic ideas slowly found some support among the Persian middle classes. Mostly, however, Iran remained weak and technologically backward during this period, as the Qajars held power by playing on rivalries between England and Russia, and between various ethnic groups within Iran.

Westernization and Islamic reaction in the 1900s. In 1925 the fragile Qajar dynasty finally collapsed and power was taken by Reza Khan, an army officer, who took the traditional title Shah (emperor) and the family name Pahlavi, meaning "ancient Persian." Reza Shah thus intended to recall Persia's glorious pre-Islamic past, and to distance Iran from traditional Islamic ways. Undertaking a massive program of modernization and Westernization, he attempted to exclude Iran's powerful Islamic clergy from political and cultural affairs. The Shah's son, Muhammad Reza, continued his father's policies after coming to power in 1941. Allying himself closely with the United States, the new Shah consolidated his power in the 1950s. With the increase in oil prices of the 1970s, Iran's revenues jumped dramatically, and the Shah used the oil money to try to make Iran into a major economic and military power. The economy, however, could not support his ambitions, and the windfall oil revenues bred corruption in the Shah's government. Also, Iran's agriculture suffered as people flocked to the cities in hopes of making quick fortunes. In the cities they found that Westerners and the Shah's rich supporters often took the best jobs and houses. At the same time the people increasingly resented the Shah's prohibition of traditional Muslim practices, such as the wearing of a veil by women.

Although many groups began to oppose the Shah in the 1970s, his enforcement of a one-party system made it impossible for a cohesive political opposition to emerge. People turned more and more to the Islamic clergy for leadership. The clergy had always opposed the secular reforms of the Pahlavis, which after all had been intended to strip them of power. In 1963, for example, the Ayatollah Khomeini (Ayatollah is a religious title) led protests in Tehran intended to challenge the Shah's programs. The next year, after further protest, Khomeini was exiled. From exile in Iraq, Khomeini continued his activity by sending tape-recorded messages to the Iranian people. As protest renewed in the late 1970s, people remembered Khomeini's refusal to compromise with the Shah, unlike other religious leaders, and turned to him as a leader, despite his long absence.

Revolution. From December 1978, when as many as four million demonstrators in Tehran called for the Shah's replacement by Khomeini as leader of a new Islamic republic, to early February 1979, when Islamic leaders consolidated their control, Iran underwent a revolution whose tone became more and more religious. The Shah fled on January 16, 1979, leaving an embattled administrative and military apparatus behind him. Khomeini's return from exile on February 1, was celebrated by millions in the streets of Tehran; for the next ten days, he led opposition in the streets to the dwindling forces of the Shah's police. On February 11, the army and police capitulated, declaring neutrality. On April 1, a national referendum declared the Islamic Republic of Iran.

Persian traditions and values remain dominant in Iran's multiethnic society, although the revolutionary leadership emphasizes Islamic and particularly Shi'ite values rather than the racial ones implied in the Shah's glorification of the old Persian empires. Centuries of rule by powerful dynasties, many of which, like the Safavids, claimed Persian descent (probably falsely), have left a legacy of tribalism and nationalism. The new leaders have attempted to replace this factionalism with a unified "pan-Islamic" state. For example, the revolutionary government always refers to its long and costly war with Iraq (1980-1988) in religious, not national, terms: Islam against the secular state of Iraq and its leader, Saddam Hussein; the spiritual against the material, rather than Iranian against Iraqi or Persian against Arab. This process of Islamization continues within Iranian society.

The hostages, the war, and the West. Despite virtually unanimous hatred of the Shah, rifts soon developed that threatened to divide Iranian society. On the one hand, many liberals and leftists believed that, with the revolution over, the religious leaders should withdraw from the political scene. They represented the part of Iranian society that, while opposing the corruption and oppression of the Shah's regime, accepted his Westernization program, at least in principle. On the other hand, the religious leadership was itself split between moderates who thought that ties with the West might be renewed without sacrificing the integrity of the Islamic state, and extremists who saw the West as the inevitable enemy of the new Iran. Two important events, the hostage crisis and Iraq's 1980 invasion of Iran, helped ensure popular support for this latter group.

In November 1979 militant Muslim students attacked the United States embassy in Tehran, taking more than fifty diplomats and marines as hostages. Anger at the United States, which had supported the Shah, had been exacerbated by President Jimmy Carter's decision to admit the Shah, now dying of cancer, into the United States for medical treatment. At the same time, the moderate prime minister chosen by Khomeini, Mehdi Bazargan, had enraged the extremists by meeting with United States officials. Unable to attack Bazargan directly, extremists used the huge anti-American demonstrations incited by the embassy take-over to force Bazargan and his liberal colleagues out of office. The hostage crisis, which lasted 444 days, strengthened the extremists' position by isolating Iran within the international community and thus creating a strong feeling of unity. Not until 1985 would the moderates gain enough popular support to challenge the power of the extremists.

Iraq's September 1980 invasion of Iran generated a similar sense of unity, one which also included both religious and national feelings. Khomeini painted the secular regime of Saddam Hussein as a tool of Western materialism, describing the conflict as a *jihad*, or holy war. Iraq, supported and armed by France, the Soviet Union, and the United States, expected a quick victory in its attempt to gain the province of Khuzestan, which contained valuable oil fields and refineries, yet the invasion ground to a halt in the face of fierce, even suicidal, resistance by the Iranians. When the war ended in 1988, Iran had retained virtually all its territory, and what little Iran lost, Hussein returned in 1990. Iran's success in the war vindicated its fundamentalist government in the eyes of the Islamic world, while Iraq's belligerence—for example, in Iraq's 1990 invasion of Kuwait—has reduced Iran's isolation without endangering its sense of unity.

Culture Today

Family life. For Persians, as for Iranians generally, the family constitutes the basic social unit. Married sons and their families often live with parents, with the father (or in his absence, the oldest son) being the chief authority figure. In Islamic law, the law of the land under the revolutionary government, a wife must be subservient to her husband, and their daughter must receive his permission to marry. A son's obedience to his father's wishes, dictated by custom rather than statute, need not be so absolute, though he will rarely marry without his father's permission. In return for his family's subservience, the father acts not only as provider but also as protector of family honor. All members of the family, both near and distant relatives, are careful to preserve this honor. Often, family honor is centered on the female members of the family. Family members also frequently work together in business or political endeavors, thus enhancing the family's reputation and position. Much of an individual's status rests on that of his or her family, whether in a rural village or a large city.

Marriages are most often arranged between a young man's parents and those of a young woman they consider worthy. (Under Islamic law, a female can marry as young as nine years of age, or after her first menstruation, whichever comes first.) In 1971, despite the Shah's attempts at Westernization, one study indicated that over a third of Iranian females married under the age of thirteen. The two sets of parents agree on a marriage payment, or *shirbaha*, which the boy's parents will pay to the girl's in order to make up for their losing a daughter. Between the agreement and the signing of the actual marriage contract, the boy performs token services for his prospective father-in-law, such as bringing him tea or running errands. After signing the contract, the two families celebrate and prepare for the ceremony, in which the boy's family arrives at the girl's father's house,

A knife-sharpener of Iran. *Courtesy of the Smithsonian Institution.*

presents him with the shirbaha, and brings the wife back to the husband's home, which is usually at his father's.

Women. An important part of the Pahlavis' attempt to build a secular state lay in their abrogation of traditional Islamic restraints on women. In 1935 Reza Shah prohibited teachers and schoolchildren from wearing *hejab* (that is, clothes that conform to the strict Islamic dress code), and forbade army officers to appear in public with women who wore the traditional veil. Later he banned hejab altogether. His son, Muhammad Reza Shah, gave women both the right to vote and to attend universities, and in 1967 introduced the Family Protection Bill, which allowed women to sue for divorce and to prevent their husbands from taking a second wife. Such measures were deeply offensive to the Islamic clergy as well as to many conservative Iranians. In the 1970s the Shah's policies regarding women became popularly identified with his regime's waste and corruption, so that for many young women donning hejab became a mark of protest.

Iranian women do not necessarily see the return to Islamic law as a curtailment of their rights. Many, for example, feel that it is proper and respectable for women to wear hejab in public. Furthermore, Iranian women have often taken an active role in Iran's economic life, running businesses and owning property. Also, the status of women has benefited from their support of the revolution, and today there are female members of the *Majlis*, or Islamic Assembly. In 1985, the speaker of the Majlis, Hashemi Rafsanjani, said that women were to be kept out of the military. Although women began serving in the army near the end of the war with Iraq, with the peace in 1989 and the normalization of relations in 1990 the old restrictions will undoubtedly return. However, it is the exclusion of women from the ranks of the *ulema,* the ruling Islamic religious scholars, that most curtails their participation in public life.

Government. The Islamic Republic of Iran is almost entirely the creation of one man, the Ayatollah Khomeini. In Khomeini's eyes, the Shah's government was *taghuti*, or illegitimate and contrary to the will of God, and thus had to be totally replaced. In writings published during the reign of the Shah, Khomeini called for the subordination of political authority to Islamic principles under a united religious, military, and political leadership. In the absence of the hidden Imam (see ISLAM), Khomeini argued that the nation's management should be entrusted to a guardian-judge, called a *faqih,* who would have supreme religious, judicial, and political authority. (The term faqih usually meant someone learned in law.) As faqih until his death in 1989, Khomeini oversaw the first ten years of revolutionary government.

Despite Khomeini's emphasis on Islamic principles, the Iranian constitution of 1979 includes many Western, republican elements. Aside from the faqih, the government features a prime minister and cabinet; the 270-member Majlis, or legislative assembly and a 12-member religious council, the *Shora-ye-Negahban*, which oversees legislation to ensure that it adheres to Islamic principles. A popularly elected president signs laws into effect and coordinates the three other branches of government. In addition, a powerful five-member High Council of the Judiciary ensures that the entire legal system remains under the control of the clergy.

Food, clothing, and shelter. Iranian diet tends to vary both regionally and seasonally, especially among the poorer people. Breakfast is usually bread and cheese accompanied by hot, sweet tea called *chai,* which is the national drink. Lunch often incorporates leftovers from last night's supper: soup made of vegetables, yogurt, and rice, or perhaps a meat stew (favorite meats are mutton and goat) or soup, or *chelo kebab,* a dish of grilled meat with rice and a dressing of spiced egg yolk. Bread, cheese, and tea are also served at lunch and supper. Between meals, Iranians eat nuts, excellent sweet melons, and sunflower seeds, along with frequent glasses of tea.

As part of his campaign to modernize Iran, Reza Shah introduced a "uniform dress law," which made Western-style clothes mandatory for Iranians. As already stated, the suppression of religious dress (hejab) for women inspired widespread resentment. The central component of such dress is the *chador,* a long cloak of thin black cotton that encloses the entire body, from the head to the ankles. The chador is held together at the neck by the left hand, or sometimes by the teeth. In public, women are allowed under the Islamic Republic to show only their faces (without makeup) and their hands. Iranian men still wear mostly Western clothes, except for the clergymen, who wear a white turban and an *aba,* a loose, sleeveless brown cloak, open in front. (Clergymen descended from the Prophet Muhammad wear a black turban and aba.)

In the 1960s Muhammad Reza Shah undertook government housing efforts in major cities designed to accommodate the large numbers of people who had come from the rural areas. In the early

1970s, housing policy shifted to provincial towns, in an attempt to attract some of the people out of the large cities. These buildings were mostly large, modern, multi-family dwellings of materials such as brick, steel, concrete, and glass. Wood is scarce in Iran's mostly arid terrain. Traditional homes in the countryside are simple one- or two-bedroom structures of stone or, more often, dried earth.

Arts and literature. Iranians have a long and varied cultural tradition, ranging from the ornate silver utensils and jewelry that survive from the Achaemenid and Sassanid periods to the famous carpets still

Planting time in northwestern Iran. *Courtesy of Dr. Nikki Keddie, U.C.L.A.*

woven by women in Iran. The Seljuq period was especially fertile for Persian culture. Under the Seljuqs, Persian potters developed new techniques, incorporating turquoise, cobalt blue, and tin-oxide white glazes into elaborate designs. Persian artists also distinguished themselves in calligraphy, miniature painting, and the intricate tile work and stylized inscriptions from the Quran that decorate the walls of the major mosques. In architecture, the distinctive Persian cupola resting on a square or octagonal base began to replace the classical Arabic design in the building of mosques.

Persian writers have contributed much to Islamic literature, at first tending to use Arabic, the language of the court. Beginning in the late 800s, however, Persian poets such as Rudaki (died c. 1020), Daqiqi (died c. 975) and Ferdowsi (died c. 1020) developed an elaborate literature in Persian. These poets, influenced by Arabic poetry and using Arabic script, nonetheless reflected a genuine Persian cultural renaissance after the shock of the Arab invasions. Similarly, the upheaval of the Mongol occupation led to another intensely creative period for Persian poets, painters, calligraphers, and historians in the 1200s and 1300s. Poets such as Hafez, Khwaju Kermani, Salman Savaji, and Obeid Zakani produced poetic masterpieces in this time of adversity. Persian poetry is highly disciplined, and ranges in content from social commentary to mysticism and the heroes of the past.

Even after the urbanization that occurred under the Shah, about fifty percent of the Iranian population remains in the circular belt of the mo'tadel. Water is scarce, and its availability determines the size of villages, which range from a few households to over 1,000 people. Farmers rely on irrigation for most agricultural production, often making use of long underground tunnels called *ganats*, which allow water to flow without loss from evaporation. This extensive system of underground irrigation dates back more than 2,500 years to the Achaemenids. Alongside the scarcity of their resources the Iranians developed a system of ceremonial hospitality called *ta'aruf*, an elaborate and formal way of demonstrating generosity and modesty. Persian folklore emphasizes acts of hospitality to strangers, especially if such hospitality involves sacrifice. Like the ganats, this tradition allowed the Persians to survive in a harsh environment, where a traveler must rely on others for food and shelter. In a more symbolic way, perhaps, Persian cultural identity itself can be compared to the ganats, both in its long life and in its ability to remain submerged for long periods, only to bubble up from below.

For More Information

Arjomand, Said Amir. *The Turban for the Crown: The Islamic Revolution in Iran.* New York: Oxford University Press, 1988.

Bausani, Alessandro. *The Persians: From the Earliest Days to the Twentieth Century.* London: Elek Books Limited, 1971.

Limbert, John W. *Iran: At War with History.* Boulder, Colorado: Westview Press, 1987.

Nyrop, Richard F., editor. *Iran: A Country Study.* Washington, D.C.: American University Press, 1978.

Simpson, John. *Behind Iranian Lines.* London: Robson Books, 1988.

IRAQI
(ee rah′ key)

Arab Muslims of Iraq.

Population: 17,000,000 (1990 estimate).
Location: Republic of Iraq.
Language: Arabic.

Geographical Setting

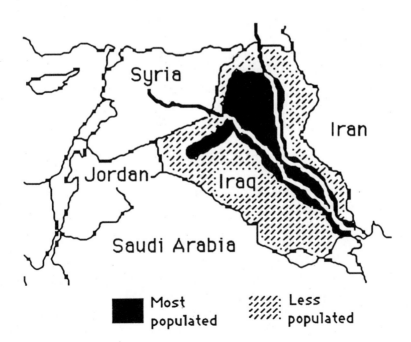

Most populated
Less populated

Lying at the head of the Persian Gulf, Iraq is bounded by Iran to the east, Kuwait and Saudi Arabia to the south, Jordan and Syria to the west, and Turkey to the north. Two geographical features have dominated the region's development: its position at a crossroads of influences from all points of the compass, and its two life-giving but unpredictable rivers, the Tigris and the Euphrates.

Iraq's terrain varies dramatically. In the south, where the Tigris and Euphrates rivers meet and flow into the Gulf, are marshes where Arab villagers live in reed huts, often on tiny, manmade islands. The nearby port of Basra is Iraq's second-largest city. Between the marshes and the capital city of Baghdad, silt deposited by the rivers has created the rich central plains that gave the region its ancient name: Mesopotamia, a Greek term meaning "between the rivers." West and south of the plains, desert extends to Jordan and Saudi Arabia. As the rivers diverge more widely north of Baghdad, the plain between them is called the Jazirah ("island"). This gives way to rolling upland, and then to mountainous highlands that run along much of Iraq's border with Iran and Turkey.

Iraq's climate varies with the terrain. In the mountainous north, snow and freezing temperatures are common in winter. Winter temperatures in the western desert can also fall below freezing. The southern plains remain quite warm through the winter, with temperatures rising as high as 120 degrees Fahrenheit in the summer. The dry heat quickly evaporates any moisture in the soil, so that agriculture has relied on extensive systems of irrigation, particularly in the southern Mesopotamian plain. The two rivers' unpredictable yearly flooding, often violent before the building of dams in recent times, was the central fact of life in the region for thousands of years.

Historical Background

Civilization and empire. Modern Iraq encompasses land on which occurred many of humanity's most important advances. Historians today see these early developments as responses both to necessity and to the benefits of controlling the Tigris and Euphrates. Agriculture began in northern Iraq over 6,500 years ago, then moved south. There, irrigation enabled farmers to grow surpluses, which in turn allowed the growth of early Sumerian cities. Although such centers probably evolved at about the same time in India and China, as well as elsewhere in the Middle East, Sumer has often been considered the "cradle of civilization." Aside from irrigation, the Sumerians passed on such legacies as the wheel, smelting of bronze, kingship, writing, and astronomy.

As early as 3500 B.C., the early Egyptians had visited this area and captured some of the city-states in the delta area of the two rivers. Around 2000 B.C. the independent Sumerian city-states in southern Iraq were subdued by a semitic people from the north, the Akkadians. The Akkadian king, Sargon I, created the world's first known empire, using conscripted soldiers to maintain his rule and work on irrigation and flood control. While Akkadian supremacy lasted only about 200 years, the fusion of Sumerian and Akkadian cultures that resulted influenced the empires to follow.

Greek and Iranian influences. The Greek conqueror Alexander the Great brought new influences to Iraq and the rest of the Middle East. Establishing new cities throughout the region, Alexander and his successors transformed the basis of Iraq's economy from agriculture to trade and commerce. Exports included barley, wheat, dates, wool,

A ziggarat, an ancient religious site at Nippur, Iraq. *Courtesy of the University Museum, University of Pennsylvania (Neg. #G8-5613).*

spices, gold, precious stones, ivory, and bitumen. The Greek rulers also increased the scale of irrigation, building complex waterways to carry water over greater distances. Such trends made rural prosperity dependent on strong central government. The Parthians, who ruled in Iraq from 126 B.C. to A.D. 227, provided this centralization. During their rule, Iraq's prosperity and population grew as Arabs and Iranians immigrated to the region. An Iranian dynasty, the Sassanid Persians (see IRANIANS), ruled from 227 to 636. Constant warfare with the Romans weakened the Sassanid administration, and Iraq fell into decay. The last traces of Sumer-Akkadian civilization disappeared, setting the stage for the arrival of Arabic and Islamic culture, which dominates today.

Islam and the Arabs. Following Muhammad's death in 632, Muslim Arab armies swept out of Arabia, conquering in the name of the new religion of Islam (see ISLAM). The Sassanid armies in Iraq, though outnumbering the Muslims, quickly crumbled. Persian rule had been unpopular in Iraq, whose people soon converted to Islam and began to intermarry with Arab soldiers and immigrants. Arabic replaced Persian as the language of government, and gradually became the spoken language of the people. However, the young faith's unity soon dissolved. Iraq became the focus of the emerging struggle between Shi'ite and Sunni Muslims (see ISLAM). Ali, the Shi'ite leader, made his capital at Al Kufah, south of Baghdad. Since that time, southern Iraq has been a traditional Shi'ite stronghold. Tensions have often existed between Shi'ites in the south and Sunnis in the north.

Abbasid caliphate. Shi'ite revolts continued in both Iran and Iraq through the 600s and 700s. During this time, the capital of the Islamic world was the Syrian city of Damascus. There ruled the Umayyad dynasty of caliphs, the political and military leaders viewed as successors to the prophet Muhammad. In the 740s, Shi'ites in Iran and Iraq united with Sunnis who resented the power of Damascus. They overthrew the Umayyads, and their leader Abbas became caliph. The Abbasid caliphs (descendants of Abbas, the prophet's uncle) moved their capital to the specially rebuilt city of Baghdad. There Persian and Arab influences combined to create a golden age of Islamic civilization. This urban-centered culture vigorously pursued philosophical, scientific, and literary inquiries, carrying out experiments and translating Greek works into Arabic. The Sunni Abbasids, who ruled from 750 to 1258, attempted to keep the loyalty of the Arab Shi'ites in Iraq by ruling fairly. At first, their strong central control maintained the necessary agricultural institutions such as irrigation. As trade increased in importance, however, agriculture declined and the countryside once again grew poor and stagnant. Repeated revolts erupted among the rural poor.

Finally, the violent Mongol invasions of the thirteenth through fifteenth centuries destroyed the legacy of Abbasid urban life. Hulagu Khan, grandson of Genghis, took Baghdad in 1258, killing the last Abbasid caliph. The Abbasids had weakened their economic position by neglecting the important irrigations systems they had inherited. Even more devastating was the similar attack by Tamerlane in 1401. During the centuries of Mongol rule, trade ceased and the irrigation systems fell into disuse. The nomadic Mongols had no use for farming, and most of Iraq's arable land was converted to pasturage for their herds. Their land useless, rural farmers also turned to nomadism. Neither urban nor rural life ever recovered from the occupying Mongol armies.

Ottoman Empire. Ottoman rule (see TURKS) lasted in Iraq from 1534 until the breakup of the empire in 1918. Ottoman armies conquered Iraq in response to hostilities between the Sunni Ottoman sultan and Shi'ite rulers who had taken power in Iran. Consequently, one result of Ottoman rule was a widening of the Shi'ite-Sunni rift in Iraq. Sunnis became identified with the Ottoman administration in Baghdad, and Shi'ites with the rural south. Kurds (see KURDS) predominated in the northern uplands. Under the Mongols, tribal loyalties had come to predominate in the countryside. This tendency grew as Ottoman central authority weakened. In the 1600s, great tribal migrations from Arabia to Syria and Iraq led to intertribal warfare, which the Ottomans were powerless to control. Ottoman reformers in the 1800s attempted to curtail the authority of the tribal sheikhs, with only partial success. The new policies changed the sheikh from tribal leader to landlord, making the people peasant tenants on the land.

British rule and independence. After the collapse of Ottoman power at the end of World War I, the League of Nations declared Iraq a mandate of Great Britain. In 1921, the British installed Faisal, a descendant of the hereditary rulers of the city of Mecca, as king of Iraq. Faisal's popular rule lasted until his death in 1933, by which time Iraq had become an independent state. After his death, however, the political situation grew unstable. Faisal's successors lacked his popularity. The growing Iraqi nationalist movement resented the monarchy's closeness to the West and increasingly considered the monarchy an imposition from the outside. In 1958, King Faisal II and his prime minister were assassinated. Several unstable regimes ensued, until the Baa'th party came to power in 1968. The Baa'th party wished to unite all Arabs around non-religious, socialist principles. Under Saddam Hussein Takriti, the Baa'th brought stability and economic development to Iraq, although while harshly suppressing political disagreement in the land. Growing prosperity slowed in the 1980s as Hussein waged a disastrous war with Iran. Following that, Iraq's occupation of Kuwait and subsequent defeat by United Nations forces brought the country to the brink of anarchy in 1991, as both the northern Kurds and some southern factions rebelled against the battered Iraqi government forces.

Culture Today

In 1991, Iraqis once more suffered a period of turmoil and economic disruption. Bombing by United States, Saudi Arabian, French, and British air forces caused unmeasured damage to industrial and civil systems. Oil production, on which the modern economy is based, has halted. Water, sewage, and electrical systems have been severely disrupted in Baghdad and other cities. In the south, Shi'ites have been in open revolt against the Hussein regime. Their revolt has been suppressed by the army, and the Shi'ites fear reprisals once the occupying allied forces leave southern Iraq. In the north, Kurds (about twenty percent of the population) remain in revolt, while Kurdish civilians flee toward Turkey or Iran. Perhaps 3,000,000 Kurds have fled their villages. Thousands have died of exposure in the northern mountains or at the hands of the Iraqi army, which has attacked them with tanks and aircraft.

Religion in society. Iraqi Arabs are historically poised between the predominantly Shi'ite Persians and the mostly Sunni remainder of the Arab world. Iraq is the only Arab country with a Shi'ite majority. The government estimates that fifty-five percent of Iraqis are Shi'ites; other sources suggest a higher figure. The largely poor and rural Shi'ite population is growing at a faster rate than that of the Sunnis. Since Ottoman times, the mostly urban Sunnis have dominated Iraq's government and economy. While the old patterns persist, in recent years

Shi'ites have become more integrated into urban society. Many have migrated from their traditional southern lands to cities such as Baghdad, where they have prospered in business, industry, and the professions. Such changes were encouraged by the government, which stepped up its efforts during the war with Iran in the 1980s. Despite attempts by Iran's Shi'ite government to win them over, the Shi'ites proved their loyalty to Iraq's national government. Shi'ite soldiers made up as much as three-quarters of the army's lower ranks, and many competent Shi'ite officers were promoted to positions of responsibility. Yet their 1991 revolt shows that, especially in the south, many are disillusioned with Saddam Hussein's Baa'thist rule.

Migration. Before 1980, Iraq's cities were expanding rapidly, as tribesmen and rural farmers sought well-paying urban jobs, often in construction or commerce. Whole families moved from the country to cities like Baghdad and Basra. The war with Iran accelerated migration to Baghdad, but cities to the south and east suffered by being close to the front. Basra, with its vulnerable oil refineries and port facilities, experienced heavy shelling by Iranian artillery. It has been estimated that the city's population shrank by more than half during the war. Rural communities around Basra also suffered. The Ma'dan or Marsh Arabs, who for centuries inhabited the marshes north of Basra, have been forced from their villages by heavy fighting in the area. They also fell prey to roving bands of Iraqi deserters who hid out in the marshes and raided the villages. Similar movements occurred along the Iran-Iraq border, as entire communities fled the fighting. The south saw further heavy fighting in the 1991 war between Iraq and United Nations forces.

Food, clothing, and shelter. Iraqi food is similar to that of other Arab countries. Simple meals among desert Arabs might consist of rice flavored with butter and perhaps a little lamb, eaten with coffee or tea. Settled villagers or city dwellers enjoy greater variety. *Kebabs*—skewered pieces of lamb interspersed with tomato and onion—are a favorite, as is *kubba*—spiced ground lamb with nuts and raisins. These and other dishes, such as spicy lamb or vegetable stews, are eaten with rice or flat bread called *samoon*. *Laban*, an unsweetened yogurt drink, might accompany the meal, with sweet coffee or lemon tea to follow. Men sometimes round out the meal with a small glass of *arak*, a potent liqueur distilled from dates or grapes.

In the cities, most Iraqis wear European-style clothing, though the women often cover themselves with a dark cloak, or *abayah*. Even in Baghdad, women will not wear pants or sleeveless dresses, which Muslims regard as immodest. Rural Iraqis wear more traditional Arab clothing. Men cover their heads with the *keffiyeh*, a checked or plain cloth secured with a double loop of cord, the *agal*. They wear a long robe (*dishdasha*), with a woolen gown (*aba*) for warmth. The men sometimes wear pajamalike clothing out doors, such as when they gather in the evening at coffeehouses to talk or play dominoes. Women wear the abayah or colorful dresses. Iraqi women love jewelry, often wearing several gold bracelets.

Houses are traditionally built of brick or dried mud for coolness in summer, with large rooms and a shaded central courtyard. The flat roof is often protected by a low wall; in the heat of summer nights members of the family often sleep outside on the roof. The government has built Western-style housing projects to help deal with the influx of war refugees into Baghdad. Many families, however, have taken up residence on vacant lots in the overcrowded city, build

Along the Tigris River, boatmen still build "Kafas" of reeds. *Courtesy of the University Museum, University of Pennsylvania.*

Iraqi build houses of reeds in the delta area of the Tigris and Euphrates rivers. *Photograph by John Henry Haynes, courtesy of the University Museum, University of Pennsylvania.*

makeshift reed and mud huts called *sharifahs.* The Marsh Arabs build houses entirely of reeds. Lattice walls are supported by bundled reed columns, arched over and spliced together to form a framework of rubs. The house (*mudhif*) is often built on an artificial island in the marsh, created by putting down a bed of reeds and dumping silt around it. The marsh villages consist of clusters of little islands, among which the Marsh Arabs travel by canoe.

Family life. As in many other Middle Eastern countries, the family in Iraq is traditionally large and dominated by the father. The household consists of a father and mother and their unmarried children, plus the families of their married sons. Often various dependent relatives also live with the family: grandparents or unmarried aunts or uncles, for example. The traditional male dominance, however, has been eroded by increasing urbanization and, above all, by the war with Iran. Where in the past it was socially doubtful that a woman would drive the family car, during the 1980s women were needed as construction workers, doctors, and law enforcement officers—occupations sometime requiring them to drive.

Arts and literature. Iraqi artists are highly respected in the Arab world. Poetry is considered the queen of the Arab arts, and Iraqis are invariably enthusiastic at public readings. The readings, which occur frequently, are like performances, and the audience responds to the poet with rapt attention, laughter, or applause. Calligraphy (decorative writing) also has a strong tradition in Arab countries. It is most often seen in mosques, where the walls are adorned with short quotations from the Quran. Painting and sculpture are also popular. Baghdad has many galleries, with high attendance at the frequent shows and exhibitions. Most public areas boast a sculpture or two. Iraqi folk musicians play stringed instruments like the *oud* or the *santur*, which are plucked, and the *josa* or the *rebaba*, which are like the flute and fiddle. When special celebration is called for, Iraqis may beat on small clay drums called *dumbugs*, while making high whooping sounds of exultation.

Education. The authoritarian government of Saddam Hussein and the Baa'th party has made great progress in improving the lives of the Iraqi people. High priority has been given to education: today six universities and twenty-two vocational institutions serve Arabs as well as Kurds and other minorities, and an eighty percent literacy rate has been achieved. During the war with Iran, the government made the difficult decision to exempt students from military service despite manpower shortages at the front.

Similar advances have been made in providing health care in both cities and villages. These developments, along with changing patterns of settlement, have done much to reduce the traditional divisions between Shi'ite and Sunni in Iraqi society. Yet the government continues to be run by a narrow group of leaders, most of whom come from Saddam Hussein's home town of Tekrit in northern Iraq. Many of them are related to each other. This situation, and the destructive conflicts into which the government has drawn the people, mean that the basic division in Iraqi society is no longer between Sunni and Shi'ite, but between the few with political power and the many without it.

For More Information

Docherty, J. P. *Iraq.* Hong Kong: Chelsea House, 1988.

Marr, Phebe. *The Modern History of Iraq.* Boulder, Colorado: Westview Press, 1985.

Metz, Helen Chapin, editor. *Iraq: A Country Study.* Washington, D.C.: Department of the Army, 1990.

ISRAELI JEWS

(is ray' lee jous)

Jewish citizens of the country of Israel.

Population: 4,000,000 (1990 estimate).
Location: Israel.
Languages: Hebrew; English; Arabic.

Geographical Setting

Israel--------

---Occupied
Territory

Egypt   Jordan

The narrow country of Israel lies along the eastern coast of the Mediterranean Sea. At its boundaries are four Arab states: Lebanon to the north, Syria and Jordan to the east, and Egypt to the southwest. About eighty-five percent of Israeli Jews live in cities. Most of the urban centers—for example, Tel Aviv and Haifa—lie along the coastal plains. However, Israel's current capital and long-time spiritual center, Jerusalem, lies inland among the Judean hills. Northern Israel is the site of mountains, fertile valleys, and the freshwater Lake Tiberias (or Sea of Galilee). Running north to south through the country, the river Jordan feeds the lake, then reaches the Dead Sea—so called because evaporation has made it too salty to sustain life. The Jordan River courses through this area between the Dead Sea and Lake Tiberias, dividing territory occupied by Israel (the West Bank) from the country of Jordan. South and west of the Dead Sea stretches the triangular-shaped Negev Desert.

Despite its small size—roughly that of New Jersey in the United States—Israel's climate is variable. The north has temperate weather: hot, dry summers and cool, humid winters (due to mountain snowfall). Farther south arid steppes lead into hot, dry desert. Most fertile is the well-watered region of Galilee in the north, but crops grow even in former swampland (Hula Valley) and, with irrigation, in the Negev Desert.

Historical Background

Diaspora. While Jews have lived in the land now called Israel for about 4,000 years (from pre-Roman times to the present), their supremacy there has been brief. Sometimes outside enemies and sometimes fighting amongst themselves defeated them. Whatever the cause, disputes gnawed at the ancient power of Israel until it disappeared in 71 C.E. (the common era of Christians and Jews). (See HEBREWS for the progress of the people prior to 71.) By this date, Rome's government had crushed a series of Jewish revolts, punishing many survivors by deporting them to foreign lands. This dispersal became an early, though not the first, diaspora (scattering) of Jews away from the sacred ground they believed their God had promised them. A stubborn few remained in the holy land, for centuries a downtrodden minority dependent on the support of fellow believers in Italy, Egypt, and elsewhere. The following takes up the story of the Jews who remained in their Promised Land during the centuries

Settlers in the Negev Desert. *Courtesy of David Tuch.*

Blowing the shofar. *Courtesy of David Tuch.*

of the diaspora, and of those who returned to found the Jewish state of Israel in modern times.

Second revolt. Jewish rebels at the rocky fortress of Masada held on until 71 C.E., when the majority killed themselves rather than surrendering to the Roman forces. Roman control was firmly reestablished, yet the spirit of resistance continued. Several decades later the Roman emperor, Aelius Hadrian (117–138), had no suspicion that trouble was brewing. Declaring there was no need to fear the Jews, Hadrain minted coins that pictured him in a toga raising a kneeling Jew. Meanwhile, Jewish workers stashed away weapons with which to fight the Romans. A group of them were supposed to build these weapons for the Roman empire. Every so often the sly workers would build a weapon improperly so that it would be rejected. They would then sweep the rejects up, quietly repair them, and stash them in mountain caves in preparation for a new revolt. Under the leader Simon bar Kochbah, the Jews finally staged this second major revolt against Rome. Several years of conflict ensued (132–135). As in the first revolt, the Romans prevailed, inflicting harsher punishment on survivors than before. Many more towns were destroyed, and Jerusalem was leveled, then repopulated by Syrians and Arabs. Jews were forbidden entry to the city on pain of death. Trying to wipe out their connection to the whole region, Rome renamed it *Palestine* after another of its peoples, the *Philistines*. Many Jews died in the revolt. Others fled or were sold into slavery (some later to perish in Roman gladiator games). Those remaining in the Promised Land faced new hardships: Roman rulers banned the burial of Jewish corpses and made it unlawful to circumcise a newborn son. So more Jews jammed the seaports, escaping to Egypt, for example. Palestine's Jewish population dropped by half, to an estimated 800,000.

Jews under Christian rule. Conditions for those still in Palestine eased over the next few centuries. Cities took on a new aspect, replete with such things as Roman style marketplaces, baths, and theaters, and so on. Foregoing city life, most Jews kept to their own villages in the countryside and a couple of towns in the Galilee region (Tiberias). Despite this low profile, the period saw vigorous achievement for Jews in and out of the Holy Land. Sages had handed down oral laws by word of mouth for centuries. Now they recorded these laws. The regulations covered every facet of life—birth, marriage, business, war, human relations, and religion. The collective work was called the *Mishnah* and it was so compact that it inspired written commentary on the law. Together the Mishnah and the commentary formed a body of work known as *Talmud*. Not all Jews accepted the oral law. A few centuries later a sect called Karaites formed from Jews who rejected it and restricted themselves to the Bible. However, most Jews accepted the oral law. The Mishnah was completed about 200 C.E., and its value as a binding force cannot be overstated. Whether inside or outside the Holy Land, the Talmud helped Jews remain one people living by one fundamental set of laws.

Meanwhile, Christianity gained popularity in the Roman Empire, becoming Palestine's state religion in the 300s (see CHRISTIANITY IN THE MIDDLE EAST). The Christians centered themselves in the city of Byzantium (Constantinople). They became known as the Christian Byzantines, a group intensely hostile to Jews. These Christians not only blamed Jews for failing to recognize Christ as the Messiah, but also held them collectively responsible for Jesus's crucifixion. Jews became outcasts in the empire's society. They could not eat with Christians, marry Christian women, or own slaves. Since all industry and most farming relied on slaves, this prohibition forced Jews to sell their land and their prosperous weaving enterprises. The Holy Land now became important to Chrisitans as the site of Jesus's birth, life, and death, bringing scores of pilgrims to Palestine. Still forbidden from living in Jerusalem, Jews encountered hostile Christian after hostile Christian in other areas of Palestine. In the face of such difficulties, the Jewish community in the Holy Land continued to dwindle.

Early years of Islamic rule. Only about 250,000 Jews lived in Palestine by the time it was conquered by Muslim armies in 638. Conditions eased under the tolerant Muslim rulers. Jews were allowed to settle in Jerusalem, and some of the refugees could return and reclaim their land. Accepted as a valued part of the Islamic community, Jews from Spain, North Africa, and the Middle East helped create a "golden age" of Islamic civilization. This period, lasting from about 700 to 1100, saw Jews reaching high positions in trade and civil life as scholars, scientists, and artists.

Crusades. From about 1100 to 1300, European Christians launched a series of attempts—called the Crusades—to win and occupy the Holy Land. For 200 years, they established a "Kingdom of Jerusalem," which at first included most of Palestine. On conquering Jerusalem in 1099, the Crusaders slaughtered nearly 40,000 Muslims and Jews who lived there, a beginning that set the tone for the rest of their occupation. Jews throughout Palestine were killed or robbed and exiled by Christian soldiers. Once more they were prohibited from living in Jerusalem. Although small numbers were later allowed to return to the city, Jewish life under the Crusader kingdoms was nearly extinguished. The handful of remaining Jews lived in a few urban centers like Acre, a coastal city with a Talmudic academy that was supported by European Jews.

Ottoman empire. The Muslims gradually drove the Crusaders out of Jerusalem during the 1200s, by which time a visiting rabbi reported only one or two Jewish families living in the holy city. For the next few centuries, once again under Muslim rule, Jews slowly returned to Palestine. There was a notable surge of immigration not only to Palestine but also to other Middle Eastern lands after Jews were expelled from Spain in 1492. They immigrated as traders, peddlers, craftsmen, or farmers. Jewish farming gradually declined in Palestine in the face of burdensome taxes. In fact, life in the Holy Land proved continually difficult: besides taxes and corrupt officials, bandit gangs would attack rural villages and even cities.

In 1517 the Ottoman Turks (see TURKS) added Palestine to their growing empire. The Ottomans welcomed Jews, many of whom were fleeing persecution in Europe. Slowly but steadily the Jewish population in Palestine grew, most of its members involved in weaving and dyeing, shoemaking, or commercial trade. The Galilean city of Safed became the spiritual and commercial center for Palestine Jews in the 1500s. A focal point for the production of textiles and farm goods, the city also attracted religious scholars and mystics. Elsewhere in Palestine, poverty remained widespread, and taxes rose as the Ottoman Empire began its slow decline in the 1700s and 1800s.

Zionism and the Jewish state. Until the mid-1800s, most Jewish immigrants were merchants or rabbis and students of religious tradition. They gravitated to cities such as Safed and Jerusalem. By now the Jewish population in Jerusalem had risen to over 7,000, or nearly half the city's total. Many of its members relied on donations from wealthier Jews who lived abroad but were dedicated to supporting those in Palestine. European Jews were among those who settled in Palestine for religious regions. The purpose changed after the mid-1800s. Now mainly Eastern European Jews began settling with the intention of rekindling nationhood; their goal at first was to establish self-supporting communities. This goal became a growing trend, culminating in a movement called *Zionism*, the drive for a Jewish homeland in Palestine. (Zion is an ancient name for Jerusalem.) In 1896, a European Jew named Theodore Herzl gave clear expression to Zionist thought in his historic book, *The Jewish State.* His activity did not stop there. The following year Herzl founded the World Zionist Organization, then sought support from Western powers and the mass of Jews in the Russian Empire

The Zionist movement gained momentum after World War I, as more Jews moved to Palestine, incurring the resentment of Arabs who lived in the region. In 1920, Palestine passed into the control of the English under a British mandate. Land transactions in which immigrant Jews bought territory occurred under British authority, increasing Arab resentment. They felt animosity not toward the Jews per se, but toward, as they saw it, the invasion of foreigners and their Western ways.

The stream of settlers grew even stronger in the 1930s, when thousands of Jews fled the terror of Nazi Germany. The tide swelled

Praying at the Western Wall. *Courtesy of David Tuch.*

after World War II. Crammed into old freighters and defying a British naval blockade, war refugees flocked to Palestine following Germany's defeat in 1945. A 1947 United Nations proposal to divide the land into an Israeli state and a Palestinian state was not well-received on either side. On May 14, 1948, the British withdrew, and Israel declared itself an independent Jewish nation. It met heated opposition from its Arab neighbors, but the United Nations approved the act. Major world leaders were convinced of the necessity of a Jewish state due to the recent wartime Holocaust. Six million Jews had been massacred in Nazi-occupied Europe during Hitler's attempt to wipe Jews out of existence. Afterwards, the victims took matters into their own hands, making Israel the solution to what was called "the Jewish problem"—the presence of unwanted Jews in other lands. World powers approved of the solution, possibly feeling collective guilt for allowing the horror of the Holocaust to happen.

Arab-Israeli conflict. Six Arab states—Egypt, Syria, Iraq, Jordan, Lebanon, and Saudi Arabia—attacked the new nation. Israeli forces rebuffed the attack, and open warfare ceased in 1949. Nearly 800,000 Arabs fled to neighboring regions, where many continue to live as refugees (see PALESTINIANS). New conflicts erupted in 1967 (the Six Day War) and in 1973 (the Yom Kippur War). Israel's military success was such that it managed to occupy some areas to which Palestinian Arabs had fled: the Gaza Strip in the south, and the West Bank between Jerusalem and the river Jordan. Ever since, conflicts between Israeli Jews and Arabs—especially the displaced Palestinians—have continued. In 1990, Iraq invaded its neighbor Kuwait. The members of the United Nations condemned this action, but Iraq refused to withdraw. Not only Kuwait but also Israel was targeted for battle. Iraqi missiles were hurled at Israel, but the country refrained from retaliating. It instead relied on United Nations forces to prevent the conflict from escalating into a region-wide religious war. Unlike earlier conflicts, this one saw Scud missiles aimed at Israeli housing. The country had to prepare for the eventuality that the weapons might release chemical gas. Therefore, Israelis who had survived World War II's Holocaust, with its deadly gas chambers, bore witness to the painful sight of their grandchildren in gas masks.

Culture Today

Law of return. Roughly eighty-two percent of Israel's population today is Jewish. The country saw five major waves, *aliyot*, of immigration that brought in Jews from 1882 through 1939. By independence in 1948, some sixty-five percent (nearly 500,000) of Israel's Jews were immigrants rather than natives. Some 300,000 more immigrants, war refugees from Europe, arrived over the next three years. In 1950, the Israeli government passed the Law of Return, which decreed automatic citizenship for every arriving Jew who claimed it. The stream of immigrants from Europe and Russia continued. Beginning in the 1950s, it increased due to a growing number of Jews from North Africa and the Middle East. Many of these Jews trace their roots to the period of Islamic rule in Spain (about 750–1250 C.E.). After winning control from the Muslims in 1492, Christian rulers in Spain expelled the Jews. They fled first to Morocco, then to other Muslim lands. These Jews became known as Sephardim, from the medieval Hebrew word (*S'pharad*) for Spain. Those from Europe were, in contrast, called the *Ashkenazim* (from *Ashk'naz*, a medieval Hebrew name for Germany). Strictly speaking, there is a third group called Oriental Jews, meaning Jews from North Africa, the Middle

Jews pray at the remaining retaining wall of the ancient temple in Jerusalem. *Courtesy of David Tuch.*

East, and India. The world tends to lump them together with the Sephardim, however, since they share major rituals and behaviors.

Over time, scores of Sephardim migrated to Israel, gradually outnumbering the Ashkenazim. In 1991, about 16,000 Jews were airlifted from Ethiopia to Israel during Ethiopia's civil war. The balance may change once again. Almost 200,000 Russian Jews arrived in Israel in 1990. Between one and two million are expected by 1995, in which case the Ashkenazim may regain the majority. The Ashkenazim were the early Zionist pioneers and settlers, and they have tended to dominate economic and political life. From them, Israel received a foundation of European culture and strong ties to Western countries like the United States. Sephardim from countries like Morocco, Yemen, and Iran, brought separate cultural traditions into Israeli society. While shared experiences and growing political power integrate them into Israeli society, they maintain certain customs. Syrian-Lebanese synagogues in Israel, for example, feature midnight and early morning singing of holy songs (*Bakashot*), performed in Arab musical styles (*maqamat*).

Food, clothing, and shelter. Israel's foods reflect its cultural diversity; restaurants in Israel offer cuisines from all over the world. Orthodox Jews observe *kashrut*, the ancient dietary laws forbidding foods such as pork and shellfish and certain food combinations (see HEBREWS). Called "kosher," food governed by laws of kashrut is served in all public buildings and many restaurants. (However, not all Israeli Jews observe kashrut strictly; most, in fact, are not Orthodox.) Often, Israelis eat a main meal—roast chicken, for example, at lunch and smaller meals at breakfast and dinner. Either of these meals might include fruits, cheeses, eggs, perhaps some Israeli salad (chopped cucumber, tomatoes, and green onions in olive oil). Specialities are *falafel, humus,* and *tahina.* The meatball-like falafel consists of ground chickpeas, herbs and garlic, deep fried, then served in flat pita bread with lettuce, tomatoes, cucumber, and a spicy sauce. Humus (chickpea dip) and *tahina* (sesame dip) are other favorites.

Most Israelis wear European-style clothing, dressing informally, especially when the weather is hot. On special occasions, Sephardim wear customary ceremonial apparel—for instance, the ornate jewelry of a Yemeni Jewish bridal costume. Some sects have distinctive ways of dress. The Hasidim, members of an ultra-Orthodox sect, wear long side-curls (*peyot*), beards, long black coats, and dark, flat-brimmed hats or fur-trimmed head coverings. Jerusalem has an ultrareligious neighborhood, *Me'a Sh'arim*, whose residents abide so zealously by old customs they might throw stones at cars driven on the sabbath or even at women who break rules by appearing in sleeveless dresses. (In different cities, equally Orthodox neighborhoods exist.) Other exceptions are recently arrived Falashas, Jews from Ethiopia who continue for a time to wear the togalike *shamma*.

In the city, most people live in high-rise apartment buildings, and children often sleep in a small room with bunkbeds. The units are not, however, apartments in the American sense. People own rather than rent them since prices are so high. City units often have a balcony and are practical rather than beautiful. They were built quickly in order to accommodate a rapidly growing population. Elsewhere, a number of Israelis live in *shikunim*, housing developments designed for groups whose members were previously acquainted. Group members might belong to the same profession or ethnic group, or perhaps they immigrated together.

Kibbutzim. The kibbutz (plural, *kibbutzim*) is a collective settlement whose members share ownership of resources. They contribute labor

An Israeli market. *Courtesy of David Tuch.*

in exchange for products that meet their daily needs. The kibbutz was first a collective type of farming settlement (the earliest was founded in 1909). Its families shared a long one-story structure with sleeping rooms, several interspersed restrooms, and a communal kitchen and dining room. Today many kibbutzim are more luxurious. They may have two-room family flats, each with a bathroom and a kitchenette, though there is still the communal dining hall. Other new attractions are a kibbutz library, a gymnasium, cafes, and tennis courts. Instead of farming, most income earned by the present-day kibbutz comes from nonagricultural sources—light industry, work-shops, and guest houses. There may be a plastic or computer factory on the premises, for example. Of course, agriculture still contributes to kibbutz earnings. Some of the most profitable products to raise are citrus fruits, vegetables, and poultry. Much of the farming, how-ever, is now done by hired Arab laborers.

While kibbutzim still wield considerable power in the nation, their membership has declined over the years. Only about three per-cent of Israeli Jews belong to the 270 kibbutzim. A fraction more belong to *moshavim*. Here, instead of one collective family, the people still operate in individual family units. The *moshav* began as a type of smallholders' farming cooperative. Families lived in a single house-hold, and farmed individual plots, but banded together when it came to buying supplies or selling crops. By the late 1980s, the typical moshav also relied largely on Arab farm labor. Its members mean-while took nonfarming jobs outside the moshav.

Family, women, and the military. Immigrants sometimes experience adjustment problems adapting to Israeli customs. Jews from other Middle Eastern lands belonged to extended families. Parents often lived with single children and married sons and their families. How-ever, the small nuclear family predominates in Israel, modeled after the European rather than Middle Eastern family pattern. Marriages are mostly a matter of personal choice, though some ultrareligious Jews still have them arranged. Generally, women have experienced fewer restrictions on their behavior here than in other Middle Eastern or Western lands. They have long participated in civil arenas, such as the Israeli military, where men serve for thirty-six months, women for twenty-four months.

While women share in most freedoms and responsibilities, reli-gion still restricts them. Customarily, the Jewish woman enjoys an honored but different-from-the-men position in rituals. This tradition is upheld today in the division of visitors to the Western (once called Wailing) Wall, the part of King Herod's temple that still stands. A fence divides women from men here, just as they are divided in Israeli synagogues. At thirteen, Jewish boys pass into adulthood by performing their bar mitzvah, and some choose to do so at the Wall. At all ages, Jews participate in the custom of wedging private prayers into cracks in the Wall, similar to the tradition of throwing a coin in a fountain.

Religion. Because it is so closely bound up in national and ethnic identity, religion plays a powerful and complex role in Israeli society. Sabbath, which falls on Friday night and Saturday, is the holiest day in the Jewish week. Business stops, while schools and shops also close on religious holidays, such as Passover. Beyond public days of work stoppage, the state of Israel declares its ties to the Jewish religion in other ways. Bible verses appear on postage stamps, and the rabbi (the Jewish religious authority) governs aspects of Israeli life. Finally, rabbinical courts rule on religious and family issues. A council of rabbis has sole authority in marriage matters. Orthodox (strictly observant) Judaism is the only kind officially approved in Israel. However, other forms of the religion (see JUDAISM IN THE MIDDLE EAST) have recently taken root in the country. Israel had nearly 7,000 synagogues by 1989, almost all of them Orthodox. About forty Conservative and

Outdoor markets are common throughout the Middle East. *Courtesy of David Tuch.*

fifteen Reform congregations had appeared in the country, but were not yet officially recognized by its religious leaders.

Religious leaders are highly influential in the country. Yet many of today's Israeli Jews have little if any contact with organized religious life. They are described as secular (nonreligious) or ethnic Jews who identify with the history and spirit rather than the religion of the people. The tension between the secular and the religious remains strong among Israeli Jews and is evident even in government.

Government. Israel's government includes a powerful prime minister and cabinet, a mainly ceremonial president, and a one-chamber parliament (the Knesset). The people elect parties rather than individuals to this parliament. Because voters cast their ballot for a party (with its list of candidates) rather than a person, the parties play the crucial role in politics. In 1984, for example, twenty-six parties competed in the election; only fifteen won seats in the Knesset.

The high number of parties means that since independence no single party has achieved an outright majority. Therefore, each gov-

An Israeli wedding. *Courtesy of David Tuch.*

ernment has in fact been a coalition, or alliance, of different parties. The liberal Labor Party and conservative Likud Party have each dominated at times. But both of these large parties have often been so equally balanced that small parties can exert great influence on government by siding with one or the other. Agudat Israel, for example, is an ultra-Orthodox party whose aim is to have the state of Israel undertake no action unless it is in keeping with Jewish law as set down in the Bible, Talmud, and later rabbinic codes. Shifting its support from the Labor to Likud Party in 1977, it helped the Likud Party come to power. In return, Agudat Israel was promised some concessions to its religious goals.

Language and education. About eighty percent of Israeli Jews speak Hebrew as their primary language. That they do so is primarily the result of one man's efforts. In the 1880s, a Lithuanian Zionist scholar named Eleizer Ben-Yehuda began expanding the Hebrew vocabulary of the Old Testament for use as a spoken tongue. Using ancient Hebrew roots, he built a written language of about 8,000 words into a spoken one that today includes some 50,000 words. Israel's 800,000 Arabs speak Arabic and Hebrew, as do many Jews of Sephardic background. English is also common, and many signs appear in all three languages.

Israelis choose from two types of public education: state schools and religious state schools. While both types teach the Bible, state schools deal for the most part with subjects such as Hebrew, history, sciences, and English; religious schools train students in Orthodox beliefs. Also, there are kibbutz schools and private religious schools, or *yeshivoth*, devoted to the study of Talmud.

Arts and recreation. In keeping with their rich heritage, Israeli Jews enjoy a lively and varied cultural life. The fine arts, dance, theatre, and movies are all popular, but Israel's classical music takes center stage. With many first-rate performers to entice them, Israelis go to more concerts than most other national groups. The small country has six major orchestras, including the world-renowned Israel Philharmonic. Famous soloists include violinists Yitzhak Perlman, Pinchas Zukerman, Isaac Stern, and pianist-conductor Danile Barenboim. Among Israeli writers, Chaim Bialik (1873–1934) was first to win renown for Hebrew poetry in the twentieth century and became the national poet. Celebrated in recent times is Yehuda Amichai (1924–). In the final verse of his poem "Jews in the Land of Israel,"

Amichai considers his generation's contribution (Bargad and Chyet 1986, p. 93).

> Shed blood is not tree roots,
> but it's the closest to them
> that we can come.

Also writing in Hebrew, the novelist Shmuel Agnon (1888–1970) won the 1966 Nobel Prize for Literature. Younger novelists include Amos Oz (1939–) and A. B. Yehoshua (1936–).

Israeli Jews participate in various sports, from skiing on Mount Hermon to the Maccabee Games' track events. Most avid, though, is the people's passion for soccer, in which sport players participate in national and international competitions.

Past and future. Jews have a longer recorded history than many other peoples, yet Israel is a young country whose first native generation has barely reached middle age. They carry the past into the future, as the physical evidence of times long gone (the Wall, Masada) surrounds them always. And they have added new physical evidence of recent times, building *Yad Vashem*, the memorial center to Jews who perished in the Holocaust and helpful Gentiles who tried to rescue Jews.

Israeli Jews carry these past legacies with them in facing present problems. Issues that embroil them in world controversy are equally

Learning to blow the shofar. *Courtesy of David Tuch.*

divisive among the people themselves. The major problem remains the plight of the Palestinians. As sympathetic Israelis point out, in their stateless situation the Palestinians resemble Jews of earlier times. For over twenty years, the occupied West Bank has been home to a large number of Palestinians (now nearly one-and-a-half million) with no political rights. Since 1987, these impoverished Arabs have carried on an ongoing protest called the *intifada*. Groups of ultranationalist Jews have meanwhile established settlements in the West Bank. Taking an opposite stand, the Jewish group Peace Now has protested in favor of negotiating a solution to the problem. Some of the country's Jews believe Israel should leave the West Bank, while others hold that Israel should absorb it completely. They all are dedicated to Israel's survival.

For More Information

Bargad, Warren and Chyet, Stanley F. *Israeli Poetry: A Contemporary Anthology.* Bloomington: Indiana University Press, 1988.

Keller, Werner. *Diaspora: The Post-Biblical History of the Jews.* New York: Harcourt, Brace & World, 1966.

Library of Nations: Israel. Amsterdam: Time-Life Books, 1986.

Metz, Helen Chapin, editor. *Israel: A Country Study.* Washington, D.C.: U.S. Government Printing Office, 1990.

Sachar, Howard. *A History of Israel.* 2 volumes. New York: Oxford University Press, 1976 and 1987.

Schenker, Hillel. "Letter from Israel," *The Nation.* January 21, 1991, pp. 45–49.

Vesilind, Prit J. "Searching for the Center: Israel," *National Geographic.* July 1985, pp. 2–38.

JORDANIANS

(jor day′ nee uns)

People of Jordan whose origins are Palestinian or Bedouin.

Population: 3,900,000 (1988 estimate).
Location: The Hashemite Kingdom of Jordan; Israeli-occupied territory of the West Bank.
Language: Arabic.

Geographical Setting

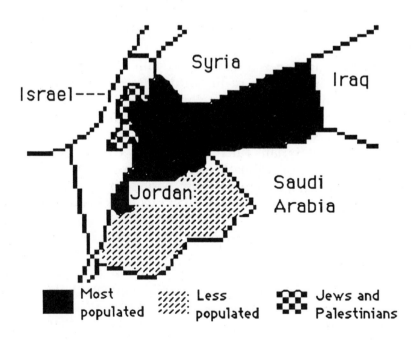

Jordan is a country in the heart of the Arab world, bordered by Israel, Syria, Iraq, and Saudi Arabia. It is landlocked except for a fifteen-mile coastline at Aqaba, a port on the Red Sea. Most of Jordan is a plateau rising from 2,000 to 3,000 feet above sea level. This plateau extends into Saudi Arabia and Syria so that there are no natural geographic features marking the boundaries of the three countries. The Rift Valley, marking the boundary between two continental plates, also forms the border between Israel and Jordan on the west side of the fertile Jordan River Valley. As this Rift Valley descends to 1,300 feet below sea level at the Dead Sea, temperatures and landscape become harsh. The major river of the region is the Jordan, which forms part of the frontier between Israel and Jordan, stretching for 156 miles to empty into the Dead Sea. Much of Jordan, especially in the south, is desert, with high sand dunes and a few oases.

Strong winds visit Jordan at some times of the year. The *khamsin*, a strong, dry, south or southwest wind comes around May and then again in September. Blowing for only a day or two at a time, this wind is still strong enough to destroy crops and make human life uncomfortable. In the summer, wind from the north or northwest, the *shamal*, lasts for longer periods of time and brings higher temperatures.

Historical Background

Ancient times. Jordan is a new nation with an ancient past. Before 2,000 B.C., the inhabitants of the Jordan River Valley carried on a brisk trade with Egypt, and developed agricultural skills, arts and crafts, mythology, religion, and a syllabic script. During the sixth century B.C. an Arabian tribe called the Nabateans established a capital at Petra while Syrians ruled in the north. Under Syrian rule, the great ancient cities of Rabbath Ammon (now Amman) and Gerasa (now Jerash) began. Except for brief periods in the fifth and sixth centuries A.D. when the land was ruled by Greeks and Romans, and again in the eleventh century when the country was controlled by Crusaders, the region remained part of the Islamic Empire ruled from Egypt.

The Ottoman Empire. In 1516, the land known in the twentieth century as Transjordan, but then as part of greater Syria, was absorbed into the Ottoman Empire, where it endured for more than 400 years. By the 18th century, nearly neglected by the central government, the area experienced some intertribal wars and raids from Arabia, as well as famine and epidemics that in some places resulted from swamplike insect-breeding grounds along the river.

Arab revolt. The history of modern Jordan grew out of Arab desires to be free of the Ottoman rule. During World War I, when Turkey was allied with Germany, Arabs in the empire rebelled. British forces who encouraged the rebellion, then joined the Arab forces to occupy Palestine. In 1920, the League of Nations placed Palestine under British administration, and in 1921 Britain defined a governmental unit called Transjordan, which is today that part of Jordan to the east of the river, thereby inventing new kingdoms. Making this an emirate, the British delegated authority to Amir Abdullah of the Hashemite family. In 1928, this authority and the British signed a new agreement giving Amir Abdullah even greater control over the country.

Petra, an ancient city in Jordan, was made famous by the filming of _Indiana Jones and the Last Crusade._ _Courtesy of the University Museum, University of Pennsylvania._

Arab-Israeli War. By the time Britain left the region in 1948, Jewish leaders had begun to establish the state of Israel in the area of the old country of Palestine. Immediately Arab forces opposed the creation of this state. The Transjordanian army, called the Arab Legion, seized the West Bank, and in 1950 it was annexed by Amir Abdullah. The annexation was recognized by only Britain and Pakistan. In 1951, Amir Abdullah was assassinated in Jerusalem by people who objected to his plans for a Greater Syria. Amir Abdullah's eldest son, Talal, took governmental control, but a year later yielded his rule to his son, Hussein ibn Talal.

Palestinian refugees. During the first Arab-Israeli war in 1948 more than 700,000 Palestinian refugees from within Israel fled to the West Bank, where refugee camps had been established by the United Nations. Jordan offered these refugees automatic citizenship and thousands entered Jordanian society. Thousands more remained in the camps, anticipating the breakup of Israel. When that failed to materialize, many Palestinians found residence in other countries throughout the Arab world.

The Six-Day War. In 1967, tensions between Israel and its Arab neighbors resulted in a brief war. Lasting six days, this battle resulted in the Arab loss of the West Bank and Jerusalem, and in an additional 400,000 refugees rushing to Jordan. These refugees began a guerrilla movement against the Israelis that endangered Jordan. The Jordanian army was instructed to drive the guerrilla activists from the country, a directive that alienated King Hussein from his Arab neighbors for several years.

Jordan and the Palestine Liberation Organization. Created in Egypt in 1964, the PLO was an umbrella group for the various guerrilla movements directed against Israel and for nationalist movements wanting to create a Palestinian state. By 1979, King Hussein and the PLO were on good terms, and in 1985 a Jordan-PLO peace initiative proposed a confederated state of Jordan and Palestine—a proposal that came to nothing. But in 1986, King Hussein severed ties with the PLO when it refused to participate in an international peace conference in response to an Israeli reluctance to participate.

The Gulf War. Again trapped between Iraq and other world governments that objected to Iraqi occupation of Kuwait, King Hussein at first participated in the United Nations embargo of Iraq. Nevertheless, King Hussein officially condemned the war against its Arab neighbor, and was supported in this action by most Jordanians.

Culture Today

Change. Never a strong, unified society, the people of Jordan have experienced great pressures in the last three decades, resulting in a loss of some tendencies and the emergence of new ones. Until the late 1940s, the Transjordanian economy was based on agriculture and the nomadic herding of livestock.

Villagers and nomads. Most of the citizens of the new country of Jordan in the 1960s lived in small villages of 400-500 people. The members of the villages were descendants of a common distant ancestor organized into a unit called the *hamula*. Since the people of that time prided themselves on their hospitality, each hamula provided a guest house for entertaining visitors. Within the hamula, several brothers and their families formed a closer unit, the *luzum*. This smaller unit was bound by common farming interests and an obligation growing out of a system that emphasized family honor. Honor of one's family was considered more important than self-advancement. A shadow cast on the honor of any member of the family demanded retribution. Settlements in the form of truce money were the duties of the luzum. This same strong family tradition existed among nomads, who earned a livelihood by herding camels, goats, and sheep rather than by farming.

Under the new king, the nomadic peoples began to supplement their income by serving in the army—an occupation in keeping with their traditions of raiding and battling one another. King Hussein encouraged this by openly courting the nomads. In the 1950s, he frequently visited them in their tent settlements for conferences and advice.

In the 1950s and 1960s, most Jordanians lived in small earth and straw or stone houses, and farmed nearby plots, raising wheat, barley, and other food products. Perhaps one-tenth of the population were Bedouins who herded animals, lived in tents, and moved from one feeding ground to another. There were no large cities in Transjordan. Amman, the largest population center, had a population of fewer than 50,000.

In this society, the tenets of Islam were strong, as were family bonds, patriarchal dominance, and respect for advancement in wealth, particularly if that wealth was benevolently used. It was a double society—men and women were mostly separate except in the home. Women visited other women and gathered at water holes or wells to do family chores and talk. While in many places the wells have been replaced by more efficient water systems, women still gather to chat and share chores. Men gathered in the village coffee shop or guest house to talk and plan. With little opportunity to meet socially, young men and women depended on their families to set up marriages. Women were expected to bear children, nurture the family, and manage household affairs. For men, divorce from an unhappy marriage was easy; for women, a bit more difficult. Males dominated, and in the event of a family break, the children went with their father.

Beginnings of change. Following the 1948 Arab-Israeli War, the now-Arab West Bank became the source of both tourist and agricultural income. The service industry—an economic category that includes trade, restaurants, hotel, transport, finance, and social and personal services—quickly surpassed agriculture as the dominant industry. But the growth of the population required foreign aid throughout the 1950s and 1960s, aid that continues in Jordan in the 1990s. The city of Amman grew rapidly. Today it is the home of more than 1,000,000 people, and two other cities, Irbid and Zarqa have populations of more than 400,000.

Economic change. The loss of the West Bank after the 1967 war was a crushing blow to Jordan's economy and society, but the country quickly set out on the path of economic recovery. The nation's productivity had multiplied nearly tenfold by 1984. Tourism in Jordan grew to surpass the 1967 level, and agriculture once again became a priority. Vast irrigation facilities were developed in the Jordan Valley.

Despite this progress, Jordan remains dependent on foreign aid. Jordan has received aid from the United States, Saudi Arabia and other Gulf states, Great Britain, West Germany, and Japan.

Influence of Palestinians. But the influx of Palestinians, first from the newly formed country of Israel, then from the Gaza Strip, and later from other regions occupied by Israel, forced changes in the social lives of the Jordanians. These people were, for the most part, more exposed to European ideas and had more formal education than their hosts. They came in such numbers that the traditional village welcomes were overwhelmed. Coffeehouses for Jordanians and guests alike began to replace the traditional guest house. Palestinians were city dwellers, and the older small home-craft industries began to give way to larger enterprises. Seeing this, villagers began to move to the cities in search of both education and jobs.

At first, these villagers organized the hamula in a quarter of the city and kept their family identity and the leadership of senior men in the family. But as young men and women began to be more formally educated and found urban jobs (the government of Jordan is the single largest employer), their economic ties to the older generation began to fade, and their willingness to take direction from the eldest family male eroded.

Meanwhile, Palestinian refugees grew in number so that they now form about sixty percent of the population. While granted full Jordanian citizenship, these people have tended to consider themselves a separate society waiting to gain their own homeland. While waiting, some Palestinians have taken important roles in business, education, and government, as others live in poverty in refugee camps—at first in large tent cities but later in shantytowns of corrugated metal, stone, and asbestos houses. The influence of the Palestinians has resulted in greater movement by Jordanian villagers and nomads to the cities, and in an increased interest in formal education.

Today, Jordan is a divided society—Jordanian and Palestinian—but moving toward common ideals and practices of urbanism and intellectual development.

Religion. In the seventh century, Muslims split into two groups over the issue of succession to the prophet Muhammad. The Sunnis held to the doctrine of selection by consensus while the Shi'ites believed in rule by divine right. More than fifty percent of the Muslim people of Jordan profess allegiance to the Sunni sect of Islam. Shi'ites represent a minority of the population.

The Jordanian constitution grants freedom of religious belief and shelters the eight percent of the people who are Christians or other minorities. Nevertheless, Islam is the pervasive force, and the constitution demands that the king be Muslim and a son of Muslims. Muslim institutions receive governmental support. While adherents to the Muslim tenets, most Jordanians have not experienced the religious fundamentalism seen in countries such as Iran.

Family life. With little ethnic or religious diversity, and with national identity still a developing concept, a Jordanian's identity still derives mostly from his or her family. In the traditional Jordanian family, several generations live together as an extended family, share financial resources, aid and protect one another, and accept the discipline of the patriarchal head. Marriages in village or rural populations are still arranged by one's elders. Often a cousin is the partner of choice in order to preserve family property rights, and also because the cousin is a familiar male in places where a woman's association with males might be limited.

Family reputation is more important than individual achievement in determining a Jordanian's status. Honor is thought to be lost through the improper behavior of one's sisters and daughters; a wife's behavior reflects not on her husband but on her father and brother. Improper behavior is sometimes unavoidable; for example, a man who makes advances to a woman may bring dishonor to her family, as well as himself, even if she has done nothing to encourage him.

Men traditionally enjoy more rights and privileges than women. Women are expected to defer to their husbands and to avoid public gathering places and social contacts with men. On the other hand, men are expected to provide for the family and to assist in the instruction of the children. The roles of men and women vary with their economic status. Poor urban women, for example, may find contact with men necessary as they find work outside the home. And nomadic women frequently find it necessary to work with their husbands and other men in caring for the animals.

Clothing. The Palestinians brought with them an interest in European-style clothes and this has gained some acceptance among the Jordanians. The older dress in the desert area of the south was the *burnoose*, a long, loosely fit garment that covered nearly the entire body and that included a hood or a scarflike head-covering held in place by a cloth band used as a face-covering for protection against the sand. This immensely practical garment for desert wear is still seen in cities, villages, and the few remaining nomadic settlements and shares acceptance in the urban society, where men go to work in suits and ties just as their European counterparts.

Forces affecting family unity. Relations within the family are changing, especially among the urban educated. Many young people prefer to establish their own households rather than live with their parents.

They now marry later in life and are not so closely chaperoned or segregated. Social security has reduced the dependence of the elderly on their children and so has begun to erode the structure of the extended family.

The role of women is also changing. One major reason has been the influx of Palestinians, who come from a Mediterranean area where Western ideas have been present for a longer period and have found more ready acceptance. Another reason has been the growth of the urban areas, which are increasingly exposed to views from the outside world as a result of tourism and international trade.

Government policy encouraging education for girls as well as boys has resulted in greater preparation for jobs outside the family. Women now work in nearly all government offices, in private commercial firms, in hospitals, as teachers, and as radio and television directors and announcers. Each year more daycare centers are created to assist the growing number of working women.

For More Information

Harris, George. *Jordan: Its People, Its Society, Its Culture.* New Haven, Connecticut: Hraf Press, 1958.

Nyrop, Richard, editor. *Jordan: A Country Study.* Washington, D.C.: American University Press, 1980.

Sinai, Anne, and Allen Pollack, editors. *The Hashemite Kingdom of Jordan and the West Bank.* Washington, D.C.: American Academic Association for Peace in the Middle East, 1977.

KURDS
(curds)

Ancestors of once-nomadic peoples living in the mountain regions
of northern Turkey, Iraq, and Iran.

Population: 5,000,000 (1985 estimate; this is an approximation since
relationships between Kurds and the governments of the countries
in which they live discourage formal and accurate population counts.)
Location: Kurdistan, an area of mountainous land stretching from
northern Turkey to the Soviet Union.
Language: Kurdish, an Indo-European language.

Geographical Setting

The Kurdish homeland lies in the mountains and foothills of the
northern part of the Middle East, following the sweeping arc of the
Taurus Mountains through Turkey then continuing the arc south of
the Zagros Mountains through Syria and Iraq before bridging the
Zagros range into Iran and the Soviet Union. For centuries, the Kurds
have been nomadic herders in these rugged mountains and foothills
where the altitudes average 6,000 feet. Summer heat and winter cold
are equally intense in this region, making the land desertlike in summer and frozen in winter. Although landlocked, the region is cut by
many streams, including the headwaters of the Tigris and Euphrates
rivers. The river valleys provide suitable land for planting. In recent
years oil resources have been developed in Kurdistan and this remains the area's primary resource other than pastureland and farmland.

Historical Background

Early history. The history of the Kurds is uncertain. However, before
1000 B.C. bands of nomadic herders known as Gutu lived in the

Kurdistan

mountains of the Middle East. In the years just after 1000 B.C. the land of the Gutu was part of Assyria. An independent people, the Gutu seem to have had their own governments within the country. The Gutu formed a union with the Medes sometime after the fall of the Assyrian capital of Ninevah in 612 B.C. These apparent ancestors of the present-day Kurds possessed a tradition of resistance to rule by other peoples. They resisted control by Macedonians, Parthians, and Sassanians. However, when not disputing outside rule, these tribesmen banded together in small units and fought among themselves.

Muslims. The Kurds became associated with Iranian tribes in the sixth and seventh centuries A.D. They came into frequent conflicts with their Arab neighbors until subdued by the forces of the caliph of Baghdad in the ninth century. Persuaded to follow the Muslim faith, the Kurds rose to their greatest power in the twelfth century. On a wave of enthusiasm to unify and spread the teachings of Muhammad following the Christian Crusades, a Kurdish officer in the

Syrian army, Saladin, took power in Egypt, then absorbed Syria under his rule.

Following the encounters with Arabs, the Zagros Mountain region was invaded unsuccessfully by Mongols in the thirteenth century, and then by the Turks and Persians in the sixteenth century. While the two powers fought for nearly half a century for control of the land, bands of Kurds herded cattle, horses, sheep, and goats throughout the mountains. Eventually, the Ottomans (Turks) claimed the land and governed it until the mid-nineteenth century. In 1826, when the Ottoman Empire was beginning to fade, the government turned on the Kurds in a quarter-century of battles and resistance aimed at

At one time Kurdish men moved about heavily armed.
Courtesy of the University Museum, University of Pennsylvania.

gaining greater power for the Ottomans. The result was the loss of much of the Kurdish land.

Struggle for independence. During the first World War, the Kurds joined their Turkish antagonists to ensure protection from the Soviet Union. In 1918, President Woodrow Wilson, proponent of the League of Nations, announced a plan for peace in the area that included self-determination for peoples in the Ottoman Empire so that each ethnic group could choose its own state. By 1920, the Empire had shriveled so that its major region of control was Turkey, in which a large part of Kurdistan lay. Turkey, in the Treaty of Sevres agreed to a split of the country into protectorates governed by Britain and France. However, Turkey had long been at odds with Greece over Greek claims to Turkish land. Led by Mustafa Kemal, the Turks initiated a Turkish War of Independence that united Turkey and ended Kurdish hopes of self-rule for the many Kurds living in Turkey.

Following this war, the Treaty of Lausanne defined boundaries in the Middle East. Under this treaty, a League of Nations delegation visited the area and recommended that it become a separate state. But Turkey rebelled and Kurdistan was divided among Turkey, Iran, Iraq, and Syria. The Kurds lost their national rights to the other governments. A year later, Turkey attempted to dissolve Kurdish culture by banning the Kurdish language in schools, broadcasts, and publications. The Kurds reacted so violently to this action that for forty years (1925-1965) no foreigners were allowed to visit this area, which Turkey had designated a military emergency. Similar battles for freedom took place in Iran and Iraq.

Kurdistan since World War II. Again in 1945, some Kurds rebelled, this time in Iran. Uniting with others from the Soviet Union, the Kurds declared independence and established their base at Mahabad, Iran. The Iranian government rallied and regained the land. The movement's leaders were imprisoned or killed. In 1958, opportunity seemed to strike again, this time in Iraq. A liberal Iraqi government encouraged free interaction among the peoples there. The Kurdish leader Mustafa Barzani, who had fled the country, was welcomed back, and Kurdish publications were permitted. However, the Kurds were thwarted once more when General al Kassem took control of Iraq. The issue was revived in 1961 when Mustafa Barzani led a war for democracy in Iraq. The Kurds were met with heavy bombardment, including napalm bombs that destroyed 1,000 Kurdish villages along with their crops and herds. Supported by the Soviet Union, Iran, and the United States, the Kurds persisted and finally signed an agreement with the Iraqi government granting Kurdish autonomy. Iraq chose to define this agreement in its own favor. The vice president of Iraq, Saddam Hussein, signed an agreement with the Shah of Iran under which the Shah agreed to ban sales of weapons to the Kurds. Iraq then destroyed more Kurdish villages and eliminated Kurdish rights.

The struggle for Kurdish independence continues. In 1991, following a disastrous attempt by Iraq to control its neighbor, Kuwait, the Kurds again revolted against a weakened central government.

Culture Today

Social organization. Early Kurds lived a nomadic lifestyle, migrating in groups that were really extended families to herd their cattle in various places depending on the seasons. Groups of related households, or *khels*, traveled together and set up leadership by a senior family member, the *agha*. Each Kurd was extremely loyal to the agha. Thus, the family became the basic social organization among the Kurds.

Several khels formed a *tira*, which was still an extended family descended from a common ancestor. The tira was large enough to be the most important political unit, determining both land rights and usage. Several tira formed an *ashiaret*. Beginning in the sixteenth century and gaining strength under British influence, Kurdish property began to come under private ownership. The aghas were encouraged to register land in their own names. The result was a settling of the Kurds in more permanent villages and a change from dependence on herds to planting and harvesting crops.

Shelter. Nomadic Kurds live in tents, usually of blackened hides, which they cluster together with others of their extended family. Kurdish villagers live in houses generally made of mud or cement with wooden poles across the top as rafters for the roofs. The roofs are wooden, serving as sleeping areas in the hot summers. These homes are generally small, but include rooms for cattle, and a courtyard. Some of the homes include underground living quarters, which the residents use in winter to escape the intense cold. In the mountains the homes are clustered so tightly in a village that people at higher elevations could use their lower neighbor's roof as additional space. A central pond or well provides water for the village.

Those Kurds who leave the villages to find work in the industrial cities of the Middle East often find themselves in shantytowns on the outskirts with no more freedom or facilities than in the village. The development of oil resources in Kurdish territory has resulted in the growth of some communities into moderately sized cities. The Kurdish city of Kirkuk in northern Iraq, for example, now houses 200,000 people. In these towns, homes vary as in most large communities, with larger homes for wealthier residents scattered through the smaller ones.

Clothing. Kurdish women do not wear the veil and enjoy considerable freedom, working and interacting socially with men, for example. However, they are not encouraged to participate in political activities. Preparing food and clothing, and bringing water to the home are part of the woman's duties. Men build the houses, and take care of the animals—sheep, goats, oxen, and horses. All the villagers help with the planting. Dress varies among the Kurdish women; in some areas, bright colors are favored, and in others, plain dress is preferred. Men dress in baggy pants bound at the ankles, along with a tunic, vest, and cumberbund. A brightly colored turban or yellow fur cap and, in traditional dress, a curved dagger and a rifle complete the dress. Even though most Kurds today wear European-style clothing with knit hats and heavy sweaters where the weather warrants them, the traditional costume is an important symbol of Kurdish unity, as is the appearance of fierceness. Among the nomadic Kurds, this is often accomplished by shaving the head and growing a heavy mustache. Today, however, many Kurds in the larger communities prefer Western-style clothing or dress similar to their Arab neighbors.

Arts. Records indicate that Kurdish literature first appeared in the seventh century. Poetry was a popular means of expression, and many great Persian poets were translated into the Kurdish language. There is a rich oral tradition, often in the form of epic poetry known as *lawj*. This poetry is often recited from memory in town cafes or meeting rooms. The poetry often describes an adventure in love or battle.

Kurds have also made important contributions to music. Ibrahim Mawsili founded the first Muslim Conservatory after introducing

Kurdish music to the ruler's court in the eighth century. Before that, music had been prohibited under Islamic law.

Religion. The Kurds are Muslims, most of them of the Sunni sect. In most places they are devout followers of Muhammad. Communal performance of rituals are important in keeping the religious tenets foremost in village life. For example, all villagers pray together, kneeling in the direction of Mecca. But in some of the more remote Kurdish regions, Islam has been blended with a belief that a presence of God is always in existence in the community. This results in adoration or near-veneration of local heroes as well as the Muslim prophets.

Conclusion. The Kurds remain voiceless in their homelands, avoided or persecuted by the rulers of the various nations in which they live, often at war with these nations, and avoided by other world powers who feel the situation is too sensitive for their involvement. Following Iraq's unsuccessful war to control Kuwait, Kurds joined in a rebellion to overthrow the Iraqi government. Failing in this attempt, two or three million Kurds fled to the mountains near the borders of Turkey and Iran, countries where the added population is not wanted. Here the Kurds lived in tents provided by the United Nations. In these makeshift camps, unsanitary conditions and a lack of food caused as many as 1,000 deaths each day.

For More Information

Chaliand, Gerard, editor. *People without a Country: The Kurds and Kurdistan.* London: Zed Press, 1980.

Kinnane, Derk. *The Kurds and Kurdistan.* London: Oxford University Press, 1970.

Pelletiere, Stephen C. *The Kurds: An Unstable Element in the Gulf.* Boulder, Colorado: Westview Press, 1984.

LEBANESE

(leb uh neez′)

People of Lebanon; Muslims and Christians who were largely rural villagers before 1970.

Population: 2,800,000 (1988 estimate).
Location: Lebanon.
Language: Arabic.

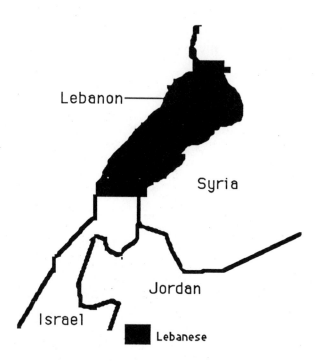

Geographical Setting

The country of the Lebanese is a small triangular area bordered by Syria in the north and east, by Israel in the south, and by the Mediterranean Sea in the west. Beyond Lebanon's rocky and steep coastline, its interior is dominated by two mountain ranges that run parallel to the Mediterranean coast. Closest to the coast are the Lebanon Mountains, whose highest peak is 11,000-foot Al-Qurnat-al Sawda. A central plain, the Bekaa, separates this range from the Anti-Lebanon Mountains. The two ranges meet at the border with Syria and Israel in the south at 9,000-foot Mt. Hermon. The coastal area is heavily cultivated with fruit and vegetable crops. The Bekaa Valley, shielded from the Mediterranean by the Lebanon range, is the main agricultural area and is watered by the Orontes River in the north and the Litani River in the south. The high peaks are snow-covered throughout most of the year and forested. Lebanon has been known throughout history for its cedar trees, and now for its ski resorts and temperate climate. The Mediterranean temperature averages ninety degrees Fahrenheit in summer and in the mid-fifties in winter. During the fall and spring, a hot wind called the khamsin blows in from the Egyptian desert, and in the winter a cold north wind blows from across Europe.

Historical Background

Ancient history. In antiquity Lebanon was inhabited by a seafaring Semitic people related to the Canaanites, who were then located along the coast. The Canaanites came to be identified as Phoenicians, traders who inhabited a series of independent city-states along the coast. These people identified themselves according to their city of origin and referred to the land as Lubnan (Lebanon).

Phoenicians. The Phoenicians became famous as the inventors of the modern alphabet, but they were also known as navigators and explorers who brought their business skills and knowledge to Europe. Although Lebanon was conquered by many foreign rulers throughout its history, the tradition of commercial trade established by the early Phoenicians continued into the twentieth century.

Traders. Since before 1500 B.C., the Phoenicians traded with the Egyptians, each independent Phoenician city-state earning a reputation for its own specialty. The Phoenician cities provided Egypt with lumber, wines, and olive oil. In return they imported gold and other precious raw materials from the Nile Valley. Tyre and Sidon were famous port cities and, along with Byblos and Berytus (now Beirut), were trade and religious centers. Commerce made these cities prosperous, but commercial competition also prevented them from uniting into a strong nation. As a result the Phoenicians fell easy prey to foreign domination and their culture was gradually absorbed into other societies. Phoenician trade declined when Egypt was invaded by nomadic Hyksos people who dominated that country as well as Phoenicia. Later, when the Egyptians recaptured Syria, the Phoenician city-states became part of the Egyptian Empire.

Independence. Around the twelfth century B.C., the region of Lebanon gained its independence and the Phoenicians flourished, growing again in trade, shipbuilding, and navigation. They became manufacturers, producing silk and other fine textiles, metalware, and glass, and trading these and cedar to other Mediterranean cultures. Their navigation took them around Africa, and led them to establish port cities on the islands of Cyprus, Rhodes, and Crete and on the coast of North Africa. During this period, Phoenicians developed the alphabet.

Assyrians. Lebanon fell to Assyrian conquerors in the ninth century B.C. The city-states were destroyed and their inhabitants enslaved. In the sixth century, the Babylonians conquered Assyria and then were, in turn, overtaken by the Persians (538 B.C.). Alexander the Great, a Macedonian leader, defeated the Persians, and the area that is now Lebanon and Syria was assigned to the Seleucid family, who continued to rule after Alexander's death in 323 B.C.

Arabs. Syria and Lebanon became part of the Roman Empire in 64 B.C. and the cities grew again, but the Phoenicians began to lose their cultural identity. Cities began to look like Roman cities. and were introduced to Christianity when it became the state religion in A.D. 313. A Christian sect, the Maronites, established a community in the mountains of Lebanon in the fifth century, (see MARONITES). However, when the Christian center at Constantinople began to waver, Arab armies invaded the region of the early Phoenicians (now known as Syrians) and, following the death of Muhammad, brought the Islamic religion to Lebanon.

Arabic rule continued until 1085 under dynasties from Egypt—the Abbasids and Fatimids. Their indifferent rule left Lebanon divided and in disarray, and enabled various Christian sects to develop strong communities. The Maronites left the upper valley of the Orontes River and settled in the Qadisha Valley in the northern sector of the Lebanon Mountains. Other Christians—Greek Orthodox, Melchites, and Catholics—also settled in this era. Another group, the Druze, an Islamic sect originating in Egypt, converted some of the people of Greater Syria (see DRUZE). Maronites, and Druze became the major religious groups of Lebanon.

During the crusades, which began in 1096, European crusaders took power in most of Lebanon and ruled it until 1291. The crusaders, encouraged by the Maronites, helped build a strong Roman Catholic presence in the area and eventually a long French interest in the region that began in the sixteenth century. About this same time, Shi'ite Muslims from Syria, Iraq, and Arabia migrated to the area that is now Lebanon and settled in the north Bekaa Valley and in the mountains northeast of Beirut.

The Ottomans. Eventually the crusaders were defeated by Saladin, ruler of Egypt, and his successor, who ruled Lebanon and Syria into the sixteenth century. They were driven out by Ottomans, an Islamic Sunni group, who added Greater Syria (Syrian and Lebanon) to the great Ottoman Empire. Allowing Lebanon some freedom of self-government, the Ottomans ruled until 1918. The indirect rule, however, encouraged two prominent Druze families, the Maans and the Shihabs, to control Lebanon. In 1593, Fakhr al-Din, a member of the Maan family, emerged as a strong leader and unified Lebanon's assorted religious groups. When the Ottomans discovered that he was pushing for independence, Fakhr was executed and replaced by a member of the Shihab family. Ottoman rule was temporarily disrupted in 1831 when Muhammad Ali Pasha, by that time ruler of Egypt, drove the Ottomans out. But his rule was contrary to British interests, so the British intervened (supposedly at the request of the Druze). With their help, the Ottomans were restored to power.

Religious conflict. The Maronite-Druze coalition erupted into conflict when the Ottomans tried to divide Mount Lebanon into Christian and Druze sections. France backed the Christians in this conflict while the British backed the Druze. In 1861, Ottomans under European pressure established a non-Lebanese Christian governor. By

World War I, the Ottomans had again taken military control of the region. When the Turks and Germans were defeated in the war, Lebanon, exploited and neglected, suffered famine, disease, and economic collapse. In 1920, the land came under French control and Maronite Christians were again installed as the leaders. Under French guidance Lebanon improved its roads, cities, ports, and educational system. Still, the Lebanese sought self-government, and in 1945 the Republic of Lebanon was formed by United Nations mandate, with the Maronites remaining in power and supported by Sunni leaders.

Palestinians. In the aftermath of the Arab-Israeli War of 1973, Lebanese Christians and Muslims clashed over a number of issues, including the support of Palestinians. Civil war erupted. In 1982, Israeli soldiers became active in the conflict and much of the capital city of Beirut was destroyed during a fifteen-month battle. Eventually the Israelis withdrew from parts of Lebanon. Syrian advisers were sent to restore order and these were followed by Syrian troops. A ceasefire was declared in 1977, but skirmishes continued and Syrian forces to maintain peace grew to about 50,000. The struggles continued in 1990 although the government structure had been destroyed and efforts to restore a workable government were beginning.

Culture Today

Effects of civil war. Before the civil war, Lebanon's cities were famous as cosmopolitan cultural centers where the educated and affluent classes enjoyed a relatively high standard of living. The capital city of Beirut, often called the "Paris of the Middle East" by the Lebanese, was a vibrant center of commerce, industry, and entertainment. Its streets and wide boulevards reflected the influence of the French, with European-style apartment blocks, office buildings and government ministries, fashionable shops, restaurants, cafes, and nightclubs. The urban dwellers shared political influence with prosperous rural inhabitants. However, since the war began, much land has become too endangered to cultivate and many rural families have moved into the no-less-risky urban areas, depriving the country of some of its agriculture and also overburdening the cities. Today, the Muslim sector of West Beirut lies in ruins and armed militia patrol sections of the city against snipers and bombing. Available food has decreased in quantity and quality.

City life. The civil war and the Israeli invasion has disrupted life in both the city and rural societies. Today West Beirut, the Muslim sector lies in ruins, with many streets and buildings reduced to rubble from frequent bombings and guerrilla warfare. The continuous violence has affected the economy and social activity of major parts of the city. Urban life begins again when fighting stops in the streets, but people have had to curtail their normal daily routines. In addition, the civil war has caused sharp political divisions in the society between and inside religious groups as well as between economic and social classes.

The migration of rural villagers, mostly farmers from the Bekaa Valley, to the urban areas has created a large underprivileged class. These villagers are Muslims who belong to the Shi'ite sect. Displaced by the civil war and by Israeli bombardment of southern Lebanon, whole villages of people are often forced to seek jobs in the cities. There they live in a state of poverty and alienation, separated by economic standing from their Sunni Muslim neighbors, but becoming the majority of the Muslims in the cities. Political differences between the Shi'ites and the Sunnis has added to the turmoil resulting from the struggle with Christians, who have long dominated political life in Lebanon. These struggles have been further pressed by the immigration of nearly 500,000 Palestinians who fled the Arab-Israeli conflicts and found refuge in Lebanon.

Village life. Before the civil war, villages were based on families or clans. In the farming areas, the leader of the village was a headman who attended to all personal and communal problems. Families owned the land they farmed, growing crops for both food and the village markets to which city people drove on the weekends. Children of farm families and coastal fishers aided in the food distribution by setting up roadside stands where they sold their produce.

Today, many rural people have migrated to the cities to find work, but these people still identify with their village. They generally send a portion of their earnings back home to help support their families. Village political leadership is organized into a system of village elders who elect a *mukhtar* (mayor). This local leadership replaces the sheikhs, wealthy landowners who once lived in the villages, but who now have become absentee landlords living in greater luxury in the cities.

Family life. Despite the political and religious divisions that have tended to upset the traditional structure of Lebanese society, the family remains at the center of all relations in Lebanese life. An individual's status is determined by family and kin through patrilineal descent, and this bond usually determines personal matters such as marriage and finance, as well as business, employment, political, educational, and sectarian matters. The family and kin group protects and supports its members, and loyalty to the family ranks as the most important factor among all groups of Lebanese society.

The traditional family is male-oriented and normally consists of a three-generation extended family unit—grandparents, husband and wife, their unmarried children of both sexes, and the married sons. These families live under a single roof or in nearby homes in the cities. The husband remains the principal breadwinner and property owner. The wife's role is to care for the children, and take care of the home. In rural areas women also provide farm labor. Increasingly, both urban and rural women find work outside the home and help support the family.

Among Muslims, marriages are still frequently arranged, usually between first cousins. The practice insures that wealth and property are kept within the kin group. This tradition is particularly strong in the villages, and tends to break down in the large cities. The traditional practices of polygyny and the payment of a bride-price are seldom carried out today.

Women. The status of Lebanese women, influenced by European education and culture differs from some of the other Arab nations, particularly those on the Arabian peninsula. Many urban women are employed in offices and have professions in communications and media, arts, sciences, and education. In recent years, however, Muslim women who had given up wearing the veil in public have been influenced by Islamic fundamentalist groups and have returned to more traditional roles. These women are often seen dressed in covering clothing from modest veils to the *burqa*, a head-to-toe black cloak. Christian women tend to be more independent and to participate in political groups and community activities—often pressed into these roles by the absence of menfolk involved in war or in migrations to other countries for better employment. On the whole, Lebanese city women are as educated and make up as large a share of university students as their counterparts in other Arab nations.

Food, clothing, and shelter. The Lebanese produce a wide variety of dishes from the locally grown vegetables, wheat, rice, lentils, dairy products, lamb, poultry, and seafood, which they sometimes stuff into grape leaves and eat with a flat bread called *khobez*. *Tabbouleh* is a cold salad of cracked bulgur wheat, tomatoes, scallions, and parsley tossed with olive oil and lemon juice. Many dishes are prepared with a paste of crushed sesame seeds, called *tahina*, that adds a rich nutty flavor to other foods. It can be eaten alone or used to make *hummus*, a mashed chickpea and garlic dip. Another favorite is an eggplant dip called *baba ghannoj*. A popular meat dish is *kibbe*, ground lamb and bulgur wheat. The Ottoman pastry, *baklava*, filled with chopped nuts and honey, is common in Lebanon.

Both rural and urban Lebanese take pride in the tradition of hospitality. In city homes, dinner parties and luncheons are regularly attended by large circles of friends, relations, and business associates. Wealthy people usually receive acquaintances and visitors for coffee and sweets in their living rooms. Rural villagers invite guests to drink coffee and share food. This tradition is practiced by both affluent and poor people. In addition, men gather in cafes to play cards, smoke, and discuss politics, sports, business, and family matters. Women gather in private homes for conversation.

Village homes are constructed of stone blocks and usually have two stories. Farmhouses are single-level structures with flat roofs, windows and doorways, and an archway that leads directly to a large open room called a *liwan*. In the plains, houses are built of adobe (mud and straw). The flat roofs are also made of adobe, and windows are equipped with wooden shutters as protection against heat. Most village houses are surrounded by a garden and vineyard.

A greater variety of living quarters is found in the cities. Affluent people own large houses and estates, as well as city apartments. Middle-income people live in modern high-rise apartments, while poor people in the cities live in shantytown suburbs. Homes in the city have televisions, electrical appliances, European furniture, and Middle Eastern carpets and ornamentations.

Similar variations occur in the choice of clothing. Urban people wear European-style clothing. Men are attired in business suits, trousers, and leisure sportswear. Women wear stylish dresses and business clothes, and carry handbags. They are fond of cosmetics and perfumes. Some villagers still wear traditional costumes. Village women wear floor-length cotton dresses with scarves on their heads. Men often wear *shalvar*, loose baggy trousers under a long, loose shirt. In the plains, some older men still wear the Arabic headdress, held in place by a crown of black cord called an *agal*. The traditional dress is seen in the cities, particularly among the older generations. This use of traditional clothing has grown with the rise of fundamentalism. Muslim women are increasingly turning to wearing the veil and the *aba*, a long coat, more often today as a witness to their faith than as a demand of modesty.

Religious groups. Lebanon's Islamic population includes both Sunni and Shi'ite sects—the largest of the Islamic groups—as well as minor groups such as Alawis, Ismailis, and Druze. Of these, the Druze make up about seven percent of the Muslim population. More than half the Druze live in rural areas. Their communities tend to be isolated and close-knit, and have been traditionally led by family confederations divided among the Jumblatt and Yazbak.

Most Muslims, regardless of sect or group follow the same religious practices: adhering to the teachings of the Quran, praying five times daily, fasting during daylight hours during the month of Ramadan, and planning to make a holy pilgrimage to Mecca once in a lifetime.

The largest group of Christians is the Maronites, founded in the fifth century by monks who were followers of Saint Maron. They retain their own religious rites and laws, and use Arabic, Aramaic, and Syriac languages in their liturgy. Other Christian groups in Lebanon include Greek Catholics, Roman Catholics, Jacobites, Armenians, Nestorians, and Protestants. These groups share Easter and Christmas celebrations although the dates vary for Greeks and Armenians.

Holidays and leisure. Lebanon was once famous for its mountain retreats and European-style ski resorts. Recreation includes weekends on the ski slopes, camping, and swimming at the seashore. Besides winter sports special festivals are held throughout the year. Christmas, New Year, and Easter celebrations are major events. Folk dancing and traditional Lebanese music is performed at many local festivals. Lebanese music features the *nai* (flute), and *daff* (drum), as well as stringed instruments—the *buzuk*, the *ud*, and the *kanun*.

Between July and September an international festival of music, drama, and dance takes place at Baalbek. Many leading orchestras, ballet companies, and film and stage stars present special performances.

Arts and literature. Lebanese craftsmen produce hammered metalware of brass and copper, tooled leatherwork, and gold jewelry. They are famous worldwide for their delicate filigree work with gold and silver, their inlaid wooden boxes, and their bone-handled cutlery. Glass-blowing and weaving of fine brocaded textiles has survived since the time of the early Phoenicians.

Lebanon is known for its high level of education, particularly in the arts and sciences. The Lebanese have made important contributions to the world's knowledge in medicine, engineering, law, poetry, architecture, painting, and the dramatic arts. Contemporary authors such as Charles Corm, Fargallah Hayek, and George Shehade produce works in French, Arabic, and Armenian.

Painting and other arts reflect Arabic influence in geometric designs or still lifes taken from nature. These designs are used in ornate metal grillwork and in stone artistry in Lebanese architecture and in the religious shrines.

For More Information

Cobban, Helena. *The Making of Modern Lebanon.* Boulder, Colorado: Westview Press, 1985.

Colello, Thomas, editor. *Lebanon: A Country Study.* Washington, D.C.: Library of Congress, 1989.

Gordon, David C. *The Republic of Lebanon: Nation in Jeopardy.* Boulder, Colorado: Westview Press, 1983.

LIBYANS
(lib′ ee uns)

The majority of the people of the country of Libya, officially named The Great Socialist People's Libyan Arab Jamahiriya.

Population: 4,200,000 (1988 estimate).
Location: North Africa; bounded by Egypt, Sudan, Chad, Niger, Algeria, Tunisia, and the Mediterranean Sea.
Language: Arabic.

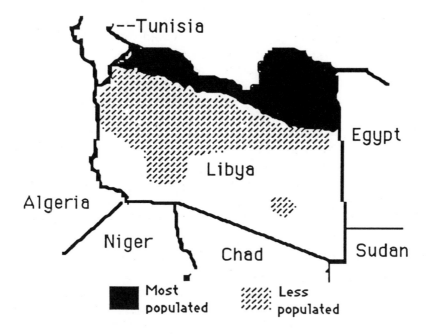

Geographical Setting

Occupying the center of Africa's northern coast, Libya's position has made the country a junction of various cultures, as European, North African, and Middle Eastern influences have interacted there. Larger than Texas, California, New Mexico, and Arizona combined, Libya has an area of 1,760,000 square kilometers—the fourth largest country in Africa. It is divided into three geographic regions: Tripolitania in the northwest, Fezzan in the southwest, and Cyrenaica in the east. Sixty-five percent of the population lives in Tripolitania, thirty percent in Cyrenaica, and only five percent in the desert region of Fezzan.

Libya's main geographical features are the Mediterranean coast and the Sahara Desert, which in the eastern part of this country is called the Libyan Desert. Virtually all of the nation's agriculture is in the coastal zones of Tripolitania and Cyrenaica. These areas receive winter rain from the Mediterranean, the heaviest rain (more than twenty-five inches a year) falling in the north of Cyrenaica. Inland Libya is hot and dry. Summer temperatures are high, averaging above 80 degrees Fahrenheit. In spring and fall, a hot dusty south wind called the *ghibli* blows into Tripolitania from the desert, evaporating much of the winter's moisture, but helping to ripen the local date crop.

The land rises inland, but there are few mountains in the country. Except at the far southern border with Chad, where Mt. Bette rises to 7,500 feet, there are no peaks above 3,600 feet in a land that lies mostly between 500 and 2,000 feet above sea level.

Historical Background

Berbers. Berbers, the earliest known inhabitants of northwestern Africa raided eastward of Libya as early as the third millennium B.C. The Egyptian name for one of these groups was "Levu" or "Libu." Greek historians later adopted the name, referring to all Berbers as "Libyans" (see BERBERS). Around 800 B.C., Phoenician traders sailed to present-day Libya and established a great trading center on the coast, Carthage.

Romans. The destruction of Carthage in 146 B.C. established a Roman presence in North Africa. In 96 B.C., the Greek king of Cyrenaica bequeathed his dominion to the growing empire, and Rome formally annexed it as a province twenty-two years later. Tripolitania, ruled for several generations by Berber client kings of Rome, was made a province by Julius Caesar in the 40s B.C. Roman rule continued until the A.D. 420s, when Vandals invaded from Spain and established a kingdom in Carthage that included Tripolitania. From Carthage, these people raided the countryside, collecting taxes and destroying crops. Roman armies under the Byzantine (eastern Roman Empire) general Belisarius won back the lost territories in the 530s. Yet Byzantine rule was confined to coastal cities, particularly in Cyrenaica. Most of Tripolitania remained, in practice, independent and Berber. The influences of the earlier Roman dominion at Carthage remained strong with these coastal Berbers.

Islam and Arab conquest. Weakened by the Vandal intrusion, North Africa was quickly conquered by invading Arabs after the death of Muhammad in 632 (see ISLAM). Muslim armies had captured Cyrenaica by 642, Tripolitania by 650, and Fezzan by 663. At first the Berbers of Tripolitania resisted fiercely, but finally some were converted to Islam by the Arab leaders. Only with the help of these converts were the Muslim armies able to overrun Byzantine garrisons at Carthage. The Arab commanders who ruled North Africa restored its prosperity, repairing the Roman road and irrigations systems. Arabic and Islamic culture predominated only in the coastal cities, however. There the Arab soldiers intermarried with Berbers to create a small governing elite. In the countryside, the Berbers preserved their traditional independence.

Most did not convert to Islam until the 1000s, when large numbers of Bedouins (see BEDOUINS) called the Hilalians invaded the land. The restless nomads had been sent by the caliph in Egypt as punishment to the Berber governors of North Africa and to rid Egypt of their presence. These Berbers, the Zirids, had abandoned the form of Islam observed by the Egyptian caliph (Shi'ite) in favor of the Sunni sect. The Hilalians ravaged the land more severely than the Vandals had done earlier, destroying urban life and converting farmland into pasturage for their herds. Perhaps as many as 1,000,000 Hilalians moved slowly west from Egypt. They Arabized the region thoroughly, converting Berbers in the country to Islam, and spreading the Arabic language and customs to as much as ninety percent of the population.

Barbary pirates. For the next 500 years, various tribes of Berbers and Bedouin Arabs fought among themselves in what is now Libya. Cyrenaica became the most Arabized, with no remnant of its Greek past. It has been said that only the interior of Arabia is more Arabic.

From Tripoli westward, Berbers and Arabs joined in creating the blend of cultures once called Moorish. By the 1500s, groups of pirates sailed from this coast to harass European shipping. Many of the pirates were European outlaws, such as the Greek pirate who became known as Barbarossa, or Red-beard. Making their headquarters in Tripoli, pirate captains like Barbarossa at times ruled the city. Europeans called the coast from Tripoli to Morocco the Barbary Coast, perhaps because they thought the pirates barbaric or perhaps because the Berbers lived there.

Turks and Italians. The Ottoman Empire (see TURKS) took control of Tripolitania and Cyrenaica in 1551. By this time the cultures of the regions had become well established. For the next 400 years Libya would remain under foreign domination, although the local Karamanli dynasty achieved some independence from 1711 to 1835. Led by the Sanusi religious order, in 1922 the Libyans mounted stiff resistance against the Italians, losing a third of their adult male population before being subdued in 1932. Allied armies of World War II expelled the Italians by 1942, and in 1951, under the United Nations guidance, the Sanusi leader Sayyid Idris became king of the newly independent United Kingdom of Libya. However, corruption in Idris' government and his failure to divide the nation's increasing oil revenues among the people, eventually caused widespread dissatisfaction with the monarchy.

Qaddafi. In 1969, a group of about seventy army officers led a quick and bloodless coup that deposed the Idris regime. The new leadership, soon headed by the twenty-seven-year-old Colonel Muammar al Qaddafi, the son of a nomadic Berber family, enjoyed enthusiastic popular support. One of its aims was to end Libya's orientation toward Western powers such as Britain and the United States, who had supported Idris since World War II. The governing Revolutionary Command Council wished instead to emphasize Arab unity, following the example of Egypt's President Gamel Abdel Nasser. Adopting these goals, Qaddafi soon consolidated his personal control of the national government.

Since then, as Chairman of the Revolutionary Council, Muammar al Qaddafi's policies have enjoyed more success at home than abroad. By the 1980s, standards of living had risen greatly, as oil revenues were used to upgrade housing, health, education, and other social services, while foreign ventures have isolated Libya in both the Arab world and the larger diplomatic community.

Culture Today

In addition to the majority Arab and Arabized Berber populations, about five percent of the population continues to speak only Berber. Considered the true Berbers, this small group lives mostly in western Libya. Nomadic Berbers such as the Tuareg dress and live in a way that is similar to the Arab Bedouin desert dwellers. Smaller numbers of black Africans such as the Tebu (about 2,600) live in southernmost Libya. Most are Muslims. Libya also has a number, estimated to be a quarter of a million, of foreign workers and residents.

Socialism. In 1973, Qaddafi introduced a "cultural revolution" aimed at combining Islamic and socialist ideas in government. Four years later, he proclaimed the *jamahiriya* or "state of the masses." The newly coined word was added to Libya's name, to reflect new institutions designed to place power in the hands of the people. Yet Qaddafi and his Revolution Command Council (RCC) remained firmly in control. The socialist ideas they imposed were meant to provide everyone with what he or she needed. Those who owned more than it was felt they needed—more than one house, one vehicle, or savings accounts of over 1,000 dinars—were to turn these items over to the government. Instead of wages, workers were accorded partnerships in the industries and businesses for which they worked. Many middle-class Libyans, such as professionals and technical workers, left the country. Today about 50,000 live abroad. Others protested or concealed their wealth. Some students and intellectuals have also criticized the regime's ideology.

Religion. Nearly all Libyans are Sunni Muslims. Among some of the Berbers, the older beliefs were integrated into their practice of the Muslim faith. The most important of these is maraboutism, the veneration of local saints. Muslims taking exception to a strict, intellectual, and legal interpretation of the religion, had earlier formed a tradition based on striving to be one with God, and more emotionally oriented. Called Sufism, this popular, mystical Muslim tradition, was brought to Libya by revivalists. The most popular of these was the Sanusi movement. Its founder Muhammad ibn Ali (the Grand Sanusi) was an Islamic religious leader who wished to return to the early purity of Islam. Popular among Bedouin tribesmen of Cyrenaica, the movement in the 1900s became the rallying point of resistance against the Italians. By the time of King Idris, the Grand Sanusi's grandson, it had lost most if its religious force.

Orthodox Islam has assumed a central role in Qaddafi's Libya. Like the Grand Sanusi, Qaddafi wished to restore the purity of early Islamic practice. After the revolution, the new government closed nightclubs and bars and banned entertainment thought immodest or sexually stimulating. Gambling and alcohol were forbidden. In 1973, Qaddafi devised a new judicial system based on *sharia* law, the traditional Islamic legal code derived from the Quran. Qaddafi stresses the Quran's authority as a guide for every aspect of social and private life, and has attempted to reduce the influence of the *ulama* (the clerical establishment).

Family life. As in many other Middle Eastern societies, family loyalty has the highest claim in an individual's social life, and a family's status dictates that of each member. The traditional extended family, in which a father rules a household that includes his married children and their families, has remained more common in Libya than elsewhere in North Africa. As economic conditions offer greater financial independence to the young, the extended family tends to divide. Still, Libyan families look after their relatives in need even when the family is separated.

When the father dies, each married son heads his own household. Society considers a man to be an adult only when he has married, and sometimes only when he becomes a father. Libyans enjoy large families, and the government encourages them to have many children. Wedding celebrations last a week, with the bride wearing a different color for each evening's festivities. The groom's family pays for the wedding, also supplying gifts of coins and clothing for the bride.

Women. The revolutionary government's greatest variation of Islamic tradition is in the treatment of women. Several laws have expanded women's rights in obtaining divorce, while curtailing those of men. Women have been encouraged to vote and have taken a place in the military. Television and the expansion of the oil economy have also contributed to changing attitudes, by exposing Libyans to Western values. An ongoing labor shortage has caused the government to try to include more women in the work force. Yet such attempts have met resistance from those with traditional values. Accordingly, women are often limited to "female" jobs such as teaching, nursing, or clerical work. Despite increased educational opportunities, few women become doctors, lawyers, or engineers. However, Qaddafi's bodyguard is made up of women. In the rural areas, women constitute a large part of the labor pool. Besides agricultural work, women in both settled and nomadic communities perform domestic tasks such as weaving.

Food, clothing, and shelter. Libyans usually eat a light breakfast—rolls, tea, and perhaps a little cheese—taking their main meal in the early afternoon. Then, a large platter of *cous-cous* (boiled wheat flour formed into tiny balls) topped with lamb and vegetables might be followed by fruit such as oranges or dates. In the evening, the family eats a light meal of cheese or yogurt. Tea, popular throughout most of North Africa, is drunk all day. It is boiled until very dark, then sweetened with sugar and flavored with roasted hazelnuts.

City people, who make up two-thirds of Libya's population, are concentrated on the Mediterranean coast, where contacts with Europeans are greatest. Here men and women mostly wear European-style clothing, but traditional clothing is acceptable and often seen. City women who dress in the old conservative style wear veils or shawls and cover their legs and arms with a long dress. The traditional outer dress for both men and women is the *barracan*, a long wool or cotton robe said to descend from the Roman toga. Men often wear the fez, a brimless, soft felt cap. Rural women, in contrast to their city counterparts, are less careful about covering themselves completely unless strangers are present. They, too, along with the rural men, wear European-style clothing. In the desert, Berbers and Bedouins wear their traditional costumes (see BERBERS or BEDOUINS). A woman of the desert might wear a brightly colored, long flowing dress and a shawl.

Libyan homes were traditionally designed to provide privacy, with high walls around a tiled courtyard and separate sections for men and women. Some lived in less well-designed houses in the outskirts of the cities, but these houses, built of material such as corrugated iron and bits of wood that were available to the poor, have been largely replaced by modern government-owned apartment houses. In rural areas, homes are built of dried mud-brick for coolness.

Arts. Islamic law frowns on the use of human images in art. That this is a law not strictly upheld is illustrated by the large pictures of Qaddafi that are posted throughout the country. Rock paintings of early cattle herders in the Fezzan region illustrate the ancient interest in drawing and painting. Cave drawings have been dated as early as 5000 B.C. Still, the art of Libya is mostly manifest in its architecture. This is as varied as the history of the country. The remains of Roman theaters and forums still stand in Cyrene and Sabratha. Italian-built cathedrals have been converted to mosques. Beautifully arched entrances mark the doorways of office buildings and government structures. Homes are decorated with ornately tiled doorways. In cities like Murzuk, long adobe walls screen equally long and low, flat-topped houses. Above these stand ancient towers and the beautifully tiled domes of more recent mosques.

Old and new. While affirming traditional Islamic values, the government has also attempted to break down old tribal loyalties. Such affiliations, paramount in the society's past, are viewed as hindering social and national development. Consequently, the land was divided across tribal boundaries in new governmental units, and nomadic communities have been encouraged to settle. The booming oil and construction industries of the 1970s speeded such change, but also helped create a movement to the cities that has discouraged food production. In response, the government initiated a program of agricultural development, which provides land for farmers. Still only about twenty percent of the people farm today, as compared with fifty percent in the 1950s.

For More Information

Blundy, David and Andrew Lycott. *Qadaffi and the Libyan Revolution.* Boston: Little Brown and Company, 1987.

Meta, Helen Chapin, editor. *Libya: A Country Study.* Washington, D.C.: Department of the Army, 1989.

The Middle East and North Africa 1991. London: Europa Publications Ltd., 1991.

Targ-Brill, Marlene. *Libya.* Chicago: Children's Press, 1987.

MARONITES
(mehr ah' nites)

A Christian-Arab group living in Lebanon, where they constitute
the largest Christian sect.

Population: 1,200,000 (1988 estimate).
Location: Northern Lebanon.
Languages: Arabic; French.

Geographical Setting

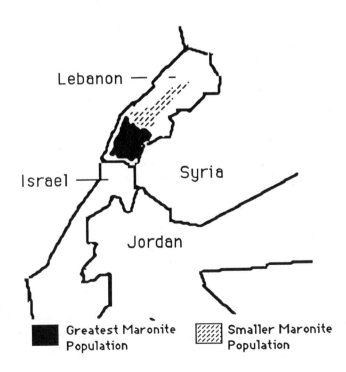

Lebanon

Israel

Syria

Jordan

Greatest Maronite Population

Smaller Maronite Population

The roughly rectangular Republic of Lebanon lies along the southeastern Mediterranean coast, bounded by Israel to the south and Syria to the east and north. The area is divided lengthwise into four alternating strips of highland and lowland: the narrow coastal plain, including the major cities of Tripoli, Beirut (the Lebanese capital), Sidon, and Tyre; the Lebanon Mountains, whose northern section (often called Mount Lebanon or simply the Mount) is the Maronites' traditional stronghold; the Biqa Valley, a section of the Great Rift geological system (which stretches from Turkey to Africa); and the Anti-Lebanon Mountains along the Syrian border, arid and less populated than the mountains and valleys to the west.

Lebanon's climate matches its varied topography. The sea moderates daily temperature ranges in the coastal plain, while inland areas experience greater extremes. Generally, summers are long, hot, and dry; winters, cool and wet, with rainfall coming in short but heavy bursts over a few days. In the summer, daytime mountain temperatures equal those of the coast, but much cooler nights and lower humidity attract coastal residents to mountain resorts. In the winter, frost and snow are common in the middle altitudes of the Lebanon and Anti-Lebanon Mountains, with snow covering the high peaks year-round.

Historical Background

Hidden origins. Maronite tradition differs regarding the group's origins. One source, accepted by modern scholars like Kamal Salibi, holds that they came from southern Arabia, perhaps around A.D. 500, settling in Syria, as many other Arab tribes did in Roman times. By the 500s, when the Maronites occupied the Orontes River Valley in western Syria and northwestern Lebanon, most of the Maronites had adopted Christianity. Probably around 950 the group began moving from the Orontes region to Mount Lebanon, which Maronites today regard as their ancestral home.

The earliest references to the Maronites, found in the works of two Muslim historians of the 900s, associate them with a Christian doctrine called *Monothelitism*, which the Orthodox Church had banned as heretical at the Sixth Ecumenical Council in 680. Most later Maronite sources deny this association, however, claiming that Maronites embraced Orthodox belies from their beginnings as a sect. Yet even among Maronites, disagreement persists about their beginnings. Three rival theories, for example, vie to explain the origins of the name "Maronite." One holds that the community took its name from a Syrian saint of the 400s called Marun; another that they were named after a monastery named for this saint; a third that the name derives from a monk of the late 600s, also called Marun, who became their first patriarch.

Contacts with French Crusaders. The Maronites retained their Christian beliefs in their new Lebanese home. (Other Arab tribal groups had adopted Islam following the conquest of the area by Islamic Arabs in the late 660s.) In 1099, about a century after the Maronites had established themselves in Mount Lebanon, the armies of the First Crusade arrived in the Middle East from Europe. The Maronites sided with their fellow Christians, establishing ties with both the Roman Catholic church, whose rites they had adopted by the 1200s, and with the French, who would play an increasingly important role in Maronite and Lebanese affairs during the nineteenth and twentieth centuries.

Mameluke and Ottoman rule. In 1169, Salah-Ed-Din Yussuf ibn-Ayud (more commonly known as Saladin), who was in the service of the Emir of Syria, became the Vizier of Egypt. His announced goal was to free Jerusalem of the Christians and his zealous pursuit of this goal encouraged the organization of the Crusade of King Richard Coeur de Lion and King Philip Augustus of France. Saladin captured Acre, Said, and Beirut, and beseiged Jerusalem, forcing its capitulation in 1197. Eventually the forces of the two kings prevailed and a truce between the opposing sides split the coastal area around Palestine. By the late 1200s, a new Islamic power, the Mamluks of Egypt (1282-1516), had driven the last Crusaders from Syria and Lebanon. Under the Mamelukes, Maronite connections with the Christian West grew stronger, as the Maronites mediated between Mameluke leaders and their Western trading partners, most notably the Venetians. This profitable three-way partnership assured the Maronites of political and religious freedom, despite heavy immigration into the region of various Islamic peoples during the period. When the Ottoman Turks (see TURKS) conquered the Mamelukes in 1516, they at first curtailed Maronite political freedom and imposed heavy taxes. Maronites appealed to the West, and in 1550 the Ottoman sultan, Suleiman the Magnificent, restored the rights of the Maronite community. A series of subsequent agreements placed the community under French protection.

In the nineteenth century, many Maronites began to migrate from their homeland in the northern mountains southward to other parts of Lebanon. Throughout the 1800s they began settling in areas occupied by Sunni, Shi'ite, and Druze communities (see SUNNI, SHI'ITE, DRUZES). In the Shi'ite and Druze regions, Maronites soon came to dominate the valuable production of silk, for which there was a ready European market. At first, labor shortages led the original inhabitants to welcome the Maronites, but as Maronite influence and numbers increased, clashes arose between the Christians and Muslims.

Meanwhile, under King Louis XIV of France (1643-1715), the French began to appoint Maronites as their diplomatic representatives in Beirut and to bring young Maronites to study in France, supplying free passage and tuition. Tensions between the by now wealthy and sophisticated Maronites and the poorer, more isolated Muslims grew and erupted in a series of bitter wars. In 1860, when the Druze massacred some 12,000 Christians, France intervened, working out with the Ottoman state a plan for Lebanese autonomy. As in the past each religious group was to administer its own laws, but now while sharing in a national government. The plan became a reality in the twentieth century. Under this program, Lebanon, which had been governed by its own amir since 1920, was for the first time politically separate from Syria.

French mandate. With the collapse of the Ottoman Empire after World War I, the victorious Allies gave control of Syria and Lebanon to France, over the objections of the native populations. France, in 1920, established the borders of modern Lebanon. In 1926, a new constitution created the Republic of Lebanon, under which the "confessional" principles—laws and representation based on religious affiliation—of the previous arrangement were extended. The system was weighted in favor of Maronites, who held all important governmental positions including the presidency of the republic.

Independence. Following the French grant of independence in 1943, negotiations between Lebanese Christian and Muslim leaders produced the National Pact, which upheld the confessional system while allowing greater Muslim participation in government. Under the National Pact, Christians would stop relying on the West for political support and recognize Lebanon as an Arab state, while the Muslims agreed to prevent a merger with any larger Arab state (such as Syria), which might threaten the rights of Maronites. This delicate balance of interests survived for barely thirty years, during which each religious community was dominated by a series of prominent families. Among the Maronites, the Khuris, Shamuns, Shihabs, Franjiyehs, and Jumayyels provided leadership into the 1980s.

Civil war. Arab nationalism had grown throughout the 1900s. In 1958, Arabs found a hero in Egyptian President Nasser, who united Egypt with Syria to form the United Arab Republic. Muslims in Lebanon, abandoning the National Pact and rebelling on a large scale, tried to force the government to join the new state. The Maronite Lebanese President Camille Shamun appealed to the United States, and President Dwight Eisenhower responded by sending U.S. Marines. This first civil war, brief but violent, left over 1,000 Lebanese dead. (U.S. forces were not involved in the fighting, though their presence helped end the conflict.)

In the years following World War II, a new presence in the Middle East had further complicated the already intricate mosaic of Lebanese politics: the Jewish state of Israel, which adjoins Lebanon's southern border. Israel's displacement of Arab Palestinians, hundreds of thousands of whom fled to refugee camps in southern Lebanon, became the point of a wedge that would eventually divide Christians and Muslims in a second, more disastrous, civil war beginning in 1975. For 20 years the refugees were quiescent, but after Israel's crushing defeat of Arab armies in the 1967 war the Palestine Liberation Organization (PLO) began to raid Israeli territory from inside Lebanon. Lebanese Muslims supported the PLO, which rapidly increased both its arsenal and its control of territory in southern Lebanon. Christians, of whom Maronites formed the majority, while fearing Israeli reprisals for the raids, tended to sympathize with Israel.

As Israel indeed began raiding PLO camps in the late 1960s, in the process killing innocent Lebanese, private militias, recruited from among the various Lebanese religious groups, began arming themselves heavily. When unidentified gunmen fired on Pierre Jumayyel, leader of the Phalange (a Maronite militia), in April 1975, Phalangists responded by ambushing a bus carrying Palestinians, killing twenty-eight. The incident touched off immediate and violent combat throughout Beirut. Fighting in Lebanon has continued since then, with 130,000 dead by the end of 1987. Although outside forces—the PLO, Israel, Arab neighbors such as Syria, and other world forces—

helped initiate and prolong the war, the intense rivalries among Lebanese themselves have also drawn it out.

Culture Today

War and survival. For Christian and Muslim alike in Lebanon, the war remains a central fact of life. The struggle has centered in the once beautiful city of Beirut, reducing entire neighborhoods to rubble, and dividing the city, with Maronites dominating East Beirut and the various Muslim Shi'ite groups controlling West Beirut. Violence has erupted throughout Lebanon, however, especially in the south, and many Maronites have sought the security of their traditional home in Mount Lebanon, reversing the outward migration of earlier times. This influx has brought a paradoxical prosperity to the Christian enclave, as it is known, with businesses and building booming during the 1980s. Cars crowd the narrow, winding roads, and once quiet villages bristle with restaurants, cafes, shopping centers, and service stations. This new prosperity contrasts with the general poverty of Muslim areas, a disparity also apparent in Beirut itself, where more of Muslim West Beirut has been destroyed, yet less rebuilt, than Christian East Beirut.

Religion and the state. Although the division between Christian and Muslim remains fundamental to Lebanese society, each faith itself presents a complex array of often conflicting religious groups. Fighting among (and within) sects of the same faith has sometimes been as bloody as that between faiths. While the Maronites (with about sixteen percent of the population) comprise by far the largest Christian sect, other substantial Christian groups include Greek Orthodox (five percent), Greek Catholics (three percent), and with less than one percent each, Roman Catholics, Jacobites or Syrian Monophysites, Armenian Orthodox or Gregorians, Nestorians, and numerous Protestant denominations introduced by Western missionaries. Principal Muslim sects are the Shi'ites (forty-one percent), Sunnis (twenty-seven percent), and with less than one percent each, the Ismailis and Alawis. (For more information see ISLAM.) The Druze (seven percent), an offshoot of Ismaili Islam, are often thought of as an element of the Muslim community, though in strict terms they constitute a separate religion. They have been special opponents of the Maronites, as the civil war has rekindled animosities from the 1800s. Though Jews have played an important role in Lebanon's confessional past, all but a few hundred Lebanese Jews emigrated in the face of growing Muslim hostility after 1975. The percentage figures given above are 1986 estimates; political instability has prevented the Lebanese government from carrying out a census since 1932, as Maronites and other minorities fear decreased representation in the confessional political system.

Government. The 1926 constitution promulgated under French auspices remains in effect, although civil war has considerably weakened the central government's authority. In theory, three branches share power: the presidency, the cabinet or Council of Ministers, and a legislative Council of Deputies (sometimes called a parliament). In practice, however, authority has tended to reside in the office of the president, who appoints the prime minister and has effective control of the legislative process. Custom, established after and according to the 1932 census, dictates that the president be a Maronite, the prime minister a Sunni, and the speaker of the Chamber of Deputies, a Shi'ite. The 1932 census also established the ratio of six Christians to five Muslims in the Council of Deputies, a proportion that has been held to despite changes in the Council's size.

This constitutional arrangement overlies an entrenched system of patronage, or clientele, in which political leaders called *zuama* control the disposition of offices within each sect. Often the zuama hold important offices themselves, manipulating elections to ensure that their supporters gain less important ones. The zuama system, common to all sects in Lebanon, arose in feudal times, when great landlords (such as the Druze and Maronite landlords in the Shouf) allowed peasants to work the land in exchange for loyalty. The power of the zuama is inherited: the influence of the Maronite zaim Pierre Jumayyel, for example, allowed his sons Bashir (president for just three weeks from August 23, 1982, until he was assassinated on September 14, 1982) and Amin (who succeeded Bashir as president) to come to power, and Amin became zaim on his father's death in 1984.

Family life. Maronites tend to emphasize the nuclear family more than their Muslim neighbors, though Lebanese of both faiths place great importance on extended kinship in conducting personal, financial, and political affairs. In the Maronite nuclear family, the father tends to be a more integral part of the domestic household than in the Muslim family. While Muslim men tend to spend much of their time away from home, in exclusively male company, Maronite men gravitate to the home, taking great pleasure in the informal company of their wives and children. Because of the Christian insistence on monogamy, and because divorce is more difficult for Maronites than for Muslims, Maronite wives enjoy greater security and independence than their Muslim counterparts. This contrast exists as well with other Christian groups in Muslim societies (see COPTS). For Maronite women the difference is greater due to both a higher degree of Westernization and the absence of men serving in various militias. The war has also affected the position of children in all Lebanese families, especially males: an atmosphere of violence and a pervasive influence of militarism have undercut traditionally strict parental authority, particularly in less affluent households.

Food, clothing, and shelter. Lebanese food is a mix of Middle Eastern and Mediterranean characteristics, to which the Maronites also add French and European elements. Breakfasts are simple, usually consisting of Lebanese flat bread or croissants with cheese and coffee or tea. Lunch and dinner dishes combine meat (mutton is a favorite) with onions, spices, and rice. Mutton is often ground, served as meatballs, in stew, or mixed with rice and vegetables and rolled in grape leaves. Before meals, Lebanese enjoy *mezzeh,* consisting of a number of hors d'oeuvres (such as *hummus,* made of ground chickpeas with tahina, olive oil, garlic, and lemon) scooped up with bread, and accompanied by *arak,* and Arab wine.

Proud of their historic associations with the West, Maronites dress in Western fashion. In formal settings, men wear suits and ties; younger people relax in jeans, T-shirts, and sneakers.

Maronite architecture also shows Western influence, with white sandstone being a favored building material for homes. In the past, the Maronities adopted early Muslim Arab houses of dried mud or Turkish-inspired wooden structures. Maronite houses are generally small and intimate, simple but elegant, often with a balcony overlooking the mountains or the Mediterranean. Villages have the look of those in Italy or France rather than the Middle East, a direct result of building habits traceable to the arrival of French Crusaders.

Conclusion. Although most Maronites would accept the classification of Arab on a political and ethnic basis, emotionally they consider themselves to be outside the Arab world. They continue to look to the West, with many speaking French or (in recent years) English. Some Maronite voices consider themselves ethnically separate as well, identifying with the pre-Arabic, Phoenician inhabitants of ancient Lebanon rather than with the Muslim Arabs. Much of the difficulty comes with the identification of Arab with Islam: the dynamic religion of Muhammad has overwhelmed other, competing strains in Arab history. Maronites fear that if Lebanon became fully democratic, with representation strictly by numbers, they would soon find themselves second-class citizens in an Islamic state. Muslim Lebanese, on the other hand, resent the disproportionate power that Maronites have historically wielded. With the recent discussions of the conflicts within the Maronite and Muslim communities, and the increasing value that Lebanon's powerful neighbor Syria seems to place on establishing improved relations with Western societies, many commentators see an improved prospect for peace in Lebanon during the 1990s.

For More Information

Collelo, Thomas, editor. *Lebanon: A Country Study.* Washington, D.C.: Federal Research Division, Library of Congress, 1989.

Salibi, Kamal S. *A House of Many Mansions: The History of Lebanon Reconsidered.* Berkeley and Los Angeles: University of California Press, 1988.

Viorst, Milton "The Christian Enclave," *The New Yorker Magazine.* October 3, 1988, pp. 40-68.

MOROCCANS

(mah raw' cans)

Inhabitants of the Kingdom of Morocco.

Population: 23,000,000 (1987 estimate).
Location: Northwest Africa; bounded by Western Sahara and Algeria.
Languages: Arabic; French; Spanish.

Geographical Setting

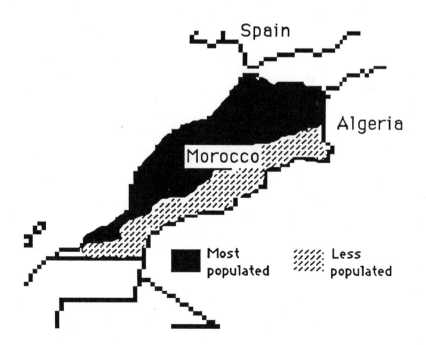

About the size of California, Morocco lies along the farthest north-western corner of Africa, with coastlines on both the Mediterranean Sea and the Atlantic Ocean. Where the two bodies of water meet stands the ancient city of Tangier; the headland east of the city is separated from Spain by only nine miles of water, the Strait of Gibraltar. The nearness to Europe has meant that inhabitants of the region have both influenced and been influenced by European cultures. South of Tangier and parallel to the Mediterranean coast lie the rugged Rif Mountains, one of four mountain chains that dominate Morocco's geography. Extending south from the Rif, like a spine through the center of the country, run the Middle Atlas, High Atlas, and Anti-Atlas ranges. All of Morocco's major cities lie to the west of these mountains, either in the coastal plains or along the coast itself. The fertile coastal plain is well watered by rivers that flow from the mountains. East of the mountains are arid and semiarid plateaus and valleys that descend gradually to the Sahara Desert. Winds from the Atlantic and Mediterranean drop rain over the mountains, ensuring a steady water supply to the plains below. Coastal regions have warm, wet winters and hot, dry summers.

Morocco is part of an area called the Maghreb (Arabic for "sunset"), the region between the Mediterranean Sea and the Sahara Desert. This area is most heavily populated along the Mediterranean coast. Inland, peoples such as some Berbers have long lived in relatively isolated areas such as the Rif Mountains. Berber life is described in a separate section of this book (see BERBERS). This section describes the lifestyles of the urban, coastal Moroccans.

Historical Background

Arabs and Berbers. Before the A.D. 600s, Morocco was the home of small societies clustered along the coast and in inland pockets near water. Of the peoples of Morocco, the Berbers were one of the most numerous (see BERBERS). Arab Muslims, spreading the new religion along the coast, first raided Morocco in A.D. 683, and by 710 had succeeded in securing the coastal areas. The Arab commander at that time, Musa ibn Nusayr, succeeded in converting the Berber people to the Islamic faith. Arabs and Berbers then joined forces and moved across the Strait of Gibraltar into Spain. Settling there they joined with the Spanish to create the culture known to Europeans as "Moorish." The Islamic civilization flourished in Spain and Morocco until Christian Europeans drove the Muslims from Spain in the 1400s.

Two cities at Fes. However, in the 700s an Arab *sharif* (a direct descendant of the prophet Muhammad), Mulay Idris ibn Abdallah, united a number of western Berber groups into what might be considered the first Moroccan state. According to tradition, Idris' son, whose mother was a Berber, founded two cities at Fes—one Arab and one Berber—which were later seen to symbolize the close relations between the two peoples. The descendants of Idris, the Idrisis, established a tradition of cultivated urban life. The Al Qayrawaniyin University and other schools and religious institutions were founded there in the 800s. However, Idrisi political influence was shorter-lived than their cultural legacy. Beginning with Idris II, the dominion was divided among various heirs.

Arab nomads. For several hundred years, Arab influence was confined to such urban centers as Fes. In these centers Arabs and Berbers intermarried to form a small elite leadership. During the 1100s-1300s, however, nomadic Arab tribes known as the Banu Hilal invaded the Moroccan countryside in great numbers. For over 100 years the Banu Hilal had ravaged the Maghrib lowlands as they moved west, Arabizing the Berber population more radically than the previous, relatively small, military outposts had done. The Arabic language came into widespread use throughout the Maghrib. Having reached Morocco, the nomads gradually took over much Berber farmland to pasture their herds. Many lowland Berbers took up the Arabs' nomadic life, and the two groups intermarried. Other Berbers withdrew to the mountains.

Dynasties of the shurfa. During the 1000s-1500s a series of Berber dynasties ruled in Spain, Morocco, and other parts of the Maghrib. But the Berber dynasties gradually weakened, and power in Morocco returned to Arab groups led by a succession of *shurfa* (the plural of sharif). Along the coast, these rulers held power over the Arab and Arabized Berber populations. However, their influence generally did not extend to the isolated, mountainous interior, the bled es-Siba. The first sharifan dynasty was that of the Saads, who came into power south of the Atlas Mountains in 1511. By 1559, the Saads had captured Fes in the north, thus establishing control over the coastal plains. This control lasted less than a century. In 1666, another sharifan group, the Alawis, captured Fes, and their leader, Mulay Rashid, became the sultan. The Alawis have remained in power for over 300 years, and the succession of Alawi rulers includes today's King Hassan II.

European influence. By the 1400s, Christian armies who had regained control of Spain began to raid Morocco. When the Alawis came into power, they successfully resisted these intrusions. However, Morocco began a period of economic and cultural stagnation that lasted into the early 1700s. Europeans with superior ships—especially France and Spain—increasingly dominated Moroccan trade through the 1700s and 1800s. Spanish fortresses, established during the Christian offensives of the 1400s-1600s, provided Spain a foothold in the north. However, exploitative French companies and speculators virtually controlled the Moroccan economy by the end of the 1700s. During the 1800s, British, German, and Spanish interests competed with the French for influence in Morocco with its strategic location at the entrance of the Mediterranean Sea.

Colonialism. In order to protect their economic interests, the French exerted increasing political control in Morocco. With French troops surrounding Fes in 1912, the Alawi ruler Abd al-Hafiz signed a treaty making two-thirds of Morocco a French Protectorate. An earlier (1904) agreement between France and Spain had recognized Spanish control of the northern third of the country—the Rif and surrounding areas. Under French occupation, the sultan remained as a figurehead, but a French Resident-General wielded all real power in the government. In the 1920s, European settlers began arriving in large numbers, taking over much of the best farmland. By 1951, Europeans owned 2,500,000 acres, and the average Moroccan-owned farm of seventeen acres was ten times smaller than the European-owned one. Without the use of their land, many Moroccans became unemployed.

Independence. In the 1920s, a number of young men from prominent urban families organized attempts to promote Arabic Moroccan culture. The French administration responded by forcing the sultan to issue an edict (*dahir*) giving equal standing to Berber culture and customs. This dahir was seen by Moroccans as an attempt to split the Arabs and Berbers, and added to the resentment of the French. Still, the nationalist movement remained mostly Arab and urban. Following World War II, this movement changed from cultural assertion to a goal of political independence for Morocco. Both Spanish and French sections won this freedom by negotiation in 1956. Since then, Morocco has reinforced its ties with the larger Arab world. In 1967, for instance, Moroccan troops supported Egypt in the Six-Day War against Israel. More recently, however, Moroccan efforts have been directed towards resolving Arab-Israeli differences. In 1982, Morocco hosted a meeting of Arab leaders to discuss the subject. Morocco also sent troops to join the multinational coalition which ousted Iraq from Kuwait in 1991. As in other Arab countries, however, the government faced popular protests from those who saw in Saddam Hussein a symbol of Arab resistance to the West.

Culture Today

Berber or Arab? The gradual mixing of Arab and Berber blood over the centuries has meant that Moroccans tend to define the two groups in cultural terms rather than racial ones, as seen by this response to a question put to an Arab from the south (Dwyer 1982, p. 119).

> Being Berber is just from language. If his origins are Berber, if his root is Berber, and if he knows the Berber language, only then is he a Berber. But if he no longer knows Berber, he's become an Arab . . . even if his roots are Berber. What, are you going to call him a Berber when he is an Arab? He was born here—that is an Arab.

Berbers who move to Arab communities and take up Arab ways become Arabs within a generation or two. The process is flexible, even reversible (Dwyer 1982, p.120).

> There was one girl from here who married a Berber in the mountains and there she became a Berber, knew their language and wore their clothes. But then she remarried here and became an Arab again.

Food, clothing, and shelter. In Moroccan cities, much social activity centers around tea. The ceremony of tea making is as important as the sweet, green, minty drink itself. A silver or brass tea service, ornate and decorated, is presented to a guest, who is often invited to prepare and pour the tea. For supper a Moroccan family might have *tagine* or *cous cous* followed by fruit. Tagine is a stew of mutton with onions, prunes, and nuts, or chicken with dates and almonds. Cous cous, Morocco's most famous national dish, consists of small, white semolina beads (similar to pasta) served in a heaping mound with bits of carrot, eggplant, turnips, and usually mutton. On formal occasions, or when a guest is present, these dishes are often supplemented with a procession of flavorful appetizers, other main dishes such as roast lamb, pigeon, or chicken pies, rich soups, yogurt, breads, pastries, and fruit.

Western dress is widespread, particularly in modern cities like Casablanca or Rabat, both of which had their most significant growth in the twentieth century. In rural areas and older cities such as Fes, with its traditional markets and walled old quarters, both men and women wear the Arab *jellaba*, a long, hooded overgarment, and felt or leather slippers. Men may wear a fez, the small brimless felt hat named for the old city, which is Morocco's distinct contribution to Arab clothing. Some women wear a veil.

Moroccan homes, which can be several hundred years old, are often built of dried mud, with high, windowless exterior walls. Often these walls surround a courtyard with shaded gardens and patios. The houses, especially in cities and towns, tend to be plain on the outside, but some are large and luxurious on the inside. Many of the

A Marrakech woman kneading bread.
Courtesy of Dr. Nikki Keddie, U.C.L.A.

urban poor—about thirty percent of all city dwellers—live in shanties made from discarded materials such as planks and flattened oil drums.

Family life. As in much of the Arab world, Moroccan perceptions of the family have changed in recent decades. Older traditions have begun to give way to newer practices. Segregation of the sexes and family-arranged marriages, for example, are no longer held to as completely as in the past. The patrilineal extended family, once the rule, in which a father heads a household that includes his married sons and their wives and children as well as the father's unmarried sons and daughters is now rare. Even in rural areas, the smaller nucleus of a couple and their unmarried children has largely replaced the old extended family.

Most Moroccans still depend on agriculture and herding for a livelihood, and for most of these people, life at home is filled with chores of food preparation and clothing making. Women grind corn and other grains, knead the grain into a dough, and cook the round loaf in an outdoor oven. This is the base of meals that must be prepared from raw ingredients. Men tend the flocks then return to join in such household chores as knitting. Water is often carried from a village fountain, or washing is done. The chores fill the days of the rural Moroccan.

A part of most Moroccan villages and towns is the *souk*. Usually, people gather at this open-air market weekly to trade their products. The souk is a center of trade and business of all kinds, including in some, the arranging of marriages.

Government. Morocco's government is a constitutional monarchy, in which the king's powers are limited by those of an elected legislature. The present constitution, drafted by King Hassan II in 1972, allows the king to take full control of the state in case of emergency. The king also influences the daily practice of government, in that he selects the prime minister and the council of ministers, and presides over the highest judicial council. The king and prime minister both have authority to prepare and suggest legislation to be endorsed or rejected by the elected legislature.

Morocco's legal system incorporates Islamic and Berber law, as well as Judaic codes. Jews played an important role in earlier Moroccan society, which absorbed Jewish artists and craftsmen fleeing persecution in medieval Spain. Although they once numbered more than 200,000, most Moroccan Jews emigrated to Israel in the 1950s so that today only about 14,000 remain.

Arts and literature. Like many other Islamic cultures, Moroccans have focused much of their artistic efforts on the design and building of mosques and religious schools. Islamic architecture, found throughout North Africa, southern Spain, and Sicily, emerged from the mixture of Arab, Berber, and Spanish styles in Muslim Spain. The style features horseshoe-shaped doorways, windows, and arches.

Moroccan craftsmen—jewelers, weavers, smiths, wood carvers, and especially leather-workers—have created intricate and beautiful objects for centuries. The city of Fes, established by the Idrisi, soon became the center of the artistic leather tradition. The tanners and bookbinders of Fes, for instance, ensured that "morocco" came to stand for the highest-quality leather bookbinding.

Moroccan literature is written in both Arabic and French. Writers mostly use classical Arabic instead of the Moroccan spoken variant; thus two of the country's spoken languages, Moroccan-Arabic and Berber, are largely oral rather than written. Arabic writers include the poet Allal al-Fassi, who wrote after World War I, and the novelist Abulhamid Benjelloun. Two authors in French, Driss Charibi and Ahmen Sefrioui, examine contemporary Moroccan culture.

Religion. Virtually all Moroccans (about ninety-nine percent) practice Sunni Islam (see ISLAM). Most distinctive aspects of Moroccan Islam, such as the important phenomenon of *maraboutism,* or the cults of local saints, suggest Berber influences. Greatly affecting religious practice in Morocco was Sufism, a movement that stressed a mystic element, and began in Iraq and Persia in the eighth and ninth centuries (see ISLAM).

The cities. Agriculture (barley, wheat, vegetables, and fruit) and herding goats and sheep have been the traditional mainstays of the Moroccan economy. In recent years, however, population growth and a prolonged drought in the 1980s encouraged many Moroccans to move to cities. Today, nearly half the population lives in urban centers. While Rabat is the nation's political capital, the busy port city of Casablanca is the center of its industrial activity. The world's richest phosphate deposits (used in fertilizers) are found nearby. With a population of nearly 2,500,000, Casablanca is Morocco's largest city. Tangier, declared in the colonial period an "international" zone, today retains a cosmopolitan flavor, and continues to attract artists and literary figures as well as tourists. Fes, with its respected university, beautiful mosques, and the contrast of newer French and older Arabic influences, endures as the heart of Morocco.

For More Information

Dwyer, Kevin. *Moroccan Dialogues.* Baltimore: Johns Hopkins University Press, 1982.

Morocco in Pictures. Minneapolis: Lerner Publishing Company, 1988.

Mostyn, Trevor, editor. *Cambridge Encyclopedia of the Middle East and North Africa.* Cambridge: Cambridge University Press, 1988.

Nelson, Harold D., editor. *Morocco: A Country Study.* Washington, D.C.: American University Press, 1985.

NUBIANS
(new' bee uns)

People who speak the Nubian language and live in Egypt.

Population: 50,000 (1985 estimate).
Location: Before 1963, in villages along the Nile River in the region of the Aswan High Dam. Now relocated to New Nubia, 20 miles north of Aswan.
Languages: Nubian; Arabic.

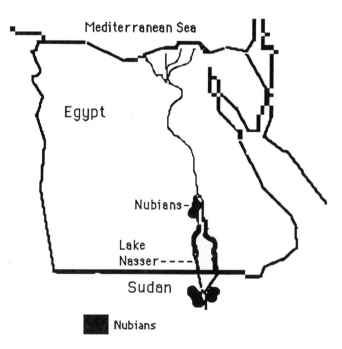

Nubians

Geographical Setting

Until recent history, "Nubian" was the name commonly given to people whose native villages were located in Nubia—a thin settlement along the Nile River that stretched for 500 miles from the first cataract (waterfall) at Aswan in southern Egypt to the fourth cataract near Dongola in Sudan. Today most of Old Nubia has been submerged by the flooding from the Aswan High Dam built in 1963. Before the water was backed up, a massive resettlement scheme relocated tens of thousands of Nubians to a new area of Egypt called New Nubia. The new land is a low-lying and fertile flood plain like the old land. Here, near the river, crops such as millet and date palms can be raised. Beyond this narrow strip, on either side of the river, the land becomes desert. In Nubia, the climate is extreme. Summer temperatures rise to 120 degrees Fahrenheit, and winter temperatures may fall below freezing.

Historical Background

Nubians are distinguished by geography, culture, and language. Having a dark skin like their inner African neighbors, Nubians are visibly distinct from the majority of Egyptians. They are, however, of a mixed Arab, Mediterranean, and African ancestry. For several millennia, foreign conquerors, alien traders, and adventurers passed through Nubia, at times settling and intermarrying within the various Nubian tribal groups. While once broken into many political units, Nubians today belong to two major societies—Kenzui and Fedija.

Ancient origin. Until the twentieth century, the history of Nubia had only been partially gathered through written records of neighboring states and foreign travelers. Then, before Nubia's archaeological past was forever submerged by the floods of the Aswan Dam, the world's largest archaeological salvage survey was undertaken. Sponsored by UNESCO (United Nations Educational, Scientific, and Cultural Organization), teams of scientists worked intensely to uncover clues to Nubian culture.

Excavations revealed a Nubian culture that existed before the time of the early Egyptian dynasties around 4000 B.C. Around 3000 B.C., Egyptian pottery and trade materials began to appear, pointing to contact between the two groups. From that time forward, Nubia's history is dominated by the pharaohs of ancient Egypt. Inscriptions of Egyptians show that Nubia was frequently attacked by Egyptian troops. When Sesostris I invaded Nubia about 1950 B.C., he named the land south of the second cataract Kush. By 1700 B.C., the Kingdom of Kush—based in the Nubian Sudan city of Napata—had broken through the frontier to take command of Aswan and begin raiding Upper Egypt. Pharaohs such as Ramses II built dozens of elaborate temple monuments like Abu Simbel, a gigantic temple south of Aswan. Nubia was subject to the changing rule of the Kushites and pharaohs until 45 B.C. In 23 B.C. Napata was destroyed by the Roman army and Nubia was divided into smaller kingdoms called the Merotic and Nobatae kingdoms. These kingdoms were the chief political units until a Nobatae king was converted to Christianity in A.D. 540.

Christian Nubia. In the sixth century A.D., a new era in Nubian history began with this conversion to Christianity. Soon most of Nubia had been converted and churches and scriptures began to appear throughout Nubia. A few of these churches have been excavated and show large frescoes of religious figures in the dress of the Eastern Orthodox Church. In the seventh century, an Arab leader of Egypt, Abdallah ibn'Said, invaded Nubia but shortly withdrew after arranging a treaty that became the basis of Egyptian-Nubian relations for 600 years. The treaty recognized the Christian kingdom, made trade relationships easier, and established a tributary relationship between the two countries that demanded an exchange of gifts annually. As Arab merchants then were allowed to visit Nubia, it became an important source of slaves for sub-Saharan Africa.

Islamic conversion and Ottoman rule. While Nubia was largely Christian, it was surrounded by Islamic powers. Gradually, over several hundred years, Nubia was converted to Islam. The last active Christian church in Egyptian Nubia was closed in the sixteenth century. Since Muslim tradition forbade the enslavement of Muslims by other Muslims, the slave trade in Nubia ceased.

The conversion to Islam coincided with a long period of distant rule by the Ottoman Empire based in present-day Turkey. During this period, from 1517 to 1805, Ottoman military stations were set up in Nubia. The Ottoman rulers of Egypt, the Mamelukes, made frequent raids upon Nubia and prevented Nubian trade across the Sahara. So suppressed were the Nubians during this time that historical records are limited to oral folk tradition. In 1811, the last remaining Mamelukes were massacred by the Egyptian Muhammad Ali, who included Nubians in his own administration.

British colonialism. From 1882 to 1922, Great Britain assumed control in Egypt and the Sudan and finally ended the slave trade that had been revived along the Nile. During this time, Nubian men, like many rural Egyptians, began to leave their village households and migrate to Cairo and Alexandria in search of work. Under the British, Nubians carved a niche for themselves as servants and guards within aristocratic homes and luxury hotels built for European tourists. Today Nubians are found in all sectors of Egyptian society, but they still dominate the service work force in urban centers, where they remain a tightly knit community. Social clubs called *gamaiyya*, provide a cultural continuity for Nubians living away from the roots of their ancestral village. The village family unit, or *nog,* remains the focus of Nubian culture as Nubian men eventually return home to their families and property.

The Aswan Dam and Nubian resettlement. Since 1898, successive dams built at Aswan at the first cataract along the Nile have left more than sixty percent of Nubian territory in Egypt and Sudan unfit for habitation. Due to increases in population in the past century, millions of Egyptians looked toward the dam to increase irrigation and open new land for farming. The dam, however, caused major shifts in Nubian society as settlements were abruptly disrupted. The first dam, initiated by the British and built in 1898, was enlarged in 1912 and 1934. By the 1960s when the Aswan High Dam was near completion, the fabric of Nubian villages had been drastically weakened. The villages were basically occupied by women, children, and the elderly living on less-than-adequate land and dependent on the urban income from Nubian men working in the cities. The Egyptian government soon initiated a resettlement scheme that moved the majority of Egyptian Nubians north of Aswan on a forty-mile stretch of land along the Nile that would become New Nubia. The massive and costly plan reconstructed Nubian village layouts and dwellings and even uprooted some of the old palm trees of Nubia to recreate the traditional environment. Services such as hospitals, along with secondary and teacher-training schools were also part of the scheme. The total cost of reconstruction was just over thirteen million British pounds (about $30,000,000).

Culture Today

The resettlement plan has brought changes and challenges to the Nubians. Yet, the foundations of the Nubian culture created over hundreds of generations—family structure, religion, and cultural traditions—have persisted. Nubian culture is centered upon the traditions that were established in the environment of Old Nubia. The Kenuzi and Fedija Nubians in Egypt share similar but often distinct cultural traditions.

The Nubian family and shared resources. Nubians speak of their land as "balad el aman"—a land of safety and security, a place where people and property are secure and where one can live in peace. The foundation of the relatively harmonious Nubian society can be found in the strength of family ties and the system of shared resources that has been the basis of Nubian social organization for several millennia. All units of family membership are called *nogs,* with the first nog being the household unit. The second nog is all kin who have ownership of shared property that has been subdivided. The third nog represents all of the smaller nogs spread over villages and districts that bear the same family name. Nubians are patrilineal; that is, they trace their descent through male ancestors. However, property and wealth may be inherited from both the father's and mother's side of the family through gifts at weddings.

The family is the basic means for acquiring wealth and property within Nubia. Shares of property are divided and exchanged through inheritance, gifts, and marriage alliances. Nubian family holdings are rarely sold. Due to the scarcity of resources in Nubia, the basic forms of property—land, cows, date palm trees and expensive water wheels called *eskalay*—are broken down into shares. For instance, each leg of a cow may be owned by different brothers and another portion by a cousin. Each owner has to play a role in caring for the cow according to his share. The complexities of dividing an extensive network of ownership of a date palm tree is evident at harvest time when Nubian owners can be seen seated under the tree dividing dates into piles. The Nubian preference for marrying amongst cousins keeps property circulating within an extended lineage. Marriage celebrations are thus grand occasions that solidify family relationships and shareholdings.

Traditional means of settling disputes. While various administrative units, military, and police have had offices within Nubia as a means for governing the territory, Nubians have developed their own system for settling disputes within families and the community. Whenever there is a conflict, a *wasta* (an intermediary, or "go-between") is used to carry messages back and forth between disagreeing groups and to help the parties reconcile their differences. It is considered the responsibility of every Nubian man or woman to intercede in quarrels between those kinsmen and neighbors with whom they share some identity or interest. Older men are usually called upon to perform the service. The wisdom of this method is illustrated by a Nubian story that tells of two men who were constantly quarreling over division of water in a stream they shared. Each man accused the other of taking more than his share of the water until an uncle overheard the argument. After thinking for a moment, the uncle picked up a stone and placed it in the middle of the channel dividing the water into two streams and effectively ending their long dispute. This art of "putting a stone in the middle" is highly valued in Nubian society as well as other Arab communities in the Middle East. Leaders within Nubian communities are recognized for their skill in settling disputes, thus preventing harmful discord from escalating.

Food and clothing. A variety of crops harvested on the Nile have become part of the Nubian diet. During the winter growing season, wheat, barley, millet, beans, lentils, peas, and watermelons are planted. Mangoes, citrus fruits, and, particularly, dates are also Nubian foods. Date trees are among the most cherished possessions of Nubians and serve both as a cash crop and as a gift of a shareholding at Nubian weddings. The leaves and trunks of the date palms are manufactured into trays, mats, baskets and ropes, utensils, and sponges. Despite the importance of the date tree, the Egyptian government has encouraged the cultivation of sugar cane as a cash crop in New Nubia.

One of the basic staples of the Nubian diet is the *dura*, a thin, coarse bread. Made without salt from freshly ground grain that is kneaded, formed into a thin disk, and baked on an iron plate, dura is also used among the Bedouin Arabs. Pieces of the bread are piled on top of one another and eaten with vegetable and sauce dishes. Specialty items include a beer made from barley or dura and a tasty jelly made from dates.

Present-day Nubians dress in clothing suited for the desert environment. Nubian men wear the traditional Arab gown (*gellabiyah*) and turban in preference to Western dress. Nubian women do not wear a full veil but they always wear a loose black outer garment called a *tob* over their head and shoulders, which may be drawn across the face when a stranger nears. Women wear jewelry as part of their bride-price and on festive occasions colorful gowns and *tobs* over their head.

The art of Nubian architecture. With the exception of the colorful, decorative tradition of painting houses, most of the artistic expressions within Nubia are associated with celebrations such as the singing and dancing at weddings. Their ceremonial traditions are perpetuated in the urban centers by young Nubian artists at Nubian social clubs.

At the resettlement villages, Nubians found the traditional household painting one of the primary means of reestablishing the cultural environment. The typical houses are spacious and consist of several large rooms surrounding an open courtyard. Built from earth and straw, or adobe, the houses are designed to catch breezes and to accommodate an extended family and guests. One of the most distinctive and admired features of Nubian houses are the highly ornamented facades which are carved into elaborate geometric patterns. The whole facade is often whitewashed and painted with colorful and intricate patterns. Rows of china dishes are often inserted into the walls to add a distinctive decorative touch. Nubian arts are family efforts, although women have a recognized talent in painting and a highly skilled woman may decorate the houses of a whole village.

Religion. Today Nubia is universally Islamic, although beliefs centered around the spirit of the Nile, ancestors, sheikhs (religious leaders) and other powerful beings are practiced alongside Islamic practices. The Nile is considered to be imbued with life-sustaining power, and because of its annual flooding, to hold the power of life and death. Amongst the Kenuz, a distinctive festival is celebrated known as the *moulid* (Saint's Day Celebration), which was once celebrated at more than 150 shrines of ancestors of the Nubians. On the fifteenth day of the Islamic month Shaaban, Kenuzi Nubians from all over Egypt come to the shrines of the first Kenuzi sheikhs, Hassan and Hussein, to present gifts to the shrine in the fulfillment of a vow made the previous year. Part of the ritual celebration is the replacement of the tomb covers of the other ancestral shrines. Colorful processions, dancing, singing and feasting are part of the festivities, which honor and reinforce the collective past of the Kenuzi. *Moulids* continue to be annually celebrated in the New Nubian settlements as a means to regenerate Nubian cultural identity.

Education. Only since the 1930s has formal education been available to Nubians, yet Nubians have exceeded the literacy rate of most rural Egyptian communities. According to a 1960 study, 60 percent of Nubia's male population was literate as compared with twenty-three percent among all rural Egyptian males. In contrast, nine percent of Nubian females are literate, a rate that is similar to other Egyptian rural populations. Alongside of Nubian languages, Nubians are learning Arabic as part of a process of acculturation into Egyptian society. The New Nubian resettlement communities have primary and secondary schools and teacher-training facilities as part of a new thrust for education.

Conclusion. While the land and historical remnants of Nubia's past have been submerged by the floods of Aswan Dam, Nubians have continued to assert their cultural identity and way of life in the settlements of New Nubia and in the urban centers of Egyptian society. Some changes were irrevocable as familial ties to the land, irrigation through the water wheel (*eskalay*), and sacred religious sites have been lost. In many ways, the resettlement strengthened Nubian cultural identity and increased an awareness of the importance of Nubian traditions and languages to maintain "balad el aman"—a land of peace.

For More Information

Adams, William. *Nubia: Corridor to Africa.* Princeton, New Jersey: Princeton University Press, 1977.

Geiser, Peter. *The Egyptian Nubian: A Study in Social Symbiosis.* Cairo: American University in Cairo Press, 1986.

Fernea, Robert. *Nubians in Egypt: Peaceful People.* Austin: University of Texas Press, 1973.

PALESTINIANS
(pal eh stin' e uns)

Agricultural Muslim and Christian people who have lived for millennia in the land that is now Israel; currently the group resides in various countries of the Middle East.

Population: 4,000,000 (1988 estimate).
Location: Occupied territories of the West Bank and Gaza; Jordan; Lebanon; Syria; Iraq; Egypt; Saudi Arabia; Libya; Morocco.
Language: Arabic.

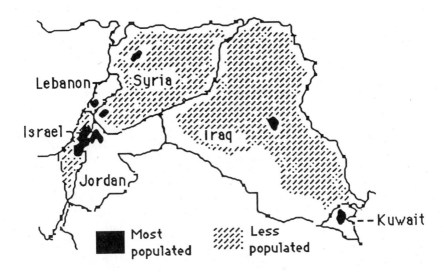

Geographical Setting

The area once known as Palestine includes modern-day Israel, the occupied territories of the Gaza Strip and the West Bank of the Jordan River, and the Golan Heights on the border of Syria. It is a small but varied region of fertile lowlands, humid coastal plains, the arid Negev desert of the south, and rocky mounds. More than half of this land has been turned into productive farmland by large-scale irrigation. In the desert, rainfall is scant, averaging less than four inches annually. Long, hot, dry summers and shorter, cold winters form a Mediterranean climate.

Historical Background

Origins. Lying on the pathways between the great societies of the Tigris and Euphrates rivers to the northeast and the Nile River to the west, the area of Palestine was a mixing ground and the scene of many of the battles between east and west. More than 5,000 years ago the land was inhabited by nomadic hunters and small agricultural societies. Merchants crossed the land from east and west bringing ideas of pictograms from Egypt, a written alphabet from Phoenicia to the north, and law and government from Mesopotamia. Before 1100 B.C., Hebrews had moved into the hill country of Palestine, and the Kingdom of Philistia had arisen in the southwest.

About 1000 B.C., King David united the region occupied by early ancestors of Arabs and Jews. Separated by vocation and religion, the Hebrews lived apart as herders, while the early Arabs lived in towns and villages as merchants, traders, and farmers. After King David, the land was again divided, with separate kingdoms of Judah and Israel. But these small monarchies were no match for Assyrians who invaded the country and for a time ruled the region.

In 586 B.C., Babylonians from the Fertile Crescent captured the land, destroyed the Hebrew temple, and exiled the Hebrew people to be servants in Babylon. When Babylon was eventually defeated by Persians from the east, some of the Hebrews returned to their homes, while others preferred to remain in Babylonia, preserving their beliefs by following religious laws contained in a scroll called the *Torah.*

There followed a succession of foreign rulers: Egyptians, Greeks, Romans, Egyptians, and in 1516, Turks. The land of Palestine was part of the Ottoman Empire for 500 years. After World War I, the

British controlled the region and in 1917, British Foreign Secretary Arthur Balfour declared British intent to reestablish a Jewish homeland in Palestine. Arab residents of the region, small-scale farmers and urban dwellers, protested this action, claiming the land as their own. They had been left alone in the land while the Jews were spread throughout the world. Between 1917 and 1930, many Jewish people did return to the region, and some bought land from wealthy non-Jewish landowners. These owners often lived away from their holdings, in countries like Syria, and rented their lands to peasant farmers. From these absentee owners, Jews purchased a foothold of six percent of the land.

Israel. By the beginning of World War II, a Jewish population was firmly entrenched in Palestine, and the Muslims, Christians, and Jews were protesting United Nations proposals for separate states. In 1948, the United States and the Soviet Union led world actions to recognize Israel—a land including much of the old Palestine—as a separate nation. Having lost some of the land they farmed and now under rule with which they disagreed, many of the Muslim Palestinians were forced to move. As many as 800,000 Palestinians migrated to Syria, Kuwait, Iraq, and other countries of the world. Most of those remaining in old Palestine were confined in poverty to the Israeli-occupied territories of the West Bank, Gaza Strip, and Golan Heights. Nearly 2,000,000 Muslim and Christian Arabs still live in Israel.

A series of battles between Israel and its neighbors has followed, as the now dislocated Arab Palestinians were supported by other countries in their quest to recapture the country. In the late 1980s and early 1990s, almost constant battles between these Arabs now known worldwide as Palestinians and the Jewish government of Israel have focused world attention on the plight of the disenfranchised Palestinians, who like the dispersed Jews before them seek to be near Jerusalem, the site of some of their holy symbols.

Culture Today

Palestinians in Israel. Once a majority of peasant farmers, the Palestinians of Israel now live in small villages or refugee camps and find such work as they can in Jewish-owned factories and farms. Increasing tensions between Muslims and Jews and the resultant tightening of Jewish military control have raised unemployment in the West Bank area. Here many Palestinians live without running water or electricity. More than 500,000 still live within Israel, outside the occupied territories. These people of the regions of Galilee, the Negev Desert, and the Haifa area, live in small towns that were once self-supporting but whose people now provide labor for Israeli agriculture (see ISRAELI JEWS). Almost all these towns are under Israeli military government control. Some Muslim Palestinians are small businessmen, shopkeepers serving the people of the towns, house painters, construction workers, or unskilled laborers in nearby Israeli cities.

Palestinian expatriates. Two million people of Palestinian origin or descent now live in the nearby countries of Syria, Iraq, Egypt, Libya, and Morocco. Here they are part of the general population of each country and work in all occupations. Palestinian business interests include IntraBank, Arab Bank, Middle East Airlines, Arabia Insurance, and many others. Many leave their families in the cities and find work in the oil fields and construction industries. A large number of these workers fled to refugee camps in Jordan when Iraq invaded Kuwait in 1991.

Religion. Seventy-five percent of Palestinians are Muslims, most of them of the Sunni sect of Islam. Seventeen percent are Arab Christians and eight percent are Druze, whose religion includes elements of both Muslim and Christian beliefs.

Strict adherence by Muslims to the teachings of the Quran varies from one location to another. Rural Muslims follow a popular form of Islam, pay less attention to religious rituals, and provide less support for their religious institutions. While they follow the teachings of the local religious leader, the *imam*, they often mix these teachings with folk beliefs, including a belief in evil spirits called *jinns*, which can take the shape of natural forms and cause mischief or misfortune. These villagers need not make a pilgrimage to Mecca unless they can afford it, but must follow such Muslim practices as fasting for the entire month of Ramadan.

In Israel, such practices as the seclusion of women, the wearing of a veil and polygyny are less commonly followed, and divorce for men is more difficult under Israeli law.

Family life. An extended family organization, the *hamula*, once regulated village society. This powerful male-dominated extended family is disappearing as families spread to find work and as land resources once distributed through the clan have disappeared.

Marriage of cousins within the hamula is still encouraged, but the once arranged marriages are more often made by choice. These marriages are no longer restricted to hamula members. Once married, the woman is expected to bear children, clean the home, cook, and care for the needs of her husband. The husband is expected to be financially able to pay a bride-price and to provide for his family. These patterns are eroding, as women become more educated and able to help support the family. In addition, Palestinian women are becoming vocal participants in their homes and communities. Some women lead workers' strikes and most demonstrate for a Palestinian state.

Village life. In the mid-nineteenth century Palestinians were mostly rural villagers under the rule of clan or sub-clan chiefs who belonged to two large confederations called Qais and Yaman. Villages were controlled by sheikhs who could collect taxes. The tax collectors, *multazim*, used this power to gain control of the lands, converting them from subsistence farming to cash crops. The Land Laws of the 1850s led to large landownings and to sharecroppers. Peasants lived in villages and worked as tenant farmers. Landed people became associated with a guild of religious leaders descended from the prophet Muhammad, the Ashrafs, and other powerful families, who gained control of the economic and religious life of the Palestinians. Under the Ashrafs, village elders chose a leader, the *muktar*, whose job it was to organize the work force for the communal harvest. Some of this unity remains today.

Palestinian villagers share a common code of honor, loyalty, and respect for their elders. In times of need they look after each other, tend their neighbors' sheep and goats, and share what they have with visitors and travelers.

Most villages and now camps are bustling places of activity. In the center of town, old men smoke water pipes and drink small cups of strong coffee while arguing or playing cards with their friends. Men gather to talk in the streets while women do their daily shopping at outdoor food and fruit stands. The main street is filled with pedestrians, taxis, and old buses while commuters weave in and out of traffic on bicycles. Young people play in the back alleys of streets that contain small shops—bakeries, meat shops, cobblers, tailors—and stands where vendors sell household supplies, soap, candles, cutlery, and clothing. Typically located on a flat hill, the old quarters of the Palestinian village contain one-story houses constructed of white stone. The houses are separated by stone-cobbled streets and small groves of olive trees.

Food, clothing, and shelter. A common house contains a kitchen, a room for bathing, and a number of small rooms for sleeping. The interior walls and ceilings are plastered in white, and concrete floors are covered with pieces of linoleum or carpet. The houses have wooden doors and window frames and are often surrounded by small gardens separated from the street by a high wall with a gateway. Affluent homes have indoor plumbing and electricity, while other households draw water form the local well and cook on charcoal stoves. Most Palestinians have radios, record players, small cooking appliances, and some have refrigerators and televisions sets.

The homes in refugee camps are tents or cinder-block dwellings built by the UNRWA (United Nations Relief Workers). These homes have no running water or electricity, and are covered with corrugated metal roofs. Doors are also corrugated metal, and windows are covered by wooden shutters. Cooking is done on a metal grate laid over a tin container filled with charcoal. Thin sleeping mats are rolled up during the day. Bathing and clothes washing are done using metal drums filled by hosing water from street-side faucets.

With the exception of the elderly, most people today wear Western-style clothing—T-shirts and jeans with sandals for the young, while the men wear trousers, shirts, sweaters, and sports jackets. Men also wear the traditional black-and-white checked *kaffiyeh* headdress held in place by a double ring of black cord. The elderly men often wear long white robes (*jallabiyeh*), a tunic (*kimba*), or a Western sports jacket under a camel hair coat (*abba*). Their wives wear long black peasant dresses (*thaub*) with an embroidered bodice. Women cover their head and shoulders with a shawl. Younger women wear knee-length skirts and dresses, often with a scarf.

A simple wheat and mutton diet had its origin thousands of years ago. Meals are eaten while seated on mats or cushions set around a cloth laid out on the floor. Most often, pieces of *khoubz*, a flat bread, are used to scoop up the food for eating.

Pork is forbidden by the Muslim religion and beef is not available. The varied diet is based on lamb or goat meat, chicken, and fish served with spiced saffron rice. For noon and evening meals, this is supplemented with home-grown vegetables, milk products, olives, citrus fruits, honey, herbs, and spices.

Breakfast may consist of cheese, olives, and bread, or it may be a bowl of a yogurtlike food called *laban*. The main meal might include one-course dishes such as meat pies (*lahem*) or a casserole called *maklube* of chicken cooked below a layer of rice then inverted like an upside-down cake to eat. *Mansaf* is a festive dish consisting of a base of paper-thin whole-wheat crust covered with seasoned rice and topped with chunks of stewed lamb. Food preparation usually demands liberal amounts of olive oil, fresh herbs, and spices.

Education. The Palestinian elite, most of whom live in exile, are a highly literate and educated group. Many have attended colleges and universities as refugees and then used their education to enter the professions in the Arab world. They belong to a class of doctors, lawyers, academics, engineers, writers, and journalists. However, educated Palestinians living in Israel find themselves severely restricted in professional and social advancement.

Children attend schools provided by the Israeli government, where lessons are taught in Arabic. Avoiding texts about Jewish heros and Jewish history, Palestinians in Israel use texts from Jordan that must be approved by the Israeli government. In recent years, schools for Arabs in the occupied territories have been curtailed as student activity in a rebellion called *intifada* has grown.

Arts, music, and literature. On festive occasions and events such as weddings and circumcision of males, men and women dance separately, singing and clapping to the rhythm of a drum called the *derbakah*. Men dance in a semicircle with their arms around each other. In addition to the drum, a lute player is accompanied by a piper playing a reed instrument, the *shebabah*. Singers sing folk songs and improvise songs of praise of family and friends.

Palestinian contributions to literature, history, art, and poetry are evident in many countries and include such famous names as Mahmoud Darwish, the poet who wrote the protest poem called "Investigation." Edward Said is a well-known historian and essayist, Afif Bulos is a musician of note, and painter Jammana Al-Husseni shows his works internationally. Author and radio personality Sabri Jiryis wrote *The Arabs in Israel,* an account of events in 1956 in one Palestinian town, Kafr Qasim.

An excerpt from Mahmoud Darwish's poem "Investigation" is an example of the angry voice that reaches out from occupied territory (Dimbley 1980, p. 221):

Write down,
I am an Arab,
I am a name without a title,
Steadfast in a frenzied world.

My roots sink deep
Beyond the ages,
Beyond time.

For More Information

Aburish, Said K. *Children of Bethany: The History of a Palestinian Family.* Bloomington: University of Indiana Press, 1988.

Bendt, Ingela, and J. Downing. *We Shall Return: Women of Palestine.* London: Zed Press Ltd., 1982.

Curtis, Michael, Joseph Neyer, Chaim Waxman, and Allen Pollack, editors. *The Palestinians; People, History, Politics.* New Jersey: Transaction Books, 1975.

Dimbley, Jonathan. *The Palestinians.* New York: Quartet Books Inc., 1980.

Johnson, Paul. *Civilizations of the Holy Land.* New York: Atheneum, 1979.

PUSHTUN
(push ton')

People of central, southern, and eastern Afghanistan known
historically for their warlike attitude.

Population: 15,000,000 (1988 estimate).
Location: Afghanistan, particularly the southern plains and eastern
mountains; Pakistan; Iran; the Soviet Union.
Languages: Pushtu, an eastern Iranian language; Persian.

Geographical Setting

Afghanistan is a rugged land of high mountains and fertile mountain valleys. More than two-thirds of the country in the north is dominated by the Hindu Kush Range, which rises to 18,000- to 22,000-foot peaks. The result of severe earth movement in the past, some of these mountains run east to west, while nearby ranges run north to south. In the north the mountains slope to the steppe lands of the Soviet Union. To the south and west the mountain ranges slope to a plateau of rolling hills. The plateau area is dry, with rainfall averaging less than ten inches per year. Precipitation increases in the east, but rarely exceeds thirty inches annually. Temperatures are extreme—bitterly cold in the mountains in winter and over 100 degrees Fahrenheit in the southern summer. The Pushtun, the largest group of Afghans, spread over the slopes and plateau of the south.

Historical Background

Origin. The people of Afghanistan claim to be descended from King Saul through his son Ishmail and Ishmail's son Afghana. The country was long considered part of Persia, and later was conquered by Alexander the Great. The Pushtun people, who make up the majority of Afghans, may be the original inhabitants of the Peshawar Valley, which stretches from Kabul in Afghanistan through the Khyber Pass into Pakistan. They inhabited the region as early as the sixth century A.D. One of the earliest pieces of literature in the Pushtu language is a history of the conquest of Swat, a kingdom on the Peshawar Valley border near Pakistan in A.D. 1413-14. The presence of the Pushtun in the valley can be traced with certainty to the 1500s.

Reputation. Early in their history, these people gained a reputation for being warlike. About A.D. 1000, Pushtun soldiers seized and ruled part of present-day Iran, and during another period warriors from Afghanistan invaded India (1525). In 1550, they fought the Usufzai who occupied most of the fertile lands of the region. From 1504 to the eighteenth century, the Pushtun resisted rule by other groups who attempted to control the region. In the eighteenth century, Marathas and Sikhs from the east took control of the area, but the Pushtun resisted their rule.

Early history. For centuries, the Pushtun were a fragmented group, living in tribal organizations and loyal to their local leaders. But between the seventh and ninth centuries, Islam reached all parts of the country and encouraged a union under a ruler at Ghazni. Another tribal kingdom, Ghor, eventually defeated Ghazni and ruled the region until the Mogul forces took control. By the end of the sixteenth century, the country was again divided, this time between India and Persia.

In 1747, a Persian ruler, Ahmad Shah, was elected Amir of Afghanistan and began to form the Pushtun and other tribal groups into a unified political group. Overthrown by Dost Muhammad in 1835, the land soon fell to the British. British control over the Peshawar Valley was completed in 1849, even though the Pushtun resisted with a skill that earned them a reputation as superior guerrilla warriors. Their continued resistance to British rule led to a declaration of independence following World War I, and King Amanullah became ruler in 1919.

Pushtun dominance. The Pushtun under King Amanullah became the dominant ethnic group in the new independent country. With Pushtun support, the king began a program of modernization that was pursued by his successors. Pushtu was adopted as the official language of Afghanistan in 1937. Educational institutions were established and cotton and textile industries were developed. A major blow to the Pushtuns was the separation of some of their people under a new government when Pakistan was formed in 1947.

A defeated majority. While the Pushtun people constitute sixty percent of the population of Afghanistan and have played an important role in its development as a separate nation, they lost power when King Zahiar Shah was deposed in 1973. Then the Republic of Afghanistan was established under the military rule of Lieutenant General Muhammad Daud. This leader was overthrown in a second coup in 1978 and replaced by the Khalzi Party, a Communist organization supported by the Soviet Union. Civil war began immediately, led by people from Pushtun villages. In 1979, the Soviet Union intervened on the part of the government.

Families of *mujahidin* rebels ("freedom fighters") from Pushtun and other groups were bombed and attacked with napalm by loyal government forces trained and equipped by the Soviet Union. Helicopter gunships destroyed whole villages. Three million survivors, most of them from Pushtun villages, fled into Pakistan. Then leaving their families in refugee camps, the men returned to Afghanistan to continue battle. The anticipated easy victory over the guerrillas by a government force based at the swelling city of Kabul, proved difficult to achieve. Pushtun rebels persisted with such success that by 1989 the Soviet Union had wearied of the struggle and prepared to withdraw its troop support. The ruler of Afghanistan, Dr. Najibullah Ahmadzai, began to reinstall a more democratic form of government and to attempt to reconcile the various rebel groups.

Aftermath of the war. Reconciliation and the rebuilding of Afghanistan, however, will be difficult. The struggle sent villagers whose farmlands had been destroyed to cities poorly equipped to deal with them. Kabul, the once small and quiet capital has swelled to 600,000 people. Meanwhile, nearly one-third of the people fled the country during the rebellion. Hundreds of thousands of Pushtun now live in Pakistan. Those villagers who remained faced, in many areas, uncertain water supplies. Only three percent of the people outside the large cities have safe water to drink. Fifty percent of children die before the age of five years, and few educated people remain in Afghanistan. More than three-fourths of the people of Afghanistan cannot read or write.

Culture Today

The Pushtun code. The Pushtun, along with nearly ninety-nine percent of all Afghans are Muslims and adhere to Muslim law. But the Pushtun also abide by their own long-standing code known as *Pushtunwali*. This code places these obligations on the people: defense of property and honor *(ghayarat)*, revenge *(badal)*, asylum and refuge to those who seek it *(nanawatee)*, and hospitality to guests *(melmastia)*. This code is sometimes translated into warlike actions. Disputes over gold, women, or land have commonly led to blood feuds between Pushtun families and clans. Murders are often avenged by killing not only the murderer but other male relatives in the murderer's family. Under these code interpretations, one-half of a village might be engaged in an ongoing feud with the other half. Today, there is a tendency for wrongdoers to appease their opponents by paying blood money.

Political organization. Pushtun villages scattered in the hill regions of Afghanistan are guided by a *jirga*, a village assembly of adult males who are called upon to settle disputes. These elders enjoy the chosen social status because of their age and experience. Larger hill communities are ruled by a local chief with little allegiance to or aid from the national government. Only in the larger cities and towns are the structures of Pakistani or Afghan national rule effective. This issue of divided rule is further complicated by the unstable nature of the population. One-sixth of the Pushtun still lead nomadic lives as herders in the mountains.

Food, clothing, and shelter. Three-fourths of the Pushtun are engaged in farming although only one-eighth of the land is devoted to agriculture. The more successful farmers raise cash crops such as cotton, along with food crops—wheat, rice, potatoes, and vegetables. The most successful of them live on large estates or in towns where they enjoy conveniences such as refrigerators and telephones. The majority, however, live in small villages with few conveniences and farm small plots of wheat and barley. Others still move with their flocks and herd sheep, goats, camels, and horses. Many Pushtun workers, however, have left their traditional occupations in farming and herding to find jobs in construction, lumber, or any of the occupations related to a big city.

The herders live in black, goat-hair tents while migrating with their animals. Village homes are built on stone foundations, with walls made of earth and straw or stone and flat earth-covered roofs. A group of houses of an extended family is often surrounded by a high mud wall with cylinder-shaped watchtowers as safeguards against enemy attack.

The home of a single family includes several rooms—for sleeping, housing guests, cooking, and bathing. It also contains a place for prayer. Almost all households keep cattle or goats for food. Buttermilk, cheese, and cream curds are popular. Fish, vegetables such as lentils and spinach, fruits, and berries such as mulberries are among the most common foods. Brown bread and tea are parts of the everyday diet.

Typical clothing for Pushtun men includes long cotton or light woolen shirts that button at one shoulder and cover baggy dark-colored trousers. Some wear sweaters under their shirts or waistcoats over them. Weapons (rifles, pistols, or knives) complete the outfit of the villagers. Men wear a turban cap that is often tied in a manner to identify the Pushtun group of the wearer.

A shirt and trousers also serve as everyday wear for Pushtun village women, but are often in brighter colors. Sometime white sheetlike coverings are worn for special occasions. It is not unusual for coins to be sewn into the garments for decoration and for safekeeping. Women working in the fields wear the *chadar*, or head shawl, while others wear the *chadry*, a sacklike veil that extends from the head to the toes, following the tradition of secluding women.

Recreation. Teams of Pushtun compete in athletic events. A popular sport is *ghosai*, a form of wrestling in which a team member hops on one leg to reach a goal that is protected by his teammates against their opponents. In *buzkashi*, the object is for a team member to retrieve a calf's body from a ditch while riding on horseback and then carry it to a goal.

Dance is popular among the Pushtun. One dance, the *attan*, is performed by fifty or more people formed into a large circle and is accompanied by singing. Pushtun music features melodies for drum and flute.

Religion. Before the Muslim conquests of the seventh to the ninth centuries, an equal number of the people were Buddhists. Today, the Pushtun follow the Sunni sect of Islam, praying frequently, visiting mosques when possible, and providing hospitality to the needy and to visitors in the manner prescribed by their religion.

Language and literature. Pushtun people speak an Asian language called Pushtu. Until the acceptance of Islam the language had no written form. The Pushtun write using Arab characters, but in their own language, which includes three more consonants than Arabic. In this language, the literature of the Pushtun is rich, particularly in history and poetry. Beginning with a history of the conquest of Swat written by Shaikh Mali about A.D. 1420, Pushtun literature tells of wars, victories, and daily events. Abdur Rahman, the best-known poet, created his masterpieces in the seventeenth century. Other poets included Khushal Khan and Ahmad Shah, the founder of the kingdom in Afghanistan. Beside writing and speaking Pushtu, many Pushtuns write Persian, which is the cultural language of Afghans.

For More Information

Fisher. W. B. *The Middle East: A Physical, Social, and Regional Geography.* London: Methuen and Company Ltd., 1978.

Western and Central Asia. Danbury, Connecticut: Danbury Press, 1973.

QASHQA'I

A confederacy of tribal groups whose members have been camel, sheep, and goat herders in the southern Iranian highlands.

Population: 600,000 (1988 estimate).
Location: Iran.
Language: Turki, a western Oghuz Turkic language.

Geographical Setting

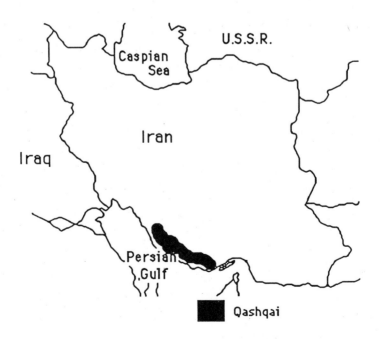

The Qashqa'i are primarily nomadic herders of sheep and goats. The people migrate great distances in southwestern Iran, with the greatest concentration of Qashqa'i located in the Fars province. The Zagros Mountain Range runs in two parallel chains through the region and plays an important role in the livelihood of the Qashqa'i. In order to find grass and water for their herds, the Qashqa'i migrate twice a year between the warm, lower-lying valleys near the Persian Gulf and the higher pastures of the Zagros. Winters are spent in the warmer areas (*garmsir*). As these pastures begin to dry up in the early spring, the Qashqa'i move their camps to the higher cooler areas (*sarhad*) where they spend the summer. These mass migrations occur over distances of 150 to 300 miles and are completed within three to six weeks each way.

Historical Background

Origins. The Qashqa'i are not a single ethnic group or tribe; rather, they are descendants from people having diverse linguistic, cultural and tribal backgrounds who have migrated into Iran from southwest and central Asia since Islamic times. In the seventeenth century, a confederacy (a united alliance) of various tribes were formed under Jani Mohammad Aqa, a leader of the Shahilu family. Historical documents about the Qashqa'i began to be recorded in Persia around this time. Some sources place the origin of the Qashqa'i among the Khalaj, one of the Middle East's largest Turkic groups from Central Asia who were moved to central and eastern Iran at the end of the fourteenth century. At this time a group of the Khalaj were said to have fled and settled in the Fars province where present day Qashqa'i live. The oral folklore of the people refers also to their origin. The Qashqa'i assert that their name is derived from the Turkic '*Qashqa Atlilar*' which refers to a lucky sign "Those of the Horses with the White Spots on Their Foreheads." This interpretation relates to the legend that the Qashqa'i were originally cavalrymen whose families tended flocks for the Mongol Emperor Genghis Khan and participated in his westward campaigns.

In fact, the origins of the Qashqa'i are likely to be as diverse as the diversity of the present-day Qashqa'i. Many of the Turks, Lurs, Laks, Kurds, Arabs, Persians and Gypsies who sought the resources in the region eventually aligned themselves with Qashqa'i leadership and over time assumed Qashqa'i identity. In the twentieth century, the major Qashqa'i tribes are Amaleh, Darrehshuri, Kashkuli Bozorg, Shish Boluki, and Farsi Madan.

The Qashqa'i confederacy. In the early 1600's, Jani Mohammed Aqa was given the title 'khan' to govern the various tribes of the Fars province. The Qashqa'i consider Jani Mohammed Aqa of the Shahilu family as the founder of the Qashqa'i confederacy. Over time, the Shahilu became the paramount rulers, or Il Khani, of the Qashqa'i and, in the earliest government documents about the area, the Shahilu family name was refered to as Qashqa'i.

Throughout the Qashqa'i's history, the Shahilu family has derived its authority from the ruling monarchies and governments of the Iranian nation. During the eighteenth century Iranian state rulers were unable to administer and control the largely nomadic, tribally organized people of the Fars province. These rulers relied on the Shahilu family to handle the difficult task of governing the various subgroups. The Shahilu's power came from the allegiance of the various subgroups of the Qashqa'i who benefited from being members of a politically unified body that served and protected their interest with the neighboring forces. By the mid-nineteenth century, the Shahilu were firmly in position as the leaders of the culturally diverse but largely Turkic peoples in the rural southern Zagros Mountains. However, it was not until the political conflicts of the twentieth century that a Qashqa'i cultural identity emerged.

Qashqa'i rise to power. The formation of the Khamesh tribal confederacy in the Fars province in 1861 initiated a new era in Qashqa'i history. Regional competition between the Khamesh and the Qashqa'i led to a greater consolidation of power amongst the Qashqa'i as an entity to be reckoned with and not just a taxable administrative body. The rivalry between the two confederacies was a source of unrest in the Fars province and led to increasing British intervention to ensure the security of the trade routes they had established through the province. These roads became a major source of conflict between the Qashqa'i and the British from 1865 into the the twentieth century.

Conflict with the British. In 1906-11 a national movement for a constitutional government challenged the Qajar dynasty that ruled Iran and weakened its administrative powers over the provinces. The Fars province became embroiled in conflict over power. The German presence in southern Iran drew the local conflicts into a wider British-

German rivalry as both sides tried to win over local powers. In 1917 and 1918, the Qashqa'i fought against British supported armies, but Great Britian assumed administrative and economic control of Iran in 1919. During this period the Il Khani (paramount leader) of the Qashqa'i began to depend more upon the tribal power of his own people than on the state and government.

Reza Shah. From 1925-1941, the regime of Reza Shah began to build a strong central government in Iran. The tribal units in the country were a threat to this unity and the Shah dealt harshly with the nomadic tribes. As the new state required political subordination of all its citizens, many Qashqa'i leaders were executed, imprisoned and exiled to ensure state control over the perceived threat of the Qashqa'i. The policy of Reza Shah was to eliminate the Qashqa'i as a political and cultural entity. The Qashqa'i people were disarmed, militarily subjugated, and forced to relinquish their traditional dress. Migration routes were blocked and nomads were ordered to settle. Many were forcibly settled on land that could not support their flocks or produce food crops. The rebellion of 1929 was an attempt by the Qashqa'i and other tribal minorities in the Fars region to fight on behalf of their interests. This unsuccessful rebellion furthered Reza Shah's military tyranny in the region, causing him to remove all of the Il Khani and their potential successors from the region. Despite the political and cultural oppression of the Persian Iranian state, the Qashqa'i identity became even stronger. With the abdication of Reza Shah in 1941, political leaders of the Qashqa'i returned and the Qashqa'i resumed their nomadic way of life.

Changes: 1956-1978. After a brief period of relative independence between 1941 and 1953, Reza Shah's son Mohammed Reza Shah regained power and formally disbanded the Qashqa'i confederacy in 1956. The *Il Khani* were once again sent into exile and military governors were installed in their place. Between 1956 and 1979, state action against the Qashqa'i was not as harsh as under the first Pahlavi ruler, Reza Shah. However, the removal of tribal leaders, government control of land, and loss of pasture, demanded changes in Qashqa'i lives, and the Qashqa'i began to move in three general directions: settled village life, a difficult form of herding nomadism, and urban wage labor. These changes resulted in a more divided tribal society.

Due to the natural richness of the Fars province and its strategic position along trade routes from the Persian Gulf, the Qashqa'i became one of the wealthiest tribal groups in Iran. While the Shahilu family of old Qashqa'i rulers no longer wielded political control, it remained a small, exclusive, wealthy elite. Shahilu income came from agricultural, orchard, and ranch lands which they owned. Due to land reform in the early 1960's, a second class of landowning Qashqa'i emerged, with upper middle and middle class urban lifestyles similar to other groups in Iranian society. The majority of Qashqa'i belonged to a third class, which relied on a combined income of animal husbandry and agriculture. A fourth class of poorer Qashqa'i owned small flocks but depended on some wage labor to supplement their income. A fifth group depended solely upon employment for their livelihood. In the 1970s, many of these Qashqa'i left for the larger Iranian cities and other Persian Gulf states to engage in contract labor.

The Islamic revolution. The Islamic revolution against the rule of the Shah in 1978-79 provided an opportunity for the Qashqa'i to seize control of their lands once again. Political leaders returned from exile, and many Qashqa'i returned to their pastoral way of life, which they found more profitable than the livelihoods adopted in the 1960's and 1970's. As the Qashqa'i were Shi'ite Muslims, unlike the Sunnis of other ethnic minorities in Iran, the Il Khannis were allowed to assert their political leadership in the region for a brief period. After 1979, the vast majority of the Qashqa'i were left unobstructed by the

A Qashqa'i camel caravan. *Courtesy of Dr. Nikki Keddie, U.C.L.A.*

government to continue their herding and agriculture livelihoods. Then, in the 1980's, military confrontations between the Ayatollah Khomeini's Revolutionary Guard and the Qashqa'i broke out when a Qashqa'i leader, Khosrow Khan Qashqa'i, was denied a seat in Parliament, arrested, and imprisoned. The Revolutionary Guards attacked Qashqa'i camps and by 1982 many Qashqa'i political leaders were killed or once again forced to flee Iran. Today, however, the Qashqa'i in the rural areas remain armed to resist the threat of state control that has continually besieged their land and way of life.

Culture Today

Family life. The majority of the Qashqa'i today are still nomadic sheep and goat herders and farmers despite the influence of settled urban lifestyles. The Qashqa'i family works together to sustain their herding and agricultural livelihood. Older boys and men take care of the daily herding while the younger boys and girls look after the young animals and dogs. Adolescent girls and their mothers do most of the cooking, milking, milk processing, weaving and child care. Men perform economic and political tasks and participate in group decision-making. All household members participate in the making and breaking of camp during migrations.

Bread making in a Qashqa'i home. *Courtesy of Dr. Nikki Keddie, U.C.L.A.*

Qashqa'i men and women view their roles as interdependent and mutually beneficial. In general there is a greater equality between men and women in Qashqa'i communities than in many Muslim and Middle Eastern rural settings. For example, Qashqa'i women do not wear veils across their face except when visiting bazaars and religious shrines, where they are obliged to conform with the prevailing customs.

Goverment. The Qashqa'i confederacy of tribes was officially disbanded by the Iranian government in 1956. Before that time the people were grouped into six major divisions known as *taifeh*. All of the taifeh were governed by a paramount chief or *Il Khan* from the ruling Shahilu family. Each taifeh was headed by a subchief, or *Kalantar*, who governed the subgroups, which were known as *tireh*. The tireh can be described as the people who share common grazing land in the summer and winter quarters. The average size of a tireh is eighty families—the equivalent of 500 people. Each tireh is headed by a leader known as the *kadkhoda,* who is responsible for law and order and for collecting taxes to be passed on to the Kalantar. Within the tireh, groups of thirty to forty tents band together in a smaller group called the *bonkuh.* The affairs of the groups are governed by a council of elders composed of leaders of nuclear households. The most basic unit, the *beyleh*, is composed of families that herd or farm together daily. This flexible unit changes according to the fortune of individual families. The single tent of the nuclear family is never seen in isolation but always together with cooperating families under the framework of the beyleh.

Food, clothing, and shelter. Qashqa'i food staples are commonly made from the dairy products of their herds and supplemented by grains, fruits and vegetables that are either cultivated or obtained through trade in the towns and cities. Women prepare milk, yogurt, butter, cheese, buttermilk and *kashk,* small balls of dried cheese, from the milk of the goats in their herd. Animals are rarely eaten but whole chickens are at times spiced with turmeric and roasted over an open fire. Rice and a paper-thin unleavened bread called *nan* are the daily staple foods, accompanied by stews eaten with the right hand from serving dishes. Tea is a favorite beverage and is served in glasses with an abundance of sugar. After meals, a water-pipe, *ghalian,* is smoked by men and women as a social activity.

The costume of the Qashqa'i distinguishes them from other villages, townspeople and nomads in the region. The typical women's costume is comprised of baggy trousers called *salvar* with six to seven layers of petticoats and a printed skirt worn on top. Over the skirt a long overdress with a high round neck and long sleeves is worn. On her a head, a Qashqa'i woman wears an open-faced veil that is secured with a distinctive sequined headband.

Since Reza Shah banned traditional regional and tribal costumes in the 1930's, the men's traditional costume has fallen out of use. Today men wear Western clothes with the exception of the distinctive felt cap which identifies Qashqa'i men from other groups in the region. This brown or grey felt cap is rounded at the top with two flaps folded up on the side. During the twentieth century, the cap has become an important symbol of Qashqa'i cultural identity.

Tent dwellings are the primary form of shelter for nomadic Qashqa'i. Three types of tents are used for various needs and seasons, all of which can be set up and packed for travel. The simplest tent is a lean-to overnight shelter which is used during the migration

A Qashqa'i woman spinning wool.
Courtesy of Dr. Nikki Keddie, U.C.L.A.

between winter and summer pastures. The summer tent is an open-fronted tent that varies in size according to the status of the owner. Large tents are used by the Il Khans and prosperous Qashqa'i. These provide hospitality during the plentiful summer months. During the winter, a third type of tent is used that is made from heavier cloth for more protection.

Tent encampments are set up near water and pastures in groupings called *beyen.* The contents inside the tent is highly organized. The left side of the tent is the woman's domain where the domestic and family activities take place. The right side is for men and the entertainment of visitors. The floor of the tent is covered in felts and carpets and the base of the tent is surrounded by bags that serve as anchors for the tent and are stuffed with possessions, including dry food supplies. For weddings specially decorated tents are constructed from the finest woven carpets of the Qashqa'i.

Arts and crafts. Weaving rugs is one of the traditional crafts of the Qashqa'i and is practiced in the camps during both summer and winter months. The rugs are woven from the wool of the sheep in the Qashqa'i herds. These fine carpets are both functional and decorative. Rich colors and geometric designs are woven in complex patterns using common themes such as flowers and birds. Patterns are handed down through family members and are used to make saddlebags and covers, bags, floor rugs, and wall dividers. Qashqa'i rugs are collector items in the West and several exhibitions of Qashqa'i rugs have been organized.

Religion. Unlike many of Iran's tribal, ethnic, and national minority groups, the Qashqa'i are Shi'ite Muslims, the primary sect within Iran. The Qashqa'i, however, are not devout practitioners of Islam. Few Qashqa'i observe the basic requirements of Islam such as the daily prayers, the Ramadan feast, or the pilgrimage to Mecca. There are no religious leaders within Qashqa'i society although passages from the Quran (the sacred scriptures of Islam) are recited at weddings and funerals. Qashqa'i men tend to be skeptical of the Islam that they have had contact with through trade and state politics and to associate themselves more specifically with tribal customs and ethics. Qashqa'i women are even farther removed from formal Islam. Travelling *dervishes* (the mystics of Islam) provide cures, prayers and protective charms for women and children. Women also attend local shrines along migratory routes and some make yearly pilgrimages to a major shrine in the urban centers to fulfill religious vows.

Education. One of the single most important developments affecting the Qashqa'i in the past few decades was the creation of a tribal education program. This program was one of the few services offered to the Qashqa'i by the Iranian government. The founder of the program, a Qashqa'i, Mohammad Bahmanbegui, served as a link between the people and the state in the absence of the state-banned position of the Il Khan. The program, however, had conflicting results. On one hand, the educational units strengthened Qashqa'i identity and awareness of their cultural heritage. On the other hand, the program was designed to integrate Qashqa'i herders into a modern, rapidly changing Iran, thus aiming to change their traditional way of life. A Tribal Teacher Training School was established to train teachers who then set up tent schools within their tribal groups. A Tribal Carpet Weaving School, a Tribal Technical School, and training programs for midwives and paramedics were also begun. As a result of Bahmanbegui work, white or orange canvas tent schools became a distinctive feature of Qashqa'i landscape. The schools offered the standard curriculum of Iranian government schools and operated during the settled winter and summer months. Persian was the language of instruction, since the schools had the goal of assimilating Qashqa'i into Persian society. Qashqa'i culture, however, was also promoted. Female teachers were encouraged to wear customary dress, and festivals that featured Qashqa'i music and dance were part of school activites.

For More Information

Bahmanbegui, Mohammad. "Qashqa'i: Hardy Shepherds of Iran's Zagros Mountains Build a Future Through Tent-School Education." In *Nomads of the World*, edited by Melville Grosvenor. Washington, D.C.: National Geographic Society, 1971.

Beck, Lois. *The Qashqa'i of Iran.* New Haven: Yale University Press, 1986.

Oberling, Pierre. *The Qashqa'i Nomads of Fars.* The Hague: Mouton, 1974.

SAUDIS
(sah oo' deez)

Urban and nomadic people of Saudi Arabia.

Population: 14,400,000 (1989 estimate).
Location: Saudi Arabia.
Language: Arabic.

Geographical Setting

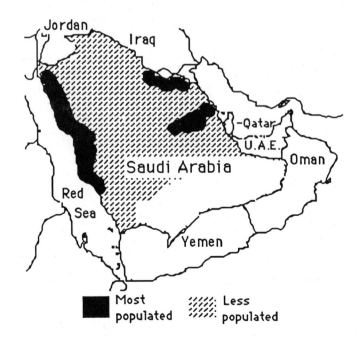

Saudi Arabia occupies eighty percent of the Arabian Peninsula, which lies between the continents of Africa and Asia. It has a long western coastline at the Red Sea, and a shorter one at the Persian Gulf. The coastal regions and oases are the main population centers; vast areas are relatively uninhabited.

With the exception of the temperate, humid lower western coast, Saudi Arabia has a desert climate, dry and hot. Daytime temperatures in the interior can reach 129 degrees Fahrenheit. The dramatic shifts in temperatures often give rise to sudden, violent winds, especially in the spring. Average annual rainfall is only four inches, which often comes in one or two downpours. Some areas are without rain for years. There are no rivers or lakes, and water is obtained from underground aquifers through springs or wells.

The mountainous west coast of Saudi Arabia is divided into the Hejaz area in the north and the Asir region of the south. The Hejaz mountains reach 7,000 feet and then drop abruptly into the sea. Most settlements in this area are on the more gently sloping eastern side of the mountains where oases are located. A gap in the mountains near the holy city of Mecca marks the end of Hejaz and the beginning of the Asir region, the most fertile part of Saudi Arabia and the only region reached by the monsoons that affect the Indian subcontinent. With irrigation, the monsoons provide enough rain to grow fruit, vegetables, cotton, and coffee. The Asir landscape is a sharp contrast to the rest of the country, with perennial streams and forests of juniper and olive. Lagoons, swamps, sandbars, and coral reefs mark the coast of the Red Sea.

Most of inland Saudi Arabia is a vast desert, but not without distinguishing features. A rocky central area of desert, isolated mountains and dry riverbeds (*wadis*) make up the Nejd region. North of the Nejd are miles of sand dunes with few oases. In the south, the Rub al Khali ("empty quarter") is a desert as large as the state of Texas that often passes several years without rain and is nearly uninhabited.

The eastern coastal region on the Persian Gulf is made up of sand and gravel plains. Once covered by the waters of the Gulf, this region was left with vast quantities of dead sea plants and animals that settled to the sea floor and, over millions of years, created the large petroleum and natural gas reserves of Saudi Arabia. Here, in the Saudi Arabian area of Al-Hasa are the largest known petroleum deposits.

Historical Background

Origins. Until about 3000 B.C., the Arabian Peninsula was more verdant and pleasant than it is today. As climatic conditions changed, the inhabitants began to migrate. Between approximately 3500 and 1500 B.C., nomads traveled to the Sinai Peninsula, Babylonia, and the Fertile Crescent, which formed an arc through the valleys of the Tigris and Euphrates rivers from Kuwait north, then along the coast to Israel. The people of the Tigris-Euphrates valley and Egyptians discovered early that two desirable elements—frankincense and myrrh—could be obtained from the south of Arabia. Frankincense was an incense essential to some religious rituals, and myrrh was used in cosmetics, perfumes, and medicine. Foreigners dominated the harvest and trade of these and other precious elements until about 1500 B.C., when descendants of Arabian migrants returned to their ancestral homeland. In addition to exporting their own goods, they became middlemen for trade from India and Africa. These traders from southern Arabia, called the Sabaens, prospered from the tenth to the first century B.C. Around 350 B.C. the Nabataens of northern Arabia and present-day Jordan gained control of some of the commercial routes, taxing caravans that carried spices along their route.

The Nabataen civilization declined during the first century B.C. The Romans had begun using ships for trade, and their new Christian society had little use for frankincense and myrrh. Arabian tribes began fighting among themselves for control of the remaining trade routes. By the middle of the sixth century A.D. the Ethiopians were able to control southern Arabia, and by A.D. 575 they had been replaced by Persians.

Muhammad and Islam. Until Muhammad, the majority of Arabians were concerned with tribal honor and loyalty. The prophet Muhammad, born in A.D. 570 in the city of Mecca, preached the destruction of statues at Mecca and called for the worship of a single invisible God named Allah. At first many people were suspicious of Muhammad, and his enemies forced him to flee from Mecca to Medina. But soon his influence had spread over much of Arabia. By 630 Muhammad was able to return to Mecca and establish it as a holy site for Islamic worship.

After his death in 632, Islam lost followers for two years, then revived in 634. Islamic warriors conquered Egypt, North Africa, Spain, Syria, part of modern Iraq, Persia, Afghanistan, and parts of

India. As the religion expanded, the political center was moved out of Arabia to Damascus. Meanwhile, Islam continued to decline in most of Arabia. Tribes outside Muhammad's region of Hejaz had been only nominally converted during his brief ministry, and soon returned to pagan practices. Southern tribes objected to the religious tax they were required to pay, and resented the power of the Hejazis. Once-powerful tribes sought the prestige they had enjoyed before Muhammad. Because Islam offered no real economic advantages, the tribes began fighting again.

For hundreds of years the peninsula had no real political center. As in the past, many people began to migrate to surrounding areas. Tribes fought continuously. During the sixteenth and seventeenth centuries, the Ottoman Turks conquered and took control of the Hejaz area but left the interior to the warring tribes.

Wahhabism. In the early 1700s, Muhammad ibn Abd al-Wahhab led an Islamic revival movement now referred to as Wahhabism. This orthodox sect was based on a literal interpretation of the Quran, the holy book of Islam. Abd al-Wahhab so alienated fellow villagers with his moralizing that, like Muhammad, he was driven from his village. Seeking refuge, he joined the chief of the Najd region, Muhammad bin Saud, with the goal of conquering and purifying Arabia. Together they captured much of the peninsula. In an effort to exercise control, the Turks sent Egyptians who invaded and occupied Nejd in 1818, but by 1824 the Sauds had reasserted their power and established Riyadh as their capital. Soon after, the Saud kingdom began to decline, troubled by interfamily disputes. By the end of the nineteenth century the house of Saud had lost its territory to the rival Rashidi family.

Unification under Abd al-Aziz. In 1901, Abd al-Aziz, a member of the deposed Saud family, returned from exile to reconquer his ancestral domain. With only 200 followers, he captured Riyadh and declared himself ruler of Najd. Then renamed Ibn Saud, indicating that he had restored the House of Saud, he used the old call to Wahhabism to unify the tribes in the south. With their help he went on to conquer other Arabian provinces and to create more than 100 Wahhabi colonies during the next fifteen years. During World War I, Ibn Saud signed a treaty of friendship with the British, but this treaty faded as the British also formed a friendship with Hussein, King of Hejaz and Ibn Saud's rival. In an intense competition, Ibn

Saud took control of much of western Arabia, and in 1926 became king of Hejaz and Sultan of Najd. By 1932, a large portion of the peninsula had been united to form the Kingdom of Saudi Arabia.

Oil. By the late 1920s, Ibn Saud was endeavoring to make educational and health services available to the Saudis. For this he needed money, and was willing to grant oil exploration rights to Standard Oil of California. When the first reserves were discovered, the Saudi government formed ARAMCO, the Arabian-American Oil Company. Shortly after the end of World War II, a consortium of American companies was at work exploring for oil in Arabia. The lives of the Saudis changed over the next twenty-five years as Ibn Saud's successors improved airports, television stations, international transportation, and communications. Saudis used the money from one of the world's largest oil reserves to improve industry and agriculture, with a view toward making Saudi Arabia self-sufficient and strong even after the oil reserves were played out. The Saudis also became increasingly involved in international affairs as a member of OPEC, the Organization of Petroleum Exporting Countries. The Saudis advocated a policy of recognition of Israel in exchange for Israeli withdrawal from occupied territories, and took positions in opposition to Iran in the Iran-Iraq War and to Iraq in its attempted takeover of Kuwait.

Culture Today

Economy. With government planning and financial aid, farmers in Saudi Arabia are growing increasing amounts of crops even though the number of people employed in agriculture declined between 1950 and 1980 before beginning to grow again at the rate of five percent a year. Still about half of the workers are in agriculture, and these workers produce about five and one-half percent of the wealth of the nation. Wheat is a principle product, as are barley and millet. In the areas of the southern oases, farmers share water and land with herders and their goats, sheep, and camels. Tomatoes, dates, and grapes are also important cash crops. However, the primary source of jobs and income among the Saudis is petroleum. This industry and related construction demands so much labor that the government is constantly attempting to control the influx of foreign workers.

Food, clothing, and shelter. As the number of families dependent on agriculture has declined and petroleum-related jobs increased,

Saudis are moving to the cities in search of employment at the rate of five percent a year. Riyadh, the seat of government has grown to more than 600,000 people, while cities such as Jeddah have grown to over half a million and have become very "new" cities.

With the variety of landscapes, and the rise of cities, the homes of Saudis have varied greatly. Most homes in the city are equipped with modern conveniences such as electricity and television, while retaining their older "compound" appearance of separate quarters for men and women sheltered from outsiders by a wall that encloses a courtyard. Many of the workers in the cities live in modern apartment buildings of concrete. The government has been attempting to stabilize the desert population by building residential settlements around

Remnants of an early Saudi Arabian village. *Courtesy of Dr. Paul Fischer.*

the oases. Some Saudis, however, cling to their nomadic life and live in goat- or camel-hair tents; low and long shelters, still with separate quarters for men and women (see BEDOUIN).

The traditional lifestyle in most of Arabia has been nomadic. In this tradition, easily stored and transported grains formed the basic diet along with milk, cheese, yogurt, and meat from the herds of goats, sheep, and camels. Flat breads, made from wheat, millet, and barley, vegetables, and mutton or lamb are the staple food of the Saudis. However, the typical meals vary from place to place according to available imports.

Lunch, the main Saudi meal, is served after the children return from school. The father takes time off from work to join them. Traditionally the meal is served on a tablecloth spread on the floor. The centerpiece of a typical lunch is a big bowl of rice covered with chunks of roasted lamb or, more rarely, camel, with eggplant or potatoes and soft flat bread on the side. Dessert might be fruit or custard with raisins and almonds. Lunch is a leisurely meal, with much talking and laughter. A nap often follows. If guests happen to be present, the mother and daughters stay in another room, quietly preparing the food. Boys may eat with the male guests but must not speak unless spoken to.

Clothing, too, varies. City men wear European-style suits and ties when appropriate and the more comfortable and traditional robes

A typical Saudi Arabian village. *Courtesy of Dr. Paul Fischer.*

when that fits the occasion. In traditional dress, a Saudi man wears a simple garment called a *thobe*. In winter it is generally made of gray or black wool; in summer it is white cotton. On his head he wears a *ghutra*, a piece of cloth to wrap around the face in case of sandstorms. In winter it is red-and-white checked wool; in summer, white cotton. Farmers and herders wear the familiar burnoose, a long garment loosely covering most of the body and with an attached headpiece.

A Saudi woman is required by Saudi interpretation of Islamic law to wear a robe that covers her entire body and a long dark veil. Increasingly though, women wear European-style clothing at home.

Now most Saudis live in cities or towns, and their houses or apartments are much like European dwellings. But the nomads, called Bedouins, still live in the desert. They ride horses and camels while they herd sheep and other animals from place to place. These nomads live in large goat or camel-hair tents, usually near wells. Today the government is encouraging these wanderers to settle by building permanent settlements near the oases.

Abandoned villages are found throughout the Nejd. *Courtesy of Dr. Paul Fischer.*

Arts and leisure. Islamic law puts severe restrictions on the arts of Saudi Arabia. Pictures are believed by some Muslims to foster idolatry, so there is little painting, sculpture, or photography of human forms in Saudi Arabia. Movie theaters are forbidden. Even the romantic poems and stories so popular before Muhammad are now frowned upon. The Quran discourages the playing of music in both religious services and private life. Nevertheless, the Saudis have found outlets for artistic expression. Non-pictorial arts like architecture and calligraphy have flourished. Storytelling and singing are popular among the Bedouin and increasingly among urban dwellers, thanks partly to radio and television. Popular music is a blend of traditional and modern styles from other Arab countries.

Saudi families enjoy visiting with friends, relaxing in parks, and watching television. They also enjoy shopping, either at a mall or at a *suq*, the long-standing open market where bargaining is the rule. Sports are becoming increasingly popular. Traditional favorites are camel and horse racing, and hunting with dogs or falcons. Since the early 1950s, western sports, particularly basketball and soccer, have become popular. Soccer is now the country's number-one sport. The Saudis have built several modern stadiums in recent years, and in 1984 they sent their first national team to the Olympic Games.

Religion. Islam originated in Arabia and is the official Saudi religion. Sunni Muslims, mostly of the Wahhabi sect, make up eighty-five percent of the population. Shi'ite Muslims make up the remaining ten to fifteen percent. There is no religious freedom in Saudi Arabia, except among noncitizens such as foreign businessmen and oil workers; any religion other than Islam is strictly forbidden.

The orthodox sect of Islam that began in the eighteenth century dominates all aspects of Saudi life. Five times a day a call to prayer interrupts daily activities as people stop whatever they are doing to face in the direction of Mecca and pray. There are restrictions on dress and behavior, while alcohol and attending movie theaters, for example, are forbidden. Wahhabism emphasizes absolute submission to an omnipotent God. It condemns *shirk*, that is, identification of any symbols with God through idolatry, religious offerings, or the worship of saints or tombs. Wahhabism also condemns sufism, a form of mysticism that attempts to gain personal relationships with God, and foregoes religious festivals of all kinds.

Islam's two holiest cities, Mecca and Medina, are located in the Hejaz region of the country. More than a million Muslims gather every year on the Plain of Arafat, near Mecca, for the Hadj. Muslims everywhere are required to make this pilgrimage to the city of Mecca at least once in a lifetime. Here social, political, and religious differences are set aside as all visitors don similar white garments to participate in the rituals.

Law. Wrongdoing is an affront to the whole community in Saudi life. Because any crime is thought to endanger the safety and unity of the *umma*, or Muslim community, punishment is sometimes harsh. A minor offender might be imprisoned or lashed. A thief might lose a hand, and a murderer most often dies. Islamic vice-squads called Muttawa routinely visit stores and restaurants to enforce closings at prayer hours, the ban on mingling between the sexes, and the dress codes for women. Punishments are rare, however, as the Saudis have one of the lowest crime rates in the world.

Tribe and family. In the near past, the Saudis were a collection of independent tribes, some living in communities near the coasts and some as nomadic tribes living around the oases of the desert. The Saud family organized these tribes, developing a growing sense of a collective identity. Rather than by force, Ibn Saud and his successors, particularly the very capable King Faisal, chose to organize the Saudis by strict religious precepts and by using the oil wealth of the country to provide necessary services to all the people. While some of the tribal identities are giving way to a national identity, the old values of the family and tribe guide Saudi conduct. Groups that trace their origins to the more ancient Arabian tribes enjoy greatest prestige; at the other end of the scale are the "despised" tribes of descendants of slaves. Each tribe is a group of related people divided into lineages, which are families descended from the same male ancestor three to seven generations back. Lineages are made up of extended families. The lineage collectively owns property, such as water wells and livestock, and is responsible for avenging the wrongs suffered by its members. The extended family, three or more generations living together, shares wealth and property. The family plays an active role in arranging marriages, with cousins as the favored mates. Even today, few Saudis lack a tribal identity, so the primary tribal values of generosity, hospitality to travelers, care of relatives, and honor to the tribe and family are dominant values among the Saudis. Honor is much tied to the purity of women and demands strict adherence to dress codes and segregation of the sexes.

Role of women. The Saudis have great respect for women and an extreme concern for female purity and hence for family honor. Girls and boys are taught to serve one another from an early age. Sexual segregation after early childhood is seen as a way to ensure the family values. Many homes—even nomadic tents—are divided into men's and women's quarters. Women cannot leave these homes alone, drive cars, gather in public, or work alongside men. Unmarried women cannot live alone, stay in a hotel alone, or go to a restaurant alone. They are discouraged from any activity that might bring them into contact with men other than their fathers, brothers, and husbands— even close male relatives. In public, women are required to wear robes that cover most of the body, and usually a veil covering the face and hair.

Urbanization and international communications are slowly bringing changes to the Saudis. Female school enrollment rose from eight percent in 1961 to thirty-seven percent in 1981. Women are not welcome in business with men or in politics, but have their own businesses and are gradually becoming involved in medicine as well as social and charitable activities. In the early 1980s there were 25,000 women working in government, mostly as teachers. But social segregation remains in force. Rather than break this segregation, the government has increased the number of exclusively female activities.

For More Information

Lackner, Helen. *House Built on Sand.* London: Ithaca Press, 1978.

Mansfield. Peter. *The New Arabians.* Chicago: J. G. Ferguson Publishing Company, 1981.

Middle East and North Africa, 1991. London: Europa Publications, 1990.

Nyrop, Richard F., editor. *Saudi Arabia: A Country Study.* Washington, D.C., U.S. Government Printing Office, 1984.

SYRIANS

(sear' ee uhns)

The Semitic people of Syria.

Population: 11,300,000 (1988 estimate).
Location: The Syrian Arab Republic, bounded by Turkey, Iraq, Jordan, Lebanon, the Mediterranean Sea, and Turkey.
Languages: Arabic. Kurdish and Armenian are also spoken in some areas.

Geographical Setting

Although small in comparison to its neighbors, Turkey and Iraq, Syria is a country of varied geography. A western section is mountainous land cut by many fertile valleys that fall to a narrow coast along the Mediterranean Sea. The Jebel Ansariya (Ansariya Mountains) form a ridge separating the coastal area from inland steppes and then, in the southeast, desert. The mountains rise to their highest levels along the southern border with Lebanon. The Euphrates River runs diagonally across the northern part of the country and into Turkey.

The temperature and vegetation of Syria varies according to the regions. In the western coastal zone, both summers and winters are mild; the interior valleys are subtropically warm; and the eastern plateau has hot summers and cold winters. Forests of pine, oak, cedar, and cypress grow on the slopes of the northern Jebel Ansariya and on the upper reaches of the mountains at the border with Lebanon, the Anti-Lebanon Range. Scrub and hardwood trees grow in the south, while the steppe is a grassland with some trees. With the exception of the western coast, rainfall is scant. In most of the interior rain averages five to seven inches a year.

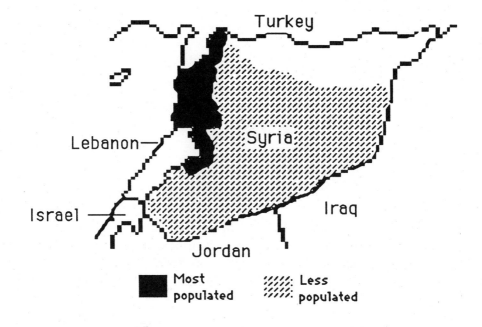

Most populated   Less populated

Historical Background

Early history. "Greater Syria" once included modern-day Syria and parts of Turkey, as well as Jordan, Lebanon, and Israel (then Palestine). This vast area was part of a booming commercial network between ancient civilizations, which traded lumber, gold, silver, and resins used in religious rites. Around 3000 B.C., this part of the world was inhabited by nomadic peoples (Semites) who had migrated from the Arabian desert and had settled among agriculturists who were already living there. As waves of Semites moved into the area and mixed with existing populations, a new culture evolved. The earliest of these new "Syrians" may have populated the Kingdom of Ebla, which existed near present-day Aleppo. Ebla was an independent kingdom whose name came from its appearance as a city of white stones. The kingdom of Ebla reached its height around 2500 B.C., and ruled in the time of the Akkads (see BABYLONIANS). Its people are believed to have been related to the Canaanites of ancient Palestine. Their offspring, the people who formed the alphabet, came to be known as Phoenicians. Ebla dominated northern Syria, and parts of Mesopotamia, Iran, and Anatolia (present-day Turkey). The center of this empire was Byblos on the Syrian coast.

During the second millennium B.C., ancient Syria was in turn ruled by non-Semitic peoples such as those from Egypt, and later by Hittites from Anatolia who settled northern and central Syria. Friction between Akkad and Byblos continued through these reigns and finally resulted in the destruction of the kingdom of Ebla in 2300 B.C. After that collapse, large waves of Semitic-speaking tribes migrated to Greater Syria. One such group, the Amorites, settled in such large numbers that they eventually absorbed the Canaanite culture and became the dominant element of Syria-Palestine. Arameans, another Semitic group, migrated to the region around 1500 B.C. and founded the kingdom of Aram near present-day Damascus. The language of these people, Aramaic, came to be spoken throughout Greater Syria. It was the language of the ancient Hebrews and of Judah and Palestine in the time of Christ. Aramaic remained the primary language of Greater Syria until it was replaced by Arabic with the invasion of Muslims in the seventh century A.D. Today the Aramaic language is used in only three towns in Syria.

The Hebrews, another Semitic tribal group, settled southern Syria in the thirteenth century B.C. They founded the kingdoms of Israel and Judah and were probably the first people to worship one God who was not somehow represented in natural objects such as the sun (see HEBREWS).

Persians, Greeks, Romans, and Turks. The city-states of Greater Syria always retained some degree of self-rule, even though they came under foreign rule. Between the eleventh and sixth centuries Syrians were invaded and governed by Assyrians and Babylonians. In 538 B.C., Syria was conquered by the Persians and was part of their empire until the arrival of Alexander the Great in 333 B.C. A year later, upon Alexander's death, his governors of the area, the Seleucid family, became rulers and held the land until overthrown by the Romans in the first century B.C.

Under Roman rule, Syria prospered and Antioch became one of the great cities of the Empire. In A.D. 395, the Roman Empire was divided into eastern and western sections and Syria became part of the empire ruled from Constantinople (the Byzantine Empire). During this period, Syria became Christianized along with the rest of the Roman Empire, and remained so until the arrival of Islam in 634. The Muslim Arabs were Semitic people whose religion was based on the teachings of the prophet Muhammad. In two years, they had command of virtually all of a Syria larger than that of today. Intermarrying with the local Syrian population, they established a Muslim dynasty at Damascus, the Umayyad Caliphate. From 660 to 750 Damascus served as the seat of government of this powerful Arabian empire, which extended from Iran and Arabia, to Egypt, North Africa, and Spain.

Invasions of Syria by Abbasids, Seljuk Turks, Christian Crusaders, and then Egyptian Mamelukes ended when the Egyptians were driven out by the Ottoman Turks, who claimed Syria as a province of the Ottoman Empire in 1516.

Ottoman rule brought stability and prosperity to Greater Syria. The Turks were Sunni Muslims; they obeyed the laws and teachings of the Quran and respected the Arabic language. Although their rule was sometimes harsh, they respected non-Islamic minority groups. Jews and Christians were allowed some autonomy under a *millet* system (a system under which people with varying beliefs were allowed to live by their own laws) and were governed by their own religious courts. Muslims of the provinces of the Ottoman Empire were governed by Islamic law administered by *quadis* along with a provencial government administered by *pashas*, governors, and *beys* (military leaders). As long as all of these people obeyed central authority and paid their taxes, they continued to live undisturbed.

Under the Ottomans, Damascus remained central to the Islamic religion and became a gateway to Mecca. The stability introduced by the Ottoman Empire lasted into the nineteenth century, when the arrival of European powers changed the traditional societies of the region.

Europeans. Because the Ottomans had sided with Germany during World War I, the victorious Allies, following a plan previously arranged between Britain and France, dismantled the empire. Under British-French agreements, Syria was divided into four separate states. France controlled Lebanon and Syria, and the British governed Palestine and Jordan.

Following World War I, Britain and France, under United Nations sanctions, divided Syria and created the present country configurations of Syria, Lebanon, Jordan, and Palestine, along with Iraq. Great Britain tried to establish domination over all the Middle East by appointing Faisal, son of their friend the king of the Hejaz area of Saudi Arabia, to be king of Syria, but the Syrians objected and

France took control of that country. Israel became a separate state in the Palestine region in 1948. In 1960, part of Mount Lebanon was carved from Syria by the French to make an easily distinguishable boundary with Lebanon.

Independence. Despite the French mandate, Syrians demanded their independence and in 1945 were admitted to the United Nations. Independence was officially declared when the French were ousted in 1946, and May 17 came to be called "evacuation day," marking Syria's independence. Lebanon became independent that same year, and the State of Israel was established in 1948.

The Baa'th party. A series of military coups eventually resulted in a political dictatorship of the Baa'th party led by President Hafez al-Assad by 1970. The Baa'thists assumed control of the government, military, and police, and are credited with modern reforms and secularization.

In the late 1970s, Syria became involved in the internal difficulties in Lebanon. Commissioned by the Arab League to intervene in search of a regional peace, Syria first sent fifty military advisers to the troubled country. The number grew so that ultimately 50,000 Syrian soldiers were attempting to control events in Lebanon. This situation has had a lessening of faith in the government by some Syrians. The disillusionment may have started when President Hafez al-Assad surrounded himself with aides from the minority Muslim sect of which he is a member, the Alawites. As unrest grew in Syria, a number of Alawite government officials were assassinated. The government's response has been powerful and suppressive. As a result authoritative information on incidents inside Syria is largely hidden.

Culture Today

Ethnic and religious composition. Eighty-five percent of Syrians are Muslims, the majority of whom belong to the Sunni sect. About ten percent of the people of Syria are members of other Islamic sects such as the Alawites, Shi'ites, and Ismailis. Non-Arabic Kurds are also Sunni Muslims. About fourteen percent of all Syrians are descendants of non-Arabic minority groups: Armenians, Jews, and various Christian Caucasian sects.

The government introduced land reforms, provided free compulsory education for all, and gave women the right to vote.

But despite increasing urbanization, the majority of Syrians outside of the large metropolitan centers, are engaged in agriculture, live in their ancestral villages, and are loyal to their kin group. While all segments of the society change, some change their lifestyles more slowly than others. Bedouins live in the desert as nomads with their camel, sheep, and goat herds; non-Sunni Alawites live in compact and isolated villages as sharecroppers in the mountains of the al-Latakia province; rural farmers and shepherds inhabit the steppe country; and Kurds maintain their ancient tribal lifestyle as farmers in the foothills of the Taurus Mountains north of Aleppo and speak their own language.

Urban life. In the large cities such as Damascus and Aleppo, people have adopted European styles and habits. They live in apartments with European conveniences, wear European-style clothing, attend schools, drive cars, and work in businesses, industries and the government. The cities are centers of commercial and cultural activity, with new residential sections, office buildings, hotels, shops, restaurants, theaters, and public transportation. The government operates railways and airports. It also owns and controls the press, radio, and television systems.

Village life. Since ancient times Syrian society has been both urban and rural, and villages and towns have been interdependent for goods and services. Towns represented law, education, financial, and government services, along with production of luxury items by artisans and craftsmen. Villages provided agricultural produce, domestic animals, and a peasant work force that farmed the land of the wealthy urban landowners.

Each town contains a central marketplace, the *suq,* its own mosque, shops, and the traditional coffeehouse where the men gather to socialize, conduct business, and resolve political issues. Living quarters are sometimes organized within religious and ethnic bounds. With change, particularly in education, a new middle class of professionals, merchants, and government workers has accelerated the creation of town suburbs, with new residential sections added to the older towns. With land reforms and new industry, many people from the rural areas have migrated to the larger urban centers and either live in shantytowns or new government housing developments. Most towns have new as well as ancient architecture, some of which dates to pre-Roman times.

Economy. Land reforms instituted in the 1960s have tended to alter the relationship between the peasant and traditional absentee landlord. Small farms and businesses are privately owned today, while large parcels of land owned by the wealthy have been sold to tenant farmers and organized into cooperatives. About one-fourth of the Syrians are employed in agriculture, and these contribute about one-third of the nation's income. The government has created irrigation projects and introduced mechanized farming in order to increase productivity, and hydroelectric power has brought energy to the entire nation. The changes have been made with the aid of a great deal of help from nearby oil producing countries. As a result, the economy of Syria has been struggling since the mid-1980s.

Religion and family life. Islamic law, the *shari'a* governs all aspects of Muslim life. As a group, the Sunnis, the majority of Syrians, do not believe in clerical hierarchies and they accept the belief that nothing stands between the individual and God. This differs from the Shi'ites and other sects whose religious leaders, *imams*, are thought to be successors to the prophet Muhammad.

Non-Muslims, who are mostly Arabic Christians, have their own law and courts administered by their religious leaders since the days of the old *millet* system of the Ottomans. The Sunnis and other Muslims, as well as Christians and other sects, often add pre-Islamic practices to their religious activities. Beliefs in saints, spirits, and folk customs cut across the different groups. Most Syrian villages have their own saints and shrines, usually the burial place of a local person who was known to have led a good life.

Muslim women are more likely than men to believe in the effects of good and evil *jinns*, or spirits. They are also more likely to pray at the village shrine and to use charms to ward off the evil spirits.

All Muslims follow the five pillars of Islam: prayer five times a day, recitation of the *shahada* (creed), alms-giving to the poor, fasting, and making a holy pilgrimage to Mecca at least one time. Local religious leaders, imams, as well as the *ulama* (teachers), *qadis* (judges), and *muftis* (interpreters of the law) are all government employees. In urban areas there are religious leaders in the large mosques, and leaders who officiate at the Friday noon services. Men pray publicly or at the mosque, and women generally pray at home. Fasting during daylight hours takes place during Ramadan, the ninth month of the Muslim calendar. The fasting is broken in the evening with a festive meal.

Family kinship ties, determined by male lineage, are the most important bonds among Syrians. Marriages are arranged between families within one's own kin-group or tribe. The traditional preference among Muslims to marry with cousins is common in rural areas but is waning among the middle class of the cities. Households usually consist of the grandparents, their married offspring, and the grandchildren. Strict seclusion of women is not practiced in most places in the nation. Outside of the educated urban elite and middle class, the honor and dignity of a woman reflects upon the reputation of the kin-group. Women are expected to look after their husbands, children, and home, and their social life is limited to female friends and relatives within the house. Loyalty to family and kin dominates social, business, and political relationships among Syrians, and being a good family member and kinsman is deeply valued.

Food, clothing, and shelter. In the villages and rural areas of the northwestern sector, beehive-shaped structures of mud-clay reinforced with straw house the entire family. Interior decorations depend on what the family can afford, but the typical home has curtains on the windows, plastered walls, and layers of oriental carpets on the floors. Cushions and sofas are used for sitting and relaxing, while most families have chairs and other furniture as well.

Homes in the eastern and southern areas are built of stone blocks. They have flat roofs, wooden window and door frames, gardens and open courtyards, and thick walls to keep out the heat.

Wealthy urban dwellers own large homes with the latest conveniences. A status symbol is the hospitality room where the men gather to socialize and smoke their *hookah,* or water pipes, in the evening. Most city dwellers own televisions, radios, refrigerators, and other conveniences.

Urban citizens wear European-style clothes, sometimes combined with more traditional attire. Muslim men often wear suit jackets and ties under their long robes, and the typical white or checked cloth Arab headdress held in place with an *agal,* a crown of black cord. Only a very few conservative women cover their faces with a veil. Younger women and those who are employed wear European-style street clothes and cover their hair with a scarf. Affluent women who do not work wear the latest European styles, jewelry, and cosmetics at home and while entertaining. However, as a mark of status, the most fundamental Muslim women cover their clothes with long overcoats and wear a veil when away from their homes. Non-Muslim women wear modest hemlines and sleeves so as not to offend their Islamic neighbors.

Rural Syrians wear peasant costumes that vary according to the locality. Men and boys wear long tunic shirts over *shalvar*, under-trousers that are fitted at the calf and ankles. They, too, wear the Arab headdress, along with sandals. Rural women rarely cover their faces with veils, but they hide their hair under scarfs. Since Syria was long a part of the Ottoman Empire, many local costumes show a Turkish influence: long printed cotton dresses and skirts worn over leggings, flowing robes, richly embroidered vests and headdresses. Children frequently wear school uniforms, often of a military style.

Syrian food, like all Middle-Eastern cuisine influenced by Turkish cooking, is varied. The basic diet of the farm workers consists of *bulgur* wheat dishes, flat Syrian bread, lentils, vegetables, yogurt, cheese, olives, meat, poultry, and fresh fruits and dates. Food is eaten with the hands, so a custom of washing before and after meals is common throughout Syria.

A few Jews live in Syria. This Jewish boy is carrying home bread in Damascus. *Courtesy of Dr. Nikki Keddie, U.C.L.A.*

The diet of city-dwellers is often more complex. Meals begin with a variety of hot and cold appetizers called *mazza*; salads of cucumber, tomatoes, olives, pickles, stuffed grape leaves, and mashed chickpeas called *hummus; tahina;* and a smokey eggplant dish called *baba ghan-nooj,* which is eaten as a spread on bread. *Tabbouleh* is an aromatic salad made of cracked wheat, chopped tomato, onions, parsley, and mint, and laced with plenty of olive oil and fresh lemon juice. Most main dishes consist of lamb, either roasted, broiled, or ground into a fine paste. A national Syrian specialty is *kibbi*, raw or cooked ground lamb and cracked wheat, seasoned with herbs and spices, and shaped into oval meatballs. Another typical dish is *sfeeha*, a firey pepper and ground-lamb meat pie that contains onions, pine nuts, and tangy homemade yogurt. Meals end with cups of strong coffee and an array of sweets, cakes, and candied fruits.

Arts and literature. Syrians are famous for their intricately carved brass and copperware. Calligraphy and geometric or flower patterns

Syrian women in peasant costumes.
Courtesy of the University Museum, University of Pennsylvania.

are used to ornament silver or hammered-copper utensils such as trays, coffee service sets, and musical instruments. Syrian craftsmen also produce decorative furniture inlaid with mother of pearl and chess sets, as well as hand-woven blankets and rugs. Calligraphy, etching, and sculpture, usually in white marble, decorate Syria's great architectural legacies, such as the churches and shrines of the ancient city of Aleppo.

With compulsory education, the level of literacy has improved. Still Syrians prefer oral literature in the form of poetry. Arabic poetry is often set to music and performed with folk dances, such as the *debke*, for entertainment during festivals and weddings. Men dance with each other and women celebrate separately by singing, clapping, and dancing.

Important literary figures of twentieth-century Syria include Omar Abu-Rishe, Ali Ahmad Said, and Nizar Kabbani. Contemporary writing appears in Arabic, along with Kurdish and Armenian languages that employ the Latin alphabet.

Recreation. Syrians are fond of playing chess and dominoes, and men engage in sports such as wrestling and soccer. Other popular activities are swimming, boxing, and tennis. In large cities people attend movie theaters, nightclubs, and discos. A sense of Islamic nationalism and fundamentalism has encouraged people to memorize and recite passages from the Quran as a form of entertainment. This form of recreation has existed for years.

Important Syrian holidays, reflecting the sense of identity following its 1946 independence, are Revolution Day on March 8, the birth of the Arab League on March 22, Martyrs Day on April 6, the commemoration of French withdrawal on April 17, and the national Day of Mourning on November 29.

For More Information

Devlin, John F. *Syria: Modern State in an Ancient Land.* Boulder, Colorado: Westview Press, 1983.

Egan, E. W., editor. *The Middle East: The Arab States in Pictures.* New York: Sterling Publishing, 1978.

Khoury, Philip S. *Syria and the French Mandate.* Princeton, New Jersey: Princeton University Press, 1986.

Syria: A Country Study. Washington, D.C.: U.S. Government Publications, 1988.

TUNISIANS
(too nee' zhuns)

Citizens of the Republic of Tunisia.

Population: 7,900,000 (1989 estimate).
Location: North Africa, bounded by the Mediterranean Sea, Algeria, and Libya.
Languages: Arabic; French.

Geographical Setting

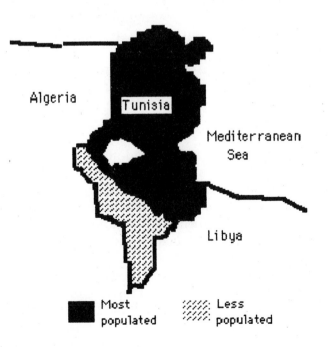

The country of Tunisia is part of the Maghreb, an "island" between a sea of sand in the Sahara Desert and the Mediterranean Sea. The term Maghreb is Arabic meaning "place of the sunset." Although smaller than its neighbors in the Maghreb, Tunisia is a land with three distinct regions and climates. Northern Tunisia, sometimes called the Tal, is a mountainous section where the Atlas range that begins in Morocco ends at the sea. Air rising over the mountains releases heavy rains and blocks much of the rain from reaching the south. Northern Tunisia is fertile, and more densely populated than the southern part of the country. Just south of the Atlas range, known in this area as the Dorsale Mountains, the soil becomes poorer and the rainfall scant. Here people live as herders in steppe lands near the Algerian border. The extreme south of the country is frequently depressed below sea level and rises at a few oases and at the gravelly coastline, before joining the Sahara Desert itself. The depressed regions contain salt marshes called *shatts*.

Historical Background

Early history. Humans or their ancestors have lived and left tools behind in the region now known as Tunisia for perhaps a million years. About 10,000 years ago immigrants from western Asia settled there, living in caves and hunting with stone arrows and blades. Eight thousand years later, settlers from Sicily brought with them bronze tools, and Minoans from Crete stopped on the coast before 2000 B.C. In the first millennium B.C., the Phoenicians (from the area of Syria, Lebanon, and Israel) established a chain of trading posts all along the Mediterranean coast of Africa (see PHOENICIANS).

Carthage. Phoenicians from the kingdom of Tyre founded Carthage (near present-day Tunis) in 815 B.C. According to Roman legend, Dido fled Phoenicia because her brother, Pygmalion, King of Tyre, had murdered her husband. She founded Carthage and became its queen. From Carthage, Phoenicians conducted trade in metals and other goods while establishing colonies in Spain, Sardinia, and Sicily, as well as North Africa.

The rivalry that existed between Rome and Carthage over control of southern Europe was played out in three "Punic Wars" in the third and second centuries B.C. The first (264-241 B.C.) was a battle for control of Sicily. In the second war, between 218 and 203 B.C., the Carthagian forces were led by Hannibal and his relative Hasdrubal.

Hannibal led armies to the gates of Rome, and at one time crossed the Alps in midwinter with 12,000 horsemen, 90,000 foot soldiers, and forty elephants to take cities in Gaul. But suffering defeats by Scipio's army, Hannibal's armies retreated and were chased in Africa about 203 B.C. The third Punic War (149-146 B.C.) saw the domination and eventual total destruction of Carthage by the Romans.

Romans. Tunisians came under Roman rule and their land was considered a part of the province of Proconsular Africa. Later, Julius Caesar ordered that Carthage be rebuilt as a Roman city. For 400 years, the province was united by a common language (Latin) and the Roman legal system. Roman forums, baths, markets, and fountains standing in Tunisia today attest to the vitality of this province of the Roman Empire. However, it was largely African tenant farmers and slave laborers who supplied food for the Roman aristocrats and were forced to build these grand structures.

During this Roman era, Jews, who had been deported by Romans from Palestine, came to Tunisia and converted many Berbers (see BERBERS) to Judaism. By the beginning of the second century A.D., Christianity had been introduced to the Jewish communities and soon Carthage became the center of Latin Christianity in Africa. Perhaps the most influential Christian leader of Africa, St. Augustine of Hippo, was born of a Christian mother and pagan father and received his early education at Carthage.

Vandals and Byzantines. Vandals, a Germanic tribe, crossed Spain in 429 enroute to Africa on the invitation of a rebellious Roman official. Like the rulers who preceded them, the Vandals collected taxes from local populations and exploited the land. In 533, their kingdom fell to Byzantine armies (Romans headquartered at Constantinople) who strove to retake North Africa for the Roman Empire. Berber nomads in the coastal regions were prevented from ascending to power during this second Roman period, but the ideal of Roman imperial unity failed to stretch far inland. Inhabitants of the marginal, outlying areas had gained autonomy during the rule of the Vandals and were able, therefore, to resist the Romans. The Roman hold on the land was thus weakened.

Arabs and Islam. Within two years after the prophet Muhammad died in 632, most of the peoples of the Arabian Peninsula had been converted to Islam, and Arab armies had begun to spread east and west to conquer and in the process to make converts to Islam. In 670, these Muslims founded Kairouan as a military base about ninety miles south of Carthage. From here, Arab rule soon grew stronger and spread, establishing unity under Islamic law and the rule of the successors of the Prophet.

The Arab armies traveled without women and married among the native populations. Arab culture and Islamic religion spread to townspeople, farmers, and nomads. Although many of the converts abandoned Islam once intimidating Arab armies had moved on, Islam has remained the predominant religion of the region.

Spaniards, Turks, and Husaynids. In the sixteenth century, Spaniards launched several naval raids on the Maghreb, and Tunisia petitioned to the Ottoman Turks for assistance. With the arrival of this help, Tunis became a regency of the Ottoman Empire and was the front line of an ongoing East-West confrontation until Husayn Bin Ali took control and led Tunisia into a prosperous, independent period. Its economy based largely on the trade of black Africans as slaves to the West, the country began to decline in the nineteenth century as slavery was abandoned. Still the country was attractive and Europeans were bidding on construction projects in Tunisia. To strengthen their position in this economic atmosphere, the French entered Tunisia from their base in Algeria and colonized the country by force.

French colonial policy. Tunisia was officially designated a French protectorate in 1881, and the French established the grid-plan towns, broad boulevards, and pseudo-Oriental buildings that mark northern Tunisia today. To assist in mining phosphates, zinc, lead, and iron deposits, the French constructed an extensive railway system across the country, disrupting some agriculture, and displaced farmers of small landholdings with larger units controlled by European settlers. The large estates with red-tiled farmhouses of these foreign owners still dot the Tunisian landscape.

It was the establishment of the Neo-Destour constitution by the National Front party's Secretary-General Habib Bourguiba that began a strong national movement, which when coupled with international support, finally forced France to withdraw and the independent Republic of Tunisia to form in 1956. Until 1970, Tunisia remained economically bound to Europe, especially France. But in 1967, the Six-Day War between Israel and Egypt began to unite the Arab countries. Tunisia reestablished relationships with Arab countries in 1970 and became a member of the Arab League.

In 1987 Bourguiba was declared unfit to govern because of ill health and Zine al-Abidine Ben Ali became president of Tunisia. Since then, Ben Ali has struggled to reform the government and increase political freedom in Tunisia.

Culture Today

Ethnic groups, languages, and religions. Because of Tunisia's long history of settlement by foreign immigrants, the country has an ethnically diverse population. The native population of North Africa, the Berbers, and the Arabs have intermarried since the seventh century. Today, a few Berbers remain (less than three percent of the population), speaking their own language, but most have been Arabized. Arabs are Islamic and speak Arabic, although traces of their Berber background can be seen in many places.

Before 1956, there were about 85,000 Jews in Tunisia; about 5,000 of these remain. Most Jews left Tunisia following its independence, uncertain of their treatment under the new regime. Also, before independence there were many French and Italians living in Tunisia. Most of these left after independence, leaving French the language of the elite and of the schools for several years. Today, Arabic, the language of most of the people, is the national language, but about half the people also speak French. .

Further diversifying the Tunisian population are sub-Saharan blacks, Muslims from Spain, and Turks.

Social organization. North African people once organized themselves into tribes. While this pattern is seen in some of the Maghreb, foreign influences have nearly eliminated tribal organization in Tunisia. Since the French wanted a strong central government, they made tribal sheikhs into civil servants who served the central government as its representatives over their own people. Nomadic tribes were forced to become sedentary farmers.

A legacy from Ottoman rule was a class hierarchy, with notables, bureaucrats, and other city dwellers forming an upper class, followed by rural villagers. Nomads are in less powerful positions. A person's class, therefore, was usually decided by birth. During the French colonial period, rich and elite French people dominated the upper classes, ousting the locals so that after independence the country was left with many professional vacancies.

Today, economics determine the class structure. Western-educated civil servants and businesspeople in addition to large landowners are the upper class, while shopkeepers, schoolteachers, skilled workers, and low-level civil servants make up a second group. Subsistence farmers and other agricultural workers living in the south and the interior form a third class, while day laborers and unemployed people, who live both in rural areas and urban shantytowns, make up a fourth class. In this arrangement, education is a significant determinant of class.

Economy. As with many people of the Middle East, many rural people of the Tunisian area have abandoned farming and herding and moved to the industrialized cities in search of work. Those who remain raise wheat, barley, chickpeas, olives, potatoes, tomatoes, melons, apples, dates, and other fruits and vegetables, or raise cattle, sheep, goats, and poultry for meat and other food products. Dates are grown around the oases in the south and are an important food for the desert dwellers. About two-thirds of the country is suitable for agriculture, but the population of the country has recently outstripped its farm productivity. The country has launched a plan to make itself self-sufficient in terms of food. Meanwhile, light manufacturing of such items as leather goods, and the mining of the country's mineral resources have slowly added to the economy of the nation.

Family life. The traditional Arab social and economic unit is the extended family, which consists of husband and wife (or wives) and their unmarried daughters and sons as well as their married sons and their families. This patrilineal family lives in a single house or in adjoining units, may hold property in common, and may work together in joint ventures that are funded by the group as a whole. This pattern still exists in Tunisia's rural interior, but the nuclear family of husband, wife, and young children is a more common grouping, especially in the cities. Today, women often act as household heads. Still, even where the extended family has given way to a nuclear unit, old traditions are apparent as migrants to the cities try to organize the suburbs along family lines.

Women. The differences between Tunisia and some other Arab states are reflected in rules and traditions related to women. Fifty percent of the college students of Tunisia are women. While Islamic law allows for a man to have more than one wife (if he can afford to), the Tunisian constitution forbids polygyny. According to Islamic law, husbands can repudiate (divorce) wives merely by declaring their intentions in front of witnesses, but the Tunisian Code of Personal Status requires that divorces only be granted by court action. Women can petition the court for a divorce—a comparatively new innovation that holds for most Islamic states. The Islamic injunction for women to live modestly, which is interpreted in the states of the Persian Gulf as demanding that women live in seclusion and work at home, is interpreted differently in Tunisia and a number of other Arab states. While women are not encouraged to speak with strangers, particularly men, girls do attend school with boys, and women are employed in mixed-sex work places in the cities.

Muslims traditionally marry within their social groups or within extended families. Marriage to cousins is preferred and was once arranged by the parents of the prospective bride and groom. Today, most young Tunisians expect to choose their own marriage partners

Tunisian Muslim woman. *Courtesy of Dr. Nikki Keddie, U.C.L.A.*

and tend to do so on the basis of educational level along with other personal factors.

Food, clothing, and shelter. The Tunisian diet reflects the wide variety of meats, dairy products, grains, and vegetables that are grown in the country, although an increasing amount of the food supply must be imported—in part due to a now abandoned attempt to collectivize farmland into state cooperatives.

Two specialties in Tunisia are *brik* and *salade mechouia*. Brik, perhaps originally the Turkish "borck," is a pastry stuffed with fried egg, vegetables, and tuna, while salade mechouia is a salad of roasted vegetables. As in much of Africa, main courses are usually combinations of a starch (*cous cous*, pasta, or potatoes, for example) with either grilled meat or fish, or a stew consisting of meat and vegetables. Whatever the combination, a hot, peppery sauce almost always accompanies it. Scrambled eggs and spicy soups are also common and meals are frequently ended with seasonal fruits or honey-sweetened pastries made with filo dough and nuts. The influence of French colonialism is seen in the restaurants, where multicourse meals are served with elaborate cream cakes and croissants. Tunisians drink very strong tea, and for snacks, enjoy hunks of French bread stuffed with meats, olives, other vegetables, and *harissa*, the sauce made from red peppers.

Dress in Tunisia ranges from European styles to long robes and dresses and elaborately tied head-coverings for both men and women. The draping clothes that are traditional in the Middle East provide essential air flow and ventilation in sometimes intense heat. These garments are also culturally appropriate in the Islamic countries where it is inappropriate to have much of the body visible. While European influence is most apparent in urban areas, there is now a resurgence of traditional dress in these areas. Many women, for example, have returned to completely covering dress, including veils to demonstrate their commitment to Islam. Many fear that their government's long-standing European approach to economic development will lead to abandonment of religious, moral, and ethical principles and values. Similar attitudes are being expressed in places throughout the Islamic world.

In larger cities, homes range from apartment houses that resemble their European counterparts to shantytown settlements that are the first urban stopping places for rural immigrants. An ecologically sound development, nearly unique to that part of Tunisia where rocky mountains approach the sea, is the subterranean home. Built into the rocks of the cliffs or in caves, these homes use cliffs and caves as walls and have terraced designs. This popular style is seen in underground dwellings in level areas. In this case, large patios are extended in front of the houses to provide a view and sky-lit expanse at the entrance of the house.

Arts. Specialized artisans produce pottery, metalwork, and leather goods in addition to woven carpets characterized by complex geometric patterns. The demand by tourists for these goods has become so great in some cases that traditional workers have been displaced by faster, mechanized production. While sculpture, portraits, landscapes, and other types of paintings are not characteristic of Arab-Islamic traditions, the European presence in Tunisia has encouraged these arts as well.

Tunisian music is largely based on songs introduced into the country by refugees from Spain in the fifteenth and sixteenth centuries. Called *maluf,* this folk music is sung in local Arabic dialects throughout Tunisia, although the prevalence of radios has made Western music very popular, particularly among the youth. This popularity has caused the government to encourage the recording of older music to preserve its tradition.

Religion. Although Islam is the official state religion, the government has conducted itself largely as a secular state since independence. The freedom to practice any religion is specified in the constitution. Still, while there are a few Jews and Christians in Tunisia, it is estimated that ninety-nine percent of the population is Muslim—most of these Sunnis.

Change. Tunisia has had a long history of foreign arrivals and foreign rule. As a result, Roman ruins, Islamic mosques, and French cuisine are all characteristic of Tunisia.

As the country strives to hold on to some ancient traditions, while incorporating itself in the international arena and participating in the world's markets, tensions build among residents who favor the two directions. Meanwhile, the secular government and the multiethnic people continue to hold to cultural practices shaped by their environment as well as by history and religion.

For More Information

Golany, Gideon S. *Earth-Sheltered Dwellings in Tunisia: Ancient Lessons for Modern Design.* Newark: University of Delaware Press, 1988.

Nelson, Harold D., editor. *Tunisia: A Country Study.* Washington, D.C.: American University Press, 1988.

Perkins, Kenneth J. *Tunisia: Crossroads of the Islamic and European Worlds.* Boulder, Colorado: Westview Press, 1986.

TURKS
(turks)

Native speakers of the Turkish language who inhabit the Republic of Turkey.

Population: 51,400,000 (1985 estimate).
Location: The Republic of Turkey.
Language: Turkish.

Geographical Setting

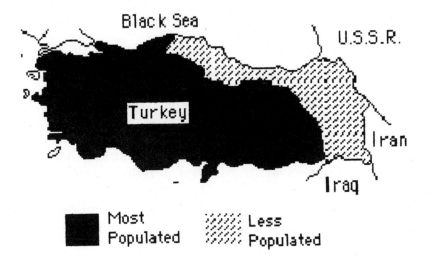

The roughly rectangular Anatolian Peninsula, bounded on the north by the Black Sea, on the west by the Aegean Sea, and on the south by the eastern Mediterranean Sea, makes up ninety-seven percent of Turkey's area. To the east and southeast, Iran, Iraq, and the Soviet Union supply a land frontier over 1,000 miles long. The Sea of Marmara and the Bosporus Strait (which join the Aegean and Black seas) divide this Asian section of Turkey from its smaller, triangular European part, which shares borders with Greece and Bulgaria.

Central Anatolia consists of high plateaus, averaging nearly 4,000 feet, interrupted by scattered mountain ranges, both of which become higher and more forbidding in the east. Mostly herders and wheat farmers, Turks live in scattered villages on these bleak plateaus, where they face harsh winters and stifling summers. Their remote and rugged life has made these central Anatolian Turks tough and conservative. In the southeast live descendants of nomadic tribes, some of whom are non-Turkish, such as the now more settled Kurds and Arabs. Though some continue to herd their flocks to the high mountain pastures in summer, most have settled in lowland villages. In the coastal areas, along the Black, Aegean, and Mediterranean seas, both climate and terrain are more even than in the interior. This mild climate encouraged the growth of trade and industry. Greater prosperity allows the farming of luxury goods—such as dates, figs, and tobacco—rather than subsistence foodstuffs. An easier life and greater contact with the outside world has brought change more rapidly to the coastal Turks, who are separated from the interior by a ring of mountain ranges.

Historical Background

Arrival in an ancient land. The Turks, who did not arrive in Anatolia until the eleventh century, are relative newcomers to a land that had seen many successive civilizations before their arrival. Beginning around 2000 B.C., pre-Hittites, Hittites, Phrygians, Lydians, Persians, Greeks, and Romans had lived or ruled in the region. After the collapse of Roman power in the west about A.D. 450, Anatolia became the heartland of the Byzantine empire (a Greek continuation of Roman rule in the eastern Mediterranean), supplying it with troops and wheat. Originally nomadic peoples from the steppes of central Asia, Turkish tribes began moving west towards Europe around the first century A.D. In the middle of the 400s, the first group, known as the Huns, reached western Europe. Others established kingdoms in Turkestan and Persia before the 900s, by which time they had converted to Islam. In the late 900s a new Turkish dynasty, the Seljuqs, came to power in Turkestan and then Persia, from where they began to make incursions into Anatolia in the early 1000s. In 1071 the Seljuqs crushed the Byzantine army at Manzikert in eastern Anatolia, capturing the emperor himself. This important battle marked the effective end of Byzantine power in Anatolia, and the beginning of Turkish dominance.

Seljuqs of Rum (Rome). The main branch of the Seljuqs continued to rule in Persia and Mesopotamia (Iran and Iraq; see PERSIANS), while another branch known as the Seljuqs of Rum (or "Rome"), quickly penetrated the entire Anatolian Peninsula. Of the original population, some fled to Constantinople or the west, a few remained Christian under the generally tolerant rule of the Muslim Turkish tribes, but over the centuries most converted to Islam. Gradually, too, these former Christians, mostly Greek or Armenian speakers, began to speak Turkish, melding with the dominant Turks, whom they had originally outnumbered.

During the 1100s the Seljuqs contended with the Byzantines and with Christian Crusaders from Europe for control in Anatolia, especially along the Aegean coast, from which the Byzantines and the Crusaders had driven the Turkish tribes for over 200 years. The strongly centralized Seljuq state reached the peak of its power in the early 1200s; shortly thereafter local internal revolts, combined with the Mongol invasions from the east, began to erode its authority. By the early 1300s it had collapsed completely.

The Rise of the Ottoman Empire. Of the ten local emirates, or kingdoms, that arose in Turkish Anatolia after the Seljuqs' disintegration, one quickly came to preeminence: that of Osman, who ruled in northwestern Anatolia and founded the Osmanli or Ottoman dynasty. Osman's son, Orhan, expanded his father's dominions in Anatolia and in the 1350s undertook the first Ottoman conquests in Europe, wresting several towns in eastern Thrace from the Byzantines and crushing the Bulgars and Serbs in battle. His successors Murad and Bayezid (nicknamed the "Thunderbolt") continued the string of Asian and European conquests.

By the early 1400s the territory of the once mighty Byzantine Empire had been reduced to a small island of land, surrounded by Ottoman territory, around Constantinople itself. As Ottoman power had increased, so had the pomp of those who wielded it. Murad, for example, had taken the title sultan (meaning "authority" or "power"), rather than the less majestic bey or emir, which were military ranks. Ottoman capitals also became increasingly grand. They included Bursa, in northwestern Anatolia, which Murad's father Orhan ornamented with sophisticated mosques and tombs; Adrianople, an ancient Byzantine city in Thrace, captured in 1361 and made the capital by Murad II (ruled 1421-51), who filled it with artists and intellectuals; and finally the great prize of Constantinople itself, which fell in 1453 to Muhammad II—known thereafter as Fatih, the Conqueror. Muhammad undertook a massive building program in the defeated city, constructing houses, baths, bazaars, inns, fountains, gardens, a huge mosque, and an imperial palace. He also encouraged the original inhabitants who had fled to return—Jews, Greeks, and Armenians, many of whom were craftsmen, scholars, or artists—and made trade agreements with Venetian and Florentine merchants. Renamed Istanbul, the old city became once again a hub of culture and commerce. Under Muhammad, Ottoman court ritual (the rules governing behavior in the presence of the sultan) also became more formal and elaborate, closer to that of the conquered Byzantines, and very different from the simple traditions of the early emirs.

Suleiman the Magnificent. By 1520, when Muhammad's great-grandson Suleiman took power, Syria, parts of Arabia, Egypt, and northern Africa as far west as Morocco had been added to the empire. It now stretched from the Danube to beyond the Nile Valley. Called the "Magnificent" by Europeans and the "Lawgiver" by Turks, Suleiman brought Ottoman glory to its peak. At home, he reorganized the system of provincial administration to define more clearly the powers of the central government and those of the provincial governors. Like Muhammad the Conqueror, he also became a great builder. His architect, Sinan, designed and built the finest Turkish mosques, particularly the Suleimaniye mosque in Istanbul. Suleiman also enjoyed a string of brilliant military successes: in Asia he conquered eastern Armenia; in the eastern Mediterranean, his admiral Barbarossa made the Turkish fleet supreme; and in Europe he captured Belgrade (in modern Yugoslavia) and most of Hungary and alarmed all of Europe by besieging Vienna. Only when torrential rains mired his heavy artillery was Suleiman turned back from capturing this city in the heart of Europe.

Stagnation and decline. Shortly after Suleiman's death in 1566, Ottoman might began to wane. In 1571 Turkish naval supremacy was interrupted for a year by Austria and its European allies at the Battle of Lepanto. The Turks regained naval supremacy the next year by destroying the Spanish fleet. In the 1600s and 1700s, Austria, Hungary, Poland, and Russia scored further military successes, whittling away Ottoman territory in Europe and the Crimea (the region north of the Black Sea). Intrigue within the sultans' households and within the elite palace guard known as the *Janissaries* led to the guard's control of succession to the throne. They continued to install and depose sultans until 1826, when one sultan destroyed them by cannonading their barracks. Beginning in 1839, Sultan Abdul Mejid at-

Topkapi was the home of a Turkish leader's harem.
Courtesy of Dr. Paul Fischer.

tempted military and political reforms, but to no great effect. Throughout the 1800s, nationalist revolts—as in Greece from 1815 to 1830—and diplomatic maneuvering by western European states progressively deprived the by now crippled Ottoman state of most of its territory outside of Anatolia. In 1914 Turkey entered World War I on the side of Germany, and defeat in that war meant that in 1918 the victorious Allies—including Turkey's biggest enemy, Greece—were poised to carve up the former Ottoman lands between them. A dynamic new Turkish leader prevented them from doing so.

Kemal Ataturk. Mustafa Kemal (1881-1938) was a general who had distinguished himself during World War I. Kemal organized the war-

In earlier times, some Turkish ladies were waited on by slaves. *Courtesy of Smithsonian Institution.*

weary and ragged Turkish army, called into being a Grand National Assembly in the central Anatolian city of Ankara, and prepared to resist the Greeks, who had occupied the western Turkish coast. Forced to retreat at first, by 1922 Kemal's army had driven the Greeks out of Turkey. In 1923 the Allies recognized Kemal's demands in the Treaty of Lausanne, which established the borders of the new state. In the same year, Kemal became president of the new Republic of Turkey and, in a symbolic break with the Ottoman past, moved the capital from Istanbul to Ankara, the heartland of his nationalist movement.

Kemal, who took the name Ataturk (meaning "Father of the Turks"), initiated a series of reforms aimed at turning Turkey into a modern, secular, industrial state, such as those in western Europe. From 1925 to 1930, he abolished religious education in schools; ordered the wearing of Western rather than traditional Islamic clothing; replaced religious law with civil, criminal, and commercial laws based on those of Switzerland; changed the Islamic call to prayer from Arabic to Turkish; and replaced the Arabic alphabet, in which Turkish had been written, with a modified Latin alphabet. In the 1930s, Ataturk consolidated Turkey's diplomatic situation by concluding agreements with major European powers. From a one-party system under Ataturk's Republican Peoples' Party, Turkey's government evolved into a parliamentary democracy which, despite interference from the military in the early 1970s, has largely managed to maintain its independence from the powerful army.

Culture Today

Goals of Ataturk. Although Turkic peoples—including the Uzbeck, Kirghiz, Turkmen, Kazakh, Azeri, and other groups who speak different dialects of the same language—occupy areas throughout Central Asia, those in Turkey feel a special pride, based not so much on tribal or ethnic considerations as on national ones.

Among Ataturk's national goals, the attempt to industrialize the nation has been less successful than he had hoped. Although in the major cities, most of them along the coast, life for the educated middle classes is similar to that in western European or American cities, prosperity has come slowly for most of the nation. Still, an improved road system has made it easier to transport goods from town to town as well as allowing easier access to cities for the rural poor.

The greatest obstacle to Ataturk's program has been resistance to secularization. In Islamic tradition, unlike in Christian, church and state have always been closely intertwined (see ISLAM). Since the time of the Seljuqs, Turks have been devoutly Muslim, and today about ninety-nine percent of Turkey's population remain Muslim, although among the urban middle classes traditional religious practices tend to be less strictly observed. Despite general affection for Ataturk's memory, Turkey's always strong religious lobby has been able to win some concessions from politicians, particularly in the general reinstatement of religious education.

Food, clothing, and shelter. For breakfast, Turks in both city and country eat bread with jam, honey, or feta cheese, accompanied by

Inside a covered bazaar in Istanbul. *Courtesy of Dr. Paul Fischer.*

coffee or tea. A favorite breakfast dish (similar to a pancake) is *koz-leme*, made from wheat flour, eggs, and water, cooked in a hot skillet and sweetened with jam. Lunch and dinner often feature meat, soup, or stew, with rice, lentils, or beans. (Lamb and veal are the most popular meats.) Salads consist of tomatoes, onions and cucumbers, dressed with olive oil, vinegar and herbs. Yogurt accompanies most meals, plain or as a sauce, or mixed with water and salt to make a drink called *ayran.* Turkish coffee (a famous and potent brew) is drunk all day, but especially after lunch and dinner. Ground very fine and heated with water and sugar, the coffee is poured into cups and the grounds allowed to settle before it is drunk.

Ataturk succeeded in making Western-style dress, at least among men, widespread in Turkey, even in many of the most remote villages. He outlawed the traditional *fez,* a brimless, conical red hat and made brimmed felt hats mandatory, because with them on men could not touch their foreheads to the ground in prayer. Despite Ataturk's injunctions, however, rural women continue to swathe themselves from head to foot. Wool is the preferred fabric among rural Turks, particularly valuable to those who continue in a nomadic lifestyle. Herders are sheltered from rain and cold in the *kepenek,* a heavy, hooded mantle shaped from a single piece of felt that serves as coat, blanket and tent.

The weatherproof material also provides homes for nomads throughout Turkey and Central Asia, many of whom live in portable felt *yurts,* circular tentlike dwellings with domed roofs that can stand up to the cold winds of the Anatolian plateaus and Asian steppes. Villagers build most often from stone, simple dwellings sometimes constructed on escarpments so that new rooms can be quarried from the live rock. In the cities, middle class families in prosperous neighborhoods are outnumbered by those who live in shanties called *gecekondu,* meaning "built in a night." Gecekondu occupy outlying areas of major cities, providing shelter for up to two-thirds of the population, most of whom have come from rural areas in search of work.

Family life. Turkish family traditions remain strongest in the villages, where the extended, patriarchal family functions both as a unit and as an interconnected part of village life. The father is undisputed master of the house, commanding deference from his wife and children, including his married sons, who usually live at home until their father's death. The oldest son then inherits and becomes head of the household, with the younger sons eventually leaving to establish their own households. Men often spend as little time as possible at home, working in the fields or, when relaxing, gathering at the *kahvehane* (coffeehouse). Aside from kahvehane, an important gathering place for men is the *misafir odasi* (guest room) of the village's headman, a strictly male precinct usually segregated from the rest of the house. Sons grow up in this male world, their education dependent in early years on the mother and later on the father, who teaches them the rules of social behavior and the farming skills they will need as adults. Among sons, a younger one defers to an older, often referring to him as *agabey*, a combination of the two respectful terms *aga* and *bey*. Younger brothers and sisters refer to their elder sister as *abla*.

Relations between men and women are constrained by rigid taboos and rules of behavior. For example, if a village man is going off on a long journey, his mother and sisters might hug and kiss him in public as they say good-bye, while his wife remains silent in the background. The women of the family are kept from contact with men outside it, interacting rarely even with those in the family. As the men spend much of their time outside the house, women remain mostly inside it, relying on each other for personal contact and amusement. Girls grow up almost entirely within the household, taught by their mothers cooking, sewing, cleaning, and other skills they will use as wives and mothers. Upon marriage, a girl moves from her father's house to that of her husband's father, a separation that can be very painful for her and her mother, particularly if her husband lives in a distant village. From marriage on, the wife comes under the immediate control of her mother-in-law, on whom she waits and for whom she performs the household's menial tasks. This relationship is the most important for her, and her life is made considerably more pleasant if they get along. The Turkish word for "bride" and "daughter-in-law" is the same: *gelin*, which originally meant "the one who comes." The new bride slowly gains status in the household, until she becomes a mother-in-law herself.

Economy. Construction and factory jobs in the cities attract many Turks from rural areas, but there are usually many more applicants than opportunities. Even those who find jobs must often settle for low pay. If he cannot find work in the city, the villager might join the many unskilled migrant workers who travel to Germany, Sweden, France, and other countries in western Europe. In 1970 almost one million Turks made such journeys, signing up at recruitment centers

Istanbul is a large modern city in Turkey near Greece. *Courtesy of Dr. Paul Fischer.*

in Turkish cities with representatives from the European country concerned. The numbers grew each year until the late 1980s, when hostility from European workers led to tensions between their governments and that of Turkey. Since then, fewer Turkish workers have sought work abroad. Unemployment remains a problem, because important labor sources (such as agriculture and forestry) offer only seasonal work. Tourism has grown substantially in the 1980s, however, particularly in coastal areas, and service industries contribute increasingly to the national economy.

Arts and literature. As with art throughout the Islamic world as a whole, Turkish art has been made primarily for some home decorations and for religious purposes, especially the design and decoration of religious buildings. Aside from Islamic influences, both Seljuq and Ottoman builders incorporated design features such as the dome from Byzantine architecture. Seljuq building in Anatolia was also heavily influenced by Persia (as was Islamic art generally in this period; see PERSIANS). Refining and developing existing elements rather than creating new ones, Seljuq architects and craftsmen built graceful minarets (free-standing spires) and mosques, with highly elaborate gateways and portals of carved stone. Sinan, the architect of Suleiman the Magnificent, brought Ottoman architecture to its peak, designing 343 buildings in all, including three masterpieces: the Shezade, Suleimaniye, and Selimiye mosques.

Folk literature is central to Turkish culture, whether in epic form, such as the *Book of Dede Korkut* (probably incorporating pre-Islamic traditions, though taking its present form in the 1600s), or in the humorous stories of the good-natured trickster Nasreddin Hoca. The *hoca* is the local religious teacher. One is usually found in each village. Ataturk reformed Turkish of its Arabic and Persian words, with the result that writers even of the 1800s are difficult for modern Turks to understand. Among these are the poet Abdulhak Hamit and the playwright Namik Kemal, despite the latter's use of Western stylistic elements and conversational language. Western influence has grown since Kemal's death in 1888, as demonstrated by the proliferation of realistic novels such as those of Halide Edip Adivar and Yakup Kadri Karaosmanoglu. Gains in education have enabled literature to reach a wider audience as well as to draw a greater variety in authorship.

Conclusion. Turkey's deepest division—between urban and rural societies—continues to make itself felt in almost every area of life. In

An open bazaar in Istanbul, Turkey. *Courtesy of Dr. Paul Fischer.*

particular, country people tend to share in the general revival of Islamic fundamentalism, which differs from the urban, secular cultural forms that Kemal Ataturk initiated and that continue today.

For More Infomation

Bates, Daniel, and Rassam, Amal. *People and Cultures of the Middle East*. Englewood Cliffs, New Jersey: Prentice Hall, 1983.

Makal, Mahmut. *Village in Anatolia*. London: Vallentine, Mitchell & Co., Ltd., 1954.

Muller, Herbert J. *The Loom of History*. New York: Harper & Brothers, 1958.

Stirling, Paul. *Turkish Village*. New York: John Wiley & Sons, 1965.

YAZIDIS
(yah zee' deez)

Iraqi people who live in near isolation in the mountain area of the
northern border of Iraq known as Jebel Sinjar.

Population: 30,000 (1985 estimate).
Location: Iraq; Syria; Turkey; the Soviet Union.
Language: Yazidi.

Geographical Setting

On the east side of the Tigris River, the border between Iraq and
Iran is marked by an abruptly rising mountain range, the Zagros

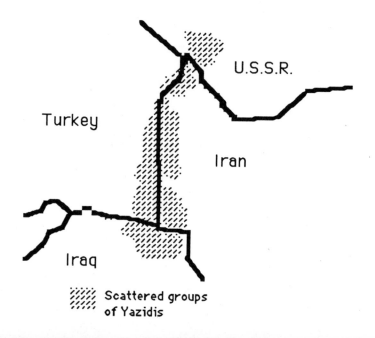

Scattered groups
of Yazidis

Mountains. In the north this range arcs across the boundary of Iran and Turkey. Here the mountains and foothills form a rugged land as high as 5,000 feet. The Yazidi live in the mountain valleys. Annual rainfall in these valleys averages twenty-five to forty inches, most of it falling in December and January. Summer temperatures are mild compared to those just south of the mountains, while winter temperatures are frequently well below freezing.

Historical Background

Origin. The Yazidis began as different groups of peoples who migrated in stages to Iraq from other areas of the Middle East. Their migrations may have begun as early as the sixth century B.C. The groups lived together in isolation, practicing a variety of religions, including Zoroastrianism and Christianity. In A.D. 750, the Omayyads of North Iraq brought Islam to the groups of the region. Accepting Islam, but adding some of their older traditions, the people began to come together as a single unit. Shaikh Adi (1072-1161) became their leader and was worshiped as a god.

Religious bonds. The Yazidis taught that there were six godly beings, including the Sun, Satan, Jesus Christ, Melak Salem, Yazid, and Shaikh Adi. They further claimed that all emanated from and were really the same being—God. They denied the existence of evil and regarded Satan as a fallen being, who will someday be reconciled with God. Satan was symbolized as a sacred peacock and their regard for Satan as a deity resulted in persecution and massacre by Muslim groups. Shaikh Adi was originally a Muslim, but the Yazidis claimed that he had eaten bread with God. Afterwards, Shaikh Adi excused his followers from saying the five daily prayers and other Muslim practices.

The Yazidis and Islam. Muslims regarded the Yazidis as infidels, issued edicts against them, and condoned holy wars to convert them. Many Yazidis were killed in 1254 by the Muslim ruler Badr al-Din. Later, the army of Prince Izz al-Din al-Bakhti waged war on the Yazidis in 1400, destroying many people, desecrating Shaikh Adi's grave, and burning his bones. The Yazidis retaliated and won, crucifying and slaughtering their captives. In the fifteenth and sixteenth centuries they acquired strength and influence, establishing a strong principality of their own and dominating other principalities where many Muslim people lived. However, repeated attacks by Muslims and others were directed against the Yazidis in the 1700s. They were killed and their villages plundered by Kurds in 1702 and by Muslims in 1732. In 1753, the Muslim leader Sulayman Pasha tricked the Yazidis by inviting them to take refuge with him. The Yazidis accepted, whereupon he confiscated their weapons and ordered his troops to shoot the hostages. Memories of this attack are preserved in Yazidi song. Seeking revenge, the Yazidis formed bands, attacked Muslim villages, burned their homes and fields, and robbed passing caravans.

Yazidis and Turks. The area was ruled by Turks of the Ottoman Empire during the 1800s and 1900s. In 1911, Asad Pasha al-Druzi led the Turks in a successful campaign against the Yazidis, and afterwards the area remained quiet for a number of years. The Turks left the area in the 1920s and were replaced by Iraqis who, in 1939, instituted compulsory military service. Yazidi chiefs refused to obey, and the people revolted, robbing travelers and terrorizing state functionaries.

Yazidis and British. When the government of Iraq fought the British in 1941, the Yazidis cooperated with the British. In laws passed in 1948, the government of Iraq awarded full citizenship rights to the Yazidis. It opened an office to direct Yazidi affairs in Baghdad in 1969. By then small groups of Yazidis resided in the cities, and fewer Yazidis were leading a traditional existence on their isolated terrain along the Iraqi, Syrian, and Turkish borders.

Culture Today

Isolation. Traditional Yazidi belief prohibits association with outsiders. Until some moved to the cities, Yazidis were not allowed to enter public baths, schools, theaters, or any place in which they might hear words that are contrary to the Yazidi faith.

Education. Learning was once a privilege reserved for descendants of the Yazidi family headed by Shaikh Hasan al-Basri, but these traditional prohibitions have been upset by recent developments in the Middle East. Improved transportation has brought contact with non-Yazidis and some Yazidis have succumbed to government efforts to educate them. Those who are more traditional live strictly according to the Yazidi holy books, *Jalwa* and *Resh.* According to the speaker of the holy scripture, every age has its own overseer who directs affairs according to Satan's decrees.

Religion. The Supreme Being is believed to participate in all affairs, including those that non-Yazidis call evil since this Supreme Being incorporates good and bad. Religious rites referred to in the scriptures recall the various earlier religions. Baptism and circumcision and the description of feasts show Christian influences. Prayers, fasting, and pilgrimages to Mecca are Muslim influences. The Hindu influence is apparent in the Yazidis belief in reincarnation and in the division of their people into castes. In spite of this reflection of influence by other religions, the Yazidi faith is closed to outsiders. Intermarriage with members of other groups is prohibited and the people are taught to be secretive with people of other creeds.

Yazidi society. In traditional society, intermarriage is prohibited between certain castes of Yazidis as well. The three highest castes are occupied by rulers. At the top level is the prince, who descends from Shaikh Adi and is his sole representative on earth. The next caste is for the Pesmrreyyah, cousins of the prince, who have acted as his advisers and have assisted him in directing the affairs of the community. At the next level are Shaikhs, or chiefs of Yazidi tribes, and elders from the house of Shaikh Adi. Below them are three castes of religious leaders. *Faqirs* have forsaken worldly pleasures and are clad in black woolen rags tied with a red belt that contains a yellow copper ring. *Chanters* recite religious songs and poems for the people, keeping their oral traditions alive. *Kochaks,* who act as advisers and guides to Yazidi individuals, dress in white turbans and white flowing robes that are tied with black or red woolen belts, and their responsibilities include the washing and the shrouding of the dead and foretelling the fate of a deceased soul. At the bottom of the social strata are the Commoners, who work for higher castes in the manner of serfs. They have been sold, handed down by families as part of an inheritance, and restricted to marriage with others of their own caste.

Family life. Marriages are arranged by a tribe's sheikh. The suitor informs the sheikh who then tells the boy's father and agrees on the amount of dowry that will be paid to the girl's father. Yazidi families may include one husband and as many as four wives and, in accordance with the teachings of Shaikh Adi, adultery is permissible. Aside from marriage and family relations, each of the Yazidis has a special relationship with an individual chosen to be a brother or sister in the afterlife. This brother or sister is with the individual in times of sickness or need.

Food, clothing, and shelter. The traditional Yazidis earn their livelihood by farming and raising animals on land that is jointly owned. The main crops are wheat, barley, chickpeas, lentils, olives, and corn, while the farmers keep mules and donkeys, and raise sheep and cattle. Nearly all Yazidis are affiliated with a particular tribe and some are nomads who migrate with their livestock at particular times of the year.

Round pieces of dried cream that have been ground to make a sort of meal are part of the staple menu. These are mixed with butter and garlic. In contrast with the usual Muslim teachings, wine is a common beverage for the Yazidis. Among the foods the Yazidis avoid eating are meat, lettuce, cabbage, cauliflower, beans, and fish.

Other prohibitions affect Yazidi housing and dress. Unmarried women wear flowers in their hair, necklaces made of coins, grain, or small pearls, and colorful clothing. Married women wear white. Clothing includes long dresses, ankle-length white cotton pants, and a heavy coat in winter. An unmarried woman may wear a red or black cloth on her head as a veil and will wear a white veil that extends downward from the chin, while the married woman wears a white turban on her head. Men wear a woolen belt and a white cloth with red polka dots on their head. Traditional summer clothing includes a coat and broadcloth pants. A cloak and pelts serve as wintertime clothing. Some Yazidi men wear a high brown cone-shaped cap covered by a black or red turban. Young people are beginning to wear Western-style clothing, another indication that fewer Yazidi are following traditional practices as time passes.

Yazidi traditions are dominated by their unique religious tenets, their attitudes toward others, and even their grooming habits. In the belief that Satanic forces reside in sewers, traditional Yazidi homes are without restrooms or sewers. And, reflective of the general distrust of others, a Muslim may not be an overnight guest for Yazidis, who also are forbidden from sleeping in the same room with a Muslim. Most Yazidis have dark hair, large eyes, and thick lips. Men grow moustaches, which they may not shave and the Chanters must never shave their facial hair.

For More Information

Ahmed, Sami Said. *The Yazidis: Their Life and Beliefs.* Miami, Florida: Field Research Projects, 1975.

Fisher, W. B. *The Middle East: A Physical, Social and Regional Geography.* London: Methuen and Company Ltd., 1978.

Gulick, John. *The Middle East: An Anthropological Perspective.* Pacific Palisades, California: Goodyear Publishing Co., 1976.

348

YEMENIS
(yem' en eez)

Rural cultivators and city-dwellers of the southern edge of the
Arabian peninsula.

Population: 10,500,000 (1990 estimate).
Location: Yemen.
Language: Arabic.

Geographical Setting

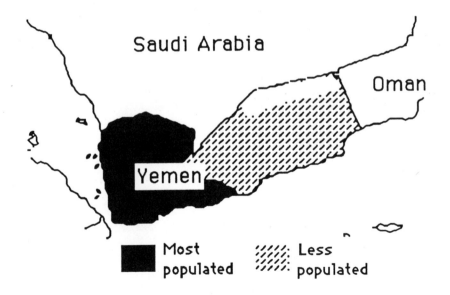

Two countries, the Yemen Arab Republic in the northwest, and the People's Democratic Republic of Yemen in the south combined in 1990 to form a single nation. The new country of Yemen forms an L-shaped region south of Saudi Arabia and bordering the Red Sea (formerly North Yemen) and the Gulf of Aden (formerly South Yemen). Both regions have narrow, hot, dry coastal zones and mountainous interiors that give way toward the north and east to the desert of the Arabian plateau. The mountain ranges rise to altitudes of 6,000 to 14,000 feet with slopes and valleys that have been irrigated for terraced farms, and are interspersed with patches of forests. Tamarind, juniper, and fig trees grow on the mountainsides in the north, while the mountains of southern Yemen are covered with shrubs, particularly along the dry riverbeds, or *wadis*. During the rainy seasons, the western wadis fill with water from an annual rainfall of thirty inches. Built on the remains of ancient volcanic activity, the ancient city of Aden, former capital of South Yemen, is the most important commercial center in the region and a major port. The other center of commerce and population is San'a, the capital of Yemen.

Historical Background

Early history. In ancient times, the area now occupied by Yemen was known as "Arabian Felix" ("happy Arabia") because the people there controlled a thriving commercial land-and-sea network of trade in luxury goods—pearls, gold, slaves, ivory, silk, and metals for weapon-making. These people had also developed dams to collect the scant rainfall and use it for agricultural self-sufficiency. This was the rich market for frankincense and myrrh, two substances valued by Egyptians and others for use in cosmetics, medicines, and embalming. These materials were brought to Aden and by boat across the Gulf of Aden to Egypt, and from India to Aden to be distributed by ship and camel caravan.

About 1200 B.C., the area was part of the Minoan civilization, but the most famous kingdom appeared in the tenth century B.C., the Kingdom of Saba, ruled at the time of Solomon by Sheba. The Sabeans were desert people from the north who controlled inland trade routes and were ruled by priest-kings, the *mukarribs.* Saba flourished for 500 years, almost constantly at war with the neighboring states Qatban and Hadramaut. Saba grew by organizing a tribal confederacy to produce and transport frankincense and began to decline when rival tribes of Hamdan and Himyar challenged its position as the major trader of the region. It reached its greatest wealth and power under Jewish kings of the Himyar, from whom the present-day leaders of Yemen claim their ancestry. Along the coast, however, the Hamdan tribe formed its own federation with the Hashid and Bakil, the ancestors of present-day Yemeni groups.

Rivalries. Rivalry between Himyar and Hamdan allowed foreign influences to gain a foothold in the region. Other native groups imposed tolls between caravan cities and distribution points, Egypt by-passed Yemen to trade directly with India, Ethiopian Christians invaded and occupied southern Yemen, and in the middle of the first century B.C. Romans took Egypt and destroyed a key incense market. The decline of the region began when traders found direct routes between Egypt and India and began to by-pass the Yemen traders. The business of supplying frankincense remained until the Roman Empire officially adopted Christianity in A.D. 325 and outlawed earlier rituals that required incense.

A part of Yemen was claimed by Ethiopians for a short time in the sixth century, and then became a unit of Persia. Under Islamic rule, first from Damascus and then from Baghdad, the tribes of the region accepted the new Muslim faith. However, they soon broke away from the central government and chose to follow their own religious leaders, *imams.* The first of these was Zaid, son of Ali Hadi.

Egyptians, Ottomans, and British. Again the area fell to foreign rule, this time by the Egyptians. The Egyptians in turn lost control to the Ottomans in the sixteenth century. The Ottomans introduced the Sunni sect of Islam in contrast to the Yemeni Shi'ite/Zaidi sect. The Yemeni imam rebelled against this religious change and enlisted the aid of the British, who took control of the port of Aden in 1609. Aden was later returned to the Ottoman empire to be reconquered by the British in the 19th century. A pact with the Ottoman Empire in 1911 left northern Yemen with a shared Ottoman and local government while the British controlled the south. The Yemens became independent in 1920.

Revolution. The old line of imams, from the family of Zaid, continued to rule North Yemen until the civil war of 1962-1970 resulted in first a military government then the legislative government that ruled the Yemen Arab Republic until 1990. Then, in 1967, the British withdrew from South Yemen, and socialists formed the People's Democratic Republic of Yemen. Following the independence of the two countries, there were repeated proposals that the two countries unite into a single Yemen, a union finally achieved in 1990.

Culture Today

Village life. The majority of the people of both Yemeni countries are Arab Muslims who are farmers and herders. Because of the port of Aden, however, forty-three percent of the southern Yemenis live in cities and towns, have had greater exposure to Europeans, and have adopted European clothing, housing styles, and patterns of education. Still, the majority of southern Yemenis live in villages and are farmers, fishers, manufacturers of homecrafts, and herders of sheep and goats.

Yemeni villages are scattered in the inland valleys near oases. Homes are built of mud-brick, three- or four-stories tall. From these villages, the people work in fields of cooperative farms owned by the government. Here wheat, millet, and sorghum along with some vegetables and fruit are grown for food, while cotton, coffee, fruit, vegetables, dates, tobacco, and grains are cash crops. Sheep, goats, camels, and poultry are raised for food and for material to create clothing.

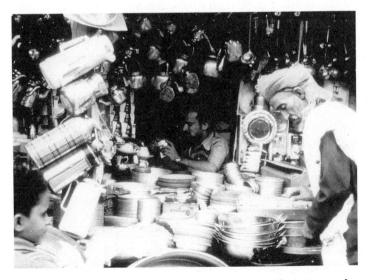

A bazaar in the Yemen capital of San'a. *Courtesy of Dr. Nikki Keddie, U.C.L.A.*

Conditions in North Yemen are similar, except that the interior city of San'a is smaller and only twenty-five percent of the population lives in the city or large towns. Northern Yemenis are mostly from one society, the Zaydis, who once ruled the land.

A village or collection of villages form a confederation of related people ruled by a sheikh (chief). Various sections of this confederation are governed by subchieftains, the *masheikh*. Both sheikh and masheikh are drawn from the traditional ruling families. The sheikh oversees the customary, but not religious, laws. Masheikh lead and mediate smaller sections of the confederation for whose protection they are responsible.

Many Yemeni villagers supplement their incomes by weaving, glassmaking, pottery work, or creating leather products. These are sold in village and city open-air markets. But it is common practice for one member of the family to move to another country, particularly Saudi Arabia, to supplement the family income.

Oil was discovered in both the old Yemen countries in the 1980s, and has since changed the economy of the country. Before that, the principal cash crops of the farmers were coffee and *gat*, a mild narcotic. Growing, selling, and using the gat leaves remains legal in northern Yemen but has been outlawed in southern Yemen.

Food and clothing. Yemeni city folk dress in European-style clothing, while the familiar Arab desert dress, the burnoose, is worn by nomads and villagers. In the cities, however, men often wear a combination of western shirts or sports jackets over a cotton kilt, the *futa*, or a saronglike garment called the *lungi*. They cover their heads with the traditional turban or skullcap and wear sandals on their feet.

Most urban women conceal their faces behind a veil and cover their dresses with a black cloak called a *shaydor* when they go outdoors. Working women may wear European dresses, skirts, or uniforms at work but cover these with a long coat, the *balto*, and a headscarf when they travel in public. Rural women wear colorful peasant dresses or blouses and floor-length skirts. They wrap their hair in a thin scarf and sometimes wear wide-brimmed straw hats. Women, too, wear sandals. Yemeni women wear necklaces, bracelets, rings, and headpieces crafted of filigree silver inlaid with stones. Often jewelry contains verses from the Quran.

Curved daggers worn by men, *jambiyya*, are handed down from father to son. These are often housed in silver sheaths and have decorative hilts. Some tribesmen may also decorate their costumes with ammunition belts.

The mainstay of the Yemeni diet is food prepared from locally grown cereals, vegetables, and milk products. Barley, wheat, maize, and rice are cooked into a thick porridge or used as stuffing for vegetables. Many dishes are spiced with zhug, a paste of chili peppers, garlic, coriander, caraway, and cardamon seeds. The paste is added to salads and used as a flavoring for lamb, fish, and chicken dishes. *Ful,* an example of a Yemeni food, is a combination of beans and garlic that is spread on bread and eaten with chopped onions and hard-boiled eggs. A village breakfast might consist of bread and *gishr,* a drink made from coffee-bean husks. A flat, round bread accompanies most meals.

In the cities, more affluent families eat meals consisting of several courses, spiced salads, fruit, vegetables, fish, and meat stews or curries, as well as milk products. Spiced water, soda, or juices accompany the meal, and strong coffee or sweetened, spiced tea follow.

Yemeni society. Most Yemeni are organized into a system of classes or castes based largely on religion. Sayyids, descendants of the Prophet, are wealthy landowners who select an imam from among them and act as mediators of disputes. Ranked below the Sayyids are the educated elite, the *Qadis,* and below them *Qabili,* who are descendants of a common ancestor within a society. A group of lower-status laborers, craftspeople, and former slaves forms the *Khadam.*

Religion. Most Yemenis are Muslim, and in spite of following different sects and teaching units, practice their religion faithfully. The Pillars of Islam, prayer, alms-giving, fasting, and pilgrimage are faithfully practiced. Most towns and villages have mosques, where men and women gather in separate sections to pray. The religion encourages cooperative action and aid to the needy.

Village family life. Membership in a kin-group is established by the line of the men. Men indicate their rank by wearing symbolic clothes or headdress and by positioning a curved dagger, the *jambiya,* in a sash. The highest rank in the villages wears the dagger on the right, the lowest on the left.

In Yemeni culture, everyone is expected to marry and establish a family to continue the lineage. Social life is defined by this lineage. Obligations to the family are most important, and much of the reputation of a family unit depends on the women. A woman is thought to bring dishonor to the family if she does not follow the customs of segregation of sexes, wearing of a veil, and recognition of the dominant position of men.

Girls are generally married between the ages of twelve and fourteen by arrangement between families. Parents choose the partners according to the principle of *kafaa,* under which a woman may not marry below her social class. When married, a woman assumes the rank of her husband.

Arts, music, and literature. Yemeni culture has a rich oral tradition of poetry and song that dates from its pre-Islamic past. To this is added spontaneous poetic compositions performed while visiting, at ritual dances, on religious holidays, and at feasts and wedding celebrations. Most poetry is recited by men, while storytellers are as skilled and well-recognized as popular artists and writers. Men also dance the Yemeni ritual dance, the *baraa.* This is a slow rhythmic dance performed to the beat of a small drum.

Yemeni authors write of subjects sensitive to the Yemenis, including loneliness, the plight of women, and political themes. Some Yemeni authors have gained international acclaim. Muhammad al-Shurafi is known for his anthology *The Tears of the Veil.* Zayd Muatee

A typical Yemen village with stone decorations around doors and windows. *Courtesy of Dr. Nikki Keddie, U.C.L.A.*

Dammaj is a short story writer known for *The Scorpion.* Historian Abdallah al-Baranduni wrote the poetic work *A Time without Quality* in 1979, and Abd al-Rahman Fakri wrote *Words and Other Words.* Many such Yemeni works have been translated into English and other languages.

Yemeni artisans are famous for silver filigree jewelry, tooled leather, colorful textiles, and decorative ironwork. This artistry and craftsmanship is reflected in a distinctive architecture. Brick and stone buildings with different-colored stones around the doors and windows mark the Yemeni village. The town of Shibam, founded in the third century, has a tiered "wedding-cake" style architecture and is called the town with the first skyscrapers of the world.

For More Information

Hansen, Thorkild. *Arabian Felix.* New York: Harper and Row, 1964.

Jayyusi, Salma K., editor. *The Literature of Modern Arabia; An Anthology.* Austin: University of Texas Press, 1989.

The Yemens: Country Studies Area Handbook Series. Washington, D.C.: American University Press, 1986.

COUNTRIES TODAY

AFGHANISTAN
(af gan' ih stan)

Population: 18,600,000 (1986 estimate).
Location: The Middle East and Asia, bordered by the Soviet Union, Pakistan, and Iran.
Languages: Pushtu; Dari.
Principal cities: Kabul (capital; only city with more than 200,000 population); Qandahr; Herat; Mazar-i-Sharif.

High mountains sweep across Afghanistan from the northeast to the west. Peaks over 20,000 feet mark the eastern mountains of the Hindu Kush range that starts near the center of the country and extends toward Pakistan (Hindu Kush means "Hindu destroyer.") Toward the west the mountains are lower and finally form a moderately high flat area in the southwest before becoming a flat desert area. In the

Afghanistan

northwest, the lower-peaked mountains extend into Iran. Rivers flow both north and south from the mountains. The Amu Darya, Morghib, and Harata rivers flow toward the Soviet Union, while the Kabul River runs east into Pakistan. The Helmand River, running from the mountains to small lakes on the Iranian border, reverses its flow in some parts each year—typifying the very rugged and unstable country. Earthquakes and small volcanic activities are frequent in the folded and refolded mountain land of Afghanistan.

The rugged and varied nature of the land has helped to isolate the peoples of Afghanistan from the outside world and from each other. Not until Ahmad Shah Abdali (1747-1772) was the land united under one rule. This union lived only a short time before breaking into smaller units, to be reunited by Amir Dost Muhammad Khan Barakzay in 1863. Dost Muhammad and his successor, Shir Ali, were considered a threat to British interests in India and, with British help, he was overthrown in 1880 after a series of Afghan-British encounters. The new ruler, Abd ar-Rahman, arranged the Afghanistan boundaries of today. In 1921, Amanullah officially declared Afghanistan's independence.

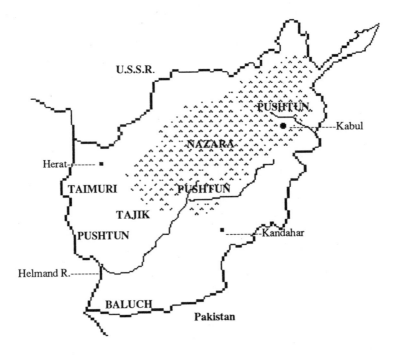

Some of the people of Afghanistan.

In the 1970s Afghanistan was struck by a long period of widespread famine, and in 1979 Soviet troops entered the land amidst a civil war in support of the government in Kabul. Rebels, the *mujaheddin,* fought with some success against the Soviet troops and the central government of Afghanistan. The struggles had lasted so long and with such little resolution of problems, that by 1990 Dr. Najibullah Ahmadzai, Chairman of the Homeland Party, had begin to seek a reconciliation among all the warring factions and the Soviets had begun to withdraw from Afghanistan.

The rugged and varied territory has separated the people so that a number of societies have resulted. While a majority of the people are Pushtun who live in the center of the country and in the south and east, there are also Ghilzays (perhaps originally from Turkey) living near Pakistan. Tadzhiks from Persia live in the northeastern mountains, Hazara in the central mountains, and Baluch in the desert region of the south and in Pakistan. For more about the peoples of Afghanistan see **Baluch, Pushtun,** and **Hazara.**

ALGERIA
(al jeer' ee uh)

Population: 23,800,000 (1988 estimate).
Location: North Africa, bounded by Tunisia, Libya, Niger, Mali, Mauritania, Morocco, and the Mediterranean Sea.
Languages: Arabic; French.
Principal cities: Algiers (capital, 1,700,000); Oran (660,000); Constantine (450,000); Annaba (350,000).

Algeria is a geologically divided land. Two branches of the Atlas Mountains sweep across the country in the north. Along the Mediterranean Sea, a thin coastal area quickly rises to the Tal Atlas Range. Farther inland, these mountains drop to a high plateau and then rise again to form the Saharan Atlas Range, which divides northern Algeria from the Sahara Desert in the south. Rainfall is only adequate

Algeria

for agriculture along the coast and foothills of the Tal. Beyond this range the land is dry and hot. The high plateau between the two mountain ranges has no permanent streams, but is drained by periodically filled washes called *shotts*.

This geography has affected the population of Algeria through the ages. Perhaps originally settled by people speaking the Berber language, the area was invaded by Arab armies in the seventh to ninth centuries. These armies moved first along the coast, and intermarried with Berber women, forming a coastal mix of Algerians. Berbers, holding to their own language and traditions, remained isolated in the Saharan Atlas and the desert.

For 132 years, beginning in 1830, Algeria was ruled by France. Then in 1962, after eight years of French and Algerian wars, the country became independent under Ben Bella, who established a socialist government with a single political party, the FLN. But Ben Bella was deposed in 1965 by military units led by Colonel Houari Boumedienne. This government reformed the educational system and began a program to industrialize the country. In 1978, Boume-

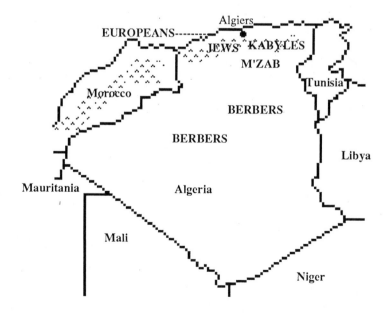

Europeans, Jews, and Kabyles live along the Mediterranean Coast of Algeria. Berbers and Mzab live inland.

dienne died and the rule fell to Colonel Ben Djedid Chadhi, who swore to continue the policies of the "irreversible option of socialism" and "national independence." The goal was to improve Algeria's economy while making it self-sufficient in food products. About seventy-five percent of Algeria's food must be imported. In 1988, young people rebelled against their government's policies with demonstrations and were repelled by the military. However, they had demonstrated the popular desire for a multi-party system and other reforms. The result was a promise of new elections in 1991.

While there is a mixed population formed from marriages of Berbers and Arabs along the coast, there are spots inland where the Berber people have kept to their own society. Farther inland, the Tuareg people are traders and herders of the desert. For more information about the peoples of Algeria see **Bedouins, Berbers,** and **Arabs.**

BAHRAIN
(bah' rain)

Population: 503,000 (1990 estimate), of which 167,000 are foreigners.
Location: Thirty-five islands off the coast of Saudi Arabia in the Persian Gulf.
Language: Arabic.
Principal cities: Manama (capital; only city with more than 100,000 population).

The country of Bahrain consists of mostly barren islands; the largest of them linked together by causeways. Another causeway links Bahrain to Saudi Arabia. Very little of the island land is suitable for agriculture. Farmers raise tomatoes, melons, and goats, while in less productive areas sheep and cattle are grazed.

Bahrain

Once the islands were the home of the ancient trading civilization of Dilmun. Archaeologists still study this civilization. For centuries an independent kingdom, the country was claimed by Portugal from 1521 to 1602 and by Iran from 1602 to 1782. But in 1783 a tribe from Saudi Arabia, the Utub tribe, settled the islands and one of their family became sheikh. The members of this al-Khalia family have ruled Bahrain since that time.

Today Bahrain is important for its mineral wealth. Oil and aluminum have been found there. In 1990 it was estimated that Bahrain had 100,000,000 barrels of oil in reserve.

Realizing that the oil reserves will be exhausted by the year 2000, the rulers of Bahrain are spending the money from the oil to develop other potential of the islands. Aluminum smelters and aluminum forming companies have been constructed, along with a shipbuilding and repairing station. Health services for the people has been improved. Education has grown so that today there are 139 elementary schools where ninety-nine percent of the boys and ninety-six percent of the girls attend. About half of these go on to high school. There

Bahrain is a cluster of islands in the Persian Gulf.

is also a technical college and a coeducational university in Bahrain. Construction and other businesses have grown more rapidly than the Bahraini population. Today, nearly one-third of the population consists of foreign workers.

Of the 350,000 Bahraini, 300,000 are Muslims. The other 50,000 are scattered through fourteen different religions. Although the al-Khalifa family follows the Sunni sect of Islam, about sixty percent of the Muslims of Bahrain are Shi'ite. For more information about the people of Bahrain, see the entry on **Arabs.**

EGYPT

(ee' jipt)

Population: 52,000,000 (1988 estimate).
Location: Northeastern Africa, bounded by Israel, Jordan, Saudi Arabia, the Red Sea, Sudan, Libya, and the Mediterranean Sea.
Language: Arabic (with some French and English).
Principal cities: Cairo, (capital, 12,000,000); Alexandria, (5,000,000); El-Giza, (1,600,000); eleven other cities with more than 200,000 population.

Egypt is one of the most distinctive countries in the world. It was one of the first places, if not the first, where people came together in towns and villages. People have lived in organized communities in the delta area where the Nile River meets the Mediterranean Sea for more than 10,000 years.

Egypt

The geography of Egypt is also distinctive. It is an almost square country (674 miles east to west and 770 miles north to south), and almost all of the land is desert. Through the middle of the country courses the Nile River, which originates deep in Africa at Lake Victoria and Lake Rudolph and runs sluggishly through Sudan before flowing the length of Egypt to the Mediterranean Sea. Over the centuries, annual floods that have sometimes raised the river level as much as sixteen feet, have widened the river channel into a valley two- to ten-miles wide. About 150 miles from the sea, the Nile fans out east and west as sections of the river cut through the silt the river has brought with it. Here, a great wedge of water-cut land provided fertile soil and was the site of the earliest communities. This narrow strip and wedge-shaped delta is the home for almost all Egyptians. Crowded into villages along the western side of this narrow valley, the people of Egypt live in one of the most densely populated regions of the world; in some places 3,000 people per square mile seek farmland on which to support themselves. Once these people grew the

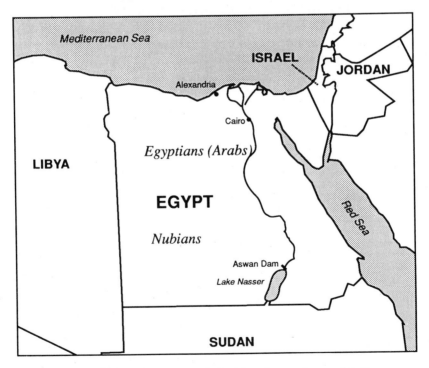

The great cities of Egypt are populated by Armenians, Jews, Christians, and Arab Egyptians, as well as many immigrants from other countries.

crops they needed for food, but today much of the land is given to cash crops such as cotton, fruits, vegetables, and flowers, and the growing population of Egyptians must import much of the food they eat.

To help the increasing numbers, the government sought to reduce the amount of land that was flooded each year, and to harness the water so that irrigation systems would allow more land to be farmed. The High Dam at Aswan, built at the only place in Egypt that the river flows through rapids, dammed the water to form a lake 350 miles long and six miles wide. Below that, flood waters were controlled but so was the flow of silt that renewed the land yearly. Now, with attention to cash crops that demand four harvests each year, the land is being depleted and Egypt must buy greater quantities of the food needed by the people, many of whom have given up their agricultural lifestyles and moved to the cities to find work.

The people of Egypt are a unique blend of older inhabitants of the delta area, Turks, and Arab invaders. Along the river upstream there are also communities of Berber-speaking peoples. Farther south, Nubians, a people with more distinctly African characteristics, have long held the valley in Egypt and Sudan. For information about the peoples of Egypt see **Copts, Egyptians**, and **Nubians.**

IRAN
(ih rahn')

Population: 49,500,000 (1986 estimate).
Location: The eastern Middle East, bounded by Iraq, Turkey, Soviet Union, Afghanistan, Pakistan, the Arabian Sea, and the Persian Gulf.
Languages: Persian; Arabic; many local languages.
Principal cities: Tehran (capital 6,000,000); Meshed (1,400,000); Isfahan (1,000,000); Tabriz (970,000); Shiraz (850,000); eighteen other cities with populations over 200,000.

For centuries a monarchy ruling a division of the Ottoman Empire that extended as far as the state of Georgia in present-day Soviet Union, and after World War I guided by British intervention, Iran came under the rule of Reza Khan in 1923, and in 1925 he became the Shah of Persia (Iran). At first a leader of revolutionaries intent

Iran

on improving the lot of the people, the Shah grew increasingly dictatorial during his tenure. Finally, in 1941 Reza Khan abdicated in favor of a new Shah, Muhammad Reza. By 1950 Muhammad Reza had amassed a very large amount of money and land, and was increasingly challenged by other leaders of sections of the country. In that year, to divert revolution, the Shah began to distribute some of his wealth to the Iranian peasants. This won him approval in a 1963 election and improved relations with other countries. However, a large Arab population continually pressed for its own independence.

In 1971, Iran celebrated the alleged 2,500th anniversary of the Persian monarchy, and in that year opposition to the Shah increased. His security police, the SAVAK, grew increasingly suppressive and ruthless in an effort to suppress the rebellion. Some of the Shah's most powerful opponents were forced to go into exile. From a town in Iraq and later from Paris, a Shi'ite religious leader, the Ayatollah Khomeini, continued the rebellion and by 1977 had succeeded so that he was able to return with popular acclaim to establish an Islamic state in Iran.

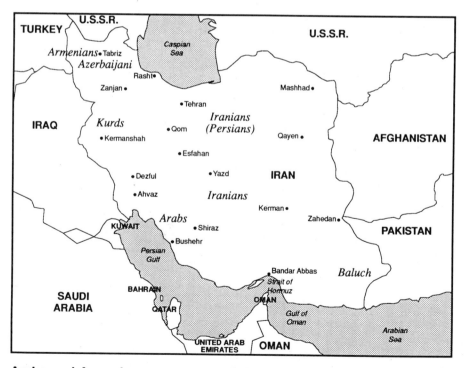

Arabs and Armenians are scattered throughout Iran.

Iran is a rugged land consisting of a central plateau ringed by high mountains. The Zagros range separates Iran from its neighbor Iraq. Oil resources lie on both sides of this boundary and have resulted in long-standing boundary disputes. In 1980, Iraq began a war with Iran to expand its territory along the boundary—a war that was to be costly and long to both countries. Ending in an indecisive cease-fire eight years later, it was soon followed by Iraq's aggression against Kuwait. In this war, Iran remained neutral, but refused to allow Iraq use of its airports or land.

In 1989 the Ayatollah Khomeini died and was replaced by a Council of Experts. In August of that year, Ali Akbar Hashemi Rafsanjani, president under the religious leadership of the Ayatollah, became the leader of a government ruled by Islamic law. This law is administered by an elected president and a 270-person Majlis (Islamic Consultative Assembly).

Under this rule, all minorities are given equal rights—even to the worship of their own religions, which include the ancient Persian religion of Zoroastrianism as well as Christianity and Judaism.

Most Iranians are city people; fewer than one-third of the population lives in rural areas. However, they represent several ethnic groups, incuding Qashqa'i in the southwest, Persians in the plateau area, Azerbaijani and Shahsaian in the northwest, and Baluch in the southeast. For more about the people of Iran see **Qashqa'i, Azerbaijani, Iranians,** and **Baluch.**

IRAQ

(ih rak')

Population: 17,000,000 (1988 estimate).
Location: Middle East, bounded by Turkey, Iran, Persian Gulf, Kuwait, and Saudi Arabia.
Languages: Arabic; also Kurdish; Persian; and Turkish.
Principal cities: Baghdad (capital, 3,800,000); Basra (1,500,000); Mosul (1,200,000); Kirkuk (535,000).

The central features of Iraq are the two great rivers, the Tigris and Euphrates, and the double valley created by them. To the east these valleys rise to the Zagros Mountains that mark the boundary with Iran, but westward, the land rises gradually to a 3,000-foot-high plateau that continues into Syria and Saudi Arabia. There are no real geological marks indicating the boundaries of Iraq and its southern

Iraq

and western neighbors. Toward the south, the land becomes desert and the Iraq boundary is vaguely marked by a neutral zone with Kuwait and Saudi Arabia that was formed to accommodate nomadic peoples who reside there. Most of the people of Iraq live in or near the valleys of the two rivers. Arising in Turkey and coursing through the northern mountains, these rivers fall quickly so that most of their routes through Iraq run through nearly flat land. Here the rivers rise dramatically in flood times and spread over great areas of the land. Since oil production began there, many flood control and irrigation projects have been undertaken to improve the agricultural land on which the country had depended. Today, with a growing dependency on oil, and a growing government bureaucracy, one-third of all Iraqis work in community or personal services. Still, one-fifth of the people depend on agriculture for a living. These people raise wheat, barley, grapes, dates, melons, and many other foods in a land that is mostly hot and humid. On the desert plateau, herders raise sheep, goats, and cattle.

While Kurds live mostly in the north, Arabs and Kurds are spread throughout Iraq.

Long a land of contrasts and disputes, Iraq was once overrun by Mongol invaders, and later was ruled by the British who held air bases in Iraq as recently as 1955. Promised their own land by League of Nations countries, the Kurdish people, who live in the northern mountains, have been in conflict with the Iraqi government since the 1970s. At that time, Iraqi officials reached an agreement with Kurdish leaders that granted autonomy to this people. However, that accord was broken the next year. Since then, several thousand Kurdish villages have been destroyed in the struggle. The struggle grew to its greatest intensity in 1988 and then again after Iraq's attempt to take over Kuwait in 1991. In the 1980s Iraq also attempted to take part of Iran. Failing, the ruler Saddam Hussein officially abandoned the idea in 1982, but fighting between these two countries continued until 1988.

Just as the land is varied, the people of Iraq represent varied lives and traditions. Marsh Arabs in the delta area of the two rivers live mostly on rafts and boats, or in raised huts built on small manmade islands. Kurds, Turkomen, and Assyrians live in the mountain areas and some of the large cities. A small group called the Yazidis live in central Iraq, and there are a few Uniate and Orthodox Christians living in the country. For more information about the people of Iraq see **Yazidis, Kurds, Arabs,** and **Iraqi.**

ISRAEL
(ihs' ra ell)

Population: 5,000,000 (1989 estimate).
Location: Middle East, bounded by Egypt, the Mediterranean Sea, Lebanon, and Jordan.
Language: Hebrew; also Arabic and English.
Principal cities: Jerusalem (capital, 500,000); Tel-Aviv (320,000); Haifa (225,000).

For such a small area, modern Israel is distinguished by its diversity. The land is marked by rugged hills and mountains in the north; the lowest place on earth, the Dead Sea, which is 1,200 feet below sea level; a fertile valley and coastline; and the southern Negev Desert. Irrigation has turned much of Israel into productive agricultural land. On this land, Israeli farmers working independently or in coopera-

Israel

tives grow more than two dozen products for export, and raise poultry, cattle, sheep, and goats.

Israel is also a manufacturing state in which products as varied as newsprint, tires, chemicals, and automobiles are produced. While one-third of the workers are involved in public services, one-fourth are employed in manufacturing, and less than seven percent in agriculture. Still, Israel is a country faced with supporting great numbers of immigrants each year, and with administering surrounding territories that are nearly one-third as large as Israel itself. The result has been that Israel's economy experiences a continual inflation of more than 100 percent yearly.

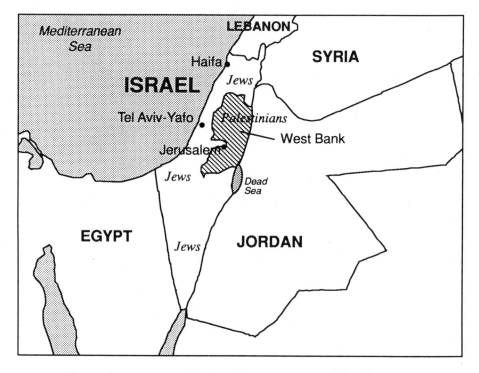

Most of the people of Israel are Jews or Palestinians. There are a few other Christians and Druze.

Israel's diversity is seen in religion. While Jews control the government, these citizens are divided among very devout and conservative worshipers and many who do not strictly observe religious traditions. One-seventh of the population is Muslim, and there are some Christians, Druze, and other religions represented in the country. The capital, Jerusalem, is a holy place for Jews, Muslims, and Christians.

Israel, formed in 1948 with the support of the United Nations, but with the opposition of its nearest neighbors, has never established a written constitution. Rather, the Knesset, Israel's parliament, has agreed to build a constitution over a long period of time from laws established by the Knesset. So far, these laws include a Law of Return, Nationality Law, State President Tenure Law, Education Law, and Yad-va-Shem Memorial Law. War with nearby Arab states has been a frequent fact of life among Israelis. The major binding force of most of Israel's population has been the commitment to reestablish and safeguard the ancient homeland of the Jews. Mindful of this commitment, Israel has over the years occupied some areas around its initial territory: the Golan Heights, which overlooks the Syrian border and was annexed by Israel in 1981; the Gaza Strip to the south; and the West Bank of the Jordan River, a bulge westward into Israel that is largely populated by Palestinians.

The Israeli population is also diversified. While nearly nine-tenths of the population is Jewish, it includes Jews who have immigrated from such diverse places as Ethiopia, Russia, and many European states, as well as Jews displaced from countries in North Africa. There is also a large Muslim population in Israel that is augmented by about 1,500,000 Muslims in the occupied territories. **Israeli Jews, Arabs, Druze,** and **Palestinians** are among the Israeli population.

JORDAN
(jor' dan)

Population: 4,000,000 (1990 estimate).
Location: The Middle East, bounded by Syria, Iraq, Saudi Arabia, and Israel.
Language: Arabic.
Principal cities: Amman (capital, 975,000); Zarga (392,000); Irbid (271,000); Salt (134,000).

The country of Jordan, by nature of its location, is one of the most pressured nations of the Middle East. Most of the country lies on the Arabian plateau that extends into Syria, Iraq, and Saudi Arabia. The semidesert plateau provides no natural features marking the boundaries between Jordan and the other Arab countries, except on its western edge, where Jordan is bordered by the Jordan River and its

Jordan

valley. This river is shared with Israel. Beginning in Lake Tiberias at the Syria-Jordan border the river runs sixty miles along the border, then ninety more miles dividing Jordan and the West Bank (claimed by the Palestinians but occupied by Israel) before reaching the Dead Sea. Both Jordan and Israel depend on this water supply for irrigation.

As a result of its location, Jordan has played a delicate balancing role in the Middle East, sometimes allying itself with Syria against Egypt, sometimes at odds with a plan to create a greater Syria, sometimes taking a role in the Arab League, and sometimes, as in its siding with the United Nations policies toward Korea, opposed to Arab League positions.

In biblical times this region was the location of a number of small kingdoms: Gilead, Ammon, Moab, and Edom. In the sixth century B.C., an Arab tribe, the Nabateans, ruled over the south, while the north of present-day Jordan was ruled by the Seleucid family of Syria. Later Jordan was to come under Ottoman influence. From the end of World War I, Transjordan was part of an Arab nation ruled by King Faisal, but in 1920 the rule of Transjordan fell to Britain. That

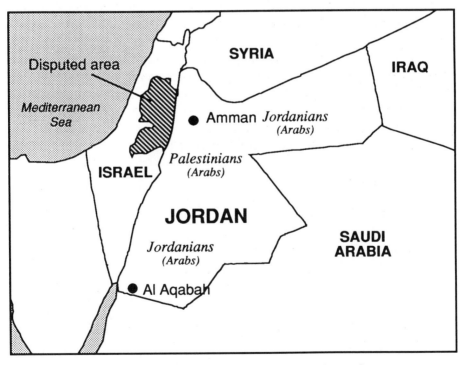

Jordan is an Arab land inhabited by its own people and many Palestinian refugees.

country began to give Transjordan a measure of independence in 1928, but it was not until 1946 that Transjordan became the Hashemite Kindgom of Jordan under King Abdullah. That family has ruled Jordan since then.

Jordan claimed a section of the land jutting into Israel on the west bank of the Jordan River, and for a time entertained the idea of a larger Arab state with its capital at Jerusalem. This sacred city for Muslims, Christians, and Jews became the center of conflict between the new countries of Jordan and Israel. Israel occupied all the land on the west side of the river, and many of the people who lived there, the Palestinians, were forced to leave. Nearly half a million fled to Jordan. By 1970 Palestinians were being appointed to key ministries in the Jordan government. The problem of the dislocated Palestinians remains an important issue in the Middle East.

Although eighty percent of the Jordanians are united as Muslims of the Sunni sect, they come from two distinct ethnic groups. Those people east of the Jordan River Valley are of a different origin than that of the people who live in the valley. Despite these differences, Jordanians lived peacefully under the king's rules for many years. But economic pressures and the problem of Palestinian immigrants created unrest that resulted in civil war in 1970. King Hussain ibn Talal suppressed this rebellion after arresting about 2,500 rebels then initiated steps to provide citizens more voice in the government. One step in 1983 granted voting rights to women. Today, deprived of good farmland on the west bank, Jordan is more than ever dependent on its oil-rich neighbors.

For more information about the people of Jordan, see **Jordanians** and **Palestinians.**

KUWAIT
(coo wait')

Population: 2,000,000 (1989 estimate).
Location: The Persian Gulf, bounded by Iraq and Saudi Arabia.
Language: Arabic.
Principal cities: Salmiya (153,000); Hawalli (145,000); Faranawiya (69,000); Abraq Khutan (45,000); Kuwait City (capital, 44,000).

The country of Kuwait is a sandy extension of the desert of Saudi Arabia and is, therefore, separated geographically from the nearby Tigris and Euphrates marshlands and valleys of Iraq. For hundreds of years the inhabitants of this area have been of six tribal families: Sabah, Bahar, Hamad, and Babtain from the Nejd region of Saudi Arabia, and Mutawa and Saleh from the north. These people lived in near isolation in their small land, herding sheep, goats, and camels,

Kuwait

and raising small vegetable crops near the few oases. In the 1700s, Kuwait was founded as a separate province of the Ottoman Empire. In 1770, Persians occupied the Iraqi town of Basra, and a concerned ruler of Kuwait, Abdullah bin Sabah, permitted the British to build a base at Kuwait City. The British influence continued until 1961.

Between 1896 and 1915, Kuwait, as a city-state was united under the single rule of Sheikh Mubarak. By 1921 Sheikh Ahmad al-Jabar had come into power in the kingdom, and in 1934 he initiated oil developments. Guided in international affairs by the British, this industry grew so that Kuwait became one of the richest nations per capita in the world. But oil riches were not without difficulties. Kuwait's population grew rapidly as immigrants from other Arab states came to find work—from 150,000 in 1950 to 1,300,000 in 1980. Today, there are about 800,000 native Kuwaitis and 1,200,000 foreigners in Kuwait.

In 1950, Sheikh Ahmad died and was replaced by Sheikh Abdullah as-Salim. This leader established, as a first priority with the income from their petroleum wealth, to improve the lives of Kuwaitis

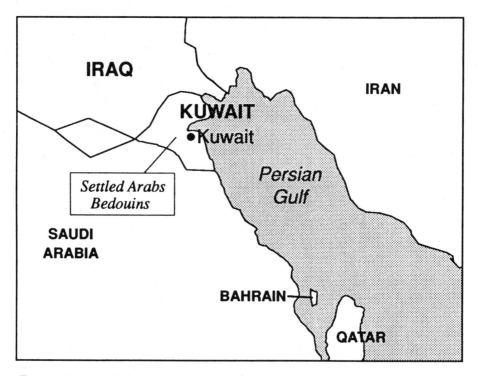

Fewer than half the people of Kuwait are native Kuwaitis.

through education and health services. From his reign to that of the present ruler, Sheikh Jaber al-Ahmad as-Sabah (Amir of Kuwait), the Kuwaiti government has been committed to providing health services, free education, and adequate housing to Kuwait citizens, and to provide adequate income to the citizens when the revenues from petroleum are exhausted. The government carefully controlled the economy of the country, establishing a number of government-owned corporations to manage the oil industry and industrial development. This management allowed the Kuwaiti government to establish a rule in exile from Saudi Arabia when Iraq invaded Kuwait with an army of 100,000 soldiers against the 20,000-man Kuwaiti military in 1991. The aftermath of this struggle, in which United Nations coalition forces defeated the Iraqis, is still unfolding. About 250,000 of the foreign workers in Kuwait were Palestinians, many of them in sympathy with Iraq. Many of these will be evicted from Kuwait. However, a large population of immigrant tribes from Saudi Arabia have been admitted to Kuwait through the years and, to preserve the riches for Kuwaitis, have been given second-class citizenship. Other foreigners, many of them residents of Kuwait for several years, remain to help rebuild the country, and are demanding a greater voice in the political leadership of Kuwait. The Amir of Kuwait has repeatedly promised to take steps to provide a more democratic political system. See also **Arabs** and **Palestinians.**

LEBANON

(leb' a non)

Population: 2,800,000 (1988 estimate).
Location: The Mediterranean Coast, bordered by Syria and Israel.
Language: Arabic.
Principal cities: Beirut (capital, 1,500,000); Tarabulus (160,000).

The land of Lebanon rises sharply from a narrow coast on the Mediterranean Sea to the Lebanon Mountains, which have peaks as high as 10,000 feet. Between the Lebanon and Anti-Lebanon Mountains, there is a narrow valley, the Bekaa, which is ten miles wide and 100 miles long. The land is warm but good for agriculture because a layer of non-porous rock under the mountains forces water to stay near the surface and provides many springs that can be used for irrigation.

Lebanon

The contour of the land helped Maronites, Druze, and other societies to remain somewhat isolated throughout history.

The home of Christian Maronites since the seventh century and of the Islamic Arab Tanukh family since the ninth century, Lebanon has long been a divided country. In the sixteenth century the land was divided between Turkomen in the north and Druze in the south, with the Maronites holding mountain lands in the center. These divergent people were united under one rule by Fakhur ad-Din II (1586-1635), of the Druze house of Ma'an. The land was later taken by the Ottomans when its ruler Bashir II sided with Muhammad Ali of Egypt in an ill-fated conquest of Syria. The Ottoman rule aggravated the separation of Maronites and Druze and threatened the region. France intervened and attempted to bring peace in 1964.

This began a long association with Western powers that, together with a real or imagined Christian majority, separated Lebanon from the rest of the Arab world. Association with the west stirred the unrest in the country and resulted in civil war, which began in 1975 and

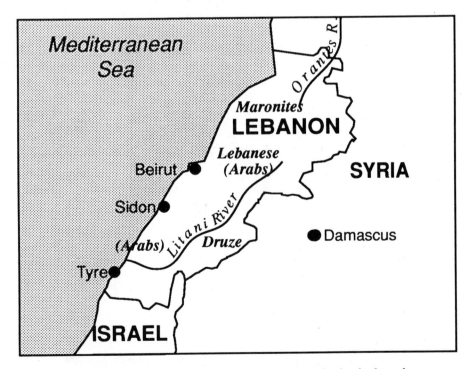

Like most of Israel's neighbors, Lebanon's people include a large population of Palestinian refugees as well as native Arabs, Maronites, and Druze.

continues today. The strife has been extended by such actions as the assassination of the Druze leader, Kamal Jumblatt, in 1977. Part of the problem is the government's refusal to take a new census as the basis for representation in the government. Lebanon has not held a census since 1932, a time when the Christians were counted to be in the majority. Until recent agreements to arrange a cease-fire and attempts to reorganize the government, the legislative apportionment remained predominantly Christian even though estimates today claim that more than sixty percent of the Lebanese are Muslim. Today about 50,000 Syrian soldiers attempt to keep a delicate peace in Lebanon.

Once Beirut was the trade capital of the Middle East and had great universities and museums. Lebanese were among the most educated people in the Middle East. But the long period of unrest has virtually destroyed Beirut's leadership. In recent years, Christians have warred against Muslims, and the various Shi'ite sects have fought among themselves. Amal (supported by Syria) and Hezbollah (supported by Iran) factions of the Shi'ites live and fight in the south. Beirut is divided among Christians and Muslims. Palestinian refugees live and claim rights in the large cities. Druze live in the mountains near Beirut. In addition, the people of Lebanon are divided between the coastal Europeanized peoples, and the interior Arabized Leba-

Shipbuilders still build vessels of ancient design from the cedars of Lebanon. *Courtesy of Dr. Paul Fischer.*

nese. For more about the people of Lebanon see **Druze, Lebanese, Maronites,** and **Arabs.**

LIBYA
(lib' ee uh)

Population: 4,200,000 (1988 estimate).
Location: North Africa, bounded by the Mediterranean Sea, Egypt, Sudan, Chad, Niger, Algeria, and Tunisia.
Language: Arabic.
Principal cities: Tripoli (capital, 481,000); Benghazi (219,000).

With coastal ports well-suited to trade around the Mediterranean Sea, Libya has been given keen attention by many peoples over the centuries. Phoenicians built the famous city of Carthage near there (in what is now Tunisia) and made it into a principal trading center in the 500s B.C. They were replaced by Greeks, and then Romans. Finally, after the death of the prophet Muhammad, Arab soldiers, in the name of Islam, established footholds in the land and eventually

Libya

won control, although the Arab control meant a succession of inter-tribal wars for 500 years and resettlement of the Berber population that had lived in the land for so long. These different influences are reflected in the population of Libya—once identified either as coastal "Libyans," resulting from the mixes of the various trading countries, or as interior "Ethiopians," who migrated from other regions of Africa.

Arab tribal leadership gave way to a unified kingdom, and to Ottoman rule. In 1912, Italy occupied Libya and held it until independence was declared in 1951.

The country is divided into three parts: an eastern section in which the coast rises sharply to hill country (Cyrenaica), the land of the early Arab forts; a western section of gradually rising coastal plains (Tripolitania); and an interior four-fifths of Libya of deserts and oases (Fezzan). Most of the land is suitable only for grazing sheep, goats, and camels, or for raising poultry. Millet is grown at the oases, and fruits in the higher country of Cyrenaica.

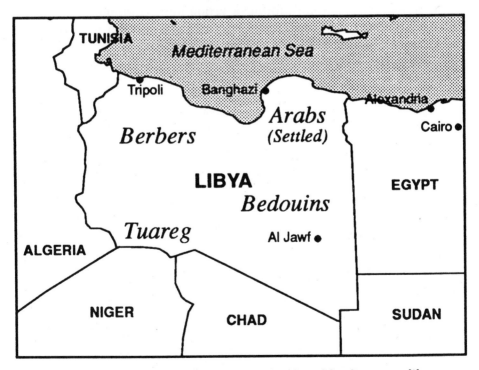

Many of the people of Libya have mixed cultural heritages, with Greek, French, and Italian influences. However, most are Arabs.

From the nomadic peoples of the Fezzan arose in 1969 a military leader, Colonel Muammar al-Qaddafi, only twenty-seven-years old but with a dream of returning Libya to its earlier Islamic ways and of restoring the economic welfare of the people. Qaddafi captured the government in a bloodless coup and set out to improve housing and other services to the people. He also began to reform the government around people's assemblies organized at all levels of government. With the development of petroleum reserves in 1971, Qaddafi found the resources to rebuild the country, even to establish permanent housing at the oases to persuade the nomadic populations to settle. In 1973, Qaddafi began a crusade for a return to Islamic fundamentalism. The economic and religious commitments made him popular with his own people.

However, with his international policies, Qaddafi experienced difficulty—fighting for rebel causes in Chad, helping to raid Tunisia, involving Libya in struggles in Uganda, squabbling with the United States, and vacillating in his dealings with most of the other Arab countries. His persistence and commitment to an Islamic Middle East, however, eventually found a grudging acceptance with neighboring Algeria and Tunisia, with whom Libya signed a 1989 proposal for a Union of the Arabic Maghreb, which never materialized.

Arabs, **Berbers**, and **Libyans** are peoples of Libya included in this volume.

MOROCCO

(mah raw' koh)

Population: 24,000,000 (1988 estimate).
Location: North Africa, bounded by the Mediterranean Sea, Atlantic Ocean, Western Sahara, and Algeria.
Languages: Arabic; Berber; French.
Principal cities: Casablanca (2,900,000); Marrakesh (1,400,000); Rabat (capital, 1,300,000); Fez (930,000); seven other cities with more than 500,000 population.

Morocco is a land divided by rugged mountain ranges. Running southwest to northeast, the Rif Atlas Range rises steeply from the Mediterannean Sea and arcs around a plain of coastland to the Atlantic Ocean. This range is separated from a Middle Atlas Range by a valley, the Col of Taza. Toward the north the range splits to form

Morocco

the High Atlas Mountains farther inland. Another depression separates the High Atlas from the Anti Atlas, a lower range that slopes into the Sahara Desert.

Phoenicians, Carthagenians, and Romans followed each other as rulers of the land. But by A.D. 684, Muslim warriors had entered what is now Morocco, and by the 700s, Arabs controlled the coast, mingling with the earlier inhabitants, the Berbers. In Morocco, Berber ranks later swelled as the Berbers fled before the Muslim crusaders.

By 788 the country and some of what is now Algeria had been united under the leadership of Idris. The rule he established lasted for nearly 200 years, and then fell to Muslim leaders in Spain and in Tunisia who quarreled over control of Morocco. Religious fervor waxed and waned, and in the 1000s was revived by the Almoravid invaders from inland Africa, then again in 1664 by the Alawi family of Berbers. This family has ruled Morocco since that time, except for a relatively short interval when the country was under French control from 1912 to 1955.

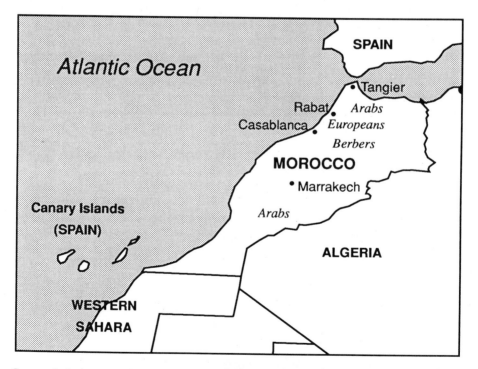

Several thousand Europeans live near Casablanca in Morocco. Berbers and Arabs live near each other in many sections of the country.

Morocco is an agricultural country, but has also developed a strong manufacturing and trade industry. Nearly one-half the workers in Morocco are involved in trade and services.

In the 1980s Morocco's leaders attempted to lead the people of North Africa into a unified Arab nation. The Oujda Treaty was signed in 1984 with Col. Qaddafi, leader of Libya, declaring a "unison of states." But this accord was short-lived as Morocco attempted to take over Western Sahara, claiming this area by the early 1980s. In 1985, the king ordered 350,000 unarmed civilians to occupy Western Sahara. Defenders of Western Sahara, the Polisario—aided by Algeria—have been at war to win freedom from Morocco since that year. This turmoil and its alienating effect with other countries has isolated Morocco and delayed the forming of a union in the part of Africa for which the Arabic term is Jezirat al-Maghreb, "Island of the West."

OMAN
(oh mahn')

Population: 2,000,000 (1988 estimate). There has never been an official census of the population of Oman.
Location: The southeast corner of the Arabian Peninsula, bordered by Saudi Arabia, Yemen, the Arabian Sea, the Gulf of Oman, and the United Arab Emirates.
Language: Arabic.
Principal city: Muscat (capital, 50,000 in 1981).

The land of Oman was known in ancient history as a trading and sailing center. Oman people sent ships into the Persian Gulf from an ancient port that may have been where the city of Muscat stands today. From there they traded the frankincense prepared from bushes that grew in the area to the people of Ur as early as the third century

Oman

B.C. The early sailors also traded in Egypt and in India. The inhabitants of Oman had come to the land earlier in two groups: the Qahtan from the south, and the Nizer from the north.

Oman is a land with a small fertile coastline along the Gulf of Oman separated from the sandy extension of the "empty quarter" of Saudi Arabia by a mountain range. A small section at the tip of the peninsula receives rainfall from the monsoons that sweep across the Indian Ocean toward Pakistan. Traditionally, as now, the people here herded sheep, goats, cattle, and camels, and raised some dates and vegetables in the mountain valleys and near the oases.

One of the first regions to be converted to Islam by Amir ibn al-As, who later took the religion to Egypt, the Omanis had established an independent imam as their leader as early as the eighth century and have remained independent, but not without interference, since that time. The first Europeans to interfere were the Portuguese, who built two forts near Muscat in 1587-88. But by 1650 the Omanis had united under Imam Nasir ibn Murhid to drive out the invaders. The imam then went on to expand Omani territory. By 1730, Oman con-

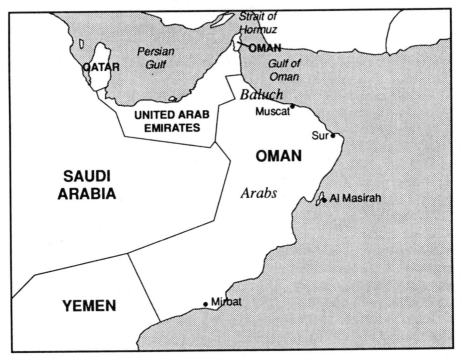

The population of Oman is a mix of Arab peoples and groups from Asia.

trolled what is now Somalia, Kenya, and part of Tanzania. In 1749, the people elected Ahmad ibn Said as imam, and the al-Bu Said family has ruled all or part of Oman since that time.

For a short time the Said dynasty profited from sailing, and Muscat became an important slave trade port. When slavery lost favor, the area of Muscat and Oman continued to keep slaves while their chief means of income declined. This is but one example of the slowness with which Oman kept pace with world changes. Another is the country's use of its oil reserves.

Not until 1970 did the ruler of Oman, Sultan Said, explore the oil potential. Even then, he refused to spend the income from the oil for any but military expenses. After three years, Sultan Said was overthrown by his son, Qataas bin Said, who began to improve the educational and health systems using income from petroleum.

Oman had also endured years of civil strife while the sultan based in Muscat quarreled over leadership with the religious leader, the imam. It was not until 1988, and not without aid from the British, that Sultan Taimur was able to declare himself ruler of all the region of Oman and Muscat and to change the name of the country from the Sultanate of Muscat and Oman to it present name, the Sultanate of Oman.

For information about the people of Oman see **Bedouins** or **Arabs.**

QATAR
(kah tar')

Population: 400,000 (1988 estimate).
Location: Qatar is a peninsula extending into the Persian Gulf from the junction of Saudi Arabia and the United Arab Emirates.
Language: Arabic.
Principal cities: Doha (capital, 220,000); Rayyan (92,000); Wakrah (24,000); Umm Salal (11,000).

Qatar is a rocky and sandy point jutting into the Persian Gulf that is dotted with salt flats. A few small valleys in the north are suitable for growing crops, but these amount to less than one percent of the land. Qatar is an independent country that did not want to be independent. Once the land was ruled by the Khalifa family that rules Bahrain, a group of islands just to the north. In 1872 it became part

Qatar

of the large Ottoman Empire. But the Turks grew uneasy as World War I began, and abandoned the country. In 1916, the British took control of the peninsula and named Sheikh Abdullah ath-Thani its ruler. Interest in the land was stimulated by the discovery of oil there in 1939, but with Britain occupied with World War II, it was not until 1949 that oil production began. In the 1970s, when Britain declared its intention to make Qatar independent, the leaders appealed to Bahrain to take control. Finding no interest, the country prepared a constitution and became independent in 1971. Through all this, the land was ruled by Abdullah ath-Thani (1916-1949), his son Ali ath-Thani (1949-1960), and his son Ahmed ath-Thani (1960-1971). Ahmed proved a disappointment as a ruler, and was overthrown by Khalifa ath-Thani, his cousin, with the approval of the family. Khalifa began a program to use the new petroleum wealth to improve the welfare of the people. Today, he governs with the aid of a thirty-person advisory council and has provided government housing for 6,000 families. Khalifa has also changed his title to "amir," a term that suggests more authority than the term "sultan."

Qatar is peopled by settled Arabs and Bedouins, along with many immigrants from other countries.

A few Qataris continue to lead nomadic lifestyles, but oil has changed Qatar drastically. Today almost all the citizens of the country live in four towns, and contend with seventy percent of the population that has immigrated to Qatar to find work in the petroleum industry.

For more about the people of Qatar see **Bedouins** or **Arabs.**

SAUDI ARABIA
(sah oo' dee uh ray' bee uh)

Population: 14,400,000 (1989 estimate).
Location: The Arabian Peninsula, bounded by the Red Sea, Jordan, Iraq, Kuwait, the Persian Gulf, the United Arab Emirates, Oman, and Yemen.
Language: Arabic.
Principal cities: Riyadh (royal capital, 670,000); Jeddah (administrative capital, 560,000); Mecca, (370,000); At-Ta'if (200,000); Medina (200,000).

Since its founding by King Ibn Saud in 1932, Saudi Arabia has been a monarchy governed by a representative chosen by the Saud family. There are no political parties and no legislature. However, there are limits to the king's authority. He is selected by senior members of

Saudi Arabia

the family in consultation with religious scholars, and can be removed by the same process, as was King Saud in 1964. An advisory council, also including many Saud family members, meets frequently to discuss governmental events and there are weekly public meetings during which citizens are free to voice opinions and complaints to Saudi princes. The royal family controls much of Saudi economic life through the government agencies and through family-held companies.

The country was once a collection of small towns in the Hejaz region and independent tribes, each with its own leaders, and many roaming from place to place in the Nejd. Rather than combine these various peoples by force, the Saud family chose to bind them into a nation by offering governmental services. Hospitals were built in the major cities, and government health service centers located near some of the most important oases. Highways made travel easier, while tending to disrupt the nomadism of some of the tribes. Now desert dwellers are as likely to use trucks to transport their camels as to use the camels for transportation. Education was improved so that, by

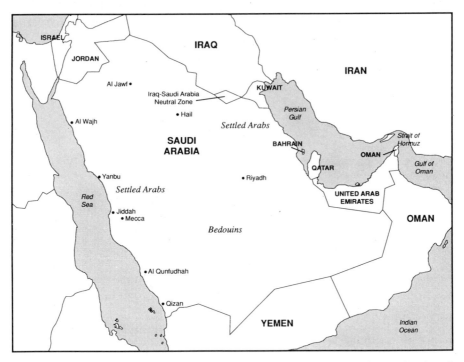

Settled Arabs and nomadic Arabs known as Bedouins share the land of Saudi Arabia.

1987, 2,000,000 Saudi children were attending school—an increase of 300 percent since 1970. The ancient and new universities at Umm al-Qura, Jeddah, and Medina have been expanded to accommodate an increasing university enrollment. To further encourage the nomadic populations to settle, the government promised all adults a plot of land and a loan of $80,000 to develop it.

While the national government does much to create a national identity and to provide services to the people, it is hampered by its own source of wealth. The petroleum industry provides more jobs than the population can support, so almost two-thirds of Saudi Arabia's work force is drawn from surrounding countries.

Saudi Arabia still manages to spend nearly one-third of its income on military equipment and training. This has been a reaction to the hostile Shi'ite government of Iran, the revolutionary government of former South Yemen, and the continuing instability of the Middle East as a result of the Israeli-Palestinian disputes. Recently the apparent interest in expansion shown by Iraq has added to Saudi Arabia's concern. The intervention with other United Nations forces in freeing Kuwait from Iraqi invaders in 1991 demonstrated the strength of the Saudi forces. For more information about the people of Saudi Arabia, see **Saudis, Arabs, Bedouins,** and **Palestinians.**

SYRIA
(syr' ee uh)

Population: 11,400,000 (1988 estimate).
Location: The eastern Mediterranean Coast, bordered by Turkey, Iraq, Jordan, Israel, Lebanon, and the Mediterranean Sea.
Languages: Arabic; Kurdish.
Principal cities: Damascus (capital, 1,100,000); Aleppo (1,000,000); Homs (350,000); Latakia (200,000); Hamah (180,000).

Long ago, Syria was a much larger land, stretching from its present boundaries into present-day Turkey, Iraq, Jordan, Lebanon, and Israel. The leaders of today's Syria often seem to think about this "Greater Syria" and to plan for its revival. Seemingly toward this goal, Syria has aligned itself at different times with various other countries. In the late 1950s, Syria joined with Egypt to form the

Syria

United Arab Republic. However, when the country found that its representation in a legislative council that was only one-third that of Egypt included many Egyptian government leaders in Syria, the alliance collapsed. A military coup eventually installed Major General Amin al-Hafiz as ruler, who appointed Hafiz al-Assad to be military leader in Syria's continuing opposition to Israel. By 1970, Hafiz al-Assad had seized power and has continued since then to be elected to office for seven-year terms. His rule has not been without difficulty. Syria has planned uniting with Libya, but that plan did not materialize. Hafiz al-Assad has sometimes allied his country with Iraq, and sometimes fought against it. He has earned some unpopularity in Arab states by sometimes siding with Iran. Most Arab states have felt uncomfortable because of his position on religion. While eighty percent of the Syrians are Sunni Muslims, Syria is the only country with a Muslim majority that has not declared the country to be an Islamic state. Meanwhile, Syrians have been embarrassed by their difficulty in defeating the Israelis, who have taken Syrian land, the Golan Heights, and annexed it to their own. It has also had difficulties

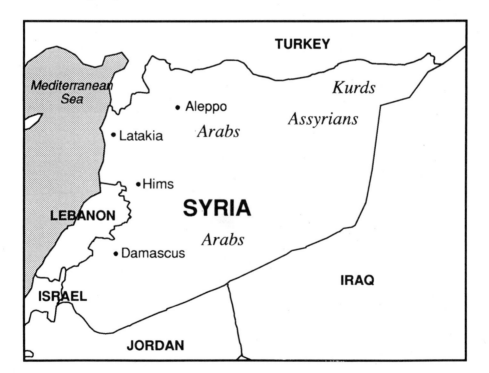

Arabs live throughout Syria; Kurds and Armenians live in the north.

resolving the conflicts in Lebanon, where Syria keeps a force of 40,000 soldiers in an attempt to bring peace to the area. However, even here, Syria has had problems with other Arab forces, often disputing and once deporting the leaders of the Palestine Liberation Organization (PLO).

Hafiz al-Assad has ruled mostly by brutally suppressing any opposition, whether it has come from a minority group within the country or from a group as large and united as the Muslim Brotherhood. The number of opponents destroyed by the government is not known, but a number of Alawites (the Muslim subgroup to which Hafiz al-Assad belongs) have been assassinated in protest to his actions. In 1991, Syria was faced with caring for thousands of Kurds who fled the conflicts in Iraq, and was concerned about the number of Kurds gathering in the north of Syria and in Turkey.

During the rule of Assad, improvements have been made in the lives of many Syrians. One major project has been the damming of the Euphrates River, a project that has greatly expanded the useable farmland of Syria.

For more information about Syria's people, see **Syrians, Kurds, Druze,** and **Yazidi.**

TUNISIA
(too nee' zha)

Population: 8,000,000 (1990 estimate).
Location: North Africa, bordered by Libya, Algeria, and the Mediterranean Sea.
Languages: Arabic; French.
Principal cities: Tunis (capital, 600,000); Sfax (232,000); Ariana (100,000).

A triangle of land with one corner pointing toward Sicily and Italy across the Mediterranean Sea, present-day Tunisia has long played an important role in Mediterranean trade. The ancient Phoenician city of Carthage was a prime seaport by 550 B.C., and by 264 B.C., had become a center of attention of the Romans. After the long Punic Wars (264 to 146 B.C.), which left Carthage in rubble, Augustus rebuilt

Tunisia

it as a Roman city and the area became again an important trade center, peopled mostly by the Berbers. By A.D. 767 a family from Iraq, the Abbasids had won control of the region. During their era the present outlines of Tunisia were fairly well established. However, by 943, the Berbers had grown weary of the Abbasid rule. After four years of rebellion the Abbasids were overthrown and power fell to the Berber Zirid family. This leadership, supported by the powerful Fatimids of Egypt, led the region through a "golden age" of development of art, science, and literature. However, their leadership was weakened and havoc reigned on the area by the Fatimids when Tunisia's rulers chose to pay allegiance to the caliph of Baghdad. By the 1100s the Zirids were in no position to combat the invasion of Norman troops in 1148. However, the Normans ruled for only twelve years. There followed a succession of rulers: the caliphs of Marrakesh, the caliph of Baghdad, and the Berber Hafsid family ruling from Algeria. By 1520 part of Tunisia had fallen to Spain, then in 1591 to the Ottomans, who ruled the area with military leaders called Beys. These Beys continued to rule after France had occupied the region

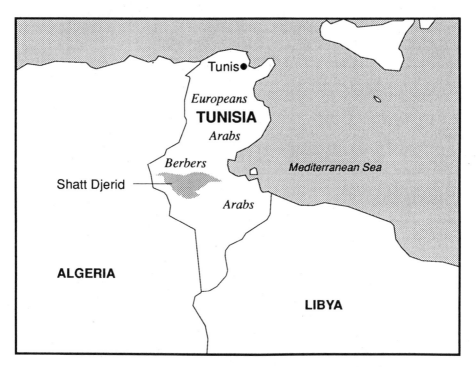

In Tunisia, Arabs, Berbers, and Europeans share the land.

in 1830. Finally, France eliminated the Bey monarchy in 1957 and established present-day Tunisia as a republic. However, since that time, Tunisia has had only two presidents. The first president, Habib Bouguiba, ruled until he was declared too ill to govern in 1987. It was a turbulent rule during which Tunisia flirted with the notion of combining with Libya, later to squabble with this country, and still later to join with it in such efforts as the generation and management of electricity in the area. Bourguiba's successor, Zin al Abidine Ben Ali, set out to reform the government and to aid the people of Tunisia. He had been largely responsible for opening two new universities in 1986 and continued to build an educational system that today finds eighty percent of Tunisian children in elementary schools. Ben Ali also used the income from Tunisian petroleum reserves to begin massive water projects to ensure the welfare of the farmland that covers two-thirds of the country. Ben Ali has worked to further the "Great Arab Maghreb" proposed by Libya's Muammar al-Qaddafi. This unity has expanded to all the Arab nations. The headquarters of the Arab League is in Cairo, Egypt; a second headquarters is at Tunis. For more information, see **Tunisians** and **Arabs.**

TURKEY
(tur' key)

Population: 55,500,000 (1989 estimate).
Location: Northeast of the Mediterranean Sea, bordered by European countries (Greece, Bulgaria, and the Soviet Union), the Black Sea, Middle Eastern countries (Iran, Iraq, and Syria), and the Mediterranean Sea.
Languages: Turkish; also Kurdish, Urdu, and Armenian.
Principal cities: Istanbul (5,500,000); Ankara (capital, 2,200,000); Izmir (1,500,000); and 15 other cities of between 1,000,000 and 200,000 population.

The languages of Turkish radio broadcasts—Albanian, Turkish, Arabic, Azerbaidzhanian, Bulgarian, Chinese, English, French, Persian,

Turkey

Romanian, Russian, Serbian, and Urdu—reflect the variety that is Turkey.

Turkey is encircled by mountains that grow taller to the east and nearly surround the Anatolian Plateau (really a series of plateaus) that covers most of the country. Here Caucasian tribes roamed the coastline in the west while Armenian-related tribes spread out through the plateau. In the eleventh century A.D., people who had populated regions farther north between the Ural and Altai Mountains began to move north, south, east, and west. In the south, these people mingled with the Anatolian tribes to become the Turks. From these tribes, three people arose at different times to lead the region that is now Turkey.

In the 1200s, one Anatolian tribal leader, Osman, assimilated the tribes around him and expanded to build the Ottoman Empire that guided the region until 1922. This empire reached its greatest expanse in the time of Suleiman "the Magnificient." (1520-1566), then began a long, slow decline as European lands began to break away from the empire. The final breakup of the old empire came as a result of

Turks, Kurds, Turkomen, and Armenians are spread throughout Turkey.

Turkey's union with Germany in World War I and its subsequent defeat.

Under the terms of surrender, Arab portions of the empire were to be separated under French and British directions. Countries were to be established for the Armenians and Kurds, and the south of present-day Turkey divided by the French and Italians. However, one man was determined to save a land for the Turkish people.

Sent as an army officer to supervise Turkey's disintegration, this man began instead to raise an army to unite Turkey. Mustafa Kemel, who is known as Ataturk, became the father of modern-day Turkey. He united the people by rebuilding an army, changing the legal system to accommodate all the different people, separating the church from the state and providing for religious tolerance, eliminating symbols of the old empire such as the wearing of the fez, and simplifying the language by introducing a Latin alphabet. Ataturk made improvements in the educational system and in the economy, and held the people together with his strong personality.

When he died in 1938, a series of unstable governments continued Ataturk's plans despite rebellions in 1960, 1971, 1978, and 1980. The economy grew, largely in agriculture, which employs half of Turkey's workers, and in mining and processing the rich mineral wealth of the country: lead, copper, chromium, and sulfur.

Today, Turkey is still divided between eastern and western styles of clothing and housing. In spite of a population that is ninety-nine percent Muslim, the country has resisted uniting church and state, so that the small minority religions are free to worship as they please.

The people of Turkey include **Turks, Kurds, Arabs, Armenians** (see entries in this book), Greeks, Circasians, Georgians, and Lazes.

UNITED ARAB EMIRATES

(you night' ed ah' rab ehm' mir ates)

Population: 1,700,000 (1989 estimate).
Location: The Persian Gulf between Oman and Qatar.
Language: Arabic.
Principal cities: Abu Dhabi (capital, 725,000); Dubai (250,000).

Before the seventeenth century, Arab tribes had established themselves as nomadic herders along the Persian Gulf of the Arabian
Peninsula. Some of the tribes had become seagoing people (the Qaw-
asim), trading on the Persian Gulf, but mostly fishing and diving for
pearls. During the seventeenth and eighteenth centuries, some of the
seagoers had joined other sailors to be pirates in the Gulf.

By 1800, there were five sheikhdoms between Oman and Qatar.
The sheikhs were constantly raiding one another on land and sea.

United Arab Emirates

But sea pirating was increasingly difficult on the shiekhdom economies since it often interrupted pearl gathering. In 1820, the five sheikhdoms united in their first agreement: to not engage in any form of sea warfare during the pearling season and to cooperate with Great Britain to suppress pirating. This agreement was so beneficial that it was continued time after time until a perpetual truce was agreed in 1853. To ensure this agreement, Great Britain was enlisted as a mediator on the condition that none of the states (at this time called Trucial States) would cede any land rights to any country other than Britain. In 1971 Britain withdrew from this arrangement, and by 1980 the Trucial States, which now included six sheikhdoms—Abu Dhabi, Sharjah, Dubai, Umm al-Qaiwain, Ajan, and Fujairah—formed a gulf cooperating council. The sheikhdoms remain independent but share a common defense force, legal system, and some economic planning.

Until oil was discovered in the region in the 1950s, the Trucial States were supported by herding goats, sheep, and camels, and by fishing and pearling in the Gulf. By the early 1900s, the population

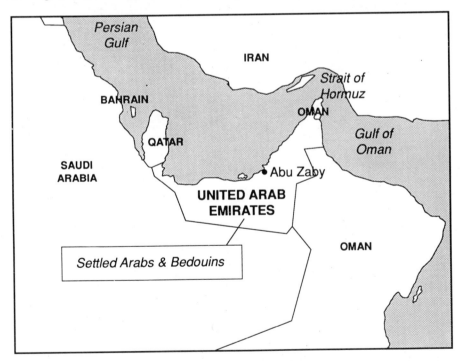

Fewer than half the residents of the United Arab Emirates are native Settled Arabs or Bedouins. The rest are workers from other countries attracted by oil.

had grown to about 150,000. However, oil brought new workers to the region. In a five-year period at the end of the 1950s, the population had grown, with added immigration, to 1,100,000. The change has made the native Arabic population of the United Arab Emirates a minority in its own country. It has also changed the population balance so that today sixty-five percent of the residents of the emirates are males.

Major support for the United Arab Emirates has come from Abu Dhabi and Dubai, the first two emirates to discover oil reserves. With their support, the central government has worked to improve education and health services to all the people.

For more about the residents of the United Arab Emirates see **Arabs, Baluch, Bedouins,** and **Iranians.**

Dubai is a modern city in the United Arab Emirates.
Courtesy of Dr. Paul Fischer.

YEMEN
(yeh' men)

Population: 9,300,000 (1989 estimate).
Location: The southwest corner of the Arabian Peninsula, bordered by Saudi Arabia, Oman, the Gulf of Aden, and the Red Sea.
Languages: Arabic, English.
Principal cities: San'a (capital, 278,000); Aden (272,000); Hodeida (126,000); Taiz (120,000).

The Republic of Yemen is the youngest political unit in the Middle East, having been formed by the union of the Yemen Arab Republic and the People's Democratic Republic of Yemen in 1990.

For centuries before that, the region had been divided at first between the Tihana tribe of the coast and the Zaidis of the highlands,

Yemen

and later by claims of the Ottoman Empire, the British, who wanted a shipping base at the port of Aden, and Saudi Arabia.

The land of Yemen consists of a narrow flat strip of coastland that rises to hill country and then, in the west, to mountains. The highlands of Yemen are among the most fertile of the Middle East. Sorghum is grown there along with a variety of fruits and vegetables. However, it was the eastern lowlands that first gave Yemen importance.

In ancient history, myrrh was a much valued ingredient in cosmetics. Coming from the sap of scrub trees that live on the hills in an otherwise barren land, myrrh was shipped to Egypt and other lands for market. When the demand for myrrh decreased, the land lapsed into economic insignificance. About this time, the ninth century, Zaidi religious leader, Yahya al-Hadi ila'-Hag, succeeded in dominating the land and forming alliances with several of the tribes who lived there. The Zaidis remained the most influential force in Yemen through the period of control by the Ottomans—an interval that lasted from 1517 to 1918. Throughout this time, the northern highlands of

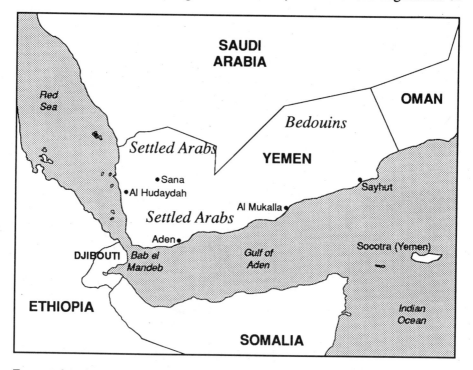

Except for dense populations near San'a and Aden, the country of Yemen is lightly settled by Bedouins and other Arabs.

Yemen formed some of the most densely populated areas of Arabia. The economy of the region continued to be poor until the British felt a need to establish a sea base at Aden to counter the French base at Djibouti.

In recent years, Yemen has been the focus of activities of three outside forces. Seeking to establish a united Arab republic, Egypt has been able to claim strong support in Yemen for many years, as has Egypt's rival for Middle East domination, Saudi Arabia. Meanwhile, Britain continued its interest in Aden at the tip of Yemen territory. During the turmoil resulting from the various claimants, North Yemen became the Yemen Arab Republic, and began to press for a united Yemen. In the early 1960s, Britain agreed and declared its intent to leave Aden by 1968. But there were some objections to Britain's withdrawal. The hesitancy created by these objections allowed for internal disagreements to come to focus and Yemen fell into civil war. Finally, in May of 1990, the two Yemens united.

The union combined the Zaidi-dominated fertile highlands with the British-influenced coastal area of the Gulf of Aden, an area in which only one percent of the land is suitable for farming. However, international aid has focused on providing water control dams in the major wadis to increase the agricultural land upon which eighty-five percent of the Yemenis depend for work and food.

However, Yemen is an indefinite country. The only fixed borders are along the oceans. Inland, Yemen has no fixed border with Saudi Arabia or Oman. For more information about the people of Yemen, see **Yemenis, Arabs,** and **Bedouins.**

Glossary

Abbasids A caliph dynasty that ruled the Muslim Empire between 750 and 1258 A.D. whose leaders claimed descent from Abbas, uncle of Muhammad.

Abraham (Ibrahim) An early Hebrew leader from whom both Jews and Muslims claim ancestry—Jews through his second son, Isaac, Muslims through his first son, Ishmael.

agal A black cord worn by many Arabs to hold a headdress in place.

amir (emir) A prince or political leader.

Arabia Felix The ancient trade and farming area of the Arabian Peninsula, now Yemen.

Ashkinazim Jews whose ancestors lived in central Europe.

Bible A holy book of Christians and Jews. For Jews, the history of the ancient Hebrews and their patriarchs represented in the part of the Christian Bible known as the Old Testament. The Christian bible includes the New Testament, which documents the life and teachings of Jesus Christ and his followers.

burza A black cloak often worn by fundamentalist Muslim women.

caliph Religious head of a Muslim state.

diaspora A scattering of people, such as the scattering of the Jews with the disintegration of Jerusalem or the scattering of Armenians by the Turks.

Fertile Crescent An arc of fertile and early-inhabited land including the Tigris and Euphrates valleys and a section of the Mediterranean coast to Lebanon and Israel.

fallahin Peasant farmers of the Nile River Valley.

fez A felt, brimless hat once popular in Syria and Libya.

frankincense Gum from trees of the Boswelia genus growing in Yemen and parts of Africa and used for incense.

Greater Syria Pre-Ottoman Empire Persia that included present-day Syria, part of Iraq, and Lebanon.

Hadj (haj) Holy excursion to Mecca required of all Muslims who can afford it.

Hejaz The fertile southwest coast of Saudi Arabia containing the holy city of Mecca.

Hellenistic Having cultural heritage from the Greeks.

intifada The uprising of Palestinian Arabs against the ruling Israelis.

jazirah Island; the region between the Tigris and Euphrates rivers north of Baghdad.

jebal Mountain (jabal, mountains).

jihad Holy war.

Kashrut Jewish dietary rules.

khamsin A hot wind blowing from the Sahara; called *khamsin* in Egypt and *qhabli* in Libya.

Kibbutz A cooperative farm in Israel.

Kush An ancient kingdom of Sudan and Egypt.

Maghreb (Magrib) Arabized western north Africa (Algeria, Tunisia, Morocco, Libya).

Mamelukes An Ottoman slave family that became rulers in Egypt.

Mesopotamia The land between the Tigris and Euphrates rivers.

Mongols Nomadic tribesman from Mongolia.

mosque Muslim place of worship.

Muhammad (Mohammed) An Arabic name; the name of the founder of the Muslim religion.

mujahidin Freedom fighters of Afghanistan.

Nabataens Early traders of Arabia and Jordan.

Nejd Central Saudi Arabia.

Ottoman Empire Turkic dynasty that ruled the Middle East and Egypt for 500 years before 1917.

patriarch A family leader of ancient Hebrews and Muslims; for example, Abraham.

pharaoh An ancient ruler by divine right in Egypt.

Quran (Koran) The holy book of the Muslims held to be God's words as revealed to the prophet Muhammad.

Selucids A ruling family of Asia Minor from the fourth to the first century B.C.

Seljuk Turkish rulers of the 11th to 13th centuries.

semitic The family of languages that includes Arabic, Aramaic, Hebrew, and Ethiopic.

Sephardim A division of Jews whose ancestors came from Spain or North Africa.

sheikh A leader of an Arab family or tribe.

shalavar Loose trousers worn in several regions of the Middle East.

sharif Arabic word that identifies descendants of Muhammad.

Shi'ite (Shiite, Shia) Muslim supporters of leadership by popular consent. They have come to believe in strong local religious leadership.

steppe A grassland dotted with wooded areas.

Sunni Muslim supporters in religious leadership of the lineage of Muhammad as represented by the fourth caliph, Ali. They have come to believe in little direction by local religious leaders.

synagogue A Jewish place of worship.

Talmud A holy book of the Jews containing regulations by the most wise rabbis and commentaries on these regulations.

wadi A dry wash that is periodically flooded.

Transjordan The area east of the Jordan River that is now Jordan.

Umayyad Muslim dynasty of the Middle East, North Africa, and Spain founded by Umayyah in 661 A.D.

Bibliography

Aburish, Said K. *Children of Bethany: The History of a Palestinian Family.* Bloomington: Indiana University Press, 1988.

Ahmed, Sami Said. *The Yazidis: Their Life and Beliefs.* Miami, Florida: Field Research Projects, 1975.

Alotaibi, Muhammed. *Bedouin: The Nomads of the Desert.* Vero Beach, Florida: Rourke Publications, 1989.

Arjomand, Said Amir. *The Turban for the Crown: The Islamic Revolution in Iran.* Oxford: Oxford University Press, 1988.

Ausubel, Nathan. *Pictorial History of the Jewish People.* New York: Crown Publishers, Inc., 1953.

Benningsen, Alexander and S. Enders Wimbush. *Muslims of the Soviet Empire: A Guide.* Bloomington: Indiana University Press, 1986.

Ben-Sasson, H. H., and Ettinger, S., editors. *Jewish Society Through the Ages.* New York: Shocken Books, 1971.

Berger, Morroe. *The Arab World Today.* Garden City, New York: Doubleday and Company, Inc., 1962.

Chitham, E. J. *The Coptic Community in Egypt: Spatial and Social Change.* Durham, England: Centre for Middle Eastern and Islamic Studies, University of Durham, 1986.

Collelo, Thomas, editor. *Lebanon, A Country Study.* Washington D.C.: Federal Research Division, Library of Congress, 1989.

Curtis, Michael, Joseph Neyer, Allan Pollack, and Chaim Waxman, editors. *The Palestinians: People, History, Politics.* New Jersey: Transaction Books, 1975.

Dafalla, Hassan. *The Nubian Exodus.* London: C. Hurst and Company, 1975.

Dimbley, Jonathan. *The Palestinians.* New York: Quartet Books, 1980.

Elon, Amos. *The Israelis: Founders and Sons.* New York: Holt, Rinehart and Winston, 1971.

Fisher, W.B. *The Middle East: A Physical, Social and Regional Geography.* 7th ed. London: Methuen & Company Ltd., 1978.

Gulick, John. *The Middle East: An Anthropological Perspective.* Pacific Palisades, California: Goodyear Publishing Company, Inc., 1976.

Hourani, A. H. *Minorities in the Arab World.* London: Oxford University Press, 1947.

Hovannisian, Richard G. *Armenia on the Road to Independence 1918.* Berkeley: University of California Press, 1969.

Jayyusi, Salma K., editor. *The Literature of Modern Arabia: An Anthology.* Austin: University of Texas Press, 1989.

The Jewish Communities of the World. New York: Crown Publishers, Inc., 1971.

Kakar, M. Hasan. *Pacification of the Hazaras of Afghanistan.* New York: Afghanistan Council of the Asia Society, 1973.

Kirk, George E. *A Short History of the Middle East: From the Rise of Islam to Modern Times.* Northampton: John Dickens & Co. Ltd., 1964.

Mansfield, Peter. *The Arab World: A Comprehensive History.* New York: Thomas Y. Crowell Company, 1976.

Marsot, Dr. Lufti al-Sayyid-Afaf. *A Short History of Modern Egypt.* Cambridge: Cambridge University Press, 1985.

The Middle East and North Africa 1986. 32nd ed. London: Europa Publications Ltd., 1985.

Mostyn, Trevor, editor. *Cambridge Encyclopedia of the Middle East and North Africa.* Cambridge: Cambridge University Press, 1985.

Nelson, Harold D., editor. *Morocco: A Country Study.* Washington, D.C.: American University Press, 1985.

Nelson, Harold D., editor. *Tunisia: A Country Study.* Washington, D.C.: American University Press, 1988.

Nyrop, Richard, editor. *Jordan: A Country Study.* Washington, D.C.: American University, 1980.

Pakistan, A Country Study. Washington, D.C.: American University Press, 1983.

Patai, Raphael. *Israel between East and West: A Study in Human Relations.* Philadelphia: The Jewish Publication Society of America, 1953.

Pelletiere, Stephen C. *The Kurds: An Unstable Element in the Gulf.* London: Westview Press, 1984.

Sachar, Howard M. *The Emergence of the Middle East: 1914-1924.* New York: Alfred A. Knopf, 1969.

Schoenbrun, David. *The New Israelis.* New York: Atheneum, 1973.

Sigal, Philip. *Judaism: The Evolution of a Faith.* Revised by Lillian Sigal. Grand Rapids, Michigan: William B. Eerdmans, 1988.

Stirling, Paul. *Turkish Village.* New York: John Wiley and Sons, 1965.

Syria: A Country Study. Washington, D.C.: United States Government Publications, 1988.

Wakin, Edward. *A Lonely Minority: The Modern Story of Egypt's Copts.* New York: William Morrow and Company, 1963.

Western and Central Asia. Peoples of the Earth, Volume 15. Danbury, Connecticut: Danbury Press, 1973.

Wright, John. *Libya, Chad and the Central Sahara.* Totowa, New Jersey: Barnes and Noble Books, 1989.

Index